THE CHAIN OF BECOMING

The Chain of Becoming

THE PHILOSOPHICAL TALE, THE NOVEL, AND A NEGLECTED REALISM OF THE ENLIGHTENMENT: SWIFT, MONTESQUIEU, VOLTAIRE, JOHNSON, AND AUSTEN

Frederick M. Keener

Columbia University Press

NEW YORK

1983

Other Columbia University Press books by Frederick M. Keener:

English Dialogues of the Dead: A Critical History, An Anthology, and A Check List

An Essay on Pope

Library of Congress Cataloging in Publication Data

Keener, Frederick M., 1937–
  The chain of becoming.

  Includes bibliographical references and
index.
  1. English fiction—18th century—History
and criticism.   2. Psychology in literature.
3. Philosophy in literature.   4. French fiction—
18th century—History and criticism.
5. Enlightenment.   6. Austen, Jane, 1775–1817—
Knowledge—Psychology.   I. Title.
PR858.P75K4   1982   823'.5'09   82-12878
ISBN 0-231-04001-6
ISBN 0-231-05573-0 (pbk.)

Columbia University Press
New York   Guilford, Surrey

Printed in the United States of America
Clothbound editions of Columbia University Press books are
Smyth-sewn and printed on permanent and durable acid-free
paper.

For Ann,
Thomas, and David

Contents

Acknowledgments

The writing of this book, I am very pleased to acknowledge, was in large measure made possible by a Fellowship for Independent Study and Research from the National Endowment for the Humanities and by a special leave and a typing grant from Hofstra University.

To name everyone who has in one way or another, over the years, helped me clarify and try to achieve my purposes in the book would be impossible, and if not that, ostentatious, but I must record my debt, for signal assistance, to the late James L. Clifford and Arthur M. Wilson. I wish I could show them, and my late father, the finished book.

More cheerfully, I must thank my family and friends. At various times, Edward Chalfant, Richard Hayes, Joseph Kissane, Elizabeth MacAndrew, John Middendorf, and John Richetti have variously and substantially assisted my work, as have others here and abroad, including students at Hofstra and Columbia Universities; colleagues from the Columbia University Seminar in Eighteenth-Century European Culture, from the American Society for Eighteenth-Century Studies and its Northeast regional association, and from the New York Eighteenth-Century Seminar; and Hofstra's excellent librarians. My education having been chiefly in English literature, I am particularly appreciative of aid from colleagues in French and in philosophy who have taken an interest in my work as it involves their subject matter. William F. Bernhardt was, as usual, a most helpful editor. Jane Churchman typed the book with notable care.

I gratefully acknowledge permission to include revised and expanded versions of two articles originally published in *Studies in Eighteenth-Century Culture*: "Conflict and Declamation in *Rasselas*," Volume VI, edited by Ronald C. Rosbottom, pp. 157–181, and "*Candide*: Structure and Motivation," Volume IX, edited by Roseann Runte, pp. 405–427 (Madison: The University of Wisconsin Press; © 1977, 1979 respectively by the Board of Regents of the University of Wisconsin System).

A Note on Quotations and Translations

Quoted passages retain peculiarities of older spelling, accentuation, and the like. To assist readers and to make sure that certain terms bearing on my argument get appropriate recognition, I have appended plain translations of my own to French passages of any length or complexity.

PART I

The Chain of Becoming

CHAPTER ONE

The Philosophical Tale
and the Novel

But though we attend with delight to the achievements of a hero
who is transported in a moment over half the globe upon a griffon,
. . . if immediately after he had vanquished a giant or a dragon, he
should leap into a well or tie himself up to a tree, . . . the story
would be condemned as improbable, unnatural, and absurd.
                    —John Hawkesworth, *The Adventurer*, No. 4

The central genre of the Enlightenment and its best literary
gift to posterity is the genre called the philosophical tale, of
which *Candide* must be the most renowned example. Yet the
genre, not closely defined in eighteenth-century criticism, still
invites clarification and thorough understanding, despite excellent
modern studies of particular tales and sets of them. The tales especially deserve full appreciation as tales, as fiction. Almost everywhere in the commentators a reader runs up against the specious
axiom that fiction, in the tales, is subordinate to ideas—that is,
secondary to what is "philosophical" about the tales, however that
may be defined. Nearly everywhere, too, it is assumed that the
genre ought to be understood in contrast to the novel, often by
deduction from it: the tales are nearly this and not quite that. Comparison of the two forms, unbiased comparison, should not be discouraged, for there are significant resemblances and differences between them befitting their fraternal twinship. The two genres came
to prominence together, both in England and in France, during the
eighteenth century. In a sense the tale complemented the novel,
performing what the novel could not or would not undertake, as I

seek to show here by the way. In another sense they were rivals, and may be so again. But the tale lost: the nineteenth century was all the novel's; the twentieth has been much the same. Critics probably tend to overemphasize the fact that the tale is not the novel because so many other critics and readers, the retinue of the victor, have presumed it should have been.

This book is not a study of all the philosophical tales of the eighteenth century, not a comprehensive history of the form. I concentrate on the major philosophical fictions: *Gulliver's Travels* (1726), *Lettres persanes* (1721), *Candide*, and *Rasselas* (both 1759). I range these somewhat diverse works together because of a particular philosophical theme they have in common, a theme that importantly reflects the course of philosophy in the Enlightenment, that in these works cooperates with fiction at every turn, and that illuminates the distinctive purposes of the taletellers as compared to those of the novelists; as compared to those of novelists in general, I would suggest. *Candide* and *Rasselas* will be discovered to have in common a highly differentiated aesthetic and historical identity as philosophical tales. The often remarked, uncanny likeness between those two tales of the same year, no "influence" linking them, emboldens me to venture the thought that *Gulliver* and the *Lettres persanes* are in some sense actual harbingers of them and, comparably, historic counterparts of each other, though I need not insist on these points, and I suppose no corresponding intention in the authors.

After being concerned with Swift and Montesquieu, Voltaire and Johnson, instead of pursuing such epigones of the tale as Marmontel or seeking to discern which nineteenth- and twentieth-century authors might be said to have produced tales conforming to the great eighteenth-century pattern, I describe what I take to be the main effect of the genre upon the novel, in several works of Jane Austen. Seeing her novels as framed by the tradition of the philosophical tale solves certain problems that critics have remarked in them, and more: it clarifies the purposes and accomplishments of a writer whose ability to profit from the eighteenth century has been neither surpassed nor completely assessed, and it demonstrates the enduring, proper force of the philosophical tale because

she so directly set the methods and assumptions of the tale in juxtaposition, even in conflict, with those of the novel. This book,
moreover, though concentrating on a manageable number of major
works, has application to the broad question of how to read the
literature of the Enlightenment, as well as to the critical questions
raised by varieties of prose fiction. Part I takes up the critical and
philosophical issues pertinent to the tale, describing them with an
eye to the different concerns of the novel. Part II explores the major
tales. Part III attends to Austen.

The task of defining the genre of the philosophical tale has
been made easier by Sheldon Sacks, whose *Fiction and the Shape of
Belief* gives close attention to the nature of *Rasselas*. Sacks argues
that *Rasselas* is neither a novel nor a philosophical dialogue but an
"apologue," which, as it progresses, formulates and refines a set of
abstract propositions about its subject, in this case the possibilities
of human happiness; thus "Johnson's task was to increase our interest in the agents [the characters, as plausible persons] to the
greatest degree possible short of obscuring the relation of the episode to the controlling theme."[1] This is a helpful distinction, but
it does not settle the question, and Sacks only sketchily comments
on the degree to which characters of an apologue must be conserved,
must remain consistent (pp. 59–60). The distinction he has made
would permit too much inconsistency in characterization from episode to episode. Moreover, it seems to encourage *a priori* underestimation of the fullness of characters; to refer to Sacks's main
example, he remarks that "Rasselas' contempt for the meretricious
teacher of morality"—the Stoic of chapter 18, defeated by his
daughter's sudden death—"does not reveal his emotional reaction
to human suffering" (p. 60; cf. p. 14). Yet neither the passage nor
its context warrants so strong a word as "contempt" to describe the
feelings of "the prince, whose humanity would not suffer him to
insult misery with reproof." He could perhaps have stayed and
comforted the devastated, mistaken philosopher, but Rasselas is
emotionally young, in this early episode has his own ends to pursue—
and has just been badly disappointed himself, having accepted the

philosopher at face value against Imlac's advice. The prince's reaction here, like that of the man who has disappointed him, is unphilosophical but human.

Sacks, in addition, implies by his statement an overall conviction of the young man's customary humaneness; like other readers who insist on the difference between philosophical tales and novels, he tends pleasantly to take the characters more seriously than not. His insufficiently explained impression that the thwarted search for the happiest state of life is still somehow consoling, not unreassuring about the human condition, may derive somewhat from the advantages he sees the characters discovering in virtue and the hope of eternal joy (pp. 52–55). But it may arise also from the resiliency, penetration, imagination, and generosity the characters display as, over the course of the story, they convincingly take disappointments in stride and come to understand themselves, each other, the consolations of companionship and education, and the universality of their condition, better than they did at the beginning. The consolations I mention are for the most part enacted rather than talked about and thus apparently tend to escape readers who take up the book expecting discursive propositions rather than fiction in any degree evocative. More than Sacks recognizes, *Rasselas* and other philosophical tales may give considerable fullness to their characters as well as to philosophical teachings; it may be that such an equilibrium best defines the apologue, rather than stress on propositions at the expense of the characters. Such a formula would, in any event, preserve the distance between Johnson's tale and a *Tom Jones* or a *Middlemarch* without giving too much away.

The question also invites more historical understanding than it has received. How fully, a hundred years before George Eliot, did fictional characters need to be developed in order to "seem real"? It is worth considering the inclusiveness of one generalization about the early history of English prose fiction, from an exceptionally literate eighteenth-century reader well acquainted with the minds of the contemporary book-buying and -borrowing public, Benjamin Franklin: "Honest John [Bunyan] was the first that I know who mix'd Narration and Dialogue, a Method of Writing very engaging to the Reader, who in the most interesting Parts finds himself as it were brought into the Company, and present at the Discourse. Defoe in his Cruso, his Moll Flanders, Religious Courtship, Family Instructor, and other Pieces, has imitated it with Success. And Richardson has done the same in his Pamela, &c."[2] Or consider how seriously Fanny Burney took Johnson's story as well as his moral (the italics are mine): "Oh, how dreadful, how terrible is it to be told by a man of his genius and knowledge, *in so affectingly probable a manner*, that true, real, happiness is ever unattainable in this world!—Thro' all the scenes, publick or private, domestick or solitary, that Nekaya or Rasselas pass, real felicity eludes their pursuit and mocks their solicitude."[3] The feeling comment about the characters indicates that the "affectingly probable" covers their sufferings as well as the logic of the tale's abstract propositions. The eighteenth-century threshold for judgments about verisimilitude in fiction was decidedly low—as ecumenically receptive as, in that time, anything approaching precise discrimination between apologue and novel was rare.[4]

Gulliver, the most implausible of the heroes in the outright philosophical tales I have mentioned, is no novel character. What has often been said of Candide, that he is a marionette serving, *ad hoc*, the shifting satirical purposes of his author, is more appropriate to Gulliver. Early in the book he protests strenuously, at length, when accused of having had an affair with a woman six inches tall, and other blatant examples of lack of realism in his character are easily noticed, were doubtless meant to be enjoyed. Yet, as I have indicated, readers' expectations of realism were lower when Swift wrote than they have become. The tradition of realistic characterization associated with the novel had hardly commenced. The chief English character in the new mode was Robinson Crusoe, and Crusoe, not the steadiest of persons in some respects (inhumanly steady in others through many years of solitary confinement), can be mindless enough to spend six months hewing out a boat that he at last finds too heavy to drag to the water. Across the book he firmly establishes himself as a character who sees not the everyday phenomenal world so much as a divine, providential plan beneath it, the evidence of things unseen. Repeatedly he discovers symbolic communications from the hand of God. The process of his being rescued becomes, in his eyes, less a chain of naturally linked events—a phrase to which I shall return—than, as he says, a "Chain of Wonders."[5] The Irish bishop who allegedly thought *Gulliver* "improbable" would not, of course, have had the same complaint about *Crusoe*. It is not a lack of realism in Defoe that I mean to emphasize, though I remain struck by Robinson's lack of concern, in the tropics, with sex and insects. It is, rather, the lack of high realistic expectations on the part of Defoe and Swift's audience, as manifested in the comment of Lord Monboddo, no fool, who said of *Gulliver* that "the character of an English sailor is finely kept up in it." He explains, ". . . Those monstrous lies so narrated, have more the air of probability than many a true story unskilfully told." James Beattie likewise pronounced the fiction absurd, particularly that of the "abominable" fourth voyage, yet said Swift "personates a seafaring man; and with wonderful propriety supports the plainness and simplicity of the character."[6]

Thus *Gulliver*, so fanciful, even seriously absurd a book, seems to have been less exclusively a satire in the eighteenth century than it has become in modern critical interpretations, where one is constantly being told that Gulliver is not a character worth considering. Cheek by jowl with such statements, however, one often finds extensive anthropomorphic disquisition on the way Gulliver reasons, wills, remembers, imagines, feels emotion, senses, acts, and reacts. The contradiction is not unproductive, leading as it may to useful distinction of Swift's work from the novel, in opposition to earlier critics' confusion, and it may lead also to rich observations on satirical rhetoric. But there remains the latent problem about characterization, deriving from the tacit or explicit generic division: "in a novel," on the one hand; "in a satire," on the other. A more satisfactory point of departure is afforded by association of the *Travels* with *Candide* and other philosophical tales, provided the same mistake, that the *dramatis personae* are inconsequential as characters, does not interfere. The prejudice against tale characters is a species of the error whereby fiction, in the philosophical tale, is said to take second place to "the ideas."

The best proof of the power of characters in philosophical tales to engage readers' interest is the frequency in the commentators of appreciative remarks about characterization—despite the denials. René Pomeau, for example, in the introduction to an edition of *Candide*, first asserts that the characters are "marionettes, silhouettes, croquis," Voltaire being "dénué d'imagination psychologique," then almost immediately adds that Candide and Pangloss provide "l'intérêt psychologique sans lequel il n'est pas de grand œuvre."[7] Comparably, F. W. Hilles stoutly proclaims that "We do not read *Rasselas* for the story" and yet proceeds to display, as W. K. Wimsatt notes, "affection for the story (character and plot)."[8] The slipperiness of the issue has long been inadvertently advertised: G. B. Hill's edition of *Rasselas*, from the late nineteenth century, faults Johnson for wavering in the characterization of Nekayah, Rasselas' sister; but a few pages earlier Hill had explained the matter differently: Rasselas' "nature is deeper than his sister's."[9] The fact that commentators show themselves not slavishly subordinate to their own ideas is a point in their favor, I think. They have sensed something but have not quite defined it and refuse to be perfectly consistent at the expense of their integrity as readers. The special way in which philosophical tale characters, but not the tales they occupy, are or may be truly subordinate to ideas is the central subject of the present book.

During the last decades the underestimation of tale characters has been variously and valuably contested, particularly in studies of what is called the *roman* in the *Lettres persanes*—that is, the element of a comprehensive plot to be found there—and in commentary on the imaginative fullness of *Candide* and other of Voltaire's tales. To the familiar dismissal of Candide and his kind as marionettes, Douglas A. Bonneville, developing hints from Yvon Belaval and turning them against Sheldon Sacks, responds by reminding us that there are many degrees of realism and by suggesting that the key to the representation of reality in Voltaire's characters is the distillation of experience: the tales require a reader who has lived sufficiently to recognize the bearing of reality upon them.[10] Bonneville does not ground his suggestion in eighteenth-century commentary on fiction. Yet a base may be discovered there, in Samuel Johnson's remarks on Shakespeare and on the nascent novel. In the *Preface to Shakespeare* Johnson questions the necessity of a playwright's observing the unities of time and place, his opinion supported by the postulate "Imitations produce pain or pleasure, not because they are mistaken for realities, but because they bring realities to mind." It is clear from the context that this generality should be taken as absolute for imaginative literature, not confined to the effects of drama, because Johnson adds that "no more account of space or duration is to be taken by the auditor of a drama, than by the reader of a narrative. . . ."[11] The point might be elaborated here; I should be surprised if most eighteenth-century readers or auditors of drama and other literary forms, especially those members of the audience well acquainted with the classical tradition ancient and modern, would think the trappings of high realism very important. And I think that many inconsistencies and excesses of characters would be regarded as no more unrealistic, or worth denomination as such in terminology of the time, than those of critics, unless the author of a work in question had taken special, conspicuous pains, as in some novels, to instill that requirement in readers against their grain.

"When the knight of La Mancha," Johnson notes in *Rambler* 2,

> gravely recounts to his companion the adventures by which he is to signalize himself in such a manner that he shall be summoned to the support of empires, solicited to accept the heiress of the crown which he has preserved, have honours and riches to scatter about him, and an island to bestow on his worthy squire, very few readers, amidst their mirth or pity, can deny that they have admitted visions of the same kind; though they have not, *perhaps* [emphasis mine], expected events equally strange, or by means equally inadequate. When we pity him, we reflect on our own disappointments; and when we laugh, our hearts inform us that he is not more ridiculous than ourselves, except that he tells what we have only thought.[12]

Unrealistic as an event in fiction may be, particularly an event in a character's mind or an action that proceeds from his thinking, it may very well bring realities to a reader's consciousness. Perhaps, even so absurd a turn of events as Gulliver's protestations in the case of the alleged little mistress is not without reference to characteristic human responses; at the least, comparable folly—though not precisely the same folly—cannot be judged so uncommon outside the book. We are hardly engulfed by sympathy for Gulliver in this instance; we laugh. We never fully share Gulliver's thoughts and feelings, but saying that is not the same as saying we find them incomprehensibly and uninterestingly alien to us, or even unrecognizable. We read his alibi closely enough, perhaps, to notice a flaw in it.[13] We really are friends of Gulliver (though friends more to truth) for we know him. The surprise we feel in this remarkable episode is due in part to our appreciation of Swift's insight into us. And the characters in *Lettres persanes*, *Candide*, and *Rasselas* are less bizarre.

Johnson's recognition of the power of nonrealistic fiction is a key to understanding the moderation of his enthusiasm for the new realistic form we have come to call the novel. He called it the "comedy of romance," and in *Rambler* 4 (not unlike many French writers of the time)[14] he pondered it with weighty reservations, worrying that it could infect the minds of "the young" but also "the ignorant, and the idle"—in Johnson's view, no doubt, a set of categories rather more than less comprehensive of mankind: heads "unfurnished with ideas, and therefore susceptible of impressions; not fixed by principles, and therefore easily following the current of fancy; not informed by experience, and consequently open to every false suggestion and incomplete account" (pp. 19, 21). This is a famous *Rambler*: readers will readily call to mind Johnson's concern that unformed persons may take for reality what the novel so realistically presents, that they may become callous about their own moral shortcomings through exposure to those of sympathetic fictional characters, and—a moralistic prescription, we may think—that novel characters ought to display "the most perfect idea of virtue" consistent with human nature (p. 24). The danger presented by realistic fiction lies psychologically in the fact that "the power of example is so great as to take possession of the memory by a kind of violence, and produce effects almost without the intervention of the will" (p. 22). That is, the novel can sow delusion which the reader vaguely but positively invites, "voluntary delusion."[15] The memory was widely regarded in the eighteenth century as the ground of personal identity. An unwary novel reader stands in peril, Johnson says, of confusing what he has read with what he has experienced outside books, thus opening his imagination to unrealistic expectations like those of Quixote, or worse. In Johnson's view, the older, unrealistic romance appeals to a reader's imagination; but the patently fantastic elements of that sort of romance keep him alert to the difference between what is actual, probable, and possible, and what he wishes were so.

It would seem that the nonrealism of the philosophical tale ought to have the same effect, distancing the reader, shielding him from delusion. Like the romance, unlike the novel, the tale may present unusual, improbable, even impossible events and characters—"giants" as in *Gulliver* or Voltaire's *Micromégas*, "a hermit" as in *Rasselas*, "a battle and a shipwreck" as in *Candide* (these quoted phrases from *Rambler* 4, p. 20). It is not, however, such trappings that Johnson finds exclusively essential to the genre of romance, though he says the genre would vanish if deprived of them. He probes deeper, in the process intimating a major point of difference between the romance and the philosophical tale: "In the romances formerly written, every transaction and sentiment was so remote from all that passes among men, that the reader was in very little danger of making any applications to himself; the virtues and crimes were equally beyond his sphere of activity; and he amused himself with heroes and with traitors, deliverers and persecutors, as with beings of another species, whose actions were regulated upon motives of their own, and who had neither faults nor excellencies in common with himself" (p. 21). As much as the marvelous events, every "sentiment," all the "motives," of romance characters are perceived as strange, alien to the reader's own, and thus unlikely to enthrall his judgment.

What I would assert about the philosophical tale, in contrast to the romance as Johnson describes it, is that alongside unrealistic and even anti-realistic narrative elements the sentiments and motives of tale characters are *not* generally far removed from those of readers, indeed constantly bring to mind realities of thought, feeling, and motivation. The novel, on the other hand, has a tendency to make the extravagant sentiments of romance seem real and acceptable. The tale, in contrast to both novel and romance, despite all that is nonrealistic about the form, seldom strays from acute, hardheaded emphasis on the actualities of mental life. Johnson ends *Rambler* 4 by allowing only two courses of action to the fiction writer: presenting paragons of virtue or trimming the sails of realism. In *Rasselas*, several years later, he exemplified a third, better solution.

Thus, whereas in the novel realism is generally a matter of form and content—I am thinking mainly but not exclusively of the eighteenth-century novel—in the philosophical tale it is centrally and most importantly a matter of theme. The term *realism* needs explaining here. One of the best definitions is Ian Watt's in *The Rise of the Novel*, a definition of "formal realism" especially useful to me because based on eighteenth-century fiction and because compound and divisible. Watt draws a distinction between realism of "presentation" and realism of "assessment." Realism of presentation, supporting the "premise, or primary convention" of the genre, "that the novel is a full and authentic report of human experience," entails a relatively plain, unfigurative, seemingly referential prose style and detailed, circumstantial representation of ordinary, contemporary conditions and individualized (if not ordinary) characters and chains of events. This is the characteristic realism of Defoe and Richardson.[16] Realism of assessment, associated especially by Watt with the novels of Fielding and Austen, has to do with pointed sociological, psychological, and moral understanding and judgment brought to bear on characters, characters taken individually and collectively; that is, "a wise assessment of life" related to "the whole tradition of civilised values"—in Jane Austen "an august and impersonal spirit of social and psychological understanding."[17]

Yet in developing and employing these categories, adeptly, Watt pays much more attention to presentation than to assessment, and very little attention to realism of psychological assessment.[18] In Watt's view, the main current of French fiction "from *La Princesse de Clèves* to *Les Liaisons dangereuses* stands outside the main tradition of the novel. For all its psychological penetration and literary skill, we fell it is too stylish to be authentic. In this Madame de La Fayette and Choderlos de Laclos are the polar opposites of Defoe and Richardson, whose very diffuseness tends to act as a guarantee of the

authenticity of their report, whose prose aims exclusively at what
Locke defined as the proper purpose of language, 'to convey the
knowledge of things', and whose novels as a whole pretend to be
no more than a transcription of real life. . . ."[19] Watt's theories are
tailored to the rise of the novel in England, where the resolution
of novels tends to be social and moral: the main characters are
usually rescued, providentially, by society or a saving remnant of
society, which has learned to appreciate their merits. By contrast,
and here I rely particularly upon Peter Brooks, the French "novel
of worldliness" lays stress on the main characters' need to don a
social mask and to penetrate, psychologically, the masks of others.[20]
Realism of psychological assessment is thus essential to the French
novel in the period, not to the English. Yet there remains a curious,
strikingly absolute limit to this quality of French novels up to Laclos: the main character seeks, indeed drives relentlessly toward,
psychological assessment of other characters, not himself. It is exactly this omission in English and French novels of the eighteenth
century, I would say, that largely accounts for the existence of the
philosophical tale.

Much more than the novel, the philosophical tale is occupied
with the theme of the main character's psychological self-assessment, at least his need for it, promoting such realism on his part
as prerequisite to all other judgments. It is in this respect that the
philosophical tale is seriously philosophical—not when a character
very loosely parodies a Leibniz. Moreover, it is in this respect that
the philosophical tale is philosophical in a particular way the eighteenth century was. Like eighteenth-century thought, the tale is
essentially concerned with the importance of psychology to philosophy (as I explain in the rest of this first Part). The tale sets
realism of psychological self-assessment against the other forms of
realism typical of the novel, English and French, just as Locke and
many of his successors, in their campaign to establish and preserve
sanity and ward off delusion, insisted that philosophy begin with
scrutiny of the rational and irrational processes of the natural mind,
the subordination for better or worse of persons to their ideas.

CHAPTER TWO

The Chain of Being,
the Chain of Events,
and the Chain of Becoming

Tant de raisonneurs aïant fait le roman de l'ame, un sage est venu
qui en [a] fait modestement l'histoire. . . .
—Voltaire, on Locke, Lettres philosophiques, letter 13

*T*he discipline we call psychology, meaning the more or
less empirical study of the mind in contrast to philosophical
or theological investigation of the soul, was just beginning when
the novel and the philosophical tale came to prominence in the early
and mid-eighteenth century. The first Englishman to use the word
other than in a translation, according to the *OED*, was David Hartley, just before 1750. The infant discipline remained a branch of
philosophy, though a branch from which the tree more and more
seemed to hang. Johnson describes the new state of affairs succinctly in the *Preface to Shakespeare*, proceeding, as in *Rambler* 4,
toward the question of human motivation and toward a distinction
between realistic and unrealistic fiction. In the late sixteenth and
early seventeenth centuries, Johnson says,

> The contest about the original benevolence or malignity of man had
> not yet commenced. Speculation had not yet attempted to analyse
> the mind, to trace the passions to their sources, to unfold the seminal
> principles of vice and virtue, or sound the depths of the heart for
> the motives of action. All those enquiries, which from that time that
> human nature became the fashionable study, have been made some-

times with nice discernment, but often with idle subtilty, were yet
unattempted. The tales, with which the infancy of learning was
satisfied, exhibited only the superficial appearances of action, related
the events but omitted the causes, and were formed for such as
delighted in wonders rather than in truth.[1]

Before this change, people seem to have been examined as if they
were characters in a romance, their development not looked at closely.
The "contest about the original benevolence or malignity of man"
which provoked new scrutiny was that lively seventeenth-century
political debate wherein, among many participants, Hobbes made
human malignity the rationale for autocracy and Locke, upholding
a more benign estimation of humanity, argued for the right to depose an unjust ruler. The new analysis of the mind was also a
component of the scientific revolution; that is, of Baconian curiosity
about natural causality in all its provinces.

In political science and philosophy, for Machiavelli, Bacon,
Hobbes, and many after them, the program was to study government as it is and man as he is rather than as either ought to be.
The project was historical in spirit. Locke describes the approach
taken in *An Essay Concerning Human Understanding* as "this Historical, plain Method";[2] he would base his appraisal of knowledge on
observation of his experience of mental processes so as to determine
what the mind could in fact know and not know. In a phrase often
used by eighteenth-century writers, the history resulting from such
observation—whether the subject was politics or another aspect of
human life—would be the history of a "chain of events." Instead
of simply listing what had happened in chronological order, the
historian would seek to discover a chain of cause and effect, and
to identify the principles of causality operative in it, the principles
other than or apart from supernatural agency. The force and novelty of such purposes come all the way home to us if we contrast
the chain of events with that other chain prominent in early eighteenth-century thought, the ancient concept of the Great Chain of
Being, sustained in the 1730s by Pope's *Essay on Man* and to be
found elsewhere in his predecessors and contemporaries, though
hardly ubiquitous.[3] This grand vertical, essentially atemporal concept proceeds deductively from the attributes of God as defined by

theology, especially the Creator's infinite goodness and wisdom. Angels, men, beasts, and other created things stand ranked in a descending, divinely appointed, best possible order. The way God is, rather than the way man is, supports the concept. The motives essentially involved are God's, and only secondarily, almost casually, does the doctrine seek support in observation of the natural world. Pope, at the end of *The Dunciad*, voiced horror at naturalistic investigation: "*Philosophy*, that lean'd on Heav'n before,/Shrinks to her second cause, and is no more."[4] A. O. Lovejoy, in his fine history of the idea of the Great Chain, provides a chapter about eighteenth-century attempts to temporalize it. He does not, however, consider the horizontal "chain of events."[5]

But Hume saw the contrast and pounced on it in this account of the new hero of the age, the historian:

> The historian traces the series of actions according to their natural order, remounts to their secret springs and principles, and delineates their most remote consequences. He chuses for his subject a certain portion of that great chain of events, which composes the history of mankind: Each link in this chain he endeavours to touch in his narration. Sometimes unavoidable ignorance renders all his attempts fruitless: Sometimes, he supplies by conjecture what is wanting in knowledge: And always, he is sensible, that the more unbroken the chain is, which he presents to his readers, the more perfect is his production. He sees, that the knowledge of causes is not only the most satisfactory; this relation or connexion being the strongest of all others; but also the most instructive; since it is by this knowledge alone, we are enabled to controul events, and govern futurity.[6]

Hume's phrase "great chain of events" can only be an allusion to the concept studied by Lovejoy, pointedly indicating a rival ground of being for reliable knowledge: empiricism. His last sentence, about understanding of natural causation as the basis for governing future events, sounds a brave new worldly note consonant with the program of the French Encyclopedists but also far from dissonant with the more moderate aspirations of writers such as Locke or Johnson. A quite comparable passage turns up in Fielding, though considering his gift for irony I shall not press the point: ". . . Besides that it conduces greatly to a perfect understanding of all history, there is no exercise of the mind of a sensible reader more pleasant than the tracing the several small and almost imperceptible links in every chain of events by which all the great actions of the world are produced." I shall not press the point except to note, again conscious of ironical possibilities, that the setting for Fielding's statement is *Amelia*, which contains (indeed is prefaced by) the promise that sensitivity to the "minute causes" of events produces the best instruction "in this most useful of all arts, which I call the ART of LIFE"[7]—or governing one's own futurity.

The image of a horizontal chain of events or causes became so frequent in the writings of the Encyclopedists that, as Agnes G. Raymond observes, it was satirized in the play Palissot wrote against them, *Les Philosophes* (1760), in which a character claims, "J'examine avec soin les principes des choses,/L'enchaînement secret des effets et des causes" ("I carefully examine the principles of things, the secret enchainment of effects and causes").[8] Enamored with the chain metaphor, d'Alembert employs it to speak of mathematical and logical relations, about the connections between the various arts and sciences, and about the processive nature of the universe ("phénomènes dont l'enchaînement tient peut-être au système général du monde"—"an enchainment of phenomena which proceeds, perhaps, from the fundamental system of the world").[9] Diderot tells Sophie Volland that conversation, no matter how casual it appears, is organized causally, like the only apparently disorganized thoughts of a dreamer or a fool, but it can be difficult to discover the links (*les chaînons imperceptibles*) that draw so many differing ideas together.[10] Rousseau adapts the metaphor to special circumstances and purposes: the imaginative prehistory in the second *Discours* is (a reminiscence of his cherished Crusoe?) an "enchaînement de prodiges," and the *Confessions* lay claim to coherence by reason of "la chaîne des sentimens qui ont marqué la succession de mon être, et par eux celle des évenemens qui en ont été la cause ou l'effet" ("the chain of the feelings which have characterized the progress of my being, and by them the chain of the events which have been the cause or the effect of it").[11] All these examples, from outside the main text of the *Encyclopédie*, do not begin to make an exhaustive list.

Nor was use of the metaphor confined to the Encyclopedists. For La Mettrie the mind is not born but made as it draws, from experience of objects and relations, "une longue chaîne des conséquences,"[12] and Condillac describes mental life as "une chaîne dont les anneaux sont tour à tour idées et desirs" ("a chain, of which the links are by turns ideas and desires").[13] Hume, in *An Enquiry Concerning Human Understanding*, after the passage I have quoted, says all the actions of a human life depend on each other, "nor is it possible to strike off one link, however minute, in this regular chain, without affecting the whole series of events, which follow," and in the earlier, more ample and less polite *Treatise of Human Nature*, Hume refers to "that chain of causes and effects, which constitute our self or person."[14] Employing a favorite English word for *enchaînement*, Johnson in *Adventurer* 107 speaks of "the whole concatenation of causes and effects" in the world.[15] A sermon on the popular topic of "Self Knowledge," by Sterne, insists on man's God-given power "of turning his eyes inward upon himself, and taking notice of the chain of his own thoughts and desires."[16] Gibbon mentions "a singular consequence in the chain of human events" in the *Memoirs*.[17] The chain of events had, like the Chain of Being, a long ancestry, having been established in Stoicism as the manifestation of destiny. Commenting on the great chain of Zeus (*Iliad* 8.18), Vico warns: "The Stoics would have the chain represent the eternal series of causes by which their Fate holds the world girdled and bound, but let them look out lest they be entangled in it. . . ."[18] Perhaps, as Raymond suggests, Montesquieu did most to give the metaphor currency, having used it early and late in his career. Readers of the *Lettres persanes* will readily recall his claim that the work is unified by "une chaîne secrète et, en quelque façon, inconnue," as if it were written to be read in a manner like the new historical or genetic method of reading the events of the world.[19]

Before taking up the *Lettres persanes* in Part II of the present book, I devote the sixth chapter to the question, familiar since our childhood book reports, of the "development of character." I ap-

proach the question not primarily in its rhetorical aspect (the revelation, progressively, of character to the reader, or the representation of changes in a character so as to make them seem plausible),
and certainly not according to the ways of post-eighteenth-century
depth psychology, but from a basis in the thought of the Enlightenment as represented by Montesquieu, who is most famous as a
great early theorist of the motivating principles of social and political structures, as set forth in *De l'esprit des lois*. That is, he most
distinguished himself as a theorist of the chain of causes and effects,
environmental and human, which leads human beings to conceive,
create, and sustain or destroy a monarchy or another form of government, monogamy or another sort of social relationship. He was
a theorist, moreover, with a passion for historical and empirical
details; and his hero in the *Lettres* seeks a comparable understanding
of the world. Indeed, Montesquieu has some claim to being considered a pioneer theorist also of the particular species of realism
in fiction that I began to explain in the preceding chapter. He conceived the possibility, as evidenced by his remarks on the *Lettres*,
of relatively autonomous growth of characters in accordance with
an empirically based theory of the natural genesis and causal progress, for good or ill or both, of characters' consciousness—a chain
of events in characters' minds corresponding to the chain of events
observed in real human minds. Later, Rousseau's *Émile* would pre-
scribe educational methods based on a comparable, though much
more elaborate, theory of relatively endogenous psychological development.

Ernst Cassirer, generalizing about the thought of Montesquieu
and other Enlightenment students of what would come to be called
the social sciences, elucidates the matter by calling special attention
to a form of logic relatively new in eighteenth-century thinkers and
characteristic of their method, a logic not of classification but of
discovery:

> This intellectual impulse was most immediately and distinctly felt
> in the theory of definitions. The scholastic method of definition of
> a concept by means of *genus proximum* (next genus above) and *dif-
> ferentia specifica* (specific difference) is more and more commonly rec-
> ognized as inadequate. The object of a definition in this sense is not

merely to analyze and describe a given conceptual content; it is to be a means for constructing conceptual content and for establishing it by virtue of this constructive activity. Thus arises the theory of the genetic or causal definition, in whose development all the great logicians of the seventeenth century participated. The genuine and really fruitful explanations of concepts do not proceed by abstraction alone; they are not content to divide one element from a given complex of properties or characteristics and to define it in isolation. They observe rather the inner law according to which the whole either originated or at least can be conceived as originating. And they clarify within this law of becoming the real nature and behavior of this whole; they not only show *what* this whole is, but *why* it is. A genuine genetic definition permits us to understand the structure of a complex whole; it does not, however, stop with this structure as such, but goes back to its foundations.[20]

The form of scholastic logic as Cassirer describes it resembles the Chain of Being: the logician defines an object by locating it in a static hierarchical order. By contrast, the new logic of discovery, instrumental and heuristic rather than final and metaphysical, defines an object by revealing in it a causal chain of becoming. A synthetic, model chain resembling the process of becoming observed in nature is used to explain how—by what causes, in what order of operation—something "either originated or at least can be conceived as originating." Between these two possible results of the method of analysis through synthesis, there is of course quite a difference, well worth keeping in mind.

It is doubly useful to set the chain of becoming against the Chain of Being in a book on the philosophical tale, most obviously because, in notable tales such as *Candide* and *Rasselas*, the philosophical Optimism associated with the Great Chain is a major foil, represented by Pangloss and by the philosopher of "universal felicity" in Johnson's twenty-second chapter. A second, more subtle and more important use of juxtaposing the chains may be drawn from Voltaire's tale *Zadig*, published twelve years before *Candide*, in 1747. *Zadig* builds vexingly and instructively to a confrontation between the character named in the title and an angel who argues that certain events, abominable as they seem, are good because of justifying causes and effects beyond the knowledge of mankind.

(*An Essay on Man* teaches: "All Chance, Direction, which thou canst not see"; ". . . To reason right is to submit.")[21] Replies Zadig, uncomprehendingly, memorably: "Mais . . ." Zadig's angel has explained, however, that if there were only good in the world "cette terre serait une autre terre, l'enchaînement des événements serait un autre ordre de sagesse; et cet autre ordre, qui serait parfait, ne peut être que dans la demeure éternelle de l'Être suprême, de qui le mal ne peut approcher" ("this world would be a different world, and the chaining of events would be a different order of wisdom; and that different order, which would be flawless, can exist only in the eternal home of the Supreme Being, whom evil cannot come near").[22]

This, it must be noted, is very much an eighteenth-century angel speaking—speaking not of the chain of events, the object of desired knowledge, but of the enchaining of events in the genetic process of trying to know that object, the chain Zadig can construct in his mind. (In having immediate celestial instruction, Zadig differs importantly from Candide and other major philosophical tale heroes.) The recognition promoted by the angel is evident too in Hume's account of the historian, who "Sometimes . . . supplies by conjecture what is wanting in knowledge," and it of course comes to great prominence elsewhere in Hume, almost everywhere. "An Abstract of . . . A *Treatise of Human Nature*" ends strikingly not just because only three principles are held to account for the way the mind associates its ideas (the three principles being those of resemblance, contiguity, and cause-and-effect) but also because, in his small peroration, Hume once more may have the Chain of Being within his peripheral view: "'Twill be easy to conceive of what vast consequence these principles must be in the science of human nature, if we consider, that so far as regards the mind, these are the only links that bind the parts of the universe together, or connect us with any person or object exterior to ourselves. For as it is by means of thought only that any thing operates upon our passions, and as these are the only ties of our thoughts, they are really *to us* the cement of the universe."[23]

The effect of such an epistemology, as Ian Ross observes, is to move philosophy, science, and everyday thought very close to art. "With respect to consciousness, causation, and self-identity, fictions meet the needs of ordinary existence. . . . It would seem, in the last analysis, that all of us are crypto-philosophers and novelists in our daily lives, forging in our imaginations fables of the self, and endlessly seeking associative links of cause and effect in our relations with other persons and the external world of objects."[24] Or as a contemporary of Hume says, on the basis of a less fully skeptical cast of mind: "The Understanding does often make its own Objects: we create a thousand Truths every Day."[25] And it will be clear that if we are novelists we must also be critics, or novelists with critical ability, lest our fictions be deluding.[26]

Hume, as much as anyone in the eighteenth century, much more than most thinkers of the period, but in some respects simply carrying the more modest thinking of others to the farthest point possible, has made all knowledge into psychology. For all practical purposes he has psychologized the world. The truly knowable chain of becoming is the chain of mental processes in the knower. The project of a science of man based upon observation of his behavior as it really is has turned into the project of a science of the enchainment of events in the mind, that enchaining a process with its own natural series, its own proper sequences of causes and effects, its own principles of change—and perhaps a metapsychology needed to understand the chains of psychology, potentially an infinite regressive series of more and more comprehensive sciences of sciences. The ancient counsel "Know thyself" has first acquired unprecedented urgency and then inexplicable complexity.

Such is the contagion of opinion on the subject of knowing the mind in the eighteenth century, however, that this doubt need not be upheld. It is not at the polar pinnacle occupied by Hume that I wish to generalize about the nature of eighteenth-century psychology. It is at a lower, more temperate and populous level, where Hume has something in common with such widely divergent philosophers, of his century and before, as Hobbes, Locke, Berkeley, Butler, Hutcheson, Archibald Campbell, John Gay, Condillac, Diderot, Hartley, Johnson, Adam Smith, and others, including Addison and numerous critics and aestheticians. What they have in common is some degree of reliance upon associationism, on the psychology tracing links or connections between ideas.[27]

Locke introduced the term "association of ideas" into the fourth edition (1700) of *An Essay Concerning Human Understanding* to explain error. Voluntarily or involuntarily, the mind can tightly join ideas that do not belong together and—the condition, Locke says, is a species of madness though prevalent among mankind and often unnoticed—can regard the new conjunction of ideas as natural, right, and true. The concept "association" is here critical in purpose, the term pejorative, probably a metaphor indicating a mindless political party spirit motivating the ideas to mob together instead of exercising responsible, independent judgment. (Political partisanship is another cause, for Locke, of misconnected ideas.) Once joined, like factional rowdies these unfortunate ideas "always keep in company, and the one no sooner at any time comes into the Understanding but its Associate appears with it; and if they are more than two which are thus united, the whole gang always inseparable shew themselves together."[28] Man may be born free but he may very well, soon afterward, be everywhere in mental chains—and may not know it. I shall return to Locke in more detail with reference to *Gulliver* in chapter 5.

Later, eighteenth-century philosopher-psychologists depending in whole or in part upon associationism accorded the concept and term constructive in addition to critical meaning, in various ways. But the central fact about these authors, from the standpoint of the philosophical tales, is their analytical attention, historical in spirit, empirical and genetic in method, to the chain of mental events as it is or may be conceived, instrumentally, to be.

The enterprise was historical more in spirit than in actuality, the study of mental development not descending to extensive individual case histories, though Hartley called for such records.[29] Similarly, social contract theorists, such as Locke in the *Second Treatise on Government*, did not begin with detailed archeological and anthropological investigation of the probable condition of mankind before the formation of political bodies. The casualness of some assumptions in such works remains astonishing, so much so that they may seem to present disguised, imaginative autobiographies:

Locke's first men comporting themselves as Locke would himself have done in the circumstances—the same for Hobbes, Montesquieu, Rousseau, and others. The method was generally to form a simplified definition of man, reducing him to a set of basic drives and accompanying conceptions related to his presumed circumstances, and then to imagine how these elements might or must have led to civilization. The social-contract theories, that is, are really psychological theories representing in brief narrative form what is fundamental in the workings of the mind.

From a somewhat different point of view, the contracts achieved in these little prehistories correspond to positive or negative associations of ideas. And from still another point of view, these prehistories are the Enlightenment's mythology: pure synthetic and genetic models so appealing that a character in a philosophical tale, which may include such a myth at some point (e.g., the *Lettres persanes*' story of the Troglodytes), might be tempted to overlook the distinction made by Cassirer between true and merely conceivable accounts of development. The difference sharply separating the genetic myths of prehistory from the associative theories that are my main subject here is that the latter, drawing more openly and directly on familiar commonplace experience, more explicitly restrict model-building to exploratory, analytic purposes. Casual about cases as the new historical psychology often was, from many exponents in England and France it forcefully promoted critical attention to the chain of becoming that has constituted much of the individual person's mind. For a knowledgeable person of the eighteenth century to know himself in some degree, he had to examine the genesis of his thinking, lest his thoughts be no more than the automatic consequences of unrecognized and uncontrolled inner forces.

It is this broad genetic method that unifies the otherwise widely divergent associationists of the century and which provides the best context for understanding its major philosophical tales, rather than the tradition of the novel. The major tales, like philosophy of the period, take as a major theme the importance on the part of the main character of attaining freedom from false mental associations—and occasionally more than that: consciousness of the natural processes of his thinking. As in eighteenth-century philosophy, the minds that figure centrally in philosophical tales are not highly particularized: the tales do not present intricate, unique case histories either. But the minds in the tales move in response to recognizable human feelings and typically are fettered by quite familiar preconceptions, and are presented by their authors in such a way as to call particular attention to these psychological matters. The heroes above all represent chains of becoming.

To illustrate the practice of associationist analysis, I rely on a relatively early, brief, and accessible essay—short but remarkably full—"A Dissertation Concerning the Fundamental Principle and Immediate Criterion of Virtue . . . ," attributed to a Cambridge clergyman, John Gay. I do not claim that it influenced any authors of tales, though the extent of its influence upon English minds may have been considerable (it had an important, acknowledged effect upon Hartley's)[30] because it was published very prominently as prefatory material to one of the century's most noted works of learning, Archbishop King's Latin treatise on the origin of evil as translated by Edmund Law (1731), the translation reprinted with Gay's essay in 1732, 1739, 1758, and 1761.[31] Curiously, we here find the chain of events, of Gay's associationism, once more in close juxtaposition with the Great Chain of Being: King's book is the major British philosophical treatise on that idea and Optimism, and I do not know why Gay's essay was included, since it differs substantially from King on the origin of moral evil in the individual heart. Arguing against an extreme, totally deterministic view of the causes of moral choice, King defended the opposite extreme of entirely free election.[32] Gay was more circumspect, more modern, proceeding from Locke but taking "association" in an amplified sense relating to all thought and emotion, not merely error—thus anticipating a number of mid-century associationists.

So narrow is the human understanding, Gay explains, that in pursuing truth, in general and with particular respect to conduct, a person does not usually compare his perceptions with the first principles of reason and ethics but adopts certain intermediate positions—"certain Truths and means of Happiness, which we look upon as RESTING PLACES"—as "*Axioms*. . . . And we are more easily inclined to this by imagining that we may safely rely upon what we call *Habitual* Knowledge, thinking it needless to examine what we are already satisfy'd in." With time the "resting places" or "axioms" come to be regarded "not as they really are, the *Substitutes* of Principles, but Principles themselves" (p. xxx). Gay gives the example of a person associating pleasure with money, money as a means to obtain advantages producing happiness. This person has a tendency to come to regard the means as a substitute for the advantages it can obtain. The advantage lies then in having money. A link in the chain of reasoning has been unwittingly dropped; a link in the personality has thereby been forged: thus the psychological origin of avarice.

Not simply the vices but the whole range of thoughts and emotions becomes grist for Gay's theory. "The same might be observ'd concerning the Thirst after Knowledge, Fame, &c. the delight in Reading, Building, Planting, and most of the various Exercises and Entertainments of Life. These were at first enter'd on with a view to some farther End, but at length become habitual Amusements; the Idea of Pleasure is associated with them, and leads us on still in the same eager Pursuit of them, when the first Reason is quite vanish'd, or at least out of our Minds." So great is the "Power of *Association*" that it can "transport our Passions and Affections beyond their proper bounds, both as to Intenseness and Duration," and can also "transfer them to improper Objects, and such as are of a quite different Nature from those to which our Reason had at first directed them" (p. xxxi). Thus, as in Locke, associations may lead to madness, but for Gay they may lead also to the sane satisfactions of life. To be safe from the dangers of association, though, Gay's thinker must be alert to the formation of his axioms: "Prejudices, both Speculative and Practical, are difficult to be rooted out, *viz.* few will examine them" (p. xxx). A person must "be at the Pains to consult his Mind" (p. xxxii), must become in effect the historian of it. This prescription, implicit in all associationist philosophy, is repeatedly made explicit toward mid-century. A treatise of 1747 attributed to James Long recommends that we "trace up all our Notions, Opinions, ways of thinking, &c. to the time of their first Existence and . . . point out the

Manner in which we came at them. The shortest and most effectual Method of getting out of an Error being to know how we were first led into it," and Hartley soon afterward declares "that the Affections and Passions should be analyzed into their simple compounding Parts, by reversing the Steps of the Associations which concur to form them."[33]

The eighteenth century increasingly realized that a person seeking valid knowledge of the world might have to make his way first through a host of mental filters and screens, chains, associations, before beginning to see clearly outside himself. Bacon's "idols" had sketched the obstacles a century before Gay: the "Idols of the Tribe," those of mankind in general, make the "human understanding . . . like a false mirror, which, receiving rays irregularly, distorts and discolors the nature of things by mingling its own nature with it," and the "Idols of the Cave," those of the individual, can compound the problem, further distorting the rays of nature, either because of the individual's innate composition, or his education and conversation, or his reading, or an admired authority, or his circumstances. "Whence it was well observed by Heraclitus that men look for sciences in their own lesser worlds, and not in the greater or common world."[34] Before successful, realistic description and assessment of the outside world could be begun, there had to be realistic assessment of oneself. Yet inexperienced or dense Gulliver, Montesquieu's Usbek, Candide, and Rasselas seek—not like most novel heroes and heroines, simply to find a mate and a home of a good sort, virtue intact or restored—but to comprehend the grand world, to know the universe, the find their place in the Great Chain of things. They are students, as heroes and heroines of novels generally are not, and would-be philosophers. They boldly and unhesitatingly stride directly out of the Baconian cave, as if the first precept of life were not "the amendment of men's own minds; for the remove of the impediments of the mind will sooner clear the passages of fortune, than the obtaining fortune will remove the impediments of the mind."[35]

In *Rambler* 4 and elsewhere, Johnson proved himself deeply heedful of the lesson of the associationists. The inexperienced or unprincipled, tale-hero-like reader must be secured especially from "unjust prejudices, perverse opinions, and incongruous combinations of images."[36] This last phrase is synonymous with associations of ideas in the Lockean sense (one may note in passing that the series of negative modifiers indicates a positive sense of the concept as well, permitting not only "congruous combinations" but also "just prejudices"). So insistent is Johnson on the importance of self-scrutiny and self-knowledge as guides to conduct that, at the end of *Rambler* 4, he defines virtue not as a transcendent principle or conventional duty but as a reward of introspective analysis, concluding "that virtue is the highest proof of understanding . . .; and that vice is the natural consequence of narrow thoughts; that it begins in mistake and ends in ignominy." There was, it seems, a third possible way for an author of fiction to deal responsibly with the hazards posed by realism. Besides retreating to romance or creating the best possible paragons of virtue, an author could tell the tale of someone not exceptionally good or evil whose adventures would be chiefly those of seeking reality inside and outside the lesser world of his head by learning first about his prejudices, opinions, and "combinations of images," the mechanism that produces them, the psychological dynamic of himself; that is, by seeking realism of self-assessment. Such assessment is a feature of *Rasselas*, which thus represents a new constructive response to the problems less adequately solved, though admirably explained, in *Rambler* 4. The other major philosophical tales variously share and encourage this accomplishment. Rasselas and his tale brethren are distinguished characters in eighteenth-century fiction, perhaps in most fiction: characters requiring self-knowledge, knowledge of the chain of events in their minds and the world, to attain whatever happiness may be found.

This theme of psychological self-assessment could not be more remote from what a reader encounters in what many would call the first and most prototypical English novel, *Pamela* (1740–1742). The most striking decision in the book, Pamela's assent to the request from Mr. *B.* that she return to him, to the master who has held her captive and repeatedly abused and terrified the little servant girl in other ways—a decision that will lead to their marriage—

is based on her explicit rejection of empirical, historical, genetic grounds of judgment. "Well, I will, I think, trust in his Generosity! Yet is it not too great a Trust—especially considering how I have been used! . . . Upon the Whole, I resolved to obey him; and if he uses me ill afterwards, double will be his ungenerous Guilt!— Tho' hard will be my Lot, to have my Credulity so justly blameable as it will then seem. For, to be sure, the World, the *wise* World, that never is wrong itself, judges always by Events." Not the chain of events for Pamela; instead a sour remark about those attentive to it. And lo! within a few pages she too sets the empirical order against the Chain of Being, in its social dimension, by recalling a passage of verse that includes these lines:

> *Nor let the* Rich *the* lowest Slave *disdain*;
> *He's* equally *a* Link *of Nature's* Chain;
> *Labours to the* same *End*, *joins in* one View;
> *And* both alike *the* Will divine *pursue*. . . .

The exclusively devout Pamela returns "with a grace" instead of being guided by her experience of the secular order, a course she can perceive only as worldliness.[37] The still more crucial matter of her knowing her own motives, as distinguished from knowing those of Mr. *B.*, does not have importance in the novel. (Fielding's *Shamela* certainly makes this clear.) Voltaire would observe that Richardson's readers love to be kept in the dark about the heroines' motives, and would, if told at the start that the heroines love their tormentors, drop the book.[38]

Clarissa, the violated heroine of Richardson's masterpiece, has still more reason than Pamela to take seriously the history of her persecutor, Lovelace, and comes much closer than Pamela to historical analysis. In a letter to Miss Howe, Clarissa ponders his record as it was even apart from the act of rape. She observes, "Let any one, who knows my Story, collect his character from his behaviour to *me before* that outrage; and then judge, whether it was in the least probable that such a man should make me happy."[39] But she is little more attentive than Pamela to the chain of her own thinking as eighteenth-century psychology would regard it, and Richardson gives little indication that she should be. (Richardson's firm printed Hartley's massive *Observations on Man* for publication in 1749 but that associationist tome left no traces in *Clarissa*, published 1747–1748, or in Richardson's subsequent *Sir Charles Grandison*.) When Diderot, in his rapturous *Éloge de Richardson*, exclaimed "Tout ce que Montaigne, Charron, La Rochefoucauld et Nicole ont mis en maximes, Richardson l'a mis en action" ("Everything that Montaigne, Charron, La Rochefoucauld, and Nicole have put in maxims, Richardson has put into fictional events"), he did not mean that it was important for Richardson's heroines to focus the beams of those mordantly psychological moralists upon the natural genesis and progress of their own thoughts and motives.[40] Nor did Johnson have any thought of that kind when praising Richardson for having "enlarged the knowledge of human nature" or saying Richardson understood the workings of the watch, Fielding only how to read its face.[41] I choose these words carefully—forcefully, to make my point about the philosophical tale in contrast to the novel, but without taking or intending to take anything away from Richardson's merits in realism of presentation, including the presentation of hearts convincingly alive and suffering, the more so because in some degree strangers to themselves.

One could say the same, I think, of that seminal French novel *La Princesse de Clèves* (1678) of Mme de La Fayette, which ends with the Princess' thoughtful, historical, skeptical assessment of the motives of the man she loves and refuses, but which nowhere shows the Princess so attentive to her own motives.[42] Somewhat comparably, *Les Égarements du cœur et de l'esprit* (1736–1738) by Crébillon *fils* begins sturdily with a preface not merely claiming that the novel will describe men as they are but also depicting the worldly young hero as "plein de fausses idées"[43]—because other characters corrupt him. Yet this unfinished novel stops before he has to take stock of his ideas, and since the preface says that he will be reformed by a good woman, he was apparently destined to have as little to do, personally, with escaping from error as he has for getting into it.

CHAPTER THREE

Self-Assessment:
Two Heads or One

. . . Thus blinded as they have been from the beginning, they never could think otherwise, at least without a vigour of mind able to contest the empire of habit, and look into its own principles, a freedom which few men have the notion of in themselves, and fewer are allowed the practice of by others; it being the great art and business of the teachers and guides in most sects, to suppress, as much as they can, this fundamental duty which every man owes himself. . . .

—Locke, *Of the Conduct of the Understanding*

*T*he earlier philosophical tales I take up, *Lettres persanes* and *Gulliver's Travels*, are forcefully ironical about the main character's attainment of self-knowledge, though amply concerned with the resources and methods of such inquiry. Gulliver achieves a "parody of awareness,"[1] in a context promoting something more substantial. Usbek, in the *Lettres persanes*, may seem to do better—while bringing on a climax worse than Gulliver's. Narration in each case is in the first person, like that of *Pamela* (Montesquieu's book being epistolary like hers as well), a mode emphasizing the main character's isolation, as does the fact that neither has a mentor most of the time. Both philosophical heroes would gladly be instructed, or so they declare, but prefer to teach, doing their learning on their own.

The self-taught person, according to the maxim, has a fool for a teacher. But the autodidact is not the only person susceptible to that misfortune. For Locke, education can be a major cause of mismatched ideas, and John Gay subtly elaborates the opinion when considering whether, as Francis Hutcheson had held, a person has such feelings as gratitude to a benefactor or pity for the distressed because there is in human nature an innate moral sense. There is not, Gay argues, though in the case of gratitude or pity or the like, including less attractive emotions, we may not have formed our dispositions consciously. In such cases

> We do not always (and perhaps not for the most part) *make* this Association ourselves, but *learn* it from *others*; *i.e.* that we annex Pleasure or Pain to certain Things or Actions because we see others do it, and acquire Principles of Action by im[i]tating those whom we admire, or whose Esteem we would procure: Hence the Son too often inherits both the Vices and the Party of his Father, as well as his Estate: Hence *National* Virtues and Vices, Dispositions and Opinions: And from hence we may observe how easy it is to account for what is generally call'd the *Prejudice of Education*; how soon we catch the Temper and Affections of those whom we daily converse with; how almost insensibly we are *taught* to love, admire or hate; to be grateful, generous, compassionate or cruel, *&c.*[2]

Education, formal or informal, can be a trap not simply for the obvious reason that the material taught may be untrue but also because human beings have a tendency to set their hearts on or against objects by imitating the desires and aversions of people they admire and wish to have think well of them—an insidious possibility.

This trait is exactly what René Girard, writing on its prominence in the novel, calls "triangular desire." Improving on Jules de Gaultier's book about *Bovarysme*, Girard shows it is not merely the externals of other characters that Flaubert's heroes and heroines imitate (the walk, the dress), but the very desires of others. The point leads quickly to a division between those novels that bring this tendency of human beings to light, exposing the contradictions of unconscious, imitative desire and the frustration and suffering it causes, and those less uncommon novels ("romantic," Girard calls these), that speciously capitalize on such feeling.[3] The distinction might have appealed to Johnson; it is a way of commenting on Jacques Barzun's remark that the novel, having after Joyce and Lawrence had enough full, realistic elaboration of "Character and Consciousness," stood in need of a "Bovariectomy."[4] Girard's argument intriguingly suggests an affinity between one of the longest and most absorbing works of fiction in existence, Proust's masterpiece, and the comparatively standoffish, succinct works that concern me. More than the philosophical tales, however, Proust may need a critic, not so much to demonstrate the point as to make readers feel it. I return to the history of what passes in the mind according to Gay.

It is striking that in describing imitative desire and in the rest of his discourse Gay raises doubts concerning two of the most common traditional means of attaining and preserving both sanity and wisdom: his "axioms," which correspond to the maxims so energetically propounded by moralists, and the mentor. The educated eighteenth-century person would derive from a mentor the maxims guiding his conduct; in a sense, a man was his maxims. The formula whereby mentor plus maxims makes wisdom is the essence of what may be the purest, neatest example of pre-Enlightenment philosophical fiction, Archbishop Fénelon's *Télémaque*, published in 1699. Tutor to the grandson of Louis XIV, Fénelon composed the tale, a prose epic, as a fictional textbook. In it, Telemachus searches for his father Ulysses, as in the first four books of the *Odyssey*, but Fénelon's narrative concentrates on the youth's activities between Homer's fourth and fifteenth books, before the meeting finally occurs.

From the beginning, when Telemachus arrives at Calypso's island, he is accompanied by old Mentor, as he thinks. In fact, as in Homer, Mentor is really Minerva in disguise, and the narrative sails forward on an almost unbroken stream of declamatory discourse between the young man and his divine elder, who unceasingly inculcates wisdom, *sagesse*: the word turns up repeatedly. Mentor is a mobile university of *sagesse* applied to questions of personal and political morality and policy, primarily morality. Each adventure provides a case to be examined, analyzed, and related to wisdom, especially wisdom in the form of maxims, and Telemachus proves remarkably docile, loyal, even reverent to his teacher. Mentor unfailingly dispels his charge's confusion, drawing the veil from general truths, the maxims, too easily unperceived by the unwise; Telemachus never seriously questions Mentor's judgment, although at one point Mentor has to hurl the youth physically, from the island of Calypso's temptations, into the sea. The consequent maxim is "on ne surmonte le vice qu'en le fuyent."[5] Telemachus will now fear his passions more than anything. Within Fénelon's world, to proceed from everyday confusion to the clarity of the maxims of wisdom is to soar above the welter of passion into the realm of the goddess, transcendent, absolute, divine ("un autre ordre de sagesse," as Zadig's angel says). Having identified herself to Telemachus, Minerva declares at the end, "Je vous quitte, ô fils d'Ulysse; mais ma sagesse ne vous quittera point, pourvu que vous sentiez toujours que vous ne pouvez rien sans elle" ("I leave you, O son of Ulysses; but my wisdom will never leave you, provided that you steadfastly believe you can accomplish nothing without it").[6] *Sagesse* is personified as if it were the Holy Spirit. Minerva, like Christ, leaves, but leaves the Comforter with Telemachus, who will live, move, and have his being only by holding fast to transcendent Wisdom, which has entered him in small infusions over the course of the tale. The unison of Telemachus and Wisdom at the end is thoroughly prefigured by the unanimity of Telemachus and Mentor from the beginning.

Maxims are important to later philosophical tales as well: moral maxims of the sort that permeate *Rasselas*, sly and satirical maxims like those in *Candide*. Maxims, however, call for the delicate art of selecting which maxim fits which occasion, and here a mentor can help. But whereas sprightly Mentor in *Télémaque* is perfect master of applications, the mentors in *Candide* and *Rasselas* are not transcendently wise, able as Imlac in *Rasselas* can be. The point of view of these later tales, more earthbound than the Archbishop's, resembles John Gay's, and hence the questions will arise: why this maxim? why this mentor? Is the maxim in question a mere prejudiced "resting place"? Is the pupil "almost insensibly" catching "the Temper and Affections of those" daily conversed with?

Association with a particular mentor can bring a character either weakness or strength. Just as one must learn to profit from maxims, one must learn to employ one's mentor. Both can serve idolatrous purposes, promoting triangular desire, becoming extensions of the hero's problems rather than aids in resolution of them, as both Johnson and Voltaire clearly recognize. (Then there is Gulliver's succession of mentors, and Usbek's mullahs.) The struggle of disciple versus mentor becomes important to the philosophical tale—another characteristic of the genre that tends to distinguish it from the novel—figuring forth, within the action of the tale, a problem like that addressed by Johnson in *Rambler* 4 concerning the power of fiction to distort a reader's mind. To the extent that a solution is reached in the tale, it occurs because the hero has achieved at least some degree of detachment from his mentor or mentors (Candide has two, reflecting his desire for comfort of the kind provided by Fénelon). And, a major though subtle feature of the art of *Rasselas* and *Candide*, not to mention Jane Austen, this struggle is paralleled by a dramatic relationship between the reader of the tale and *his* mentor, the narrator—a third-person narrator in each case and a narrator with a pronounced mind and character of his own and a part to play.

We associate the philosophical tale with the Enlightenment, famously described by Kant as entailing a refusal to employ someone else to think for oneself. Locke wanted much of the thought of the past to be sifted in the new sieve he had provided. Hume and others were more dogmatic, on occasion, about the need for thorough change in the general way of thinking. In the tales, the hero, with little traditional baggage, is transported to worlds well beyond what he has known. The mentor tends to take on the responsibility of presenting to him what at least some portion of mankind has adopted as wisdom; the hero has to decide what, in new circumstances, may be worth preserving. The more militantly Enlightened Montesquieu and Voltaire, like the quite resolutely not Enlightened Swift (if I may speak so bluntly for the present), employ heroes who will seem to preserve very little. The more moderately Enlightened Johnson will seemingly preserve more, though much of it on a new, post-Lockean foundation. But the tradition of wisdom, neither omniscient nor silent, addresses itself to the meeting of generations as well as to every other human subject, more or less adequately.

To everything there is a season, runs Ecclesiastes' maxim, bearing like many other maxims on the theme of the ages of man, the concept of a set of phases or chain of events typical of human character and personality through a lifetime. Bacon echoes the motif frequently in the *Essays* (subtitled "Counsels"), for example, "Wives are young men's mistresses; companions for middle age; and old men's nurses," from "Of Marriage and Single Life." (Both this title and the essay's sentiments anticipate the marriage debate between Rasselas and his sister.) Noteworthy for wariness about the human capacity for delusion, Bacon is also daringly constructive in thinking there may be a natural program in human, mental growth, and in the Second Book of *The Advancement of Learning*, with a memorable phrase, he declares the need for a science promoting cultivation of the best possible growth in that quarter, a "Georgics of the mind."[7] Here and elsewhere the concept of the ages of man shows, itself, remarkable longevity; Hume rhetorically asks, "Are the changes of our body from infancy to old age more regular and certain than those of our mind and conduct?"[8]

A commonplace in European literature and art from long before the eighteenth century, the ages topos could sometimes have a Polonian irrelevancy about it.[9] But like any general notion it will serve different masters in different ways, as Pope shows, updating Jaques' speech in *As You Like It*, when putting the theme in the service of the long views taken by *An Essay on Man*:

> Behold the child, by Nature's kindly law,
> Pleas'd with a rattle, tickled with a straw:
> Some livelier play-thing gives his youth delight,
> A little louder, but as empty quite:
> Scarfs, garters, gold, amuse his riper stage;
> And beads and pray'r-books are the toys of age:
> Pleas'd with this bauble still, as that before;
> 'Till tir'd he sleeps, and Life's poor play is o'er.[10]

When the limits of the concept are recognized, when it is handled with discretion and imagination as a model for conceiving of human nature rather than as a set of direct, universal truths, the concept can be useful in the service of shorter views, as Aristotle thought when comparing the characteristics of "youth, old age, and the prime of life" in the *Rhetoric*.[11] I bring in the ages of man because of the concept's application to questions of continuity and discontinuity between the viewpoints of younger and older characters in the philosophical tales, and because of the related fact that the concept was given new application and force by eighteenth-century philosophers.

The logic of discovery described by Cassirer occupies itself with the ages of man as well as with the comparable issues of the chain of mental events in psychology and political science, in contrast to the older logic of hierarchical classification. Shakespeare's Jaques classifies, marking the boundaries between the various successive ages, unconcerned with suggesting causes of change (except perhaps in the character of the no-longer-innocent justice), and Pope, indicating there is no change to speak of, conflating Jaques and Prospero, buries change in continuity. For Shakespeare, the forces bringing about change in the person are as external, or as impersonal, as the steps of a stairway (with wordplay on "stage") leading up on one side and down on the other; Jaques does not "sound the depths of the heart for motives of action." In the eighteenth century, by contrast, prominent thinkers tend to subject the ages of man to genetic definition—a major Enlightenment enterprise too grand for full description here, bearing on Rousseau's *Émile*, on the awakening statue of Condillac, Buffon, and Charles Bonnet, and on much else.[12]

To say the least, such definition becomes a very attractive way of tracing natural human progress from origins with reference to the individual person. It has a major part in Hartley, Long, and their successors; it will burgeon for literature in Wordsworth, the child "father of the man," and in Keats's Miltonic sense of the successive "Chambers" of consciousness.[13] There is an early trace of the concept as a genetic model in Matthew Prior's comical *Alma*, wherein the soul moves upward from the child's feet to the man's cranium with characteristic pauses along the way. A more sober version, but Pauline rather than Popean, appears in Hutcheson: "Nay, let us consider the different *Ages* in our own Species. We once knew the time when an *Hobby-Horse*, a *Top*, a *Rattle*, was sufficient Pleasure to us. We grow up, we now relish *Friendships, Hon-*

our, good Offices, Marriage, Offspring, serving a Community or Country.
Is there no difference in these Tastes?"[14] There is, he asserts; indicating a genetic model, there is an enlargement in the desire and
satisfaction which a virtuous man feels with respect to these successive classes of objects.

A remarkable genetic model of development through the ages
distinguishes *Rambler* 151, where, noting the observations of physicians and physiologists on "the several stages by which animal
life makes its progress from infancy to decrepitude," Johnson observes, "It had been a task worthy of the moral philosophers to
have considered with equal care the climactericks of the mind; to
have pointed out the time at which every passion begins and ceases
to predominate, and noted the regular variations of desire, and the
succession of one appetite to another."[15] Which Johnson proceeds
to do, not without allowance for individual differences (nor omitting
mention of a person's changing taste in fiction along the way). "Nature will indeed always operate . . ." (p. 42). First, regarding the
progress of consciousness, he comments that three faculties each
take their turn, youth being characterized by novelty-seeking imagination, maturity by "judgment or reason" which settles a person's
principles, and old age by memory—and cranky stubbornness. He
then turns to the passions and appetites in a second series: "In like
manner the passions usurp the separate command of the successive
periods of life." Actually, the passions have come into the scheme
already, witness the stubborness, but that inclusion represents no
oversight on Johnson's part, for they precede and motivate the suc-
cessively dominant faculties.

First the pleasure of "freedom from restraint" (p. 40) makes
the child's world a "banquet," whereupon the force of "our senses
and appetites" drives a person toward the delights of "art and contrivance," until curiosity is exhausted. The succession of "interest"
to pleasure enthrones ambitious prudence and foresight, to achieve
wealth, power, and fame in the second age of the mind, but when
"fame is observed to be uncertain, and power to be dangerous,"
and when abilities are felt to wane, all that remains is the desire
for wealth and the power it brings (p. 41). "Avarice is generally
the last passion of those lives of which the first part has been squan-

dered in pleasure, and the second devoted to ambition. He that sinks under the fatigue of getting wealth, lulls his age with the milder business of saving it" (pp. 41–42). The old man closes his mind to preserve his established tenets against novelty; that is, according to Johnson's not especially cheering scenario, against precisely what the youngest seek most—the snake spits out his tail. This is not Erik Erikson's lively "epigenetic cycle," or is a short version suggesting some critical failures. But of course Johnson does not himself regard this progress as determining fully and exclusively what the pattern of a life must be, far from it; he concludes with the precept that "nature may be regulated, and desires governed" (p. 42). Knowing the genetic cycle he has described, evidently an important part of the self-knowledge enjoined in *Rambler* 24, must be useful for that regulation and government, as the chart of a river will enable the voyager to prepare for, and guide himself during, his journey down it. Moreover, not unimportantly, a genetic definition of the ages suggests ways of understanding what may make another traveler, older or younger, differ in feeling and thought from oneself.

The perfect synthesis achieved in the other-worldly world of *Télémaque* is not to be expected from the considerably more realistic confrontation of mentor and pupil in later philosophical tales. Fénelon magically implants an old head between young receptive shoulders. In the worlds of *Candide* and *Rasselas* that operation cannot work. Ironically—and tellingly—it seems to be desired and attempted by the young person himself at the outset of each of these tales, in vain, like Boswell's resolution to ape Addison's propriety of sentiment.[16] Instead, in *Rasselas* and *Candide*, the heroes with time achieve a distancing of self from the mentors they would like to have become, or more precisely, a distancing of self from the image of the mentor initially in the young person's imagination. The heroes achieve still more, certainly Rasselas does, attaining an active combination of critical distance from and sympathetic understanding of the mentor that resembles the pupil's developed attitude toward himself.

This process and its culmination help distinguish the philosophical tale from a genre with which a reader may confuse it, the (largely) nineteenth-century *Bildungsroman*. At the outset of a moving study of that form, Jerome Hamilton Buckley conveniently draws its most general outlines:

> A child of some sensibility grows up in the country or in a provincial town, where he finds constraints, social and intellectual, placed upon the free imagination. His family, especially his father, proves doggedly hostile to his creative instincts or flights of fancy, antagonistic to his ambitions, and quite impervious to the new ideas he has gained from unprescribed reading. His first schooling, even if not totally inadequate, may be frustrating insofar as it may suggest options not available to him in his present setting. He therefore, sometimes at a quite early age, leaves the repressive atmosphere of home (and also the relative innocence), to make his way independently in the city. . . . There his real "education" begins, not only his preparation for a career but also—and often more importantly—his direct experience of urban life. The latter involves at least two love affairs or sexual encounters, one debasing, one exalting, and demands that in this respect and others the hero reappraise his values. By the time he has decided, after painful soul-searching, the sort of accommodation to the modern world he can honestly make, he has left his adolescence behind.[17]

In ensuing comments Buckley lays stress upon "the defection of the father [which] becomes accordingly the principal motive force in the assertion of the youth's independence," linking him with "heroes of romance and folklore" and propelling him toward "self-education" and exalting, transcendent love.[18] The presentation may be very realistic—a full map of London or Paris derivable from it—but the plot goes unfathomably deep, into the most insistent and impossible longings associated with the family romance, just those longings which the philosophical tale holds unrealizable, regressive, and dangerous. From the standpoint of the tale, the element sharply lacking in the economy of the *Bildungsroman* is, above all, the mentor who may become a friend of the hero but will be neither his father nor his mother, nor the deluding succadaneum of either, yet will take a helpful interest in him.

The philosophical tale promotes the delicate state of affairs that Eliot would wish for, learning "to care and not to care." Adam Smith defines it in a philosophical treatise of the same year that produced *Candide* and *Rasselas*, *The Theory of Moral Sentiments* (1759), which, according to a model I shall examine more closely in the next chapter, describes the subtle interplay between self and other. Through mutual attentiveness, Smith's associates can approach shared feeling and definite satisfaction from it, though the exact same emotion cannot be felt by both. Between the feelings of each there "will never be unisons," yet there "may be concords." And concords, Smith comments in a tone cooler than that of the book as a whole, are "all that is wanted or required."[19]

We stand a little apart from Tristan and Isolde, Manon and des Grieux, Julie and her mentor. Whether the Enlightenment philosophical tale eventuates in a concord or not, between hero and himself, hero and mentor, hero and narrator, narrator and reader, it is in a place where concord is the most that can be expected, where Fénelon-like or novelistic or romantic unisons are unrealizable, that the tale has its being. Jean Ehrard brings together most of France's prominent early novelists in the observation that Crébillon, like Marivaux or Prévost, dreamed of a perfect love unifying a person's being in the harmony of mind and heart.[20] Candide would like to think he can perform that feat of unison with himself by virtue of his professed feeling for Cunégonde, an error which the narrator, by focusing the logic of discovery upon the interesting associative genesis of that passion, keeps the careful reader from bringing into concord with his own responses. Instead of pursuing Eros—or in contrast to that pursuit, as in Voltaire and especially Montesquieu, who has available the possible raptures of Usbek's harem—the tales concentrate on friendship, typically across a pronounced barrier, that of nationality (of species in *Gulliver*) or most of all that presented by differing ages of man. Older Usbek, younger Rica in the *Lettres persanes* together give this theme great prominence and in happier moments may remind readers of an illustration from Smith employing an "ages" maxim: "The young, according to the common saying, are most agreeable when in their behaviour there is something of the manners of the old, and the old, when they retain something of the gaiety of the young."[21]

The failure to achieve workable concord with self and other in circumstances which everywhere shriek its desirability may be the subject of a philosophical tale, as in Swift and Montesquieu, in different ways; the attaining of detachment from drastic, premature, fallacious unison, as in Voltaire; the achievement, with difficulty, of concord, as in Johnson. Yet in all these writers the civilized concern with the psychological practicalities of the pursuit of personal and social concords is the most important, still revolutionary, ground of identity for the genre called the philosophical tale. Since transcendent unisons are beyond the *ne plus ultra* of the tales, they typically come to more of a stop than an elaborate conclusion; any sign of the latter is a sign of real trouble, as in Swift and Montesquieu. In the end the tales are unending, emphasizing throughout and afterward the fallacies of mindless idealization, disseminating doubts about the allure of the romantic and novelistic, single-minded ideal, going about the business of promoting inner and outer concords when practicable.

"Hushed be every ruder Breath." Fielding was drawn sufficiently toward *Sagesse* to name the woman he thus begins to introduce, the beloved of Tom Jones, *Sophia*, and of all the early novelists he comes closest to sharing the concerns of the philosophical tale. Scrutiny of his novels from the point of view of the tale does not bring out what is best in them. It does not do justice to his artful, ironical ways with plot, narration, and commentary, nor does it sufficiently admire more particular merits, such as the sophistication Ronald Paulson discovers in Fielding's play with conventions—for example, depiction of his heroes as something other and more than a host of analogous literary, iconographical, and historical figures, including Fénelon's Telemachus.[22] (That Telemachus hovers near Richardson's heroines too.)[23] But passing, economical attention to Fielding here can clarify what philosophical tales positively do, and the fact that Fielding was somehow attracted to doing something approaching it brings additional, circumstantial evidence for my contentions about the tale, the novel, and eighteenth-century thought.

Fielding begins, as a writer of prose fiction, with satirical works of fairly abstract characterization: *Shamela* (1741), *Jonathan Wild* (1743), and, at least at the outset, when the hero appears as a fairly undifferentiated figure of Chastity, *Joseph Andrews* (1742). With its preface showing some of the concerns voiced by Johnson in *Rambler* 4, *Joseph Andrews* in several respects resembles works generally labeled philosophical tales. The interpolated story of Mr. Wilson differs from Hogarth's *Rake's Progress* by reason of, among other things, Wilson's desire to reform himself, indeed to be wise. An interval of reflection makes him forsake his drinking cronies to join a club "frequented by young Men of great Abilities," who discuss "the deepest Points of Philosophy," significantly throwing away "all the Prejudices of Education," belief in God as well, establishing "in his stead a certain *Rule of Right*, by adhering to which they all arrived at the utmost Purity of Morals."[24] The wiser, older Wilson is speaking, with the clarity of bitter experience, for these young philosophers quickly prove capable of actions disappointingly base. The experience prefigures that of Rasselas when he encounters, among a "coarse" group of learned men, a philosopher who speaks grandly about a life led "according to nature" but cannot make his doctrine specific enough to be comprehensible, to Rasselas' dismay. Similarly, Rasselas' encounter with the Stoic who cannot bear the death of his daughter recalls the scene in *Joseph Andrews* of Parson Adams, who has just discoursed on strict control of emotion, weeping at news of his son's supposed death by drowning (4.8.309). In both cases the younger man recalls the older to his professed doctrines. Although we know and like Adams much better than we do the Stoic, the two scenes resemble each other more than they differ.

Comparably, both narratives indicate intellectual growth on the part of the hero, growth, moreover, assisted by a mentor. To Rasselas in these respects I return later. Joseph may be considered apart from him, and briefly; there is not a great deal to say. At the beginning he pleases the scholarly, mentorial Adams by having read "the Bible, the *Whole Duty of Man*, and Thomas a Kempis," and Baker's *Chronicle* (1.3.24); Joseph enters the book fortified with Christian piety and morality. Like most heroes of romance, he has nothing much to learn, though with experience of the world he will show himself more adept than he is at first in dealing with its deceptive Lady Booby's. (But this too is not a theme of paramount importance for Fielding, who can exhibit considerable suspicion of the suspicious.) A little on in the volume, writing to his (he believes) sister Pamela, Joseph attributes his stalwart chastity not to the books he has read, which cover the subject well, but to Adams' teachings and Pamela's letters (1.10.46). Fielding does not become concerned overmuch with the genesis of Joseph's thinking. It is easy to imagine Adams as Joseph's mentor, so suited is he to the role in age and profession, morals, and—to a large degree—temperament. Adams casts himself thus, reproving Joseph when, in opposition to the regulations of the Church regarding banns, the youth wants an immediate wedding (2.13.160), and later debating with him the advisability of public-school education, a scene broadly reminiscent of Fénelon except for Adams' obstinacy and, as the narrator explains, extreme vanity: "Indeed if this good Man had an Enthusiasm, or what the Vulgar call a Blind-side, it was this: He thought a Schoolmaster the greatest Character in the World, and himself the greatest of all Schoolmasters; neither of which Points he would have given up to *Alexander .the Great* at the Head of his Army" (3.5.232).

Joseph appears wiser as the story progresses. When, toward the end of Book 2, Adams credulously accepts the rash promises of a stranger who suddenly befriends him (a scene like that in which Candide will drink in the blandishments of some army recruiters), Joseph proves wary. Adams the schoolmaster insists, ". . . Knowledge of Men is only to be learnt from Books; *Plato* and *Seneca* for that; and those are Authors, I am afraid Child, you never read." Joseph has not, he admits, but says there is "a Maxim" among servants "that those Masters who promise the most perform the least" (2.16.176). This is a classic confrontation, wisdom divided between book learning and shrewd observation of experience, but Joseph, not deluded by vanity about his skill and resources, has the better of it and continues to have the better in exchanges with Adams to the end of the novel. What I have said thus far about Joseph parallels the argument employed by one commentator to show "a noticeable and sympathetic change and development of character into maturity." Joseph acquires "a personality of his own, a stature and force and meaning in the novel, which contribute to its thought and richness of characterization."[25] That development can be overstated, however, for at most it begins to bring "realities to mind," and not the reality of genetic change. Fielding is as little concerned to say or otherwise indicate how Joseph constructs his increased wisdom, which sets him apart from his would-be instructor, as he was concerned earlier to account for the genesis of Joseph's thinking.

Instead, over all, he makes Joseph seem wiser by giving him less to say, moving him to the background somewhat (a tactic adumbrating Clarissa's rise to relatively mute ineffability late in her novel), while giving Adams greater prominence than he has had and increasing our sense of his foolishness. Joseph appears to grow in wisdom because Adams is revealed to be less stably wise than he first appears. The characterization of Adams begins in earnest when he re-enters toward the close of Book 1, having been introduced fleetingly in chapter 3. Chapter 14 presents him unnamed, simply as a "grave Person." Joseph is lying upstairs at an inn, wounded by robbers, attended by a pompous surgeon, comforted by an uncouth parson, Barnabas, and despised by the innkeeper's wife. The grave person's reaction to her is gravely expressed: "It is not easy to say, whether the Gentleman had conceived a greater Dislike for his Landlady, or Compassion for her unhappy Guest. He enquired very earnestly of the Surgeon, who was now come into the Kitchin, 'whether he had any hopes of his recovery?'" With characteristic uprightness, Adams says the surgeon ought to give the best care he can even to the penniless. What is particularly interesting, though, is that the surgeon soon berates Adams for not having read Galen and Hippocrates, which the surgeon claims to know by heart and usually to carry about with him in his pocket. Adams replies, "They are pretty large Books," in the tone of a moral frontiersman.

My direction will be apparent. When the vainglorious surgeon says, "I suppose . . . you understand *Latin*," Adams remains the eiron: "A little" (1.14.61–63). He maintains anonymous gravity. But when later in the book he flowers as a comic character himself, it is significantly as an outgrowth of seeds planted in this scene, in different pots. The Adams who out of vanity supposes aloud that Joseph has not read Plato and Seneca has his origin in the surgeon prating of Galen and Hippocrates, and in the pocket of Adams, as yet unrevealed during the encounter with that surgeon, lurks the redoubtable Aeschylus. By the same token, the clergyman Barnabas, in the scene at the inn, foreshadows another of Adams' comic traits. When Joseph shudders at the sorrow Fanny will feel upon discovering he is dead of his wounds, Barnabas observes "that such Fears argued a Diffidence and Despondence very criminal; that he must divest himself of all human Passion, and fix his Heart above" (1.13.59). It is just such unfeeling consolation that Adams will offer Joseph at length when Fanny is kidnapped (3.11.264–66), again when the young people seek immediate marriage (4.8.308, the prelude to the Abraham-Isaac scene), and again when it appears they are brother and sister (4.13.330). Thus Joseph seems to develop because he appears graver as the book progresses, in contrast to Adams, who is—but I use the word only technically, as it is applied to Gawain—degraded, in the service of the comedy of romance.

I bypass *Tom Jones* (1749), Fielding's masterpiece of comic romance and more, with virtually silent admiration, only observing that if Richardson's Clarissa says too little about some of her feelings, Tom occasionally says or thinks too much, as when, Walpole-like, he begins to wonder whether a "Sum of Money" will buy him release from the affections of Molly Seagrim.[26] Molly is pregnant, by him he believes, and he believes she loves him extremely; given what he believes, he cannot make Molly the offer he contemplates without taking the risk of seriously and permanently harming her. A turn of plot saves him, yet the scene of his calculation un-Ferdinands Ferdinand somewhat. Extenuation of Tom's calculations through both plot and commentary will keep the narrator pretty busy in the pages to come. There is nothing unnatural about Tom's changing his mind now that he has come to love Sophia, or about his scheme, which takes into account Molly's poverty and her vanity; if I may seem paradoxical for a moment, his thinking is as natural as Candide's. But besides departing from what generally occurs in romantic comedy, this episode might have been called to mind by Tom (or by the narrator), and is not, when much later we find Tom lecturing to another young man whose situation resembles Tom's with Molly, except not apparently so serious: it

is not known yet that the woman has a child on the way. Here
Tom permits himself to explain "Lookee, Mr. *Nightengale*, . . . I
am no canting Hypocrite. . . . I have been guilty with Women, I
own it; but am not conscious that I have ever injured any—nor
would I to procure Pleasure to myself, be knowingly the Cause of
Misery to any human Being" (14.4; 2.755). It is just possible that
Tom's plans for Molly, if they had been put into practice, might
not have been expected, from his point of view, to cause her misery.
Defining that possibility would keep a casuist as busy as the narrator was when distracting us from Tom's scheming. The campaign
of distraction continues here. Tom's general reformation at the end
of the book has as little to do with realism of psychological self-
assessment as this speech does, a speech in which the narrator evidently sees nothing amiss. Tom remains something of a Skinnerian
pigeon who has pecked the charged wire often enough to "learn,"
as is acceptable in the genre of the book.

It is, however, one of the points of permanent interest in Fielding that he would make incursions where angels do not, as C. J.
Rawson particularly has taught us, displaying the nerve Fielding
manifested in continual wrestling with hard questions.[27] In his last
novel, *Amelia* (1752), the author who in *Shamela* had been so crude
and shrewd about Pamela's motives comes closest to the realism of
Richardson and Defoe, and closer than they to emphasizing realism
of psychological self-assessment. The narrator is subdued, the
Fieldingesque intrusiveness and facetiousness at a minimum, the
style plain, the subject sober—the story of a family oppressed by
poverty, debt, and social manipulation, deadening circumstances
rendered with historical particularity. The opening scenes, with
the hero in prison, have special force because of the drama created
by the psychological insight of his fellow inmate, the beautiful se-
ductress Miss Matthews, who has read "Mandevil"[28] and who clev-
erly retails a version of her life history imaginatively analytical and
persuasive, to pierce the hero's defenses. She would be at home in
a French novel of the period; like Jonathan Wild she has "a wonderful knack of discovering and applying to the passions of men."[29]
But I move on to more central matters in *Amelia*.

The hero, Booth, is also a psychologist, or appears to be. In jail he converses with yet another prisoner, a fatalist named Robinson—chapter 10 of Voltaire's *L'Ingénu* could be a variation of this scene—and declares "himself to be of the same opinion with regard to the necessity of human actions; adding, however, that he did not believe men were under any blind impulse or direction of fate, but that every man acted merely from the force of that passion which was uppermost in his mind, and could do no otherwise" (1.4; 1.15). Booth professes a view possibly derived from Hume, "Reason . . . the slave of the passions" which obey an iron law of cause and effect beyond the power of a person to direct or even modify them.[30] But from the point of view of the philosophical tale an important consideration has been omitted. Is the uppermost passion of which Booth repeatedly speaks to be taken definitely as one of several that govern a person by turns? Or is the uppermost passion one that has more or less supremacy over the other passions, giving the person a definite personality? Pursuing these questions will reveal Booth to be much less a psychologist and the Fielding of this novel to be much less concerned with psychology than they seem.

There is another eighteenth-century psychology possibly bearing on *Amelia*, more important in some respects than Hume's. *An Essay on Man* makes it clear that Pope thought each person has a "ruling passion" of the second sort, dominating the other passions permanently and thereby distinguishing one person from another. Further, Pope says a person's central moral duty is the difficult but possible identification of his own ruling passion through genetic self-assessment of a kind, so as to guide that passion toward the most estimable ends: "to rectify, not overthrow" the ruling passion.[31] The point is reinforced by the first of Pope's *Moral Essays*. In *Amelia*, curiously, the idea like Hume's of a series of passions ruling by turns is not distinguished clearly from Pope's sense of a distinctive, personal ruling passion. Several of Booth's statements about what he variously calls "the reigning passion" (3.7; 1.125), "my ascendant passion" (2.2; 1.61), and "that passion which was uppermost" (3.4; 1.108) could admit both meanings, especially because for Pope the characterizing passion in a person may remain obscure or only slowly manifest itself. None of Booth's statements refers univocally to the Humean view. When, however, Booth declares, of Miss Matthews, "Vanity is plainly her predominant passion . . ." (4.6; 1.187), the psychology is definitely Popean, and may be too in Booth's contention "that all men . . . act alike from the principle of self-love," which may eventuate in benevolence, as it does in some, or in another "passion" (10.9; 2.214).

Believing as Booth does that the ruling passion acts as it will by necessity and cannot be guided (a point about which Hume could vacillate, or hedge his pronouncements: "it being *almost* impossible for the mind to change its character in any considerable article, or cure itself of a passionate or splenetic temper, *when they are natural to it*"[32]—italics mine), it is understandable that Fielding's hero would not investigate Popean rectification. My point is not to prove that Booth belongs more to Pope's camp than to Hume's, but to expose the murkiness of his psychologizing. It is definitely odd that Booth, among all his pronouncements, does not seek to justify the choice he has made, in effect, between different versions of ruling-passion theory, and that, to the extent his opinion follows Pope's, Booth never—even if simply out of curiosity, or pride of intellectual position, or boredom in prison—says what his own characteristic passion might be or so much as wonders about it. A ruling passion must be at the root of his philosophy, which really functions as expressive description of his suffering. The lack of formal introspection in Booth is all the odder because he historically and rhetorically trades autobiography with Miss Matthews at such great length. A more fundamental oddity, though, lies in the narrator's not calling attention to the varieties of ruling passion psychology, an omission which signals the definite (also expressive) absence of the theme of psychological self-assessment from the eighteenth-century English novel that approaches it most closely.

Prudence, love, and Christian faith and morals are the truly important themes in *Amelia*. Like Tom Jones, Booth tends to be imprudent, but his wife, Amelia, proves as strong as he is weak and contributes substantially to the family's salvation. The major architect of that happy resolution, however, is the mentorial clergyman Dr. Harrison, who continually arrives at the right moment, or soon enough after, to bail out the Booths—literally or figuratively. Robinson the fatalist turns up unexpectedly at the end as another providential instrument, whereby Amelia receives the family property. Much may be said about this ending and about such, strictly speaking, romantic endings in general. Whereas the complication of *Amelia* is realistic, unprecedentedly so in Fielding, and the realism of assessment approaches being psychological as well as moral and sociological, another new departure for Fielding, nevertheless the ending is as pointedly symbolic or emblematic or allegorical as those of *Joseph Andrews* and *Tom Jones*. It will be useful for me in long- as well as short-term ways to return to *Tom Jones* for a moment.

A crucial part of the resolution there places Sophia, regarded as angelic (e.g., 18.10; 2.962), in exactly the position regarding judgment on the basis of the chain of events that we have seen Pamela and Clarissa occupy. Sophia says to Tom, ". . . What Happiness can I assure myself of with a Man capable of so much Inconstancy? . . . If I am to judge . . . of the future by the past, my Image will no more remain in your Heart, when I am out of your Sight, than it will in this Glass when I am out of the Room" and she proceeds to assign Tom a year of probation. Whereupon, to the reader's pleasure, Sophia's bumptious father, Squire Western, bursts in to rebuke Tom for giving "way to a Parcel of maidenish Tricks.—I tell thee 'tis all Flimflam. Zoodikers! she'd have the Wedding to-Night with all her Heart. Would'st not, *Sophy?* Come confess, and be an honest Girl for once," and she agrees, not without some talk of obliging a parent, to marry Tom the next day. The mechanism of the scene is perfect for a book like this, not bringing us into Sophia's mind as we were brought into Tom's when he was meditating on Molly, externalizing and allegorizing Sophia's inner conflict by deputing Western to play the part of her desires, outside her generally maidenly, comic-romance head.[33]

The interlude preempts realism of self-assessment, hardly to the reader's dismay, and Fielding gestures toward such realism by making Sophy, who is not a prude, incline herself in Tom's direction before her father enters, the year's probation to end, she says, "Perhaps . . . something sooner" (18.12; 2.972–74). The comic-romance tactic of bifurcating the mind of a character for external, allegorical resolution of problems involving self-knowledge, self-interest, and calculation (in this scene Sophia, oddly recalling Johnson's comment, is a timepiece telling years, days, and hours) survives to some extent, though not so schematically as here, in several novels of Jane Austen, a fact indicating why, in the final chapters of the present book, I concentrate on other novels of hers, which more thoroughly confine assessment of self and other within the mind of the heroine. Often considered a stepping-stone between Fielding and Austen, Fanny Burney's *Evelina* (1778) centers on a young woman who, within her circle, is among the last to know she is in love, and whose state of mind as she finally prepares to marry is "thrice-happy"[34] because the marriage has been approved by her elderly, old-fashioned mentor, her disreputable father, and her young, alert suitor: a trio representing the ages of man and the faculties of the mind allegorically supporting her decision.

To return to *Amelia*: From the standpoint of psychological realism, if the future is to be judged at all by the past, it is good that Booth has been given a home in the country, out of the wicked city, where Amelia and Harrison can keep an eye out for him, and perhaps on him. But allegorically, not without reference to the ages of man, by settling down with Harrison as well as with Amelia, Booth has embraced wisdom in addition to virtue, Harrison Booth's sage alter ego. ". . . No greater advantage, I am convinced," Booth comments early in the novel with Harrison in mind, "can arrive to a young man, who hath any degree of understanding, than an intimate converse with one of riper years, who is not only able to advise, but who knows the manner of advising. By this means alone, youth can enjoy the benefit of the experience of age, and that at a time of life when such experience will be of more service to a man than when he hath lived long enough to acquire it of himself" (3.12; 1.152). It is a not unwise comment, including as it does the mentor's need to know how as well as what to advise.

But the sensitivity of that comment can be misleading, creating the wrong expectations in a reader, for the transmission to Booth of the comfort of Harrison's wisdom is something Fielding asserts rather than investigates and demonstrates. Metaphorically, Booth is a watch that needs Harrison, periodically, to wind it up and reset it. Harrison appears less as mentor than as father to the Booths, whom he pointedly calls his children (3.10; 1.140), and he approaches being a perfect father in many respects, though neither omniscient nor without small failings (e.g., his susceptibility to flattery, 10.4; 2.188). The narrator, more subdued than earlier Fielding narrators (who tend themselves to be paternal, even paternalistic), would as clearly have us see Harrison as a father figure. And near the end of the book it is to this type of Harcourt-Reilly that Booth confesses he has forsaken his attachment to the determination of passion and has embraced Christianity, not on the basis of thought about psychology but because, in prison again, he has seen the truth while reading Isaac Barrow's sermons—another order of wisdom. Booth says appropriately, "If ever an angel might be thought to guide the pen of a writer, surely the pen of that great and good man had such an assistant." This is the Minervan moment. (The narrator, at one point in the book, has discoursed like Fénelon's Mentor on the sole remedy for sexual temptation: "To run away is all that is in our power"—6.1; 1.260.)

Most significantly, until this late scene of confession Harrison has been ignorant of Booth's apostasy and his fatalism; had Harrison known, he might have been given the part played by Barrow, and he might even have acted it ably: before the scene ends he shows he could have turned Booth's philosophy against him, for he observes pointedly that religion fits men's acting from passion by applying "immediately to the strongest of . . . passions, hope and fear" (a view much like Hartley's).[35] Had Harrison and Booth been characters in a philosophical tale, they would have debated the issues occupying Booth's mind, probably repeatedly across the narrative, clarifying the issues but, even more, disclosing and emphasizing why the exponent may need to hold one opinion rather than another. Instead, Booth and Harrison, in this long book, say comparatively little to each other. They and the narrator cannot wait to get this very short scene over with (its two pages—12.5; 2.287–88—have the three speakers say "need not be expatiated on," "ashamed to see you," "will defer this discourse"). Elsewhere Fielding takes pains to avoid confrontations between the apparent mentor figure and Booth, going so far, it appears, as to displace arguments with Harrison that might have involved Booth to scenes with other characters including learned Mrs. Atkinson (10.4; 2.185–87), an unnamed nobleman otherwise unimportant to the book (11.2; 2.225–32), and even Amelia (9.5; 2.131–33), whose main function in the novel, like that of the Redcrosse Knight in Spenser, is to maintain her original high moral ground, not without the Knight's unsteadiness at times, rather than debate theology with Una.

In the oddest of these episodes of displaced confrontation, Harrison contends with an upstart young scholar while the youth's venal father looks on—this pair of characters having been brought into the book almost exclusively for the present purpose—and the narrator lingers with father and son after Harrison has departed—a departure from the narrative norm too, attracting critical attention. The youth, in effect continuing his disagreement with the absent Harrison, besmears his father in a negative "ages" way, even referring to the classical ineffective counterpart of Mentor: "It is the common failing of old men to attribute all wisdom to themselves. Nestor did it long ago . . ." (9.10; 2.162). This little scene is the controlled saturnalian counterpart of the Minervan moment in *Amelia*, a novel in which, despite an interesting show of psychology, one single-minded head, provided that like Harrison's it is transcendently authoritative, in unison with truth, must be judged better than the alternatives, and the hero's deferring to that mentor, rather than—as in a philosophical tale—becoming significantly his own mentor—appears the adequate resolution of his difficulties.

CHAPTER FOUR

The Rub of Self-Love

"There is no alloy of self in what I feel for you."
—David Copperfield, to Agnes

*I*n describing the philosophical context of the tales thus far, I have
almost entirely kept back the most troublesome element in
eighteenth-century psychology. Bacon had warned, "Let every
student of nature take this as a rule,—that whatever his mind seizes
and dwells upon with peculiar satisfaction is to be held in suspicion."[1] The great source of prejudice, in a phrase everywhere in
eighteenth-century thought about the mind, is "self-love," that
favorite quarry of Mandeville, Swift, and, before them, a host of
witty seventeenth-century French moralists. In *Amelia* it is not surprising that Booth must confront a justice of the peace who "perfectly well understood that fundamental principle so strongly laid
down in the institutes of the learned Rochefoucault, by which the
duty of self-love is so strongly enforced, and every man is taught
to consider himself as the centre of gravity, and to attract all things
thither."[2] The play here with Newtonian physics as a model for
psychology deserves underlining: I shall return to something like
it in Part II, regarding the *Lettres persanes*; but I wish to call attention
also to the wide diffusion of comparable analogies in Enlightenment
psychology, in Hume and other thinkers whom Peter Gay calls
"Newtons of the Mind."[3] (The name for the magnet in French,
l'aimant, could not have discouraged that conception.) Voltaire most
memorably expresses the century's fascination with and embarrassment about self-love in a quip from the *Dictionnaire philosophique*,
that it resembles the organ of generation: we need, value, and enjoy
it—and have to hide it ("Amour-propre").[4]

Adam Smith, saying "concords not unisons" are the best that
can be expected in relations with others, may seem regrettably cool-
tempered, recalling that overwrought remark of D. H. Lawrence's
against Austen, that she promotes "the sharp knowing in apartness
instead of knowing in togetherness," or that other morsel, ". . .
They whose love is thin and wise," in place of meeting Helen in
Hell, "May view John Knox in paradise."[5] That would be to misread Smith, certainly to mistake his intentions, for his *Theory of
Moral Sentiments*, as the title says, is based on feeling, especially the
pleasure of "sympathy" (which should not be confused with *pity*).[6]
In Smith's view, "Nothing pleases us more than to observe in other
men a fellow-feeling with all the emotions of our own breast . . ."
(p. 14). *Sympathy* he defines as follows, "Whatever is the passion
which arises from any object in the person principally concerned,
an *analogous* emotion springs up, at the thought of his situation,
in the breast of every attentive spectator," and he immediately compares that emotion to enjoyment of "the deliverance of those heroes
of tragedy or romance who interest us" (p. 5). A parallel with Johnson on readers and theatergoers springs to mind, justly, but for
Smith the principle holds in all actual human relations. These depend on what he sees as a natural human tendency not to share
another's emotion but, on the basis of our understanding of the
circumstances which have produced his emotion, to feel one like
it, brought to the spectator's mind by his perception of the realities
of the other's situation. The qualifications are important, protecting
a spectator from necessarily having feelings analogous to those witnessed in another who is deranged. Moreover, a deranged person
could not perform the part nature assigns him in social relations,
because the achievement of "concord" (Smith's negative opposite
being "dissonance") requires the person feeling the primary emotion
to become aware, in turn, of the circumstances of the spectators
who sympathize with him.

In order to produce this concord, as nature teaches the spectators
to assume the circumstances of the person principally concerned, so
she teaches this last in some measure to assume those of the spectators. As they are continually placing themselves in his situation,
and thence conceiving emotions similar to what he feels; so he is as

constantly placing himself in theirs, and thence conceiving some degree of that coolness about his own fortune, with which he is sensible that they will view it. As they are constantly considering what they themselves would feel, if they actually were the sufferers, so he is as constantly led to imagine in what manner he would be affected if he was only one of the spectators of his own situation. As their sympathy makes them look at it, in some measure, with his eyes, so his sympathy makes him look at it, in some measure, with theirs, especially when in their presence and acting under their observation: and as the reflected passion, which he thus conceives, is much weaker than the original one, it necessarily abates the violence of what he felt before he came into their presence, before he began to recollect in what manner they would be affected by it, and to view his situation in this candid and impartial light.

The mind, therefore, is rarely so disturbed, but that the company of a friend will restore it to some degree of tranquillity and sedateness. (pp. 38–39)

Social relations thus perceived become a dance, but not a trivial or, in our sense, a sentimental one. They require full, realistic attention to and assessment of the causes of feeling evident on both sides, and a concomitant consciousness, assessment, expression, and governing of self. The person, to achieve concord with others, must have developed a spectator within himself—seeing himself, in the words of another Scotsman, "as others see us." The developed self is thus permanently divided not only from others but from itself, though concords within and without are possible and indeed only become possible because of the division, between sympathy and critical detachment, that has been achieved within the self. But inner and outer concords, despite the permanent, real barrier to unisons, are not at all lukewarm in their representation here. Indeed, Smith believes "the chief part of human happiness arises from the consciousness of being beloved . . ."; a husband whose wife behaved perfectly toward him out of dutifulness alone would be dissatisfied (pp. 87, 300). It must follow that love of self is a chief source of happiness too. The theory and certain statements in the book would have one think so (e.g., that "we love ourselves for our own sakes"—p. 298).

Yet Smith, although tough-minded in many respects, is not so here with regard to this topic, arguing feebly against an element

of self-love in sympathy (which operates so spontaneously that it
leaves no time for calculation, and which manifests itself even on
"frivolous occasions": his example, to lift both Freud's eyebrows,
is a man's dismay when only he "laughs at his own jest"—p. 15).
A sympathetic critic of Smith, attentive to Smith's circumstances,
will readily see why he blanches. It is clear from his text in several
places, early and late, that he knows he is sailing into the cannonry
of the moralists while holding the age's leviathan by the tail. Apart
from Smith's understandable aversion to a hard look at self-love,
however, his psychology in the *Theory*, which proves very attentive
to associational activity in self and other, and the sociology which
rests on that psychology, draw together many of the chief themes
in eighteenth-century thought about the mind and are ideal for
illuminating the philosophical tales, to which the philosophical themes
I have assembled could not be more relevant.

Smith's blind spot is as evident in John Gay. Before concluding
the "Dissertation," he examines the mechanism of envy, a thorn in
the side of the benevolist Hutcheson—examines especially the curious psychological fact that a person envies only some, not all,
prosperous people. The real genesis of that passion will disclose
itself as a reward of empirical inquiry:

> If a Man will be at the Pains to consult his Mind, or to look into
> the World, he'll find that these particular Persons are always such
> as upon some account or other he has had a *Rivalship* with. For when
> two or more are Competitors for the same thing, the Success of the
> one must necessarily tend to the Detriment of the other, or others:
> hence the Success of my Rival and Misery or Pain are joined together
> in my Mind; and this connection or association remaining in my
> Mind, even after the Rivalship ceases, makes me always affected
> with Pain whenever I hear of his Success, though in Affairs which
> have no manner of Relation to the Rivalship.[7]

This is a curious passage, in which Gay seems to lose his purpose momentarily. The pains of consulting oneself seem repaid by
the discovery that rivalship is a necessary condition of envy, and
thus—as La Rochefoucauld or Pascal or Hobbes or Swift would
immediately surmise—that the bone of contention is not the ostensible, external object both parties seek but the pleasure to be

enjoyed in achieving it oneself. Gay, however, does not admit, or seem conscious of, that explanation. The problem for him is permanent association of the ideas of another's success and one's own resultant failure. News of the other's later success reactivates the sense of one's former disappointment, that is all. One's own present self-regard is not at stake. Gay now digresses to venture the thought that his explanation may shed some light on the motivation of the fallen angels! (The subject of angels has a curious tendency to enter discussions of self-love, as we shall see.)

Yet what Gay says afterward implies some concern with self-love, for he remarks that we envy also those who refuse to be guided and persuaded by us, this relation being "nothing else than a Rivalship about the Superiority of Judgment; and we take a secret Pride both to let the World see, and in imagining ourselves, that we were in the right" (p. xxxiii). By what association do we require superiority in judgment? Gay does not explain, yet here the secret desire for supremacy, missing in his preceding explanation, is given as the motive, not an error caused by short-sighted association. Both elements are involved in his thinking, not fully sorted out. The mechanism of human reactions becomes obscured by the unclarified interaction of both Hobbesian egoism and Lockean associations. Like Smith, our philosopher manifests the psychologist's equivalent of that sudden, keen interest in ceilings shown by newcomers to a steambath.

The tracing of thoughts back to motives might seem no innocuous matter when psychology was unseparated from moral philosophy and from theology. In the early eighteenth century many philosophers and theologians held to what F. B. Kaye terms a "rigorist" definition of virtue, whereby only "unselfish and dispassionate" actions could be considered virtuous. Thinkers apparently so different as Mandeville and Shaftesbury approach agreement on this issue, differing particularly in the extent to which they thought human beings could attain so high a standard.[8] The satirical Mandeville and La Rochefoucauld doubted they could, and enjoyed showing why. Others, such as Shaftesbury and Hutcheson, held that by reason of an innate moral sense, human beings are naturally disposed to benevolent altruism. The persons represented in their examples are so well-bred and right-thinking that they resemble the heroes and heroines of eighteenth-century English novels. In *Paradise Lost*, to comfort Eve after her dream of pridefully rising above her station, Adam says,

> Evil into the mind of God or Man
> May come and go, so unapprov'd, and leave
> No spot or blame behind. . . .
>
> (5.117–19)

Yet Pamela and the most prominent other English novel heroines and heroes are generally far, far above selfish thoughts of even the unapprov'd variety, as if these characters would be tainted in readers' eyes by an experience through which their unfallen first mother, we are told, innocently passed.

Rigorist ethics, of course, did not necessarily rule out some self-interested actions, and in theory did not differ from Adam's doctrine that only approval of a base thought makes it blameworthy. But it appears that, for minds not inclined to satire, so strict a criterion of virtue (not to mention the underlying emphasis on regular achievement of virtuous actions) tended to discourage unprejudiced introspection and tolerance for what it might turn up that would not satisfy the highest moral standards. In opposition to rigorism, certain philosophers attempted to establish what Kaye broadly calls a "utilitarian" standard of virtue.[9] Emerging in Hutcheson, Gay, Hume, Smith, and others, this standard measures actions by the quality of not their motives but their consequences, that is, in relation to the individual and social pursuit of happiness (defined in one way or another)—the pursuit motivated by some sort of concern for self. The "utilitarian" standard, in contrast to unsatirical rigorism, seems paradoxically to have encouraged relatively free introspection because, being comparatively unconcerned with motives, it could promote a degree of disinterestedness in the person attending to what passes in his mind—a degree only, since most "utilitarians" of ethics proceeded in reaction to rigorism. Smith may be responding to the pressure of the times when he comments that the "perfection of human nature" requires us "to feel much for others and little for ourselves" (p. 44).

But alongside deferential statements of this sort, in Hume, Smith, and others one finds ample discussion, not unlike the description typifying modern psychological inquiry, of interesting peculiarities of human perception, cognition, and motivation. Why is it, Smith asks, that though we agree the intention rather than the outcome is what causes gratitude or resentment, nevertheless we are influenced greatly by the nature of the outcome? "This irregularity of sentiment, which everybody feels, which scarce any body is sufficiently aware of, and which no body is willing to acknowledge; I proceed now to explain . . ." (p. 210). Or why is it that we blame a person for an injury done without malice, say by his failure to control an unruly horse, yet would accuse the person of timidity if he refused to take the risk which led to that failure? (pp. 235–37). This novel, refreshing curiosity about motives is of a sort that Moll Flanders might display, but does not, when she finds she has just stolen a horse and has no idea what to do with it—or Crusoe, when he decides to carry off the gold from the wreck to his desert island. In brave eighteenth-century moralists such as Butler and, particularly, Johnson, there is active concern with the issues raised by rigorists and utilitarians; that is, with placing standards of morality in what might be called a realistic relation to the natural history of the mind, "dear self," and its desires and associations of ideas.

Bernard Harrison's study of *Tom Jones* is an unusual and useful book by reason of its attention to the issues of selflessness and self-love as perceived by eighteenth-century moral philosophers. According to Harrison, the career of Tom demonstrates a possible continuity between desire and virtue: Tom's desire for Sophia leads him to put her interests above his own; yet the conclusion of the novel dissatisfies a "Puritan critic" because Tom does not confess himself a reprobate, does not renounce self-love in all respects, but repents his sexual offenses on the merely practical grounds that they have apparently deprived him of Sophia's love. In scorning this interpretation, appropriately, Harrison nevertheless misses something when he classifies Johnson with the Puritans and Richardsonians who are said to believe that Tom should suppress his desires.[10] Johnson, it is true, probably would have been happier, out of concern for the effect of the novel on unprincipled readers, had Tom governed his desires more firmly throughout the novel. Yet the side of Johnson's thinking given emphasis in the present book would demand that Tom—if only the end of the novel should be taken as realistic in this way—not suppress his desires but know his mind historically as a basis for governing it in the future. This desideratum of eighteenth-century philosophy provides a context other than the "puritan" for understanding both the conclusion and the genre of *Tom Jones* and, in calling for characters to attain consciousness of the genesis of their thinking, introduces a consideration which, as Harrison briefly indicates, Fielding does not have clearly in mind.[11]

And for Johnson, as for his contemporaries, self-love remained something of a Medusa. Paul Kent Alkon notes a curious point of neglect in Johnson's writing on morals: "It is striking that one major form of self-delusion remains almost entirely neglected by Johnson. His assertion that we always think ourselves better than we are leaves no room for those dejected moments in which we think ourselves worse than we really are. Johnson himself was certainly no stranger to such depressions, and yet, so far as I am aware, he never deals explicitly with the problems of unwarranted self-depreciation." For Alkon, Johnson's "moral essays do not explicitly recognize the relationship between obsessive feelings of inferiority and the various methods of compensating for such felt inadequacies by endeavoring to become—or feel—superior to others. Johnson never explains that it is often exaggerated feelings of inferiority which first mobilize diverse methods of compensating for real or imaginary inadequacies." Alkon accounts for this omission by citing the explicitly religious purposes of Johnson's moral writings (e.g., his effort "to make his works, as he had said he had made the *Rambler*, 'exactly conformable to the precepts of Christianity.'"): "The reason . . . is surely that, as a Christian, Johnson regarded any feeling of religious unworthiness—even if exaggerated—as a useful corrective against the dangers of moral complacency."[12] This is most likely.

One wishes Johnson had looked at the psychological question squarely, extending the sensitivity shown in Imlac's rhetorical question, "for who is pleased with what he is?" or, another example, expanding upon one subject prescribed for biographers in *Idler* 84, how a person "became discontented with himself."[13]

Edward Young was more forthcoming in yet another work of 1759, the celebrated *Conjectures on Original Composition*, addressed to Richardson, where readers are told to "reverence" as well as know themselves, and particularly to avoid the danger of "thinking meanly . . . without just cause" of their own abilities. Young announced that he would write a sequel on ethics, but none was published— possibly another testament to the force of Medusa's stare.[14]

It is odd, I think, that the idea or ideas signified by the terms *self-love* and *amour-propre*, particularly as they apply to eighteenth-century fiction, have not been the subject of a full-scale study: the concepts are ubiquitous in the period, often salient, too, as in *An Essay on Man* and particularly in Rousseau's famous distinction between detestable, selfish *amour-propre* and decent, prudent *amour de soi*.[15] Voltaire did not limit his dicta on *amour-propre* to quips; it is at the center of his prolonged quarrel with Pascal. Perhaps self-love has become so universally cherished now that we do not care to look into it. On the other hand, the snaky inhibitions surrounding it probably have not entirely lost their traditional fearsomeness. Leslie Stephen, in the last century, gave left-handed tribute to the importance of the issue while chiding Bishop Butler for one "unfortunate concession to the general spirit of the age. He expressly promises in the beginning of the eleventh sermon that 'all possible concessions' shall be 'made to the favourite passion' of his age— namely self-love."[16] (This is not one of Stephen's more economical and graceful passages.)

I have been a little slow to say what *self-love* and *amour-propre* may mean—intentionally, to give readers a taste of the uneasiness about the question widely felt in the eighteenth century. Those terms were then radically ambiguous.[17] The *Oxford English Dictionary* distinguishes between common and philosophical uses of *self-love*, which are, respectively, negative and positive. In common usage during the period 1563–1875 as signified by the illustrative quotations, this "Love of oneself" shifted from a usual meaning of "partiality to oneself, Amour-propre" to "regard for one's interests or well-being; chiefly with definitely opprobrious implication, self-centredness, selfishness." (The *OED* definition of *amour-propre* is "Self-love which is ready with its claims and sensitive to causes of offence; good opinion of oneself, self-esteem"; I shall return to the French term.) The "philosophical," positive meaning of *self-love*, on the other hand—the first *OED* quotations dating from 1683, 1688, and (Butler) 1726, the ambiguity in the eighteenth century being relatively new—is "Regard for one's own well-being or happiness, considered as a natural and proper relation of a man to himself." An array of related terms can bear the same philosophical meaning, indicating concern for oneself without entailing lack of concern for others. These terms would include *interest, self-interest, self-esteem, self-regard,* and *self-confidence,* but like *self-love* they are extremely ambiguous and risky in the period. *Self-respect* does not carry a favorable meaning until the 1790s. The term *self-esteem* appears particularly slippery since, to put the matter briefly, *esteem* shifts from neutral *estimation* toward positive *valuation,* especially on moral grounds: a high regard for standards of behavior regarding right and wrong. Earlier usage would call for adjectives of approbation or disapprobation, as in *good esteem*; later, for adjectives of measurement, as in *much esteem.* The substantive acquires positive and moral significance, thus becoming too highly charged for neutral, non-prescriptive psychological description, as *self-love* tended to remain.

The slipperiness of the term *self-love* and what he sees as the shiftiness of some writers employing it vex Shaftesbury in 1711; more than a century later, Hazlitt has exactly the same complaint, only with regard to Helvétius rather than, as in Shaftesbury, Hobbes and his successors. Shaftesbury despises La Rochefoucauld and others as

> petty retailers of this wit, who have run changes, and divisions without end, upon this article of self-love. You have the very same thought spun out a hundred ways . . . that "act as disinterestedly or generously as you please, self still is at the bottom, and nothing else."

Now if these gentlemen who delight so much in the play of words, but are cautious how they grapple closely with definitions, would tell us only what self-interest was, and determine happiness and good, there would be an end to this engimatical wit.[18]

Hazlitt complains,

Surely, when self-love by all accounts takes so very wide a range and embraces entirely new objects of a character so utterly opposed to its general circumscribed and paltry routine of action, it would be as well to designate it by some new and appropriate appellation, unless it were meant, by the intervention of the old and ambiguous term, to confound the important practical distinction which subsists between the puny circle of a man's physical sensations and private interests and the whole world of virtue and honour, and thus to bring back the last gradually and disingenuously within the verge of the former. Things without names are unapt to take root in the human mind.

Both Shaftesbury and Hazlitt want to preserve the concept of legitimate "philosophical self-love," Hazlitt using that very term.[19]

The words *self-love*, *self-interest*, and the like sprawl, battered, across the eighteenth-century discursive landscape, victims of that period's long battle over *a priori* positive and negative valuation of the self—at the extremes, human depravity versus human perfectibility. There was no term or set of terms that would univocally designate the range of more or less positive meanings touched by *self-love*, including ordinary noninvidious concern for one's own well-being and happiness, even an attitude of empirical neutrality towards oneself. Much less was there a term or set of terms permitting unequivocal designation of the pleasure in being and remaining oneself or of feeling affection for, or confidence in, oneself. Needless to say, there existed no unequivocal term for any of these individual dispositions. Even the new eighteenth-century "philosophical" definition stops short of them. Indeed it appears that the philosophical definition circumvents the root issue of affection for self. That definition concentrates on what the self loves—its well-being or happiness and those things which, when acquired by the self, bring about its well-being or happiness. But the self wants those things and states of being because of an antecedent affection for itself. The self must first be loved if those attributes of the self, well-being and happiness, are to be loved. The unavoidable logic of this priority, however, remains only implicit in the philosophical definition, which therefore appears to concentrate on a comparatively untroublesome branch of self-love so as to make the quite troublesome root acceptable.

Thus all the available terms can bear traces of selfishness and even Luciferian or pharisaical pride; most involve the issue of moral approbation and disapprobation. A. O. Lovejoy, in *Reflections on Human Nature*, is at pains to separate out the varieties of what the eighteenth century generally called "pride," and distinguishes the passions for "praise," for "emulation," and for "self-esteem."[20] He does not, however, make mention of a positive or neutral philosophical meaning of *self-love* such as the *OED* provides, nor indicate the range of comparable meanings that I have separately educed, what may be called a psychological sense of the term as contrasted with an ethical or theological sense. But, as I have said, psychology in the eighteenth century had not yet been recognized as a discipline distinct from moral philosophy and moral theology.

Hume proves keenly aware of the problems I have sketched as he seeks to define a species of self-love not opprobrious.

There may, perhaps, be some, who, being accustom'd to the style of the schools and pulpit, and having never consider'd human nature in any other light, than that in which *they* place it, may here be surpriz'd to hear me talk of virtue as exciting pride, which they look upon as a vice; and of vice as producing humility, which they have been taught to consider as a virtue. But not to dispute about words, I observe, that by *pride* I understand that agreeable impression, which arises in the mind, when the view either of our virtue, beauty, riches, or power makes us satisfy'd with ourselves: And that by *humility* I mean the opposite impression. 'Tis evident the former impression is not always vicious, nor the latter virtuous. The most rigid morality allows us to receive a pleasure from reflecting on a generous action; and 'tis by none esteem'd a virtue to feel any fruitless remorses upon the thoughts of past villainy and baseness. Let us, therefore, examine these impressions, consider'd in themselves; and enquire into their causes, whether plac'd on the mind or body, without troubling ourselves at present with that merit or blame, which may attend them.[21]

This is a passage that could bear a long commentary; I confine myself to remarking the irony or mischief of Hume's choice of words, *pride* and *humility* being the most incendiary terms available in Christendom to promote Hume's professed purposes of dispassionate scientific inquiry. Elsewhere, later, Hume writes more moderately on this subject. Notably, in *An Enquiry Concerning the Principles of Morals*, he argues that self-love is estimable if the effects are good for society, and, further, that human beings are capable of good actions untouched by self-love.[22]

The lack of a vocabulary for psychological discourse, especially discourse on emotions held traditionally to be fraught with moral danger, is lamented temperately by Smith when, in the *Theory*, he touches on the

> ambiguity of language. There are some of our passions which have no other names except those which mark the disagreeable and offensive degree. The common names of the love of pleasure, and of the love of sex [footnote: "Luxury and Lust"] denote a vitious and offensive degree of those passions. The words temperance and chastity on the other hand, seem to mark rather the restraint and subjection which they are kept under than the degree which they are still allowed to subsist in. (pp. 483–84)

Jeremy Bentham would later elaborate this complaint in the course of an ambitious attempt to chart the *terra incognita* of human motivation.[23] Indeed, during the eighteenth century the "spring" of human action is increasingly referred to as a "motive" rather than as a "passion,"[24] evidently—among other causes—so as to encourage neutrality in consideration of it (a hard case of association breaking). *Motive* also carries with it a Copernican-Newtonian analogy of mental mechanism not unsuitable to a natural science of the mind.

The associationists tend to have at least one foot in Kaye's "utilitarian" current and thus do not automatically react to the question of self-love as if they had just placed a bare toe on something animate. Directing their attention toward the pursuit of happiness in one form or another (Hutcheson invents the locution "the greatest Happiness for the greatest Numbers"),[25] they had to be concerned with the human desire for it. Hutcheson speaks tolerantly of self-love.[26] Butler calls self-love "in its due degree . . . as just and morally good, as any affection whatever."[27] Archibald Campbell finds self-love "at the Bottom of every Rational Mind, and . . . universally the first Spring . . . that awakes her Powers"; a polemical preface to Campbell's book by Alexander Innes asserts that Mandeville has confounded

> *Self-Love* with *Pride* and *Flattery*. For I am very much mistaken if this one *Principle* of *Self-Love*, under proper Restrictions and Limitations, will not as clearly resolve and explain all the *Moral Relations* and *Proportions* between the several Agents in the Intellectual World; as the Incomparable Sir *Issac Newton*, by his Noble Principle of Attraction (which we may call the *Self-Love* of Inanimate Beings) has unravell'd the several *Phænomena* of the Material World.[28]

Gay thinks ethical merit consistent with seeking one's own ultimate private happiness.[29] *Amour-propre* is the original, fundamental love experienced by Condillac's genetic statue.[30] For Hume, though as in Smith sympathy is not based on self-love, though custom endears us to ourselves and accounts for "pride," and though "*selfishness*" remains the most pressing problem besetting our "*natural temper*," nevertheless, "generally speaking, the representations of this quality have been carried much too far; and . . . the descriptions, which philosophers delight so much to form of mankind in this particular, are as wide of nature as any accounts of monsters, which we meet with in fables and romances."[31] Smith I have said enough about already. Hartley constructs a ladder of progressively more enlightened self-interest whereby the mind can ascend from "gross," to "refined," to "rational" self-satisfaction.[32] As I have said, there are many important differences between these various philosophers. They differ with regard to the issues of freedom and necessity, of progress (as perfectibilitarian or merely cursive), and of hedonism in its various forms, to cite several major topics in them. As they do not agree in detail with each other about the process of association, they do not share a definition of self-love. But, and this is all I must establish, just as they further investigation of associational activity, they together promote the new philosophical and psychological, neutral-to-positive attitude toward self-love and comparable dispositions.

A useful attempt to explore eighteenth-century thought about issues related to self-love, from the point of view of economics and politics, is represented by Albert O. Hirschman's short book *The Passions and the Interests*. Hirschman seeks to explain how the pursuit of economic self-interest central to capitalism was legitimized between the seventeenth and eighteenth centuries; how the motive of personal gain that had generally been regarded as evil or at least suspect became acceptable and even praiseworthy, for reasons other than those supplied by theorists of the Protestant ethic. Early on, according to Hirschman, the word *interests* did not have its current, predominantly economic meaning whereby it has to do with "the material aspects of a person's welfare." Rather, when the term first came to prominence in the sixteenth century, "it comprised the totality of human aspirations, but denoted an element of reflection and calculation with respect to the manner in which these aspirations were to be pursued."[33]

In political theory, especially in Montesquieu, the pursuit of self-interest on the part of individuals and groups within a state came to be regarded as a potentially salutary counterforce to arbitrary governmental power. Before Montesquieu, beginning mainly in the seventeeth century, in the province of ethics, interest became identified with those passions of an individual that might usefully be set against worse passions. Hirschman quotes Bacon, from *The Advancement of Learning*, on an aspect of the georgics of the mind whereby a person may learn "to set affection against affection and to master one by another. . . . For as in the government of states it is sometimes necessary to bridle one faction with another, so it is in the government within." Interests thus came to stand for "countervailing passions," a major subject in moral philosophers of the eighteenth century. The *Moral Discipline* in the title of Alkon's book on Johnson, explained very fully in the climactic chapter, entails advice about fighting one passion with another, and Johnson turns up in Hirschman with the remark, "There are few ways in which a man can be more innocently employed than in getting money."[34]

From our long perspective, the enthusiasm of some later eight-eenth-century minds for economic self-interest as the one necessary good—not Johnson's mind, of course—may appear horrendous, as may the narcissism of an occasional proponent of self-love. From a sympathetic historical point of view, the milder version of the doctrine whereby a Montesquieu hoped to raise self-interest as a counterweight to pre-Revolutionary French government will prob-ably seem less dreadful. And to a mind pleased with the emergence in the eighteenth century of a psychological perspective on oneself distinct from ethical and theological considerations, yet not nec-essarily divorced from them, the century's recognition of the im-portance of self-love in oneself and others—not by any means an untempered or uncritical recognition—may seem positively engag-ing and, in a broad sense, historically crucial. I can here touch only briefly on reasons for this statement.

The reasons center in the fact that, from the Reformation on, the individual Englishman was century by century increasingly subjected to the burden of choice, which implies the burden of living with himself before and after he has made up his mind. "Doubt wisely; in strange way/To stand inquiring right, is not to stray . . ." are Donne's words to the religious seeker.[35] The "contest about the original benevolence or malignity of man," in Johnson's words, had commenced in connection with the rise of a less authoritarian state, church, society, and morality than England had known before the Reformation. The proliferation of religious sects and the increase in social and commercial mobility beginning by the seventeenth century; the institution of political parties and of more nearly re-publican government in the seventeenth and eighteenth centuries, and the concomitant rise of concern for personal affection apart from dynastic ambition as the basis of marriage; the advancement of learning into various philosophies and sciences over two centuries and more—all these developments had increased the possibility and necessity of making choices and in effect had focused attention on the self as unavoidably antecedent to the religious, political, social, and philosophical forms to which it might become and remain at-tached.[36] From a political point of view, as Lovejoy and Hirschman say, the possibilities of anarchy might be curtailed by devising governmental and social mechanisms whereby the efforts of contending factions would neutralize each other, as the conflicting forces of the physical universe balance the earth.

From the point of view of the individual person, susceptible to the mental counterpart of anarchy, the degree to which he had to govern himself with the aid primarily of knowledge of his desires—that is, with reference to self-love in the philosophical definition—had over the centuries been vastly increased. Governed by absolute authority from without (or reacting against it), the individual could possibly afford to regard all sorts of self-love as evil; required to govern himself, he had to believe that, examining at least some of his desires, and his capacity to make judgments, he could be pleased enough with what he saw to make his choices and live with them. And these assertions about, of course, relatively privileged Englishmen and Englishwomen would hold in some degree, regarding freedom of thought if not of overt action, for the French and the inhabitants of some other European nations, at least by the early eighteenth century, when Montesquieu, Voltaire, and other authors had widely publicized a range of alternatives to the common ways of thinking, many of these alternatives drawn from the English example as in the *Lettres persanes* and Voltaire's *Lettres philosophiques*.

Yet attractive as the possibilities of freedom unquestionably could be, the psychological burden of choice could, I believe, weigh much more heavily on the eighteenth-century mind than may appear, and the necessary philosophical, qualified, critical self-love could be more difficult to sustain than we may imagine. The issue of rigorism in ethics only begins to suggest the drama of the struggle. Douglas H. White comments that "the reputation of self-love was never, at least in Christendom, very high."[37] Indeed, to introduce the topic was, at best, to totter but a step away from denial of the Christian doctrine of man's natural depravity and from the Pelagian heresy that a man, on the strength of his good actions, his works, could justify himself in the sight of God. To Christians, as most eighteenth-century English and French authors and readers were, at least in the early years of their lives, and as many remained, the peril of a false step here, into damnation, could be terrifying

and might remain so at some level of consciousness even for un-
believers. A highly qualified self-love could be sanctioned or tolerated by Christianity—one is to love one's neighbor as oneself, a
precept that the eighteenth-century apologist for self-love would
not overlook and perhaps might adapt to his purposes ("so it is the
great principle of nature to love ourselves only as we love our neigh-
bors, or, what is the same thing, as our neighbour is capable of
loving us"—Smith, of course; p. 44).

The preceding century, however, had been more severe than
others in discouraging emphasis upon that text: self-love was the
summum malum to many Puritans, Jansenists, and even less extreme
Christians motivated by the prudential concern that Alkon perceives in Johnson, the self not to be given an inch. The seventeenth
century outdid itself scourging the issue. The prefix "self-," as the
OED is unusually voluble in suggesting, then became a four-letter
word of quite unprecedented breadth and variety of application.
Pejorative compounds beginning thus sprang up as from dragon's
teeth in that century of verbal as well as physical violence, political
and religious, when the English word *selfish* was invented. (*Selfless*
had to wait for the nineteenth century.) To urge the legitimacy of
self-approbation in the face of this heritage, as some rigorists did,
was perhaps unwittingly treacherous, since that move covertly per-
petuated confusion of self-justification with self-love.

We have seen evidence that the Great Chain of Being subtly
haunts the idea of the chain of events. I wonder whether it does
so for a reason in addition to that of metaphorical resemblance, or
that of a resemblance referring to the chain of events in philosophical Optimism (evil mysteriously eventuating in good), the spu-
rious reading of which chain is one of Pangloss's specialties. An
additional reason may lurk in the way the Great Chain idea, in the
first half of the eighteenth century, or by the middle, may have
appeared to epitomize the coldly impersonal theological-philosoph-
ical absolutism so characteristic of some major seventeenth-century
thinkers, whether or not they were Optimists. Materials powerfully
suggesting such a response, including words displaying eighteenth-
century passions at their most exercised, are readily at hand.

Voltaire's rejoinders to Pascal appended to the *Lettres philoso-*

phiques harp on the necessity, legitimacy, and value of self-love—overdoing it, we may think, as a person will against what seem somewhat gleefully pessimistic statements from the opponent. Voltaire does anything but keep self-love modestly covered here; the genitals, though, may serve purposes other than joking, including illustration of the ways of genetic thought. To Pascal's assertion that we are all born unjust, each favoring himself against all order, Voltaire replies that, on the contrary, *amour-propre* makes for order in the world, being as necessary to the formation and subsistence of society as sexual desire is to the begetting of children and as appetite is to nourishment. "C'est l'amour de nous même qui assiste l'amour des autres; . . . c'est le fondement de tout commerce; c'est l'éternel lien des hommes. . . . La loi dirige cet amour propre & la Religion le perfectionne" ("Love of ourselves helps us love others; . . . it is the base of all commerce; it is the permanent tie between men. . . . The law guides this self-love and Religion makes it perfect"). God might have made men solely altruistic but did not, giving them this "instinct" instead, to be satisfied as God wishes.[38] The argument is reiterated, varied, and extended throughout Voltaire's responses. When Pascal comments that man, if trying to be like an angel, becomes a beast, Voltaire replies that the person who wishes to destroy the passions instead of guiding them (*les regler*) wants to be an angel.[39]

Somewhat like Candide, Voltaire himself was drawn toward philosophical Optimism, but he came to discard it as scientifically false about a Great Chain, gratuitously pessimistic, an invitation to complacency about evil, and symptomatic of the presumptuousness of metaphysicians.[40] In the *Dictionnaire philosophique*, he and the alphabet juxtapose the articles "Chaîne des êtres créés" and Chaîne des événements," he alone associating the former with something he held infamous, the Catholic hierarchy; the idea of a Great Chain appeals to those who enjoy watching "le pape et ses cardinaux suivis des archevêques, des évêques; après quoi viennent les curés, les vicaires, les simples prêtres, les diacres, les sous-diacres; puis paraissent les moines, et la marche est fermée par les capucins" ("the Pope and cardinals, trailed by archbishops, then bishops; after whom come the pastors, the vicars, the ordinary priests, the deacons, the subdeacons; then the monks, and the procession is completed by the Capuchins").[41] Optimism and its appurtenances Voltaire had come to regard not merely as false but as cruel.[42]

As did Johnson—Lovejoy pairs him with Voltaire as a major eighteenth-century critic of the Great Chain[43]—Johnson making his mark when reviewing Soame Jenyns' *Free Inquiry into the Nature and Origin of Evil* (1757), the review a triumph of demolition: of the Great Chain and of Jenyns' pretensions to natural theology, on logical grounds and, most memorably, on grounds of outrage at Jenyns' astonishing complacency about human suffering. Jenyns had had the temerity to imagine that beings above man in the Chain may torment man for their own pleasure or advantage (utilitarian angelology extended). In one of Johnson's more restrained responses to this fancy, he observes:

> The only end of writing is to enable the readers better to enjoy life, or better to endure it: and how will either of those be put more in our power by him who tells us, that we are puppets, of which some creature not much wiser than ourselves manages the wires. That a set of beings unseen and unheard, are hovering about us, trying experiments upon our sensibility, putting us in agonies to see our limbs quiver, torturing us to madness, that they may laugh at our vagaries.[44]

I wish to emphasize this: what Jenyns is most damnably insensitive to are the horrors threatening fulfillment of just those "utilitarian" desires, for personal, mental, physical, material, social, and spiritual well-being and satisfaction that are signified by the new philosophical meaning of *self-love*. Jenyns, because of his own prideful, excessive, and injudicious self-love, self-love old style, arrogates to himself an authority that is above humanity; though having no high idea of angels—witness the "set of beings" Johnson mentions—Jenyns wants to be an angel. So Voltaire would say. Johnson himself almost says so of Jenyns, with reference to Pope on fools rushing in: "I am in doubt whether those who stand highest in *the scale of being* speak this confidently of the dispensations of their maker."

I would suggest that Chain-of-Being metaphysics was felt by

Voltaire and Johnson to be especially vexing in its relation to self-love, because, with that metaphysics' logically necessary, prominent, yet evidently indifferent or hostile angels, it turns so easily into a cause for anxious self-hatred on the part of human beings, who cannot contemplate themselves and their desires without calling to mind not only the woes of flesh and spirit but also, especially, the incomprehensibility of a universe and a deity orderly and yet utterly impersonal in dealings with mankind. The thoughtful person, most himself in his desires, least a hypocrite in his pleasures, must find this scheme and its mentors abhorrent. Voltaire says Pascal has traded Christianity for metaphysics.[45] Johnson says the same of Jenyns. Enlightenment thought begins to be remarkably personal in its regard for empirical psychology, its concern for the small chains of becoming that are human beings; in the transcendent, impersonal Chain of Being and that Chain's exponents it sees its antithesis.

This particular point of mine remains somewhat speculative, yet support for it comes also from Hume—we have seen him writing with the Chain of Being at the corner of his eye—from a passage, like Johnson's, more heated than was characteristic of him. Philo, of the *Dialogues Concerning Natural Religion*, after delivering the opinion that metaphysicians are given to the wrong association whereby they apply their *a priori* methods to inappropriate subjects, soon addresses philosophical Optimism (Hume's footnote mentions King) and directly protests its blindness to the terror of human suffering—protests not simply obtuseness but, it appears, the insidious additional effects of Optimism's impersonality, in a manner that recalls Johnson on Jenyns. Besides mental and physical illness, besides dejection and despair, there is man's capacity to torment himself by summoning "*imaginary* Enemies, the Dæmons of his Fancy, who haunt him with superstitious Terrors, and blast every Enjoyment of Life[.] His Pleasure, as he imagines, becomes, in their Eyes, a Crime."[46] Again we find philosophical self-love, especially, threatened by the species of thinking that employed the Great Chain. Hume's enemies here are not angels but creatures of self-tormenting brains that recoil before the prospect of themselves as they are.

It will perhaps be clear after this highly selective review of opinions regarding the range of feelings denominated as self-love, that debate over the matter was not straightforward. The covert, disputed issue was the wisdom and propriety of studying man as he is rather than as he ought to be. It was empirical assessment of self and others that was being opposed and defended. While mankind and individuals could be studied psychologically, many thought they should not, for to do so was to accept them as they are. More liberal Christians and philosophical utilitarians could tolerate such enquiry; stricter Christians, stern moralists, and satirists could not. To be attentive to or forthright to oneself about one's own natural desires was, probably, to give in to the worst of them. Pamela, when married and a mother, writes a series of letters to her husband assessing Locke's *Some Thoughts on Education*, demurring when Locke gives "this one Rule, Not to think meanly of ourselves, and not to think meanly of others." It is an "excellent" rule, she says, yet she quickly expresses a preference for the "bashful" rather than the markedly confident temper and, further, descending to the most practical application of the rule, she adds, concerning a friend for their son, ". . . Were I to chuse a Companion for your *Billy*, as he grows up, I should not think the worse of the Youth, who, not having had the Opportunities of knowing Men, or seeing the World, had this Defect [the defect of "Sheepishness," hence the punning association that follows]. On the contrary, I should be apt to look upon it as an outward Fence, or Inclosure, as I may say, to his Virtue."[47] But, as I have suggested, the practical consequence of such thinking in the vastly expanded world of decision-making presented by the eighteenth century was likely to be very burdensome for those who had to make choices.

In Meredith's *The Egoist*, a century later, a novel largely about an overweening hero who thinks himself the favorite of obscure celestials, another young man, somewhat stiffly philosophical, comments warily on the dilemma of the heroine, who finds she cannot stand her engagement of marriage. "The question then is, whether she keeps to her word, or breaks it. It's a dispute between a conventional idea of obligation and an injury to her nature. Which is the more dishonourable thing to do? Why, you and I see in a moment that her feelings guide her best. It's one of the few cases in which nature may be consulted like an oracle." There follows from his companion, the guardian of rectitude, a perfectly chilling reply: "'Is she so sure of her nature?' said Miss Dale."[48] The earlier Pamela, Clarissa, Sophia, and their like, in different degrees, generally cannot bear to give empirical attention to what they want (or, as is more the case with Sophia, cannot be shown doing so with full attention to her associations). Clarissa, as Mark Kinkead-Weekes notices, resembles Sir Charles Grandison in this respect,[49] and the fact that Sir Charles's fortunate beloved, Harriet Byron, is notably unlike those two becomes less striking in view of the accompanying fact that her loving the all-but-perfect Sir Charles is like loving Gloriana.

In eighteenth-century French novels, by contrast, self-love gets direct, ample attention, but the term is slippery in French too. Robert Mauzi's history of the idea of happiness in eighteenth-century France broadly illuminates the related idea of *amour-propre*; Lester G. Crocker investigates it more particularly when probing the idea of self-interest in the period. Although the general attitude of seventeenth-century moralists was quite negative on the subject, certain writers—Jacques Abbadie and Malebranche among them— saw love of self, when properly distinguished from selfishness, as potentially valuable, possibly moving the mind in virtuous directions. By contrast, at certain extremes such as that represented by d'Holbach, the eighteenth century in France cheerfully made simple undiscriminated self-interest the fundamental human motive.[50] For most eighteenth-century French writers, Jean A. Perkins adds, although "the consensus was that *amour-propre* cannot be condemned since it is a natural component of human nature," apprehensions about possible justification of evil on such grounds produced "infinitely convoluted ways of proving that this was not the only or even the logical development of their principles."[51]

In eighteenth-century French novels, *amour-propre* tends to bear a highly restricted meaning: the desire to have other people think one important, to have them accord oneself *considération*; as Ronald C. Rosbottom comments with regard to the *amour-propre* of Marivaux's heroine in *La Vie de Marianne* (1731–1741), after sustained deception of others she can see only her mask in the mirror. When Marianne "has been recognized by those people she has fooled, her quest does not end. She must still find out about herself, a task made more difficult because, in deceiving others, she has simultaneously deceived herself. And she slowly disappears from the reader's view, her unfinished story standing as testimony of her fruitless quest." Her lack of self-knowledge, however, is not a point Marivaux emphasizes.[52] Author and readers have another quest in view, for the excitement of watching Marianne's social adventures and perhaps the pleasure of vicariously participating in her self-satisfaction.

The French novel tends to be comparatively honest about self-love—at least regarding one species of it—and about the main character's calculations, while dismissing wisdom other than that of the most worldly kind. The English novel promotes unworldly virtue and wisdom at the expense of candor about self-love in the conscious thinking of the main characters. In both English and French novels, empirical self-knowledge goes mostly by the board—and in a sense has to. It is a question of genre; the novel could not permit intensive and candid self-scrutiny by hero or heroine. There would necessarily be literary as well as moral objections, for the main character would have to be (or would seem troublingly wrong not to be) scrutinizing and unwriting the romantic element at the same time that the author was trying to bring it to full existence.

This complex dilemma casts a long shadow over the history of realistic prose fiction. Reviewing Zola's *Nana* in 1880, Henry James complains, "The figure of the brutal *fille*, without a conscience or a soul, with nothing but devouring appetites and impudences, has become the stalest of the stock properties of French fiction . . ." while the English novelists, even the best (James mentions Thackeray, Dickens, Eliot), though "better psychologists" than the French, almost thoroughly confine themselves to subject matter suitable for "young unmarried ladies," to the detriment of the novel "when the novel is regarded as something more than a simple *jeu d'esprit*, and considered as a composition that treats of life at large and helps us to *know*."[53] Throughout the present book I try to use only such psychological concepts and terms as were current in eighteenth-century philosophy but will here make an exception. It appears that in the eighteenth century and long after, in the novel and in life, the vexed issue of self-love (made still more troublesome by the confusion of terminology affecting it) was a main cause of psychological distortion, denial, and repression and thus one of the chief obstacles to self-knowledge. But the problem can be described very well in terms the eighteenth century called its own: self-love— too much of it, or not enough, or a combination of the two—could cause prejudice, misperception, misunderstanding, and worse, delusion, in one's thinking about oneself and everything else.

Self-love, though an issue generally avoided or scanted in novels, is the major, fundamental issue and problem in all the philosophical tales I concentrate on in this book. All represent the movement in eighteenth-century philosophy away from ethical rigorism; all begin in rigorism at its most patent. All the heroes present themselves as extraordinarily selfless in motivation—Gulliver fleeing the corruption of fellow surgeons in London, Usbek decamping from what he describes as a vicious Persia and soon imagining a perfectly just society (that of the Troglodytes, derived in part from Fénelon's *Télémaque*), Candide regarding himself (he says) as "le meilleur homme du monde," Rasselas fancying the image of a government of immaculate probity administered by himself. But as quickly as these motives are professed, the narrator or another device of the authors raises questions about the characters' candor and wisdom and, beyond that, sets readers thinking about the origins of such professions, tracing back the characters' associations, unwinding the chain of becoming in the characters' minds.

The characters in time do the same for themselves more or less overtly, with varying degrees of perceptiveness. *Candide* illustrates the point rather symbolically: the tale of a person freeing himself from mentors to whom he has attached himself, with whom he has associated himself, so as to maintain disabling, "selfless" preconceptions. *Rasselas*, from a comparable position, proceeds to illuminating discourse on the mechanisms of desire, imagination, delusion, and satisfaction, discourse put to work within the fiction for discovery of the hero to himself: self-assessment taking self-love into account. As I have said, these are rare, distinguished heroes of fiction. Nor were the tales entirely without influence upon later fiction in their central philosophical preoccupations, though these do not distinguish some amusing, unrealistic later works that superficially resemble the tales, such as the novels of Peacock and Flaubert's *Bouvard et Pécuchet*.

For two reasons, I conclude this book with a pair of chapters on Jane Austen—not all of Austen, mainly *Northanger Abbey* and *Persuasion*, to some extent *Mansfield Park*. First, despite the widely known fact of Austen's admiration for Johnson, the extent to which *Northanger Abbey* and *Persuasion* are formed by mechanisms proper to the philosophical tales of the eighteenth century has not been adequately recognized. Reading her novels with the tales in mind can illuminate them considerably, among other things suggesting explanations for some much-criticized peculiarities in them, including odd shifts in the narrator's tone and odd quirks in characters—for example, Anne Elliot's stalwart defense of her original, unhappy "persuasion." Second, the emergent business of eighteenth-century psychology, promoting consciousness of association and of its history, and recognition of the value and wisdom as well as the danger of self-love, is very much Austen's business, strikingly so. Seen as sustaining and developing the tradition of the philosophical tale, her writing may increase our sense of the significance of that tradition while the tales' realism of psychological self-assessment clarifies hers, and may clarify her stature as an architect of the novel, in the history of which she has often been accorded a decisive role. She very notably appreciates the intimate connection between empirical self-knowledge, self-love, and the knowledge and love of others. For purposes of contrast, and to maintain to the end my reference to the novel as distinguished from the tale, I begin the chapter on Austen with some attention to Laclos' *Les Liaisons dangereuses* (1782), which unlike the most prominent novels before it has explicit concern with genetic development of character. From the point of view of self-assessment, what *Amelia* is to the tradition of the English novel—its nearest miss—Laclos' fine book is to the French.

Otherwise I stay at the center of the tale's mainstream. The banks, the outer limits of the genre, could not be more neatly de-

marcated both formally and historically than they are by yet one
more work originating in 1759 and another it soon, in some degree,
called or provoked into being. Before concluding this part, I look
briefly, from the point of view of the tale, at these two strange
books, Laurence Sterne's *Tristram Shandy* and Denis Diderot's *Jacques le fataliste*. The first, one might say, represents the novel taken
about as far as it can go, a work designed to absorb the reader
totally, entirely disarming him of the power to distance himself
from the text. Tristram designs the text to go on forever, two volumes a year indefinitely.[54] The narrative, beginning well before
the event of the narrator-hero's birth, might never catch up with
his adulthood. The concept of the association of ideas, it is true,
becomes more prominent—at least more talked about—in this novel
than it does in any of the philosophical tales, important as it is
there, as I have begun to show; essential to the tales, however, is
the notion that a person can and ought to recognize and break the
tyranny of associations. That is out of the question in *Tristram
Shandy*, and that it is becomes and remains the chief joke of the
book, which thus becomes the polar opposite of a philosophical
tale.

Tristram, the narrator, can recognize the process of association
that threatens to hold his mind captive, presumably the reader's
mind also in some ways (*nose* does not mean *nose* alone for the reader
either),[55] and also the mind of just about every character in the
book. But the main characters cannot liberate themselves for a moment from the mechanical process of their associations. Those characters, Tristram's father and Uncle Toby, can perceive the oddness
of each others' minds without thinking to note anything amiss in
their own. Every attempt to decide their own destinies or communicate discursively with someone else marches in a closed circle;
repeatedly it looks as though the column of one character's thoughts
will fall into line with that of another, but at the last moment there
will be a misunderstanding in keeping with each person's preoccupations, whereupon each train will circle away independently of
the other. From the ashes of failed discourse, however, springs just
as frequently the phoenix of sympathy for each character's well-
intended, ineffectual efforts. Despite (and because of) the unfailing

humor of the situation, Mr. Shandy, Uncle Toby, Tristram, and the reader brim with sympathy for each other, and as volume succeeds volume the desert of associational solitude draws upon it an ocean of warm fellow-feeling. In view of such consolation, there is no importance accorded to critical and historical self-assessment, which may well be impossible or fruitless in the world of Sterne's book.

Jacques le fataliste, on the other hand, may be called an anti-novel; it is certainly an anti-*Tristram Shandy* (Diderot makes several pointed references to *Tristram* in it);[56] and, in a sense, as much as Sterne's book may be thought the most novelistic of novels, *Jacques* is that for the philosophical tale: a curt celebration of freedom from inhibiting preconceptions. Instead of the placid, helpless, mildly teasing narrator-hero Tristram, we are presented with a most aggressive narrator bent, from the first sentences, on frustrating a reader's cozy expectations. He will tell us neither how Jacques and his master met nor even what their names are. The narrator knows what the reader wants, a love story, Jacques's love story, and throughout the book the reader will be kept waiting to hear it through, and finally will be given a choice of three different versions, none with authorial sanction. One implication of this uncommon narrative manner is that there is something wrong with the reader, who seems to prefer hearing about others' love lives to having one of his own.[57] Through much of the book the reader will be regaled with more and more compelling love stories, especially those of Mme de La Pommeraye and *père* Hudson—both of these characters, whether successful or not, being models of shrewd, free, calculated, self-interested activity, of dynamic purposiveness in love and revenge, unrestrained by altruism. By contrast, the reader sees himself as inert, the prey of the narrator and a counterpart of Jacques's pallid master, who is interested in such matters as the freedom of the will while letting Jacques make the decisions.

Then Jacques, in the latter part of the book, suddenly turns into a different character, or is transfigured in a sort of apotheosis. The narrator forgot to tell us, he says, that when in doubt Jacques always consults the bottle—consults, that is, a counterpart of Rabelais' oracular bottle—and in a page Jacques has become the Dionysian equivalent of Télémaque inspired by Mentor-Minerve, with a Christian reference comparable to Fénelon's: Jacques "prétendait que l'Esprit Saint était descendu sur les Apôtres dans une gourde; il appelait la Pentecôte la fête des gourdes" ("claimed that the Holy Spirit descended on the Apostles in a flask; he called Pentecost the feast of flasks").[58] Jacques the inspired Panurge, however, is but a heightened version of the natural figure of fun he was earlier. We are told from the first that he is a fatalist, that he believes what will happen is written in a heavenly scroll; but it is clear that there is no substance to this belief. Jacques could not profess it more lightly. It never interferes with his doing just what he wants (a policy less refined here than in Rabelais' Abbey of Thélème). It is difficult not to conclude that, unlike Candide's Optimism, the very remoteness from actuality of Jacques's fatalism, its complete inapplicability to moral decision-making, is the reason for its consummate worth to him. Rather like Hume as well as Spinoza, Jacques's putative authority, Jacques believes that, "si l'enchaînement des causes et des effets qui forment la vie d'un homme depuis le premier instant de sa naissance jusqu'à son dernier soupir nous était connu, nous resterions convaincus qu'il n'a fait que ce qu'il était nécessaire de faire" (p. 236; "if the chaining of the causes and effects which constitute a man's life from the instant of his birth to his last breath were known to us, we would remain certain that he did only what it was necessary for him to do"). Thinking the future will take whatever course it pleases, he is liberated from having to worry about what course to take himself or how to justify it, and can concentrate on pursuing his desires with no shame anywhere near. The fatalism which at first seems a ponderous load to carry is discovered to be a bag of helium lightening his every step, the divine afflatus of unqualified self-love.

As a tale, *Jacques le fataliste* is a *Candide* unmitigatedly aimed at the midsection of the novel reader, scorning his wish that the narrator be an automaton like Jacques's master (pp. 87, 33)—be so good as to provide a story with a chain of events appropriate to the conventional novelistic pattern of associations. Not Diderot; he reduces the mentor-pupil relation of narrator reader to a game of power and triumphant bad faith invited by the self-hatred lurking in the audience, and in the process he transcends the philosophy of the philosophical tale as I have described it.

I would sum up Part I of the present book, as bluntly as possible, in this way: The philosophical tale is not realistic in presentation or, generally, in sociological assessment. It "brings realities to mind" rather than, like the novel, simulating "authenticity of report." Unlike the novel, it concentrates on realism of psychological assessment, such assessment of self more than of others.

Realism of psychological self-assessment in the tradition of Locke, Johnson, and others requires that characters: 1) notice what they are actually thinking and feeling; 2) notice in their thought and feeling any patterns characteristic of their personalities (i.e., how the characters typically form and join ideas and attach feelings to them, especially when such patterns tend toward distorted perception of self, others, and the rest of the universe); 3) trace the tendency to produce those patterns back to forces within themselves and the historical origin of those forces (their chain of becoming); and 4) try to rectify characteristic tendencies toward distortion of thought and feeling, and to strengthen tendencies toward valid thought and feeling, with the help of historical knowledge of those forces. Realism of psychological self-assessment becomes a theme in a work of fiction when 1) a character manifests, or approaches manifestation of, these abilities, and/or 2) characters are presented in context which clearly indicates that they ought to manifest these abilities, even if failing to do so or doing so perversely.

The "context" I mention may involve prominent use of terms from empirical psychology, as in nearly all the tales, tale-like fictions, and related works studied here. Still more fundamentally, the context will involve pointed analogies, tropes, and other fruitful or delusive associations of ideas which, when compared with the author's main philosophical convictions, invite not only special attention but also examination by way of empirical psychology. These associational figures of speech and thought, in the texts taken as wholes, should harmonize with the figures constructed by the hero or heroine to understand self and world; the character, moreover, when constructing his figures—Gulliver's "Similitudes," Usbek's analogies, Candide's synecdoches, and so on—should realize that that is what he is doing, forming associations, providing himself with instrumental genetic models for knowing himself and his world, not automatically acquiring plain, direct, necessarily valid facts about either.

The context promotes consciousness of the associational element in mental life. The philosophical tale has extraordinary integrity as a genre despite the differences between individual tales, because the distinctive theme of the genre, the need for such consciousness, is, in another aspect, the manner and almost the method whereby works in the genre should be read. The mind's associating ideas is both object and subject, beginning and end.

Thus the philosophical tale is philosophical not because it may be written to oppose a particular philosophy or idea, but because the topics central to eighteenth-century philosophy, still of interest, are central to the tale. The most central topic is the increasing qualification of eighteenth-century philosophy by psychology, by natural psychology based on empirical observation of the way the mind actually, not prescriptively, joins its ideas. The other topics near the center of the tale follow from this: the topics of understanding human motivation and the positive as well as negative parts in it played by self-love, and of attaining a modicum of reliable knowledge of the world outside one's own mind, the world embracing the minds of others, in a way not doomed from the start by preconceptions deriving from deluding motives, but, on the contrary, in a way wisely attentive to the characters' fundamental predilections and to the limited but considerable resources of wisdom—mentors, models, and maxims. The tale is a genre in its own right, uniquely and artistically promoting a permanently double view of the hero and, through him, of his world, a view characterized at best by concords not unisons, of both positive sympathy and definite detachment, revolving together into the future beyond the confines of a book.

PART II

The Major Philosophical Tales

CHAPTER FIVE

Gulliver's Habits
and Prejudices

But in spite of all temptations
To belong to other nations,
He remains an Englishman!
—*H.M.S. Pinafore*

*A*fter having lived among the giants of Brobdingnag, Gulliver
perceives his countrymen as tiny. A land of giants is unrealistic, and so is Gulliver's extreme loss of perspective. Gulliver, it
has often been said, lacks enough plausibility as a character to satisfy
the requirements of realistic fiction. *Gulliver's Travels* is decidedly
not a novel. On the other hand, a certain semblance of characterization attaches to this odd hero and narrator, who has local hab-
itations and in other respects is not unhuman. If, in line with my
description of the tale hero in the first chapter of this book, one
allows Gulliver to be a character to the extent that he brings realities
to mind—if one will suspend awhile the extreme opinion that,
because he is not a novel character, he has no character at all—one
will not find oneself set apart from all able readers of the *Travels*.
Gulliver has been likened to Rasselas in the best essay available on
the degree to which he may be said to develop psychologically,
slowly revealing "his propensity to dream, to imagine himself in
lofty positions of power and prominence." Because of "self-deception, or lack of self-knowledge, Gulliver gradually loses his sense
of values. . . . The more he looks around, the less he looks within."[1]
The thought has even been advanced, with proper wariness, that,

beginning in Lilliput as a *tabula rasa*, Gulliver illustrates (and Swift may thus satirize) Locke's conception of "the evolution of mind" from sensation to reflection.[2] That this thought, though interesting, represents a markedly abstract reading will be clear, if only from the fact that Gulliver is nearing forty when he enters Lilliput.

But both theories of Gulliver's development are questionable because they assume dearth or absence of experience in the Gulliver shipwrecked at the beginning of Book 1. With help afforded by the commentators who have emphasized the qualified positivity of his character, I shall argue that he enters Lilliput bearing the practical equivalent of innate ideas, that is, with ideas he has thoughtlessly acquired and brings from afar, ideas he unwittingly imposes upon everything he "explores." The denial that Gulliver is a character may be set upon the assertion that "he is someone to whom things happen," as if he never invites what happens, and upon the contention that he seems incapable "of living beyond the covers of the book. Gulliver begins at the beginning of his book and ends at the end"[3]—as if he initially appears and finally departs with no force of motivation, as if he has no characteristic way of thinking, and as if he has no "passions." On the contrary, I think, Gulliver's habits of thought, his tendency to "associate ideas" (as Locke would say), and his implicit motivation and general, enduring ignorance of these traits compose a major theme of the book, signaled as such not only in that Gulliver repeatedly finds fault with the quality of thinking exhibited by other characters but also, and more importantly, in that he is heavily dependent, in his criticism, on the terms of seventeenth-century epistemology.[4] His being somewhat informed about such matters gives prominence to the theme.

It is owing to the "*narrow Principles* and *short Views*," caused by insular "*Prejudices*, and a certain *Narrowness of Thinking*," that, in Gulliver's opinion, the Brobdingnagians are so resistant to his instruction.[5] "As to Ideas, Entities, Abstractions and Transcendentals, I could never drive the least Conception into their Heads" (2.7.136). The simple laws and ways of the giants resemble those practiced by the Lilliputians in better times, being adapted to "the common Size of human Understandings" (1.6.59). Because Gulliver scorns simplicity, the Brobdingnagian king forms "a very mean

Opinion of our Understandings" (2.7.135), and charges against the quality of "Understanding" are brought to bear on Gulliver by the Laputans and, by the Balnibarbians, on Munodi (3.2.160, 3.4.175): "a very mean Opinion of my Understanding," "a low contemptible Understanding." But the philosophical leitmotiv of the volume is the term "ideas." Gulliver shows himself repeatedly (although not constantly) aware that a person's ideas, like currency brought to a foreign market, must be adapted to the ideas of any stranger he addresses if conversational exchange is to be achieved. Hence, in telling us of conversations, he has frequent recourse to the terminology of ideas and conceptions. As we have seen, he cannot "drive" certain conceptions into Brobdingnagian heads. The giants' sense of morality is such "whereof in *Europe* we can have no Conception"; the king is amazed by Gulliver's "inhuman Ideas" (2.7.135,134). The odder Gulliver finds the beings he visits, the more he is conscious of the intermental gulf ideas must cross (the Laputans cannot be told about "Imagination, Fancy, and Invention" because they have no words for "those Ideas"—3.2.163) until, in Houyhnhnmland, he is mentioning ideas and conceptions every few pages. The Houyhnhnms have not the "least Idea" of, or find "past their Conception," or cannot "understand," nearly everything Gulliver has to communicate: ideas "of Books or Literature" (4.3.235), "of the Desire of Power and Riches" (4.4.244), of command (4.10.280), of any country other than their own (4.10.281), as well as of moral evil (4.8.267) and of lying (4.3.235).

In all these references to ideas and conceptions Gulliver uses the terms in the limited seventeenth-century sense of images in the mind, never in the older sense of a pattern of perfection or in the Platonic sense of transcendent, real being. The rarity in English of "transcendental" as a substantive (*OED*) makes Gulliver's one use of it, without explanation, the exception that proves the rule: abstract, general ideas are the only transcendent things he knows. (Much of the drama of the fourth book springs from the question whether the general idea and term "Yahoo" applies to mankind, especially to Gulliver.) It is possible, indeed, that there is a close tie between the *Travels* and *An Essay Concerning Human Understanding*. I would say it is likely, especially because the recurrent mention of "ideas" that characterizes Gulliver is at once very uncommon in fiction and notably characteristic of Locke—so egregiously a mark of his writing that it made him self-conscious. He apologizes for "the frequent use of the word *Idea*" in the Essay.[6] By the time the *Travels* appeared, of course, the term had turned up in many places, but Swift is on record as attributing philosophical dependency on it particularly, satirically, to Locke. Ricardo Quintana judiciously explains Swift's mixed feelings about Locke and the *Essay*, expressed in a few scattered passages; from an obscure, posthumously published work of about 1707, Quintana quotes Swift's amusing comment—quite germane to my purposes—on the new, "refined Way of Speaking" Locke has introduced. Whereas philosophers before Locke were content to enquire about objects, "Since our modern Improvement of Human Understanding, instead of desiring a Philosopher to describe or define a Mouse-trap . . . I must gravely ask, what is contained in the Idea of a Mouse-trap?"[7] And as I have suggested, the term "idea" is but the center of a constellation of terms that appealed to Locke and Gulliver.

But let us begin with a comparatively simple, relatively early example of the Gulliverian understanding at work, the scene already mentioned of his thinking his countrymen tiny when he returns from Brobdingnag.

> I looked down upon the Servants, and one or two Friends who were in the House, as if they had been Pigmies, and I a Giant. I told my wife, she had been too thrifty; for I found she had starved herself and her Daughter to nothing. In short, I behaved my self so unaccountably, that they were all of the Captain's Opinion when he first saw me; and concluded I had lost my Wits. This I mention as an Instance of the great Power of Habit and Prejudice.
> In a little Time I and my Family and Friends came to a right Understanding. . . .
>
> (2.8.149)

Gulliver, as has been recognized, is not the most coherent of writers,[8] or has peculiar notions of coherence; here, as Hobbes says of a strange train of thought, "the coherance to me was manifest enough."[9] Gulliver's "This I mention as an Instance of the great Power of Habit and Prejudice" might better have come before the sentence preceding it. Then it would refer to only his own behavior. Where he does place it, the statement refers also to the inability of friends and family to understand him. Accustomed to a Gulliver who does not regard them as Pigmies, they cannot immediately adjust their minds to the strange phenomenon he presents. They as well as he, he thinks, must rectify their "Understanding."

Whether or not Swift had Locke in mind here, that last word and others nearby give the passage a Lockean quality. Gulliver and those about him are in a state of reciprocal error resembling madness. The Human Understanding is at fault, and the cause of error—Gulliver's in combining the idea of his wife with the idea of a Pigmy's extension, and so forth—is "the great Power of Habit and Prejudice." The diagnosis neatly fits Locke's account of error in the chapter "*Of the Association of* Ideas"; Swift's passage has to do with errors of the understanding, with the misjoining of ideas, with resemblance of the actions to those of someone mad, and with the causal explanation "Habit and Prejudice." For Locke, it will be recalled, the term "association" indicates error. Locke says the association of ideas is "really Madness," though often manifested "in the steady calm course" of people's lives. Whereas ideas properly joined "have a *natural* Correspondence and Connexion one with another," improper conjunctions or "associations" occur only because of "Chance or Custom." And while "Prejudice is a good general Name for the thing it self," in seeking a deeper comprehension of the process of error Locke concentrates on custom, explaining it by repeated mention of habit:

> Custom settles habits of Thinking in the Understanding, as well as of Determining in the Will, and of Motions in the Body; all which seems to be but Trains of Motions in the Animal Spirits, which, once set a going continue on in the same steps they have been used to, which by often treading are worn into a smooth path, and the Motion in it becomes easy and as it were Natural. As far as we can comprehend Thinking, thus *Ideas* seem to be produced in our Minds; or if they are not, this may serve to explain their following one another in an habitual train, when once they are put into that tract.[10]

Locke provides Swift's passage with an entire gloss, in terms almost the same as Gulliver's. A few pages before the account of reunion with his wife, Gulliver says of the sailors who rescued him that they too seemed "so many Pigmies" because his eyes had been "long accustomed" to giants (2.8.143). And the philosopher even includes a section on time's causing associations to decay, disuse annihilating habit. ("In a little Time," Gulliver's account concludes, "I and my Family and Friends came to a right Understanding.")

Generally, Locke was not at all sanguine about "the power of reason to help us" in disassembling an association, which people may sustain "often without perceiving it themselves."[11] *An Essay Concerning Human Understanding* stands in contrast to John Gay's "Dissertation" of 1730, where it is said, as it would be said later by Long and others, that the mind may recognize and disunite associations through tracing up its ideas to a suspect, habitual combination, then analyzing that association and perceiving its falsity.[12] Yet one does not have to wait for Gay and others to find the germ of this remedy, for Locke himself advanced it in the posthumous *Of the Conduct of the Understanding* (1706). This practical companion piece to his epistemology Locke originally planned to be, like the chapter on association, an addition to the *Essay*;[13] he returns to the question of association here after a warning about the dangers of projecting resemblance by "analogy." "And where then shall one with hopes of success begin the cure? Many men firmly embrace falsehood for truth; not only because they never thought otherwise, but also because, thus blinded as they have been from the beginning, they never could think otherwise, at least without a vigour of mind able to contest the empire of habit and look into its own principles."[14] There is a strait gate, then, for the vigorous mind, the mind more vigorous than Gulliver's. From beginning to end Gulliver remains morally blind to his own motives, though at one point (a point I shall return to) he says he will be candid about them, and he remains psychologically blind to the possibility that forces of habit may seriously and enduringly distort his thinking; he sees that possibility only in the thinking of others. Yet he feels he has developed an "enlarged . . . Understanding" (4.7.258) and by saying so once again invites attention to the concatenation of his ideas across the *Travels*.

In speaking of Locke I do not need to argue that Swift had Locke specifically in mind. The concepts of the "connexion" and "association" of ideas were not uncommon in the decades between Locke's writings and Swift's book.[15] I do mean to argue that *Gulliver's Travels*, especially because of its emphasis on epistemological and psychological considerations and terminology, asks to be read with reference to the deepened concern about psychology consequent upon Locke yet flowing from other contemporary sources. Scrupulous introspection was a major counsel of the seventeenth century to the eighteenth. Stanley Fish writes, "By the last quarter of the seventeenth century 'the duty of Self-Observation' has acquired the status of a science and an apparatus that is the counterpart of the analytical method developed in connection with the new empiricism," and he illustrates the point with these words from Edmund Arwaker's *Thoughts Well Employ'd* (1697): "For this considerate thinking on our ways, separates and discriminates things that are confusedly huddled together, . . . gather and collects those that are scattered and dispersed, . . . traces and finds out truth, examines likelihoods and appearances, and discovers and explores pretences that are feigned and varnished."[16] Throughout the present chapter I employ Locke simply as the most important writer on psychology in the years preceding *Gulliver's Travels*.

There is a danger of overestimating Locke's departure from the general psychological theorizing of his time, of underestimating the degree to which he represents psychology in general as Swift's contemporaries knew it. It has been said that Locke's theory of association "removes mental disease from the province of the moralist" because his explanation proceeds from the determinative effects of experience, not from failure of the will to control the passions. Thus, although Locke says associations may occur "voluntarily," he never develops that explanation: ". . . The examples he gives of wrong association all suggest that it is something which happens to the mind, rather than something the mind imposes on itself."[17] This description resembles that of Gulliver the

non-character already quoted, "someone to whom things happen."
But where are the passions and the will in this scheme? Locke made
a place for them in the *Essay*, and it is probable that he did not
expatiate on the idea of voluntary error simply because, though in
different terminology, it had been developed and illustrated so fully
by moralists before him, in a multitude of sermons, pensées, and
tracts.[18] He concentrated on elaborating his new idea. But by allowing that association could also be formed voluntarily, and initially remarking that the extravagant and irrational thinking to which
the chapter on association is devoted proceeds "not wholly from
Self-love, though that has often a great hand in it,"[19] he added his
new theory to the traditional moral explanations; he did not seek
to supersede them.

The early eighteenth-century sermon on "The Difficulty of
Knowing One's Self," which may be by Swift, similarly fuses counsels from traditional morality with psychological theory, theory
resembling Locke's.[20] The imagination, according to the sermon,
is normally so wild "that every Man may be said to be mad."[21] The
remedy is to be carefully conversant with the minute movements
of one's heart. Custom and false opinion may have led a person to
sin; a sinner by custom will do well if he traces "a Habit into the
very first Rise and imperfect Beginnings of it"; a sinner by false
opinion should call "to Mind what wrong Apprehensions he hath
had of some Things himself; how many Opinions, that he once
made no Doubt of, he hath upon a stricter Examination, found to
be doubtful and uncertain; how many more to be unreasonable and
absurd."[22] Among habits of thought imposed on him are prominently those imposed by himself through ill-judged self-love:

> Conversation with his own Heart may discover some Vice or some
> Infirmity lurking within him, which he is very unwilling to believe
> himself guilty of. For, can there be a more ungrateful Thing to a
> Man, than to find that upon a nearer View he is not that Person he
> took himself to be? that he hath neither the Courage, nor the Hon-
> esty, nor the Piety, nor the Humility that he dreamt he had? . . .
> These are very unwelcome Discoveries that a Man may make of
> himself; so that it is no wonder that every one, who is already flushed
> with a good Opinion of himself, should rather study how to run
> away from it, than how to converse with his own Heart.

What, really, is Gulliver's "insatiable Desire of seeing foreign Countries" (1.8.80), his "Thirst . . . of seeing the World" (3.1.153)? Even if a man stays to confront his heart, motives, and habits of thought, the sermon continues, he must overcome difficulties, among them "Prejudice and Prepossession."[23] For example, it is hard for a person to change his mind about someone he dislikes, "But how much more difficult then must it be for a Man, who taketh up a fond Opinion of his own Heart, long before he hath either Years or Sense enough to understand it, either to be persuaded out of it by himself, whom he loveth so well, or by another, whose Interest or Diversion it may be to make him ashamed of himself?"[24] By *another*—such as the King of Brobdingnag, after Gulliver has offered him gunpowder? In the remainder of this chapter what I shall emphasize is the habits of understanding, those habits so important to Locke and contemporary psychology, that Gulliver sets out with and that largely determine his ends, without his ever vigorously contesting them and looking into his "own principles" of thought, though at the end he thinks he has. His habits of association are the *fons et origo* of the text Gulliver writes.

Who does Gulliver think he is, and what does he think his ideas and motives are? The first paragraphs of the first book certainly give the impression that he is someone to whom things happen. He says he was apprenticed to a London surgeon after his Cambridge education became too expensive for his father. Later, after three years aboard ship, Gulliver settles in London, encouraged to do so by his former master. He marries, having been "advised to alter my Condition." But after two years, his physician's practice unsuccessful for lack of patronage and friends, and also for his having a conscience which "would not suffer me to imitate the bad Practice of too many among my Brethren," he goes to sea again for several voyages over six years, first having consulted wife and acquaintances about this venture. Three more years gone by, the business of physic again not prospering, the veteran Gulliver sets sail yet once more, into the adventures of Book 1, in response to "an advantageous Offer" from a captain.

He presents himself as someone to whom things happen, a

child of those narrow or adverse causes which direct or advise him to curtail his college years, take a profession, marry in accordance with that profession, and embark upon a series of voyages though he would seemingly prefer to stay at home in London. Really, he mentions no desires. He believes he will travel, but he does not say he wants to. He needs to make a living. The closest he comes to stating a desire is in his wish to avoid the unspecified evil characteristic of fellow London physicians, a reactive desire at best and perhaps suspect because his sense of failure as a physician precedes, at least in the order of telling, the condemnation of his colleagues. The second time he decides to settle in London, he does so because he has not prospered at sea either. "The last of these Voyages not proving very fortunate," he says, loosely, "I grew weary of the Sea, and intended to stay at home with my Wife and Family," as if not succeeding at something and growing weary of it were the same. Yet despite his distaste for London physicians, and the tonelessness of the remark about wife and family, during the first several books Gulliver mainly presents himself as devoted to both family and country. It is with the ideas of them that he couples the idea of excellence, as if moved to do so by patriotic and paternal love. Later he stresses his love for mankind, rather transiently, and he increasingly asserts love of truth and virtue. (As for self-love, he gives it no thoughtful consideration.) Home and nation deserve our initial attention as the anchors of his identity.

Where Gulliver's character is concerned, the many strange lands he visits are finally not so important, remarkable as they are, as the one familiar land he keeps leaving, leaving so regularly and casually despite repeated protestations of affection. When he commences his third series of voyages (we are still in the first paragraphs), he makes no mention of consulting his wife, nor does he indicate the size of his family, those hostages to fortune next noted only at the end of Book 1: "It is not easy to express the Joy I was in upon the unexpected Hope of once more seeing my beloved Country, and the dear Pledges I left in it," who include a son, Johnny, and a daughter, Betty (1.8.79–80); they are never named again. Gulliver tells the reader about the profit he made in England showing and selling Lilliputian cattle; he says nothing about the time he spent with his family before desire finally does swell his phlegmatic breast: "insatiable Desire of seeing foreign Countries would suffer me to continue no longer." Domestic life, as for Moll Flanders, is not worth recording—it seems; Gulliver's unfolding narrative, more than hers, will make us wonder about this. He leaves his family with enough money and expected income. His motive is not their economic survival or a will to be rich; it is Gulliver's strangely sudden, new Wanderlust, more Crusovian than Gulliverian when judged by what Gulliver has said thus far. As with Robinson, Wanderlust is now to be Gulliver's "insatiable Desire" and his cursed "evil Destiny" (2.8.149). Describing himself now as "condemned by Nature and Fortune to an active and restless Life," in the first sentence of Book 2 he steps forward as, almost, the archetypal haunted old salt.

In the second book, unlike Book 1, Gulliver when abroad sometimes thinks of his family, three times. Terrified by the Brobdingnagians, to whom he imagines he must seem as vulnerable as an insect, or a child, he bemoans "my desolate Widow, and Fatherless Children: I lamented my own Folly and Wilfulness in attempting a second Voyage against the Advice of all my Friends and Relations" (2.1.86). "Widow" and "Fatherless" call attention to his own plight as much as to that of wife and children, and the concluding clause introduces new information about the tears, on one side at least, shed at the close of Book 1; so he had consulted his wife after all, or she had consulted him.

Much later, in a rare example of memory exercised upon the materials of another of his voyages, Gulliver dwells upon his grandeur in Lilliput and his insignificance among the giants, who treat him kindly yet, he thinks, unbecomingly: "I was the Favourite of a great King and Queen, and the Delight of the whole Court; but it was upon such a Foot as ill became the Dignity of human Kind. I could never forget those domestic Pledges I had left behind me" (2.8.139). He has not mentioned his family for a long time, however, not since he recorded a dream about it in the first chapter, and it is hard to escape the inference that he recurs to thoughts of it now in a way at least as self-reflective as before. Those Pledges (again the language of Baconian calculation) come to mind now perhaps because in their circle he is king, not below the royal dwarf. Oddly, they do not come to mind when the king, earlier in the same paragraph, wishes he might find a woman Gulliver's size, to "propagate the Breed." Subsequently, Mrs. Gulliver says again, firmly, he must not go to sea, yet once more, again in two months, he has gone, having secured his wife's consent "by the Prospect of Advantage she proposed to her Children" from the profits Gulliver expects, her consent obtained "at last" (3.1.154).

The nuptial career of the Gullivers adds significance to the story told in Book 3, chapter 2, about the errant wives and daughters of Laputa, who "contemn their Husbands, and are exceedingly fond of Strangers." Gulliver appears perplexed by such traits, so beautiful is the flying island, upon which the women enjoy plenty, magnificence, and extraordinary freedom. The Laputan husband is so wholly given to enrapt speculation that his wife may cuckold him before his face, "if he be but provided with Paper and Implements, and without his *Flapper* at his Side." Indeed, the prime minister's wife left him and their children, disappeared, and was later discovered, content though in rags, attached to an aged "deformed Footman, who beat her every Day," whom she was separated from with difficulty, and whom she rejoined as soon as she could. Pontificates Gulliver: "the Caprices of Womankind are not limited by any Climate or Nation" and "are much more uniform than can be easily imagined." Our imaginations should not be so limited, he implies; the irony of his obtuseness rides on Chaucerian undercurrents—a "Merchant's Tale" of cuckoldom in broad daylight as if told by a diminished version of the knight in "The Franklin's Tale," who, having promised to heed his new wife's every wish, before long went off jousting for two years. Still more tellingly, the proximate context of this episode has Gulliver's complaints of being neglected himself by the King of Laputa, who in the next paragraph is said to lack curiosity about his guest's travels (3.2.165–66). Soon, like the prime minister's wife, Gulliver resolves to descend from the flying island, determined in part to do so because "I thought my self too much neglected" (3.4.173).

By the end of chapter 6, Gulliver has exhausted his interest in the mainland too and says he "began to think of returning home."

Later, after three months in Luggnagg, he is enjoined by the king to stay, "But I thought it more consistent with Prudence and Justice to pass the Remainder of my Days with my Wife and Family," whom he finds "in good Health," in—he uses the phrase twice during the final chapter of Book 3—"my Native Country" (3.9.206; 3.11.215,218). The reiterated "dear" of earlier references to wife, children, and country has been dropped for good. A reader may wonder whether that word may not be of a piece with Gulliver's too ready acquiescence in what he perceives as his role at other times. The King of Luggnagg has appreciated Gulliver and has rewarded him substantially, yet Gulliver, again weary, wants to leave—motivated, however, not by reawakening of affection but by an express determination to be prudent and just. These are not notably domestic virtues, but they are virtues flagrantly absent from the countries visited in this book. He has been away from home five and a half years this time, and now he stays with his family a full five months, contentedly he says (says in a curious way, to which I shall return).

And—not *but*—in the next sentence, ever upwardly as well as horizontally mobile, he accepts a captaincy and goes off again, Mrs. Gulliver's feelings unrecorded yet imaginable: she is "big with Child" (4.1.221). Weariable Gulliver, tired of being a surgeon, begins to proclaim himself a Lover of Mankind (4.2.230) and of course will quickly come to regard "my Family, my Friends, my Countrymen," and himself as Yahoos (4.10.278); will resist good Don Pedro's abstract appeal to principles like those that motivated Gulliver's return from Luggnagg (Don Pedro "put it upon me as a Point of Honour and Conscience, that I ought to return to my native Country, and live at home with my Wife and Children"); and will quite hopelessly go back to confront their joy with horror: "by copulating with one of the *Yahoo*-Species, I had become a Parent of more" (4.11.288–89). Earlier he had railed, to the Houyhnhnm master, against "ranting, lewd, expensive Wives" (4.10.277) and still earlier had accused his own wife of luxury (4.6.253). Now he swoons at Mrs. Gulliver's odious kiss, more affected by it than by the female Yahoo's onslaught, and so forth. That five years will pass before he can bear his Penelope's presence at the far end of a long dinner table is probably more familiar to readers than the details I have drawn together of the lengthy connubial prelude to that moment. For the first eleven years of his marriage, Gulliver had been literally at sea only a little more than half the time. But upon returning from Houyhnhnmland he says he has been a voyager during the past sixteen and a half years, and he has been with his family for only about nine months all the while (4.12.291).

Gulliver the husband interested and amused at least one of Swift's fellow Scriblerians enough to prompt composition of a frantic pastoral in which desolated Brobdingnagian Glumdalclitch, her little pet gone, torments herself with thoughts of his enjoying "thy tiny Spouse."[25] Where would she have gotten that idea? More interesting is a companion poem, "Mary Gulliver to Captain Lemuel Gulliver," in which, according to the argument, "Mrs. Gulliver, apprehending from his late Behaviour some Estrangement of his Affections, writes him the following expostulating, soothing, and tenderly-complaining Epistle." At one point the modern Eloisa exclaims:

> My Bed, (the Scene of all our former Joys,
> Witness two lovely Girls, two lovely Boys)
> Alone I press; in Dreams I call my Dear,
> I stretch my Hand, no *Gulliver* is there![26]

Not only does she show jealously comprehensive knowledge of his adventures ("Was Flimnap's Dame more sweet in *Lilliput*?"); she also, as if struck by the passage about female caprices, energetically asserts her fidelity, perhaps excessively. Gulliver never thought to record the issue of the pregnancy before the final voyage; he apparently took no special notice of the twins, as Mary's lines indicate they are, though by the time he returned and first saw these children they were nearly five years old. Lest this reflection seem too arch, however, I freely own it to be Scriblerian, not mine, and accord it whatever doubt should be raised by Gulliver's prefatory complaint to Captain Sympson about changes in the text fathered upon the author without his leave.

The Scriblerian verses on *Gulliver's Travels* are seriously useful to the interpreter because in them characters from the book, especially Glumdalclitch and Mrs. Gulliver, but also a Lilliputian, a chorus of Houyhnhnms, and the King of Brobdingnag, speak from their own experience in a way Gulliver the narrator never permits, as if they had lives centered on something other than him. Although minor characters do speak in the book, their speeches very little qualify the reader's sense of hearing a monologue. Gulliver gives no one but himself credit for having a history of thought and feeling— certainly not his wife. The single apparent exception to this generality is Munodi, the unfortunate nobleman of Balnibarbi who tells his story in the fourth chapter of Book 3: he confesses himself weak for maintaining his estate in the old, productive way despite the contempt of his newfangled, exceedingly foolish countrymen. This recognition by Gulliver, with some fullness, of another person's separate existence would be truly exceptional if Munodi did not so closely resemble Gulliver, both of them terribly concerned about whether others esteem them. Indeed, one of the cleverest devices in *Gulliver's Travels* (comparable as we shall see to Montesquieu's presentation of the major character in the *Lettres persanes*) is Swift's disguised enlistment of the reader's childish egotism, the invitation to fall in with the narrator's insensitivity to others' foreseeable natural feelings.

As early as the third chapter of Book 1 a cloud appears in the person of the Lilliputian Admiral Skyresh Bolgolam, "who was pleased, without any Provocation, to be my mortal Enemy" (p. 42). It never occurs to Gulliver that the arrival of a superman would cause resentment in Lilliput or anywhere, especially resentment by those whose station and power the newcomer threatens. The particular resentment of Gulliver by the Queen's dwarf in Brobdingnag is another case in point—though Gulliver explains it (as well Gulliver might) by saying the dwarf is proud of being taller than he (2.3.108). Very little imagination on the part of Admiral Bolgolam would be required to anticipate the maritime uses to which the giant shipwrecked mariner will soon be put against Blefuscu, making the Admiral's navy obsolete at a stroke. Gulliver behaves and thinks as if Lilliput and other lands had been created to appreciate him—and the reader may not notice Gulliver's puerile cast of mind. Considerations such as these may have led Swift to print the Scriblerian verses in editions of the *Travels* after the first. The verses wisely set Gulliver, a character adamantine proof in portable isolation, a flying island, to the test he continually avoids, of comparison and exchange with others less insular, others allotted the dignity of having their own lives and minds, given space for their points of view in a manner Gulliver evidently cannot tolerate, and allowed to be amusing in ways quite alien to his perceptions and discourse.

Locke stresses the shortcomings of Gulliverian provinciality early in *Of the Conduct of the Understanding*:

> Those who live thus mued up within their own contracted territories, and will not look abroad beyond the boundaries that chance, conceit, or laziness has set to their enquiries, but live separate from the notions, discourses and attainments of the rest of mankind, may not amiss be represented by the inhabitants of the Marian islands; who, being separated by a large tract of sea from all communion with the habitable parts of the earth, thought themselves the only people of the world. And though the straitness of the conveniences of life amongst them had never reached so far as to the use of fire till, the Spaniards . . . brought it amongst them, yet in the want and ignorance of almost all things, they looked upon themselves, even after that the Spaniards had brought amongst them the notice of variety of nations abounding in sciences, arts and conveniences of life, of which they knew nothing, they looked upon themselves, I say, as the happiest and wisest people of the universe.[27]

Most of the countries Gulliver visits fit this description, even Houyhnhnmland, where self-satisfaction is a major natural resource. But Gulliver outdoes them all, maintaining such insularity while traveling. The England he keeps leaving and talking about, describing it as if it also corresponds to Locke's example of complacency, constitutes his major, sustaining idea. "He sees his *Britain* with a Mother's Eyes;/Softens Defects, and heightens all its Charms . . .," says the King of Brobdingnag in another of the Scriblerian verses.[28] It is a perceptive comment, for Gulliver applies terms of endearment to England more frequently and persistently than he does to his Pledges, and his doting loyalty to it dies a slower death.

As late as the close of Book 4, Chapter 3, in an immediate context of resisting identification of himself with the Yahoos, he can imagine returning to England as an instance of "good Fortune"

(p. 238), and still later, though his unexamined loyalty has begun to crumble, he can mention having earlier described "our *excellent Constitution*" to his Houyhnhnm master as "deservedly the Wonder and Envy of the whole World" (4.6.254). What a curious displacement of affection, or instance of antique Roman virtue. The naturalist of human nature would suppose that the tide of a person's love bathes those nearest him before washing the polis. But Gulliver is of two minds, from rather early in the volume: startled by the intrigues of the Lilliputian court, he allows that "I had indeed heard and read enough of the Dispositions of great Princes and Ministers; but never expected to have found such terrible Effects of them in so remote a Country, governed, as I thought, by very different Maxims from those in *Europe*" (1.7.67). A few pages later he is deterred from the thought of standing trial because of "having in my Life perused many State-Tryals, which I ever observed to terminate as the Judges thought fit to direct" (1.7.73). These scruples in Gulliver's memory are oddly general—Europe, not England, or unlocated. But would not his reading have followed his affection for that "dear native Country" of his?

Although Gulliver is unreflecting about his family life, the opposite is true concerning his attitude toward England, yet he begins to reflect on that attitude very slowly and sporadically. In the first book there is but one instance, in Chapter 6: he says he would attempt to justify certain Lilliputian laws and customs "if they were not so directly contrary to those of my own dear Country" (p. 58), and in the volume's initial sign of a pattern emphatic later, he reports the little king's being morally outraged at Gulliver's verbal defense of a criminal who had committed "only a Breach of Trust." Gulliver's comment is worth pausing over, longer than he does:

> And truly, I had little to say in Return, farther than the common Answer, that different Nations had different Customs; for, I confess, I was heartily ashamed.
>
> Although we usually call Reward and Punishment, the two Hinges upon which all Government turns; yet I could never observe this Maxim to be put in Practice by Any Nation, except that of *Lilliput*.
>
> (pp. 58–59)

Thus he immediately begins a new paragraph on the subject of another Lilliputian custom, his shame quickly passed by. But the transition remains incomplete, for the question of different nations' different customs lingers in his thoughts, and the new paragraph rapidly casts belated, exculpatory qualification back upon that question. Is the abhorrence of fraud a "custom" sustained only in Lilliput, and is acceptance of fraud not a peculiarly English failing? And the shame Gulliver has acknowledged—is it on England's account or his own? His sentences neatly blur and diffuse responsibility for the shameful remark. He will shortly modify his celebration of Lilliput by observing that he praises only its old, formerly established ways, not the abuses to which it has fallen because of the "degenerate Nature of Man" (p. 60). Scapegoats multiply while Gulliver's associations cooperate to depress Lilliput's worth and to spare both England and himself direct blame for the countenancing of fraud.

Apart from this passage, its remarkable power somewhat muted by the force of the marvels surrounding it, Gulliver delivers no criticism of England in Book 1, and he generally shows to such moral advantage in contrast to the pusillanimous natives that they, not he, draw the reader's censure. Gulliver is seemingly not the main object of scrutiny here, so the scapegoats of general English, European, and human depravity can be held in reserve—by him; he does not need them yet. Although the political allegory suggesting broad parallels between Lilliput and England is blatant, it of course goes unnoticed by Gulliver, and the mistreatment he encounters (and, as is typical of "philosophical" heroes in tales, often credulously invites) he accounts for by hitting on still another scapegoat: the courtier, butt of English satire for centuries and hence a customary, easily available, seemingly safe resting place for Gulliver's mind. He calls attention to that mind's progress in the slightly ambiguous remark, "And this was the first time I began to conceive some imperfect Idea of Courts and Ministers" (1.5.54). He means, hatched the idea that they are imperfect; that they, like England, are perfect is one of the ideas he brings to Lilliput. But the statement can also be taken to mean that he has yet to perfect his idea of what courtiers are really like.

Either way, the idea is more dangerous than he realizes. The king, Gulliver says, suspects him of "Disaffection" after he has opposed the royal will to subdue Blefuscu completely and after he has very cordially entertained the enemy ambassadors (1.5.54). Of disaffection in the sense of conscious disloyalty Gulliver is not guilty; his detractors at court malign him. But in the root sense of the falling off of Gulliver's originally undivided good feelings toward the king, the accusation is true. On the same page he has said as much: "Of so little Weight are the greatest Services to Princes, when put into the Balance with a Refusal to gratify their Passions." In the proximate context it is a petulantly universal remark. What dealings with a prince has Gulliver had before? None. But he is speaking, again in the proximate context (the narrative has yet to arrive at Gulliver's several later exchanges with foreign monarchs), not as a plain sea-surgeon but as a courtier himself. The king has made him a *Nardac*, and now Gulliver has been so naively impolitic as to give evidence, unwittingly, for accusations of disloyalty that have some basis in his feelings and actions, if not in his thoughts. Like satirical courtiers before him, the unfortunate Nardac flees the wicked court in a flurry of protestation—"having never been designed for a Courtier . . . Neither had I so soon learned the Gratitude of Courtiers" (1.7.72–73). He will not trust the King of Blefuscu either, for he has "resolved never more to put any Confidence in Princes or Ministers, where I could possibly avoid it" (1.8.77), again a remarkably broad statement, especially for a man who has already found a boat to make for home in—where it is very unlikely that he shall ever see a prince or a minister again. It is clear that he continues to think of himself as a courtier without quite realizing it. Reflections against courtiers therefore do not fully provide the un-self-critical explanations of evil that he seems to seek, while generalities about the evil in courts clearly, though unbeknownst to him, set him on a collision course with his "own beloved Country."

The second book immediately develops that plot, the central chapters presenting Gulliver's impassioned celebration of his homeland and the Brobdingnagian king's famous Juvenalian reply. The scenes are too familiar to need summary, but several points about

Gulliver's behavior deserve emphasis. Initially, he has moments of flexibility and reasonableness. When the king jokes about English self-importance, Gulliver, in time and "upon mature Thoughts," suppresses his indignation and admits to himself that, from the perspective of the giants, "the most courtly Manner of Strutting, and Bowing and Prating" in England seems laughable (2.3.107). He forthrightly protests to the king that size of body does not necessarily indicate breadth of mind; in Brobdingnag too much an insect, he adduces the examples of the industrious, artful, and sagacious bee and ant; and he sees the king soften toward him, grow curious, and ask for enlightenment about English ways—the cue for the five radiant discourses leading up to the king's explosion. Only seemingly reasonable, Gulliver has taken advantage of the king's unbending. The king explodes because he has a sense of human motivation that cannot be reconciled with Gulliver's explanations. But more important than the king's rejoinder, from my point of view, is Gulliver's reaction to it. He belittles the king's mental provinciality, especially his ignorance of political science, and he offers him—gunpowder, a gift about which it may certainly be said the intention is what counts. (Throughout the volume Gulliver proves a missionary of gunpowder; he had told the King of Lilliput that it could blow up his palace [1.2.37]—this mariner whose ship was wrecked on Guy Fawkes Day.)

A reader should notice that the giant king, when roundly condemning England, had politely spared Gulliver by specifying "the Bulk of your Natives" (2.6.132); now the king's counterblast to the gunpowder offer is overwhelmingly direct and personal—"so impotent and groveling an Insect as I (these were his Expressions)" (2.7.134)—and he threatens death to Gulliver should the horrid invention ever be mentioned again. Gulliver responds by conveying, not to the king to but to the reader, some additional disparagement of the giants' backwardness in understanding, with a digression that recalls and twits the treatise of some Brobdingnagian Pascal on the defects of humanity, Gulliver like Voltaire wondering why moralists are always so ready to quarrel with nature. Gulliver will think well of mankind, and he almost immediately begins to think of leaving Brobdingnag. No further conversations with the

king are recorded, though Gulliver styles himself a "Favourite"
(2.8.139). He longs for his "Liberty"; there is every reason to suppose it is the freedom to see only what he wants to see. As I have
said, he has stopped calling his family, or his country, or anything,
"dear."

In the next book Gulliver travels among people his own size,
doing so without much eagerness, and those he sees are on the whole
not very interested in him. He has almost no occasion to describe
his homeland again until commanded to, in Book 4, by the
Houyhnhnm master, when—in contrast to the deference toward
England and its foibles that Gulliver displayed in Brobdingnag—
he proves unmitigatedly censorious of England's vices. To be sure,
the argument prefixed to Chapter 7 mentions "The Author's great
Love of his Native Country"; the text of the chapter, however, puts
the matter querulously, as Locke might have done: ". . . Who is
there alive that will not be swayed by his Byass and Partiality to
the Place of his Birth?" Both "Bias" and "Partiality" are titles of
cautionary sections in *Of the Conduct of the Understanding*.[29] Now
Gulliver, as he sees it, has contested the empire of habit once and
for all:

> The Reader may be disposed to wonder how I could prevail on my
> self to give so free a Representation of my own Species, among a
> Race of Mortals who were already too apt to conceive the vilest
> Opinion of Human Kind, from that entire Congruity betwixt me
> and their *Yahoos*. But I must freely confess, that the many Virtues
> of those excellent *Quadrupeds* placed in opposite View to human Cor-
> ruptions, had so far opened mine Eyes, and enlarged my Under-
> standing, that I began to view the Actions and Passions of Man in
> a very different Light; and to think the Honour of my own Kind
> not worth managing; which, besides, it was impossible for me to do
> before a Person of so acute a Judgment as my Master, who daily
> convinced me of a thousand Faults in my self, whereof I had not
> the least Perception before, and which with us would never be num-
> bered even among human Infirmities.

(4.7.258)

Having disengaged his idea of goodness from those of his family,
England, and all mankind, Gulliver sacrifices "every thing" to truth,
and as if moved by contemplation of an act of such grandeur he

speaks in a new way about himself and his relation to us: "Let me deal so candidly with the Reader, as to confess, that there was yet a much stronger Motive for the Freedom I took in my Representation of Things." He has resolved never to return home but to stay in Houyhnhnmland; now in his heart's home he can be candid about his motives. He has not made such distinctions before; he speaks from an "enlarged . . . Understanding."

This change has not simply "happened to" him. Comparatively cursory as Book 3 may seem in some ways, it is vital to Gulliver's mental reformation. The end of Book 2 had portrayed him as vaguely disaffected, returning home not out of desire, particularly, but because he was unsatisfied in Brobdingnag, was not taken seriously enough—a complaint voiced again in Laputa. He had made a brave show of defending his dear illusion of England; it had not succeeded. Consistent with his childishness in the second book as a whole, he had not then faced up to his errors but had brazened them out. In the fourth book he is ready to confess, to own up, to acknowledge his vacuity as the Englishman he had so prided himself on being—ready because in Book 3, the transitional book, that vacuity had come home to him, in two main movements. The first, minor change occurs in the Academy of Projectors. The new, speciously noncommittal Gulliver observes various absurd experiments in natural science without criticizing them, but in the School of Political Projectors he reacts with scorn to those scientists intent upon schemes to promote honesty in government. They make him "melancholy," those "Professors . . . out of their Senses" (3.6.187). Yet the efforts of those who would reform government by physic and surgery so captivate him that he rewards one with news of Tribnia's way of discovering treason through "Acrosticks, and Anagrams." It is not enthusiasm for his own profession or for mischievous irony that prompts his response; Gulliver has neither in his character (and that he does not is a corollary of his having a character in some ways). His interest is best explained as last-ditch hope in a desperate remedy.

The more important episode that follows, however, is Swift's negative counterpart of the descent to the underworld that gave Aeneas his enabling vision. In Glubbdubdrib Gulliver learns how inferior is a modern governing assembly to the Roman senate of old. He feasts on the sight of Brutus and the rest of that remarkable Sextumvirate and, in a moment of elation, "chiefly fed mine Eyes with beholding the Destroyers of Tyrants and Usurpers, and the Restorers of Liberty to oppressed and injured Nations" (3.7.196). He is wholly taken up with exemplars of extreme political reform, not surprisingly in view of modern parliamentary corruption as well as the failings of princes and ministers. Inclusion of parliament extends the satire farther down the political scale, and before Gulliver leaves Glubbdubdrib coverage will become virtually complete, taking in the degeneracy of aristocrats and even of his Country's Pride the yeomanry, now as corrupt as the courtiers. Though unrecalled by Gulliver, the terrible judgment of the King of Brobdingnag resounds here—that twofold judgment, first against England, then against Gulliver. The single, ephemeral ray of hope that shines on him in Book 3 comes when he imagines that, were he an immortal Struldbrugg, he might be able to reform humankind—a dream with a distinctly self-serving side.[30] Gulliver admits to having "been often apt to amuse myself with Visions of what I should do if I were a King, a General, or a great Lord" (3.10.209).

What has happened to him by the time he enters Houyhnhnmland is that the associative hobbyhorses of family and nation have been shot from under him; the third hobbyhorse, his love of mankind, is about to go, sacrificed to Gulliver's enlarged understanding when the Houyhnhnms "opened mine Eyes" (4.7.258)—a phrase from Genesis. Almost like Adam and Eve, Gulliver will discover that everyone else is naked. Houyhnhnmland is to Gulliver, in some respects, what the state of nature was to some broadly contemporary political philosophers. It is clear by now that he has been riding a secret association all this while, the association of himself with salient goodness; he will have that pride to retreat to when his love of humanity stumbles. But, as I trust is also clear, nothing has "happened to" him, really: the hobbyhorses have not been shot. In Gulliver's efforts to establish and preserve something, his self-esteem, he has ridden them into the ground, retreating from association to association, bending his mind to the task. The twists his mind takes as the tale progresses become more and more intricate, and Gulliver, though he does not fully explain his processes of thought, is attentive enough to them to draw the reader's attention there as well.

Early he praises himself for "great Facility" in languages (1.1.20), suggesting responsiveness to the minds of others, but he says too, near the beginning, that he lacks "Presence of Mind": he hits on the way to extinguish the palace fire "by a Presence of Mind, unusual to me" (1.5.56). This deficiency gains thematic prominence because it is common among those whom Gulliver visits: they often fare forward intellectually by imposing the customary upon the new, explaining it by simple resemblance or contrast. The Laputans despise Gulliver because he has no Flapper; the Houyhnhnm master is sure a "Brute" like Gulliver cannot sail a boat (3.2.160, 4.3.235). But the Lilliputians stand out for mechanical mental reactions, initiating the charge of adultery. Only Gulliver excels them in absence of mind. He is as quick as they are to neglect the discrepancy between his size and theirs, and he rapidly becomes a Lilliputian to do so—for example, taking proprietary pride in the wine of that kingdom ("the *Blefuscudians* call it *Flunec*, but ours is esteemed the better Sort"—1.5.56), or lapsing into Lilliputian when he measures the Emperor's heels by "a *Drurr*" (1.4.48). Upon first encountering the Houyhnhnms, though he imagines them conjurers (it is not long since his experience of magicians in Glubbdubdrib), he is sufficiently confident in imported notions to ask to ride one of the horses—to *ask!* some presence of mind here—and to offer them trinkets he has brought to placate "Savages" (4.1.223). Five years later, when returning from Houyhnhnmland, he will think it odd to see human beings speaking (4.11.286). Yet the "strange Effects of Habit and Prejudice" only begin to explain his thinking, which is trickier than it may seem.

Since Gulliver lacks "Presence of Mind," one could imagine that he sees his countrymen as tiny when he returns from Brobdingnag because he is used to seeing giants; that, as we have seen, is his explanation. As a result of his experience, his customary idea of others is that they are larger than he; when he sees people his own size, he thinks them small. But if this were the true explanation, he would have thought his countrymen giants when he returned from Lilliput. The explanation, then, may be that he tends to regard others as he is used to being regarded. The longer he is in Lilliput, the more the Lilliputians take him for granted, and the more he behaves as if he were the same size as they—praising the emperor as if he were as superb as he is described, and so forth. In Lilliput Gulliver forgets how big he is. But if this trait generally explained his thinking, when returning from Brobdingnag he would think his countrymen large, or no bigger than he, for the Brobdingnagians have never regarded him as anything but small. He has not adopted the Brobdingnagian view of him. In fact he has resisted it as much as possible, constantly trying to appear larger and more significant than he is. One may despair of a consistent explanation of his thinking, and hence of a basic, general consistency in his character.

But there is a third explanation possible, and I believe it adequate. Gulliver tends to regard those he meets, abroad and at home, in conformity not with the qualities of the beings he has visited last, and not with the way those beings have regarded him, but with the way that, during his most recent lengthy stay somewhere, he has seen himself in comparison to others. Returning from Lilliput, where he fit right in, he sees his countrymen as of ordinary size like himself. He tends to view himself—such is the over-riding implication—as less significant than others unless he can become comparably significant by being extraordinary. He returns from Brobdingnag regarding himself as he wished to there, larger in stature than the provincial giants. He sees his countrymen as small because he is accustomed, not to seeing giants but to maintaining an inflated idea of his own size and importance. While telling about Brobdingnag, he provides, himself, a nearly full explanation of what is "happening to" him; what he is doing to himself. Once the Queen placed him "upon her Hand towards a Looking-Glass, by which both our Persons appeared before me in full View together; and there could nothing be more ridiculous than the Comparison: So that I really began to imagine my self dwindled many Degrees below my usual Size" (2.3.107). It is interesting and amusing that Gulliver's imagination finds this means of denying the Queen's hugeness—only temporarily, however, for in a moment he effaces the image of his littleness altogether by deprecating the stature of the merely thirty-foot dwarf, an "Urchin."

Later he realizes and explains what was happening: "I could never endure to look in a Glass after mine Eyes had been accustomed to such prodigious Objects; because the Comparison gave me so despicable a Conceit of my self" (2.8.147). *Conceit*, of course, means conception or idea. "My Ideas," he continues later in the paragraph, "were wholly taken up with what I saw on every Side of me; and I winked at my own Littleness, as People do at their own Faults." The influence of ill-judged self-love upon the selection and association of ideas recorded here is as if in an epitome of Locke and the sermon on "Knowing One's Self." And Gulliver flies from the recognition and never even approaches it again.

When he returns home, weary, at the end of Book 3, he has nothing much to report about England. His family is healthy, and— he adds, most peculiarly—he "continued at Home with my Wife and Children about five Months in a very Happy Condition, if I could have learned the Lesson of knowing when I was well" (4.1.221). The retroactive conditional clause can mean only that he was not happy, and how at this time or later the Gulliver we know could imagine he might have been happy is a puzzle (the comment may be his sanest in the *Travels*). The wholesale disillusionment and general neglect he has suffered in Book 3 have depleted him. He leaves his wife "big with Child," no regrets mentioned—on either side. And he enters Houyhnhnmland in this worn mental condition, a man who, if he could have had his way, would now be securely and permanently passing his days "in the Conversation of those superiour Beings the *Struldbruggs*" (3.10.208), as he first imagined and desired them to be, perfectly rational animals, in another form the Houyhnhnms he has yet to discover but whose existence he already wills.[31] His pattern of thought persists, on into Book 4: now wishing, rather forlornly, to be important and interesting, he is uninterested in family, nation, and mankind—just as earlier, wishing to be large, he saw them as small—but he lacks the strength of character to exert active, solitary misanthropy. Something must happen to him: he needs a new master to be a new man.

Houyhnhnmland provides a master and more, a neat binary set of categories to think in. Because of the way he thinks in them, Gulliver remains interesting as a character. The critical questions become, not what a Yahoo is, or whether Gulliver is a Yahoo, but what Gulliver thinks a Yahoo is and whether he sees himself as a Yahoo, how and why.

A recurrent, comparatively tense moment in Locke is the confrontation with strange creatures—especially man-like animals, sometimes those beings encountered "in a new-discovered Country"—which must be sorted out as human or not, or the same as (or different from) each other.[32] I forbear quoting the *Essay's* many lively illustrations entailing centaurs, horses, men, monkeys, drills, "*Cassiowary*, and *Querechinchio.*"[33] Nor do I think it necessary to enter upon the grounds of distinction involving real and nominal essences, the significance of perceived shapes, and the formation of "*our Complex* Ideas *of Substances.*" What I would emphasize is the prominence of such Gulliverian scenes in Locke and his concern for prudent wariness, especially regarding analogies, when the investigator approaches a decision. For as Locke says, sternly, "The highest Probability, amounts not to Certainty; without which, there can be no true Knowledge."[34] Gulliver indeed discovers a quite similar principle among the Houyhnhnms, who hold that "*Reason* taught us to affirm or deny only where we are certain; and beyond our Knowledge we cannot do either" (4.8.267).

In the early chapters of Book 4, the question of whether Gulliver is a Yahoo remains unsettled; neither Gulliver nor the Houyhnhnm master is sure. When Gulliver first sees the nasty beasts, he finds them "very singular, and deformed" (4.1.223), but he says nothing about their resembling mankind. The Houyhnhnms, however, perceive *some* resemblance: "The Beast and I were brought close together; and our Countenances diligently compared, both by Master and Servant, who thereupon repeated several Times the Word *Yahoo*" (4.2.229)—though whether the Houyhnhnms think Gulliver and the Yahoo are of the same or only of similar species is not clear. At just this point Gulliver, with what he says are feelings of horror, recognizes the resemblance. The differences between the two perplex the Houyhnhnms; they do not know what to make of Gulliver's clothing. But Gulliver jumps, temporarily, to the judgment that he and the Yahoo are of the same species: "For as to those filthy *Yahoos*, although there were few greater Lovers of Mankind, at that time, than myself; yet I confess I never saw any sensitive Being so detestable on all Accounts . . ." (4.2.230). Then, while the Houyhnhnms continue to puzzle over the question, Gulliver resists his own judgment, thinking of "Escape to some other Country, and to Creatures of my own Species" (4.2.232). That the Houyhnhnms somehow preserve the notion of a difference between their visitor and the Yahoos is clear from their lodging Gulliver apart from the Yahoos' stable (4.2.233).

In time, still not knowing what to make of Gulliver's good qualities, the master becomes convinced that he is a Yahoo, though Gulliver does not learn of this judgment until much later (4.3.234). Interestingly, the judgment is quickly followed in the text by the master's wrong, analogical assertion that there can be no country beyond the sea and that sailing is beyond Gulliver's capacities. (The reader has reason to be wary of the Houyhnhnms' habits and prejudices.) Other Houyhnhnms, because continuing to wonder about the surface Gulliver's clothes present, remain doubtful: "could hardly believe me to be a right Yahoo"; Gulliver prudently keeps his clothes on "to distinguish myself as much as possible, from that cursed Race of Yahoos" (4.3.236)—whether to preserve the distinction in his own mind, as well as in the minds of the Houyhnhnms, is not clear. When the master, finally seeing Gulliver partly undressed, concludes him a "perfect *Yahoo*," Gulliver objects to the appellation. Yet it is most important for the reader to note that the master's conclusion is equivocal, for he means much by the word *perfect*, being "more astonished at my Capacity for Speech and Reason, than at the Figure of my Body, whether it were covered or no" (4.3.237).

It is between chapters 4 and 6 that Gulliver tells the master about England, a bitter, more intense reprise of the recitation before the Brobdingnagian king, and by the beginning of chapter 7, as we have seen, Gulliver has decided to renounce England and his kind, and the Houyhnhnms (but it is Gulliver who says this) have perceived an "entire Congruity betwixt me and their *Yahoos*." Had they become certain? If so, how? The transition—in Gulliver's mind, at least—is subtle yet not unclear. It is Gulliver himself who persuades the Houyhnhnms that he is a Yahoo, or at least who confirms their original suspicions to that effect—but first he somewhat unwittingly persuades himself.[35] Before he begins to describe England, the master is struck by the rationality which distinguishes Gulliver from the brutes. When Gulliver's discourse, or rather, series of diatribes, is ended, this formerly striking mark of difference has faded to relative insignificance: the master now "looked upon us as a Sort of Animals to whose Share . . . some small Pittance of *Reason* had fallen" (4.7.259).

The critical turn occurs as a result of Gulliver's strategy for explaining matters utterly unfamiliar to the Houyhnhnm. Because what Gulliver has to tell him does not resemble what the Houyhnhnm knows, Gulliver—having a little epistemological learning—hits on an ingenious idea: ". . . I doubted much, whether it would be possible for me to explain my self on several Subjects, whereof his Honour could have no Conception, because I saw nothing in his Country to which I could resemble them. That however, I would do my best, and strive to express my self by Similitudes . . ." (4.4.243).[36] This accomodating expedient is Gulliver's petard, for to make human beings (as Gulliver understands them) comprehensible to the master, Gulliver from this point repeatedly calls them Yahoos—"I was Commander of the Ship and had about fifty *Yahoos* under me," and so forth—as he unrolls his awful account of English depravity through two chapters. The analogy takes possession of Gulliver. In Locke's *Of the Conduct of the Understanding*, the hidden pitfalls of analogy are explained directly before the renewed consideration of the association of ideas.

The enlarged understanding to which Gulliver lays claim after disburdening himself about human depravity is countered by a like advance on the part of the Houyhnhnm. Although it has always been thought in his country that the Yahoos hate each other for their deformity, which each perceives in others but not in himself, the master now sees there is a deeper, more essential reason, to which Gulliver's diatribes have opened the Houyhnhnm's eyes—the Yahoos' Hobbesian selfishness (4.7.260). Thus Gulliver accomplishes much, not only persuading himself and his master that he is a Yahoo but also enabling the master to see that the local Yahoos are worse than was realized. The master still preserves some sense of a distinction between his guest and the Yahoos, being persuaded that Gulliver sufficiently hates the brutes not to be corrupted by going among them (4.8.265). Also, the master is finally disinclined to agree with the assembly's decision that the stranger ought to be banished (4.10.279). Yet in presenting Gulliver's case to the assembly the Houyhnhnm gives much less emphasis to the crucial distinction of Gulliver's rationality than he had before hearing Gulliver out: the master tells his peers that "he observed in me all the Qualities of a *Yahoo*, only a little more civilized by some Tincture of Reason; which however was in a Degree as far inferior to the *Houyhnhnm* Race, as the *Yahoos* of their Country were to me" (4.9.272). Gulliver's diatribes, on top of the analogy, have worn down the master's sense of this man's redeeming distinctiveness. Almost as his calling card, Gulliver in beginning to hold forth had rather tactlessly told the master about human domination and castration of horses; the master, addressing the assembly, mentions these facts of European life but does not mention, much less dilate upon, Gulliver's good qualities. It is not surprising that the assembly, thus instructed, would think it best for Gulliver to go.

Gulliver, whose delicate, not entirely witting strategy of saving himself by repudiating his species has failed, finds the Houyhnhnm decision to banish him more rigorous than reasonable, which in a sense it is. It represents an "association" of a familiar kind: the master's conversing with and keeping "a *Yahoo* (meaning my self) in his Family more like a *Houyhnhnm* than a Brute Animal," is, the assembly determines, "a Practice . . . not agreeable to Reason or Nature, or a thing ever heard of before among them" (4.10.279): it is against precedent, whereas the assembly's association of Gulliver and the Yahoos, and the Houyhnhnms' association of themselves and European horses, are comfortably based on resemblance and, ultimately, custom.

The Houyhnhnms' phrase "not agreeable to Reason or Nature," moreoever, recalls the terms of Locke's objection to associations of ideas—"Unreasonableness," "wrong and unnatural Combinations of *Ideas*"[37]—and the Houyhnhnms' associating Gulliver with the party of the Yahoos, whom it is feared he may lead "in Troops," literalizes the political metaphor underlying Locke's word "association"[38]—as in the philosopher's comment that "the whole gang [of associated ideas] always inseparable shew themselves together."[39] Gulliver suffers, one might say, from "guilt by association," the Houyhnhnms' associating the ideas of him and of the Yahoos. But the assembly's banishment of this self-proclaimed tame wolf is not imprudent, and what is central to the tale is not the Houyhnhnms' association of ideas but Gulliver's. The rhetorical strategy of similitudes has permitted expression of his own, latent, ferocious conviction of identity between human beings and Yahoos—persuasive expression. He has failed only in attempting to convince the Houyhnhnms at large that he is the distinguished exception to the rule. (The latter effort foreshadows his still more precarious later campaign to evangelize the countrymen he so outspokenly despises.)

Thus it is Gulliver himself who convinces himself and the Houyhnhnms that he is truly a Yahoo, but he does so in character, again having formed a wishful mental habit, a voluntary delusion like that of adopting equine gait and gestures. His "Memory and Imaginations were perpetually filled with the Virtues and Ideas of those exalted *Houyhnhnms*" (4.11.289). True to form, he returns to England seeing human beings in contrast to the way in which, as a would-be Houyhnhnm, he wishes to see himself. He gives a new twist to an established phrase when condescending to find in the Portuguese captain a "very good *human* Understanding" (4.11.288). The habitual ideas clinging to Gulliver's conception of human beings are hard for him to contest, yet in his state of enlarged understanding he may be victorious: ". . . Although it be hard for a Man late in Life to remove old Habits; I am not altogether out of Hopes in some Time to suffer a Neighbour *Yahoo* in my Company, without the Apprehensions I am yet under of his Teeth or his Claws" (4.12.295–96). He does not consider the possibility that a rooted association of humanity with depravity may have motivated his long career as a fugitive, at least since the time that, at the beginning of

Book 1, he found the morals of fellow London physicians unspeakable.

En route to this parody of Lockean enlightenment, Gulliver's brain is always at least one voyage in back of his body. Thus the traveler reveals himself to be a Lilliputian in Brobdingnag because he had been incapable of acting with appropriately large-minded honesty, forthrightness, and strength in Lilliput, where he proved himself not magnanimous in proportion to his comparative greatness of size. Unlike the giant king, Gulliver is above joking and hence doomed to pretentiousness. "But, I confess," he tells us regarding an early conversation with that monarch, just before the queen held Gulliver up to the mirror,

> that after I had been a little too copious in talking of my own beloved Country; of our Trade, and Wars by Sea and Land, of our Schisms in Religion, and Parties in the State; the Prejudices of his Education prevailed so far, that he could not forbear taking me up in his right Hand, and stroking me gently with the other; after an hearty Fit of laughing, asked me whether I were a *Whig* or a *Tory*. Then, turning to his first Minister, who waited behind him with a white Staff, near as tall as the Main-mast of the Royal *Sovereign*; he observed, how contemptible a Thing was human Grandeur, which could be mimicked by such diminutive Insects as I: And yet, said he, I dare engage, those Creatures have their Titles and Distinctions of Honour; they contrive little Nests and Burrows, that they call Houses and Cities; they make a Figure in Dress and Equipage; they love, they fight, they dispute, they cheat, they betray.
>
> (2.3.106–7)

The trouble is, the king is addressing a man who not only seems to have blind pride in England, despite its openness to such criticism, but also himself takes pride in the Lilliputian title of Nardac; who has described his adjustment to the garb and domestic arrangements of Lilliput in satisfied detail, not omitting his privy moments; who has told us of his making a figure despite or because of rent breeches; and who, if he has not, in Lilliput, committed the other offenses mentioned, has not spoken out against them, though of course in one rampage he could have laid all Lilliput flat.

He was there (as he goes on to say he was not in Brobdingnag) "in a Condition to resent Injuries," in a position to take up Flimnap or Skyresh Bolgolam, stroke him, laugh, ask if he were a high heel or a low heel. Instead, in Lilliput, Gulliver can subscribe "with great Cheerfulness and Content" to articles that begin, ". . . Most Mighty Emperor of *Lilliput*, Delight and Terror of the Universe . . . Monarch of all Monarchs"—it goes on (1.3.43).

The mind that responds to the King of Brobdingnag, in the interview I have just described, is a Lilliputian mind (tinged even with covert hatred as king, minister, and minister's mast of a staff can conjure up the image, for an instant, of Milton's gigantic Satan, Beelzebub, and Satan's spear so much huger than that pine hewn "to be the Mast/Of some great Ammiral"). Gulliver rounds off the scene: "And thus he continued on, while my Colour came and went several Times, with Indignation to hear our noble Country, the Mistress of Arts and Arms, the Scourge of *France*, the Arbitress of *Europe*, the Seat of Virtue, Piety, Honour and Truth, the Pride and Envy of the World, so contemptuously treated" (2.3.107). In other words, Gulliver was really a Lilliputian before he got to Lilliput, and he remains a Lilliputian in Brobdingnag, stubbornly.

Then, after the scolding he endures in Book 2, as he begins to lay emphasis on truth and virtue, his chief motive is a desire to become the Brobdingnagian he could easily have been in Lilliput had he possessed the presence of mind. The King of Brobdingnag is Gulliver's best (virtually) human mentor, and Gulliver spurns him, yet in Houyhnhnmland, when Gulliver has forsaken his attachment to family, nation, and species, he belatedly has given assent to the giant king's terrible judgment, with two modifications: Gulliver condemns his entire species, not just the "Bulk of" the English, and he makes an exception only of that "groveling . . . Insect" himself. So vehement a judgment as Gulliver's against all-but-unanimous mankind is sterner than the King's and is of course far different from the Houyhnhnms' temperate disdain for the Yahoos.[40] Moreover, for all Gulliver's breast-beating in Houyhnhnmland he never accuses himself of any specific fault. His vagueness on the latter score resembles that of his generality about physicians in Book 1, chapter 1, except that by the fourth book he has purged that profession with, as it were, specifics—and has, as he says in the first chapter of that book, become a captain instead of a surgeon!

From a Lockean perspective, it is deficiency in memory that chiefly explains Gulliver's laggard, absent mind. "*Memory*," writes Locke in the *Essay*, ". . . is necessary in the next degree to Perception," being "of so great moment, that where it is wanting, all the rest of our Faculties are in great measure useless," and he proceeds to describe two defects which may weaken that faculty. The memory may fail to retain ideas or may fail to recall them fast enough. The latter defect, "if it be to a great degree, is *Stupidity*," while strength in this capacity makes for "*Invention, Fancy*, and quickness of Parts."[41] The distinction suits Gulliver's character perfectly; he has, as he says, "a very faithful Memory" (3.2.161) in the sense that his memory is remarkably retentive, as his detailed narrative shows. He is facts' magpie. But he has no quickness (even the unusual "Presence of Mind" on the occasion of his putting out the fire may be a Swiftian joke since, as Gulliver tells the story—drinking much "very diuretick" wine the night before, having voided none, the heat of the flames and of his exertions—the decision may have owed more to sensation than to reflection).

His memory, which should help him keep a sense of proportion between one land and the next, between himself and others, serves only for self-pity and self-regard, intensifying his feeling of vulnerability when he first encounters the giants and deepening his impression of the giants' grossness in comparison to fine Lilliputian complexions (2.1.87, 91–92). He reminisces about England most in Brobdingnag, not very much. But memory never aids him. It does not prompt him to question his fear that the giants will eat him, though he himself, having threatened to do so to some Lilliputian miscreants, had not (2.1.87, 1.2.31). He trips over a snail while "thinking on poor England"—odd hypallage (2.5.118). And there is the still stranger, Proustian moment at the end of Book 2: when his domestic box, floating aside ship, is wrecked by the sailors, he says he was relieved not to have been "a Spectator of the Havock they made; because I am confident it would have sensibly touched me, by bringing former Passages into my Mind, which I had rather forget" (2.8.144). Poor sentimentalist.

Yet Gulliver the retentive narrator seems to record every detail he witnessed. His "realism of presentation" appears submissive to the actualities of his experience, all-receptive—up to a point. A secret, inner Gulliver first ventures forth, disguised, in the story he tells about "Tribnia" and its plots, ciphers, acrostics, and anagrams (3.6.191);[42] wordplay covers this unusual effusion of anger, its surreal animus more evident in retrospect when the reader comes upon that most peculiar *Tale-of-a-Tub* passage (not an un-Lockean passage, however) spoken to the Houyhnhnm master: "Difference in Opinions hath cost many Millions of Lives" in Europe, "For Instance, whether *Flesh* be *Bread*, or *Bread* be *Flesh*," and so on (4.5.246).[43] That marvelously retentive yet, by Locke's standards, ponderously stupid memory ticks away like a watch, but it is a time bomb. The show of reserved respect for the separateness of facts becomes, ultimately and conspicuously, only camouflage. The Houyhnhnm master cannot imagine what "Motives" could make English lawyers as evil as Gulliver says they are (4.6.251); how should the facts about them be joined? But Gulliver had learned in Glubbdubdrib about the "Springs and Motives of great Enterprizes" (3.8.199). He is now perversely dedicated to the eighteenth-century maxim that mankind is the same in all times and places. And he has remade the world to conform to the demands of, one must suspect, his own deepest idea of himself, the image he flees from, the idea deeper than those of family, England, or humanity, deeper and worse.

There is a problem, too, about the retentiveness of his memory, for it overpowers his judgment as much as his slowness of parts undermines it, exploding Gulliver the sober narrator. It is England that remains the major pivot of his parodic development, for his narrative is not simply an account for the benefit of the world at large but is addressed, with a fine last irony, to just that nation which Gulliver is so extremely of two minds about, expressing his mixed feelings continually in alternation of bitter condemnation and fulsome praise. His most dominant trait through all four sections of the volume has been adherence to preconceptions, a tenacity often nevertheless joined with surface submissiveness in deed and thought. Throughout the tale Gulliver shows constant eagerness to please, to harbor and demonstrate loyalty. The equine master in Book 4 is the last, or next to last, in a long series beginning with the amusing Bates and the Lilliputian king; Gulliver simply grows more ardent in his urge to kiss hands, fingers, hooves, and whatnot, and never ceases in the main text. In Luggnagg, despite the putative, recent abatement of his "profound Veneration" for "Persons of high Rank" (3.8.200), he makes no objections, even in narrative retrospect, to licking the floor in front of the throne; it should be noted that the occupant of that throne, unlike the monarch of Laputa, "was much delighted with my Company" and variously rewarded and paid attention to his visitor (3.9.206).

According to the fiction of the fiction, the intended audience of the prefatory letter is his cousin Sympson, who, like Captain Mendez in Book 4, is of no account to Gulliver. The intended audience of the letter is not the English nation. But the main text of the volume was written for Gulliver's countrymen to read and, unlike the letter, shows both sides of Gulliver's character—his "Pride that licks the Dust," as Pope said of Sporus. The letter is nearly all denunciation of mankind. It was Gulliver's intention, he says in the first paragraph, to praise no Yahoos whatsoever, not even Queen Anne. The praise of her that turns up in the main text is the work of some treacherous "Interpolator"; likewise, in a few other places Sympson or his minion has softened the text, avoiding satirical "*Inuendo*." Yet even here, mentioning Queen Anne, Gulliver adds, "of most pious and glorious Memory; . . . I did reverence and esteem her more than any of human Species."

When tracing the fiction of the fiction—a typical Scriblerian paper trail, witness the *Dunciad* and its apparatus—a reader must doubt the full reliability of Gulliver's accusation of tampering. Idealistic, futile praise of dead Queen Anne, praise probably ingratiating to the living reader, finds its way even into the severe prefatory letter, while in the main text remarks appreciative of and deferential to European Yahoos are so common as to have kept an interpolator very busy. These remarks alternate with Gulliver's railing, and this alternation is so typical of his conversational and reflective habits regarding the persons he meets while traveling that he would have to change his character to behave otherwise when addressing his countrymen.[44] From the first, with very few exceptions, he has unwittingly shown himself to be the worst sort of politician, cordial to the characters he represents himself as speaking with in his story, critical in asides about them to the reader. In the long run, though, he must try to turn everything inside out when, as narrator to the English with whom he must stay, he has to swallow or minimize what he has said about his English readers to the characters whom he met abroad. A politician equal to this dilemma Gulliver can never be, although he evidently thinks he has no choice but to try. The letter to Sympson is his last aside, and Sympson has, at best tactlessly, published it.

By contrast, the main text of the volume *was* written for Gulliver's countrymen to read, proceeding half by denunciation, half by ingratiation, in alternate spurts, more emphatic as the voyages succeed one another, flagrant at the end. There the hapless narrator offers terms of rapprochement to the readership he cannot escape, promising tolerance of all lesser Yahoo vices if, like the narrator himself, his countrymen will only renounce their pride, and, a page earlier, weighing the advantages and disadvantages of English colonization of lands the narrator has discovered. In quick succession he remarks that the Houyhnhnms might better be the colonizers; that European princes have dreadfully abused their colonies (a savage list of atrocities being introduced with the groveling mention of Gulliver's "few Scruples"); that he is confident the British do not behave so ignominiously (here, characteristically, a full-throated passage of enthusiastic nationalism: "the *British* Nation . . . an Example to the whole World for their Wisdom, Care, and Justice in planting Colonies," so forth and so on); and, closing the circle, that he stands willing to depose, upon solicitation, if the court "think fit to be of another Opinion" (that is, if an English master asks him to revise his own opinion), "That no *European* did ever visit these Countries before me" (4.12.294–95), so that English colonization may proceed apace and, implicitly, so that Gulliver may be richly appreciated in his own land. 'Ban, 'Ban Caliban—this the stalwart, enlightened soul who had declared to the Emperor of Lilliput that he "would never be an Instrument of bringing a free and brave People into Slavery" (1.5.53). Self-hatred and social hatred, he reveals, are the same.

The King of Brobdingnag, when he first laid eyes on Gulliver, before Gulliver had begun to speak, "conceived I might be a piece of Clock-work . . . contrived by some ingenious Artist" (2.3.103). We are not told so, but it seems likely that this was also the king's final opinion on the subject. That mechanical Lockean Gulliver in turn finds the king a lamentable example of the "Effects of a *confined Education*" (2.7.134).[45] For Swift's humanoid traveler is himself, as Leibniz wrote extending Locke, an example of "perception without apperception"—of, according to still another commentator on the *Essay*, a person thrall to "confused impulses, in which we have no idea of what we need, but which act like springs when they try to unbend, making us machines."[46] The reader of *Gulliver's Travels* sees, as Gulliver does not, how far "the great Power of Habit and Prejudice" extends through Gulliver's narrative. What makes Gulliver tick is what makes Gulliver run, a violent inclination not to stay put and examine what he is and the way he thinks, a passion not to be Gulliver, and an ignorance of the degree to which he, like anyone else as described by eighteenth-century psychology, has a tendency to let his clockwork self prevail.

Which is not to say that the Houyhnhnms become less exemplary, or that the hero's delusions sap the book's satire against Yahoodom. We recognize Gulliver and his species. It is only to say that, ranged with heroes of philosophical tales and with a particular, non-novelistic sort of fictional realism, that of psychological self-assessment, here invited by conspicuously Lockean terminology, Gulliver the tale character brings the mind's realities to mind, and the *Travels* is the richer, though not the simpler, for his doing so.

CHAPTER SIX

The Spirit of the
Lettres persanes,
and of Enlightened Characterization

If we will trace the progress of our Minds, and with attention observe
how it repeats, adds together, and unites its simple *Ideas* received
from Sensation or Reflection, it will lead us farther than at first,
perhaps, we should have imagined.

—*An Essay Concerning
Human Understanding*, 2.12.8

*T*he *Lettres persanes*, by the French nobleman Charles-Louis de
    Secondat, baron de la Brède et de Montesquieu, who is much
better known as a political philosopher than as a writer of fiction,
was first published in 1721, five years before *Gulliver's Travels*.
The two works, despite many differences, call insistently for
comparison, at first only because of an underlying close similarity
in theme: that of the notable explorer of strange lands who cannot
bear to stay home. Montesquieu's chief characters are two Persian
visitors in France, a young man named Rica and a somewhat older
man named Usbek. The volume as we have it is composed of 161
generally short letters by and to these and a good many other correspondents, on a multiplicity of topics high and low, ranging from
meditations on the nature of the universe to risqué sidelights on
French and Persian sexuality. Like *Gulliver*, like philosophical tales
in general, the *Lettres persanes* is strikingly miscellaneous, an "anatomy" in Northrop Frye's sense of the word ("A form of prose fiction
. . . characterized by a great variety of subject-matter and a strong
interest in ideas")[1]—another reason for comparing the two books.

Whether Montesquieu's collection of letters had any direct influence on *Gulliver*, I do not know. Gulliver's calling the holy scripture
of the Lilliputians "their *Alcoran*" catches the eye; "leur Alcoran"
is an expression used more than once by Montesquieu's Moslems
to describe the Bible. Why Gulliver would make that comparison
is hard to say, except possibly as a result of his early "Voyage or
two into the *Levant*."[2] (The only reference I have found to Persian
Letters in close association with Swift has to do with the imitation
of Montesquieu's book by George, Lord Lyttelton, published in
1735 and sent to Swift that year by a friend.)[3]

My purpose in comparing the two books is to fathom the points
of contrast beneath the similarities. For the significance of the *Lettres
persanes* to the history of eighteenth-century fiction, while easily
ignored, seems great and also fascinating. The fact that the book
is so little read outside France seems deplorable as well as—because
Montesquieu is so enlightening and entertaining—regrettable. That
fact would justify my treating the two books out of chronological
order. I have, though, a better reason than simply the general advisability of going from the well known to the less well known, a
reason I shall get to detail about soon. Broadly, the *Lettres persanes*
is as much a harbinger of the Enlightenment as *Gulliver's Travels*
is not, as much about human possibility as Swift's book scorns to
be. I rely on readers to appreciate the relativity of those equations:
flexibility must be maintained by anyone reading both books, for
they are both fearsomely difficult to interpret.

Gulliver, we know, was meant to be vexing, the essential difficulty being that Gulliver proves a Yahoo while telling us we are—
which does not by any means indicate that we really are not. As
I have sought to show, in one sense the book is all about the flight
from self-assessment of a hero whose way of speaking defines his
failures. In another perspective Gulliver can seem "Plac'd on this
isthmus of a middle state," poised like the subject of *An Essay on
Man* between the angels and the beasts, condemned to bestiality
by any fall from duty yet condemned to the same abyss by any
attempt to transcend his condition. One "soft" moral may be that
a person ought, with temperance and other virtues, to know and
keep his place in the Chain of Being.[4] The *Lettres persanes* is a work

of the Enlightenment in part because it cannot be read to support an interpretation of this sort. The oppositions Swift positively revels in, Montesquieu regards differently.

But how he does so, it is very difficult to say. Whereas *Gulliver* is vexingly indeterminate because of its fundamental antitheses, fiendishly playful, and, I believe, ultimately paradoxical though not an iota less true and forceful on that account, the indeterminacy of the *Lettres persanes* resides mainly in its variousness. Like *Gulliver*, it can be read well in several different ways, according to what chain of meaning the reader concentrates upon—and Montesquieu's intriguing hint that there is a "secret chain" has not discouraged commentators in their search for new readings. There is a semblance of infinity in the book's miscellaneousness. *The Spectator* may be a minor source, especially No. 50, in which the impressions formed of England by several visiting American Indians are humorously transcribed (Swift claimed to have given Steele the idea for this essay, which was written by Addison, and added that he regretted having done so—"I intended to have written a book on that subject. I believe he has spent it all in one paper").[5] *The Spectator* is certainly an analogue. Grave Usbek, sprightly Rica, are respectively the Persian Addison and Steele, and page for page the multifariousness of their and other correspondents' topics and opinions is as full as Mr. Spectator's. Yet no one reads Addison and Steele seeking the unity of the whole, much less seeking a plot—unlike some readers of Montesquieu, whatever that author's total design and plot may actually, finally, seem to be.

Clearly, the *Lettres persanes*, like *The Spectator* on the "Pleasures of the Imagination" and other themes, contains discursive subsets. Its gross anatomy obviously includes several unified series of letters: on the Troglodytes, whom Usbek employs to describe the origin and decline of fruitful political life (11–14), on civil and political justice (94–95), on monarchs (102–04), on the progress of the arts and sciences (105–06), and, the most prominent of all, on the causes of growth and decline of population (112–22, 124). More sets large and small could be enumerated, though many letters would remain unaccounted for. And, besides the discursive subsets, there is clearly another group of letters composing the story, evident at the end if not very conspicuous earlier, pervasively important on a second reading. The last fifteen letters record a devastating rebellion in Usbek's seraglio back home; in retrospect, it is apparent from intermittent small signs going back to the beginning of the book that trouble among his wives and eunuchs was likely.

But the reader of fiction will wonder why more was not made of this theme earlier. Perhaps the book really is mainly a witty philosophical miscellany with, literally, an appended, not fully integrated element of plot. Like commentators on the philosophical tale in general, critics of the *Lettres persanes* have frequently remarked that the fiction is subordinate to the ideas.[6] Such a view, however, could be more receptive to the relations between Montesquieu's story and his ideas that commentators have been exploring especially since the 1960s, relations such as the analogy between the seraglio and social and political institutions in Europe.[7] Such analogies—such associations of ideas—abound in the *Lettres*: for example, that *dervish* is but priest writ differently and that *eunuch* (the "wild card") is too, and also may signify a minister of state and other things. The *Lettres persanes* is not so much a store as it is a mine; the meanings must be dug out, not simply picked off the shelves. And like the stuff of a mine, they lead off in various mysterious directions, and they take different shapes, depending on how they are extracted. They ought to be cut, as much as possible, in the spirit of Montesquieu; that critical truism becomes especially important and productive in his case. As commentators have suggested, it appears that the *Lettres persanes* looked much different to Montesquieu when he reviewed, revised, and commented on the book in the 1750s than when he composed it thirty years earlier.[8]

Indeed, the book differed from itself when it was first published: there were two editions in 1721, significantly unlike each other. An edition of 1754 brought the collection close to its present form, yet a number of the letters were there printed in a supplement, not fully joined to the main text. Only in the posthumous edition of 1758 was the whole collection brought together virtually as we read it now. And there were also textual changes in individual letters along the way.[9] Historically considered, the text recalls Pope's "To a Lady": "Shakes all together, and produces—You"—kaleidoscopically.

And there is yet another tier of complication, a double tier of it, for the letters are dated, though the order of them in the collection is not strictly chronological, especially at the end. The climactic letters about the woes of the seraglio are bunched together, yet some bear dates years earlier than those of other letters preceding them in the collection. Redoubling the complication, the letters are dated according to the Moslem calendar, or, more precisely, according to a modification of it whereby European months have the names of Persian counterparts.[10] The dates of some letters, moreover, changed from edition to edition. The work was protean in time as well as space. When at last the text attained its relatively final form in the posthumous edition, there remained alternate orders within it: a rhetorical order, the order of contiguity in which the letters are presented out of strict reference to chronology, the order that presents the terrible seraglio letters as a jolting climax followed by silence; and an historical order, open to the reader patient enough to attend to the dates of the letters.[11] The former order, it is clear, represents an interpretation by the translator and compiler (as Montesquieu describes himself in the introduction), and seems most fundamentally explicable by his desire for a sensational ending. The latter order, the historical, is "purer," more nearly "raw," and is organized not so much by desire for rhetorical effect as by desire to simulate a "natural" pattern of events, a version of the chain of events.

The indeterminacy of *Gulliver's Travels* is satirically critical, that of the *Lettres persanes* constructive, even in a way prophetic. In one important sense, Montesquieu's career after the first publication of the *Lettres persanes* was devoted to learning to read it differently from the way he had done so then, learning to read a primarily satirical, spectatorial miscellany as, to employ the word he used much later, a *roman*; his more guarded way of saying that is "une espèce de roman."[12] It is this chain of interpretation that I shall trace.

The main key to the opinion that, as Montesquieu's thought developed, the *Lettres persanes* changed its significance for him, is to be found in the two brief commentaries—thirty years apart—which he wrote about the book. The first, the introduction that appeared in 1721, is, to put the matter very bluntly at the outset, the work of a young man who, up to this point, as Robert Shackleton says, had given "no indication at all of unusual intellectual powers or literary skill,"[13] and who in composing the first version of the *Lettres persanes* had scented possibilities for satire, especially against formal religion, in an ironically veiled miscellany of letters by exotic foreigners.

The second commentary, "Quelques réflexions sur les Lettres persanes," was published as a supplement to the edition of 1754. Like strands of a loosely woven piece of cloth, the two commentaries bunch the *Lettres* differently, depending on which strand is pulled. The author of the "Réflexions" was no longer a beginner in literature but had acquired international fame as the author of *De l'esprit des lois* (1748), not to mention an earlier book, *Considérations sur les causes de la grandeur des Romains & de leur décadence* (1734), a study anticipating Gibbon. (Montesquieu also wrote for the *Encyclopédie*, which had begun to appear in 1751, but his article, "Essai sur le goût," did not appear until 1757.) The later Montesquieu, the author of the "Réflexions," was no longer mainly an arch, satirical representative of the early, predominantly critical Enlightenment but one of the founders of its later constructive phase.[14] In the most positive sense he was a philosophe, a philosopher especially remarkable for an early, naturalistic theory of political and social structures, that of *De l'esprit des lois*.

His theory is naturalistic in that he tried to predicate it not on religion or on an *a priori* ideal but on empirical, historical study and comparison of actual societies, as they are found to be, not as they "should" be except in relation to what they seem constructed to achieve. He sought especially to understand how the various laws and institutions of a given form of government function in relation to each other, and to bring to light the comprehensive purpose they serve, obscure as it may be, particularly to a thinker accustomed to a different form of government (one parallel of *De l'esprit des lois* with the *Lettres persanes* will be immediately obvious here).

A pioneer social scientist, Montesquieu investigated the laws of nature as they apply to societies and to the constructive or de-

structive development of societies as positive laws and other institutions change, though he laid more emphasis on synchronic structural relations than on diachronic processes. However, he did address
himself to the latter, and in doing so he joined forces, broadly
speaking, with other early naturalistic analysts of becoming, such
as Locke (as quoted in my epigraph) and, to mention but two others,
Condillac on the formation of the mind, more or less according to
Locke, from the first moment of mental activity (*Essai sur l'origine
des connaissances humaines*, 1746; *Traité des sensations*, 1754), and Rousseau on the development of the arts and sciences and of society in
his two early discourses (1750, 1755). Through what consequential,
"natural" stages must a society or a person pass in its development,
and why? By the mid-eighteenth century, this was a question increasingly raised. At the beginning of *De l'esprit des lois* Montesquieu
attacks Hobbes's view of the state of nature. So complex is the idea
of the domination of others, Montesquieu argues, that it could not
have occurred to the earliest human beings. They must have been
driven, first of all, by consciousness of vulnerability, which, when
a person recognized it in others as well as himself, and when he
felt the pleasures of companionship, including sexual pleasure, would
lead him to form a society, necessarily.[15]

Refinement of the foregoing description of Montesquieu the
naturalist of human behavior over time, and detailed analysis of the
natural laws of such development as he perceived them, laws comparable to those of the physical universe, would be required for
full understanding of his place in the history of social science. Allowance for his peculiar mixture of conservative and radical sym-
pathies would have to be made, rather delicately, if his place in the
intellectual history of the Enlightenment were my subject. It is only
his interest in broad, natural, consequential theories of links between elements of society and of the individual, and between phases
of each, that I mean to adduce here. That his social-contract theory
was really unhistorical and rationalistic in some important respects
is evident enough from what I have said of his response to Hobbes.
But it is his *esprit* that I wish to emphasize: the desire for a natural,
causal explanation of human structures and historical change, perceived not simply by an alien, critical spectator but by an analyst

sympathetic to the point of view of the people studied, odd as they may seem in other perspectives. Not for Montesquieu Addison's minimally interested conclusion to the paper on the peculiar ways the Indians perceived London, with the faint allowance:

> That amidst these wild Remarks there now and then appears something very reasonable. I cannot likewise forbear observing, That we are all guilty in some Measure of the same narrow Way of Thinking which we meet with in this Abstract of the *Indian* Journal; when we fancy the Customs, Dresses, and Manners of other Countries are ridiculous and extravagant, if they do not resemble those of our own.[16]

Please explain the reasons and motives for those peculiarities, Montesquieu would ask.

Addison accords Montaigne's cannibals Lockean "Toleration." But the witty, ironic, yet inquiring spirit of the author of *De l'esprit des lois* was seldom single-minded about anything. Montesquieu could perceive the function served, and the valuable object achieved, by so strange and seemingly capricious a judicial instrument as trial by ordeal or by combat.[17] But first, with imaginative sympathy, he had to give serious thought to the motives that might, from the point of view of the human beings who adopted such a bizarre practice, have been the reason for its existence. How did the practice appear to those people? Why would they adopt it? How did the practice combine with their other customs? Why, later, did it lapse? What latent motives account for the adoption and the discarding of it? What possibly obscure modification in the relations of the elements of a society became the principal cause of a conspicuous change in custom. Between the first publication of the *Lettres persanes* and the time of the "Réflexions," Montesquieu had become renowned by reason of his interest and success in taking up and attempting to answer historiographically novel questions, such as these, of natural human causation. "The adumbration of notions of historical causation" is, in Shackleton's view, the most original element of the *Lettres persanes*.[18]

It was the later Montesquieu who reexamined the *Lettres* in the early 1750s and, writing the "Réflexions," described an *esprit* in the early work which had obscurely motivated it, which he only now could recognize—though, like the *esprit* of a primitive, barbaric, seemingly foolish custom, it had been present, operative, and not inestimable from the beginning, causative though itself unperceived. One helpful commentator on the *Lettres persanes* sees the "Réflexions"—I believe, incompletely—as indicating "an interesting change in Montesquieu's attitude towards realism. He is no longer concerned with hiding his voice behind a fictional editor but with introducing a tale whose characters and themes are realistic." Now Montesquieu

> insists that his oriental observers be appreciated as artistic creations. He has made an effort to present characters and events which are psychologically sound and which correspond to models in real life. They are more than mere *porte-parole*; they are carefully planned characters whose reactions to western life are logical within the framework of their Persian origins. Montesquieu has tried to think like a Persian in his characterization of Usbek and Rica and in his portrayal of the harem. In other words, the reality of artistic creation is essential to the understanding of the novel.[19]

There is definitely a change in the notion of realism presented in Montesquieu's two sets of remarks. In the 1721 introduction he out-and-out says the letters are absolutely real because actually written by some Persians who had stayed with him. He himself has simply copied, translated, and abridged the work. In this way the *Lettres persanes* is realistic in the primitive sense in which Defoe says *Moll Flanders* is. And Montesquieu briefly indicates another sense in which the collection is realistic: the letters show detailed knowledge of even the most minute details of French morals and manners.[20] But just what sort of details these are, and why they are significant, Montesquieu does not explain. A sophisticated theory of realism inhabits this statement without divulging itself.

The "Réflexions," on the other hand, are more forthcoming, somewhat. They begin with the observation that nothing has pleased readers of the *Lettres persanes* more than the unexpected discovery that it is "une espèce de roman." But the subsequent explanation is rather elliptical, the connections a little loose, requiring full quotation and analysis to reveal what the "Réflexions" say and what they do not say, and what they suggest, about Montesquieu's idea of realism. Here, I think, the commentator I have quoted is vague and possibly misleading when he says that Montesquieu wants the characters to be "carefully planned" (a paragraph before, there is the comment that Montesquieu "reveals the care which went into the planning of what appeared a random collection").[21] There is reason to think that full, conscious "planning" on Montesquieu's part occurred well after the fact of first writing and publication. The plan he half-created, half-discovered may, however, be plainly described.

Here are the first three paragraphs of the "Réflexions":

> Rien n'a plu davantage, dans les *Lettres persanes*, que d'y trouver, sans y penser, une espèce de roman. On en voit le commencement, le progrès, la fin. Les divers personnages sont placés dans une chaîne qui les lie. A mesure qu'ils font un plus long séjour en Europe, les mœurs de cette partie du Monde prennent dans leur tête, un air moins merveilleux et moins bizarre, et ils sont plus ou moins frappés de ce bizarre et de ce merveilleux, suivant la différence de leurs caractères. D'un autre côté, le désordre croît dans le sérail d'Asie à proportion de la longueur de l'absence d'Usbek, c'est-à-dire à mesure que la fureur augmente, et que l'amour diminue.
>
> D'ailleurs, ces sortes de romans réussissent ordinairement, parce que l'on rend compte soi-même de sa situation actuelle; ce qui fait plus sentir les passions que tous les récits qu'on en pourrait faire. Et c'est une des causes du succès de quelques ouvrages charmants qui ont paru depuis les *Lettres persanes*.
>
> Enfin, dans les romans ordinaires, les digressions ne peuvent être permises que lorsqu'elles forment elles-mêmes un nouveau roman. On n'y saurait mêler de raisonnements, parce qu'aucun des personnages n'y ayant été assemblés pour raisonner, cela choquerait le dessein et la nature de l'ouvrage. Mais dans la forme de lettres, où les acteurs ne sont pas choisis, et où les sujets qu'on traite ne sont dépendants d'aucun dessein ou d'aucun plan déjà formé, l'auteur s'est donné l'avantage de pouvoir joindre de la philosophie, de la politique et de la morale à un roman, et de lier le tout par une chaîne secrète et, en quelque façon, inconnue.[22]

(Nothing has been more pleasing in the *Persian Letters* than finding there, without expecting it, a sort of novel. One sees in it the beginning, the development, the end. The different characters are placed in a chain which links them. The longer they stay in Europe, the less remarkable and strange they find the ways of that part of the world, and they are more or less affected by what is remarkable and strange according to their different characters. From another point of view, disorder increases in the Asian seraglio as Usbek prolongs his absence—that is, as anger grows and love wanes.

What is more, these kinds of novels are usually thought appealing because in them the characters themselves give an account of their present condition, a point of view which makes their emotions affect us more than all the third-person narrative an author could provide. And this is a cause of the success enjoyed by some charming novels which have appeared since the *Persian Letters*.

Finally, in ordinary novels digressions may be permitted only when they form a new story themselves. The author should not add passages of philosophical discourse because, none of the characters having been introduced to each other for such disquisition, that would upset the nature and purpose of the work. But in a collection of letters, where the characters are not chosen, and where the matters discussed do not flow from any intention or plan formed in advance, the author has the advantage of being able to join philosophy, politics, and morality with a novel, and to bind all with a secret and, in some manner, unknown chain.)

The paragraphs raise questions. Why is the book a novel?—according to the second sentence, it has a beginning, middle, and end. The "chaîne" which connects the characters, mentioned in the next sentence, would seem to be the chain of plot from beginning to end as recognized by Aristotle and most theorists of fiction. The last sentence of the first paragraph addresses the plot as an overall plan of the interaction of the main characters, specifying a proportion and suggesting a link of causation between the growth of the disturbance in the seraglio and the length of Usbek's absence from it. But the preceding sentence addresses the plot in a different way, seeming to define the chain that links the characters not as the combination of events in the seraglio and in France but as the series of events in the minds of Usbek and the others who have left Persia. "The longer they stay in Europe, the less remarkable and strange they find the ways of that part of the world, and they are more or less affected by what is remarkable and strange according to their different characters." The *tale* then seems to have two causal strands, the group psychology of Usbek versus his wives, heading toward a bloody end, but also the individual psychology of Usbek and others as they variously, in character, adjust their thinking in response to Western ways. What is the connection between the two strands? Is Usbek's individual development simply his half of the social equation he makes with his wives? Montesquieu's transition, "D'un autre côté," is casual when it might have been causal. It might have bound Usbek's mental development to the seraglio catastrophe; instead it simply suggests that connection and does not rule out others.

Nor does the next paragraph, beginning with the comparably insouciant "D'ailleurs." The person in question, who is he?—not a frivolous question. Although the paragraph begins with the matter of the work's succeeding, which seems to imply that the subject is the effect of the work on the reader—a subject like that of the first words of the "Réflexions," about the reader's surprise and delight— the subject here is actually the characters. "These kinds of novels are usually thought appealing because in them the characters themselves give an account of their present condition, a point of view which makes their emotions affect us more than all the third-person narrative an author could provide."

The second sentence of the second paragraph casts an oblique, appreciative, and somewhat self-satisfied glance at Richardson's *Pamela*; in the sentence I have just translated, Montesquieu praises the dramatic force of what Richardson called writing "to the moment." (Realistic fiction being new and undifferentiated in the world, Montesquieu compares two works—his own and Richardson's first novel—that later criticism would keep thoroughly separate.) But the sentence I have just translated is interesting also for what it almost says. The generality of the nouns, with the initial reference to the effect of the book, hints that the person spoken of could be the reader, and that the charm of the book could reside especially in the fact that this story is set not in a fabulous or far-off land but in the reader's own Paris, "sa situation actuelle," investigating feelings actually engendered by that real place and giving the work a realism of immediate familiarity for the Parisian reader. This proximate hypothetical implication is but a step from praising the work for realism of sociological presentation, as Montesquieu had done thirty years before in the introduction, when he singled out the fine eye for details of French ways that his Persians had demonstrated (*Persian Letters*: Parisian Letters). However, here Montesquieu does neither, and in what he does he again leaves a string hanging. To translate the main part of the sentence again: "the characters themselves give an account of their present condition, a point of view which makes their emotions affect us more than all the third-person narrative an author could provide." Is the force of the emotions more evident because of the consonance between them and the characters' account of themselves, or—an especially plausible possibility given the nature of the main character of the *Lettres persanes*, as we shall see—because of the discrepancy between what a character says at the moment and what he is obviously feeling?

And now the third paragraph, with its mysterious reference to the secret and in some manner unrecognized chain. In this paragraph not realism but *bienséance* is the issue. The *roman* by its nature does not permit digressions on miscellaneous, discursive topics; they are foreign to the genre. The author of a *roman* has not convened the characters for debate. But in a mere "espèce de roman" like the *Lettres persanes*, the author can, with a secret and subtle chain, bind "all," including philosophy, political theory, morality, and perhaps more, most obviously the events of the story. Such a book is not one of the "romans ordinaires" mentioned as the paragraph begins. It is special, and the distinctive trait the paragraph goes on to furnish is that such a book is in the form of letters, "where the characters are not chosen, and where the matters discussed do not flow from any intention or plan formed in advance." This odd comment may simply continue the fiction of the preface that the Persians and the letters are real, though Montesquieu's more or less admitting here that the collection is a *roman* diminishes the force of that explanation. The context of the remark, the paragraph, suggests the guiding consideration should be that of genre; thus viewed, the statement means that the nature of a miscellany permits an author to proceed casually and serendipitously. The sentence would be more determinate if "choisis" were governed by "ne sont dépendants d'aucun dessein" and so forth; there is some coyness here. Montesquieu did not choose the Persians, they came to him.

Recall, however, the peculiarity of the first sentence of the "Réflexions": "Nothing has been more pleasing in the *Persian Letters* than finding there, without expecting it, a sort of novel." Pleased whom? Readers? If so, then the fiction of the Persians' being real is sustained because Montesquieu is not saying the book is a *roman*; he is observing that readers have thought so, that is all. On the other hand, the absence of an object for "pleasing" will permit a reader to think that Montesquieu includes himself in the generality—especially when the reader considers the third sentence of the "Réflexions": "The different characters are placed in a chain which links them." If this is so, then another statement I have been worrying here, that "the characters are not chosen, and . . . the matters discussed do not flow from any intention or plan formed in advance," is not true, unless "placed in a chain" implies an agent outside the author's conscious will, a motive beyond his intentions at the time of composition. But most strictly speaking, the two statements are not really contradictory since the subject of the third paragraph is the literary form "collection of letters" and the advantage that form gives an author; the paragraph does not say but only implies, indeterminately, that Montesquieu acted on that possibility in writing the *Lettres persanes*.

The main burden of the three paragraphs is not that Montesquieu bound everything with a secret chain but that readers, not excluding Montesquieu himself, have discovered signs of such a chain in the book, made possible by its peculiar form. That the chain is "secret and, in some manner, unknown" indicates that readers, not excluding Montesquieu himself, all sense its presence but have not determined, certainly have not agreed upon, what it fully and exactly is, though it is felt to link everything: philosophy, politics, morality, and *roman* (in the broad, inclusive French meanings of those terms). The secret and not fully known chain is that of the nature of things and not merely a literary contrivance. The book is discovered to adumbrate the chain of natural causation, the chain of events in the world.

Montesquieu's undoubtedly calculated coyness in the "Réflexions" has a serious purpose. He did not want to claim more knowledge of the secret chain than he had achieved; there was still work to be done, though he had done about as much as he would himself, in his analysis of Roman history and of the spirit of the laws. The secret chain, in many ways still unknown, is the chain linking actual human beings with the concerns of philosophy, politics, morality, and history. The *Lettres persanes* had, from the start, brought up these subjects and their possible points of linkage. The author of a miscellaneous, epistolary "espèce de roman" could join these subjects. But to say that does not mean the author has made the chain in the book with full knowledge of its nature, any more than it means he fully knows the true or best way of joining philosophy, politics, and morality. Reviewing the *Lettres persanes* some thirty years after he wrote it, Montesquieu perceived with delight that there were relations in it that, at the time of initial composition, were unrecognized shadowy beginnings of what, with many years of additional scholarly labor, he had in *De l'esprit des lois* brought to the level not of mere symbolic hint and possibility but of reasoned nomenclature and discourse. Partly on the basis of that accomplishment he could see an "espèce de roman" where once he had perceived mainly a satiric anatomy.

If, as I have argued, the secret chain is the chain of natural human events, individual and social, mental and extramental, traced to the secret springs of characteristic motivation—the chain that may be reflected in a miscellaneous sort of novel though remaining somehow unknown—then Montesquieu could not have *planned* the chain in any full sense of the word. And he himself was the first to say as much about the history of his own mind, in the preface to *De l'esprit des lois*, a passage reminiscent of parts of Locke's preface to *An Essay Concerning Human Understanding*. Montesquieu writes movingly of his gropings, false starts, and final illumination:

J'ai bien des fois commencé, & bien des fois abandonné cet ouvrage; j'ai mille fois envoyé aux vents les feuilles que j'avois écrites; . . . je suivois mon objet sans former de dessein; je ne connoissois ni les règles ni les exceptions; je ne trouvois la vérité que pour la perdre. Mais, quand j'ai decouvert mes principes, tout ce que je cherchois est venu à moi; & dans le cours de vingt années, j'ai vu mon ouvrage commencer, croître, s'avancer, & finir.[23]

(I have many times begun and many times abandoned this work; I have a thousand times given the pages I have written to the winds; . . . I pursued my subject without any plan; I knew no rules or exceptions; I hit upon the truth only to lose it. But when I discovered my principles, everything I sought came to me; and during twenty years I have watched my book begin, extend itself, and come to completion.)

To the extent that valid knowledge of the chain of events entailing human nature, philosophy, politics, morality, and history—the subjects of *De l'esprit des lois*—required such understanding, Montesquieu did not choose the chain in accordance with a preliminary design but in time began to discover it, *inter alia* in the *Lettres persanes* he had begun to compose long before those "twenty" years of fitfully heuristic intellectual progress had commenced.

But I have noted several loose strands in the retrospective "Réflexions" without trying to tie them in myself. There is no stress here on the fiction that the Persians are real and their letters genuine historical documents. The emphasis in the introduction indicating realism of sociological presentation also does not recur here. Questions of *bienséance* have arisen, as we have seen, but they seem present for no important reason. And of what significance is Usbek's mental development, apart from its bearing on the climactic bloodbath in the seraglio?—the psychology of Usbek as distinguished from the group psychology of his relations with his wives. The best way to deal with the loose strands is to return to the "Réflexions" and see what Montesquieu does with them, in the few additional paragraphs. The questions of realism of asserted genuineness and particularly of sociological presentation do not, of course, go away. The introduction was republished in the edition of 1754, and sociological considerations were always important to Montesquieu. But the "Réflexions" emphasize what was finally most important to him in the *Lettres persanes*.

After two short paragraphs opposing unauthorized sequels and additions to the text, he defends the work against those who think it too bold—an Enlightenment refrain. Perhaps the whole remainder of the "Réflexions," the last two paragraphs, is but a smokescreen for the censor. Yet the relevance of these paragraphs to the questions left hanging earlier suggests that such is not the whole or the main explanation. The boldness some have complained about is in remarks against Christianity; the objectors, Montesquieu asserts, have simply not paid enough attention to the sort of book this is. He continues,

> Les Persans qui devaient y jouer un si grand rôle se trouvaient tout à coup transplantés en Europe, c'est-à-dire dans un autre univers. Il y avait un temps où il fallait nécessairement les représenter pleins d'ignorance et de préjugés: on n'était attentif qu'à faire voir la génération et le progrès de leurs idées.

> (The Persians who had to play so large a role in the book found themselves suddenly transplanted into Europe, that is, into another universe. There was a time when it was necessary to show them as full of ignorance and prejudices; the author was concerned only with making evident the generation and progress of their ideas.)

The "need to represent" the Persians in a certain way finally dispenses with the claimed reality of these characters. The assertion that they are ignorant is a smokescreen in part since, as the introduction indicated, in their naivety they perceive truths unnoticed by those to whom Europe is familiar. The book founds itself on realism of sociological presentation and assessment, up to a point. But one note here is new: the main business was to make evident not just the ideas of the Persians, sometimes humorously naive, sometimes naively perspicacious, but also "the generation and the progress of their ideas." This attitude toward characterization, specifying the importance of the natural process of becoming affecting characters' consciousness, is to the best of my knowledge entirely new in the history of fiction, realistic and otherwise; and it is not set forth mildly: "on n'était attentif qu'á faire voir," insistence on making that generation and development prominent. Whatever else is realistic about the Persians, Montesquieu is saying, the chain of the progress of their consciousness is, according to a theory of the natural psychological development of consciousness;

that is, a theoretical genetic model, as described in Part I of the present book, of the chain of becoming in characters' minds.[24]

The "Réflexions" conclude,

> On prie donc le lecteur de ne pas cesser un moment de regarder les traits dont je parle comme des effets de la surprise de gens qui devaient en avoir, ou comme des paradoxes faits par des hommes qui n'étaient pas même en état d'en faire. Il est prié de faire attention que tout l'agrément consistait dans le contraste éternel entre les choses réelles et la manière singulière, neuve ou bizarre, dont elles étaient aperçues. Certainement la nature et le dessein des *Lettres persanes* sont si à découvert qu'elles ne tromperont jamais que ceux qui voudront se tromper eux-mêmes.

(The author begs that the reader not fail, even for a moment, to view the characteristics I mention as the effects of surprise in people who had to feel surprised, or as paradoxes devised by men who were in no condition to make paradoxes. The reader is asked to realize that all the diversion offered by the book proceeded from the continual contrast between things as they in fact are and the manner—idiosyncratic, unusual, or strange—in which the Persians perceived them. Certainly the nature and design of the *Persian Letters* are so obvious that they will deceive only those who want to deceive themselves.)

This statement to the censor is a two-edged sword. Do not blame the Persians for what seem sly, satirical remarks on their part. These foreigners know no better and mean no harm. Everything they say is innocuous, explainable by the congruity of their perceptions with their imported, original conceptions, and the incongruity of those conceptions with the actualities of French life. The Persians are quixotic, entertaining; only someone looking for trouble will find trouble in what they say; only someone who wants to fool himself can be fooled. That statement, though, is wholly reversible. While to the censor it says consider the *Lettres* naive, to the non-censorious reader it says the opposite, including: please reverse the significance of the book as just described. For as unfathomably alien as the Persians are by reason of their distant origin, they are in another, particularly important eighteenth-century way not foreign at all, for they are human beings, members of a species basically the same, wherever found, at the most elementary level of its being. It is customs, French or Persian, that are basically contingent on humanity, not the other way around.[25]

Montesquieu has entered sympathetically into the minds of his Persians: the "Réflexions" mention taking account of their seeing everything in a foreign perspective and the claim of psychological soundness. Yet at this point a critic should not be content with assertions of the author's artistry in characterization. Montesquieu is more particular himself: "la génération et le progrès de leurs idées." The words indicate an orderly natural process motivated from within (like the Great Chain of Being unified, gradated, full—but temporal), in some sense logical and causal, and to some degree comprehensible. "Génération," particularly, it should be noted, was a favorite word of the geometer d'Alembert, much in evidence with its cognates (including "genius") in the "Discours préliminaire" of the *Encyclopédie*. The "Discours," attempting to return "jusqu'à l'origine et à la génération de nos idées," begins with a description of the natural, original order, or chain of events, whereby man conceived and developed his ideas: his sensations led him to the recognition of his existence; recognition of his existence led to the recognition of the existence of other things. . . .[26]

D'Alembert's account of the process is not unlike Montesquieu's at the beginning of *De l'esprit des lois* under the heading Laws of Nature. In Montesquieu's state of nature man realizes his need to preserve his being, then, flowing from this, his need for nourishment, then his need for society. The process is generative and developmental because the first idea is a cause of the second, the second a cause of the third; the pattern of cause and effect unrolls from the first cause, naturally. The human being's natural desires are the principle of the generation and development of his ideas. The theory is naturalistic especially in that it does not begin with a theological definition of man. The Encyclopedists concentrated on the autonomy of natural processes and the practical value of knowing their proximate causes. They begin from the bottom up with the most general human wants, according to the notion that man must eat to think. The naturalism of the theory, aggressively untraditional, begins with the condition man shares with animals.

This natural history of human perceptions and thought is originally and radically secular, though it need not be so and is not so for Montesquieu in every respect. The history begins in perception of universal human alienation, like Descartes' doubt or Locke's "uneasiness."

From the point of view afforded by Montesquieu's mature generative naturalism, it is crucially important to see the distinction between his Persians as Persians and his Persians as human beings: different from Frenchmen because shaped by Persian customs but deep down like Frenchmen because human and framers of customs. The customs of Persia, at bottom, intersect with—are or naturally would be engendered by—the laws of need common to mankind. The surface meaning of Montesquieu's paragraph in the "Réflexions" about the utterly foreign, subjective, bizarre thinking of the Persians cannot survive confrontation with his fundamental theory of basic natural laws of human behavior, the foundation of *De l'esprit des lois*. In that work he gave attention not so much to the forms of government as to the active causes of those forms. According to the third book, each pure form of government—monarchy or republic or despotism—depends for its existence upon a particular principle (*principe*): in a monarchy, for example, the people's desire to be honored, in a despotism the people's being afraid. But interacting with the principle of the form of government in any real political state is another major cause of the form that state takes, a cause centrally described in the nineteenth book and called the "esprit général": that is, the motives or desires of a particular historical nation, such as the Romans or the English, and expressed in its customs, conditioned in some degree by soil and climate and by the fundamental needs and wishes of humanity. The genetic *principe* and *esprit général* of any particular, actual political state are thus complicated and latent, difficult to discern.

Hence, *De l'esprit des lois* presents an epistemology of political science as much as it does an account of politics. To understand the spirit which forms a particular political structure, according to Montesquieu, one must triangulate back from the relations constituting the visible form, so as to identify the invisible, functional causes. But *De l'esprit des lois* is mainly about large groups of people.

For understanding Montesquieu's parallel notion of the generation and progress of the ideas of an individual, the best source is his "Essai sur les causes qui peuvent affecter les esprits & les caractères," like *De l'esprit des lois* a product of the years between the initial and final editions of the *Lettres persanes*. First he takes up physical influences; the visions of the desert fathers are explained, as in *Lettres persanes* 93, by excessive fasting and sleeplessness.[27] But the common mind identifies his thought too exclusively with environmental explanations based on climate and the like. He turns to "causes morales," especially education, which he conceives to be a two-stage process, initial domestic and formal education followed by a general education in society. The first stage entails two phases: "1° à nous procurer des idées; 2° à les proportionner à la juste valeur des choses" ("first, getting ideas; second, adapting them to the real value of things"). But ideas, he adds, are tied one to another, associated like the elements of a form of society. The general Lockean cast of the philosophy will be evident; the "faculté principale" of the mind is that whereby it combines ideas, and a paucity of ideas will impede that faculty.[28] The multiplication of ideas, however, results in the multiplication of feelings prompted by them. And as the mind must learn to link ideas according to just comparisons, it must learn also to respond emotionally in accordance with the real value of the ideas to which it responds (3:415).

Adequate intellectual and emotional harmony is elusive, and the difficulties Montesquieu mentions sharply illuminate his notion of the generation and progress of ideas in the individual mind— and of the subordination of a person to his ideas, for the worse. (It should be noted that the term "progrès," for Montesquieu, means "becoming," not necessarily "improving.")[29] The "Essai" explains,

Il est rare que les hommes reçoivent les impressions des objets d'une manière proportionée à leur valeur. La première impression que nous recevons nous frappe presque toujours sans retour, & cela est bien aisé à comprendre: les premières idées sont toujours reçues dans un esprit, parce que, ne pouvant les comparer à d'autres, rien ne les lui fait rejeter. Or la seconde idée ne peut guère le faire revenir de la première, ni la troisième de la seconde; car ce n'est qu'avec la première qu'il juge de la seconde, & qu'avec la seconde qu'il juge de la troisième. Ainsi les premières choses qui l'ont frappé, quelle qu'en soit la valeur, semblent devoir être, en quelque façon, indestructibles.

(3:415–16)

(It is rare that men form impressions of things in a manner proportionate to their value. Our first impression nearly always takes permanent hold of us, and that it does so is easy to understand: the first ideas are always adopted by the mind because, having no other ideas to compare them with, it has nothing to prompt it to reject them. For the second idea can hardly call the first into question, nor the third the second, for only by the first idea does the mind judge the second, and by the second the third. Thus the first things which strike us, whatever their worth, seem necessarily in some way indestructible.)

Thus may a person be thoroughly subordinate to his ideas, without knowledge of the fact—like some of Locke's victims of association. Montesquieu proceeds to enumerate causes of the diversity of individuals' opinions: a favorite teacher, or a loved one; differences in native disposition, with an interesting reference to fiction and delusion:

Un homme qui a de l'imagination & un homme qui n'en a pas voient les choses aussi différemment que deux héros de roman, dont l'un seroit enchanté, & l'autre, non: le premier verroit des murs de cristal, des toits de rubis, des ruisseaux d'argent, des tables de diamans; celui-ci ne verroit que des rochers affreux & des campagnes arides.

(A man with imagination and a man without it perceive things as differently as two heroes of romance, one of whom is under a spell and the other not: the first sees walls made of crystal, roofs of rubies, brooks of silver, tables of diamonds; the latter sees only horrid rocks and arid plains.)

The peculiarities of individual native or acquired disposition are to some degree correctable by good education or by later experience of the world, set against earlier influences, but adequate correction is all too rare. Montesquieu explains that only seldom is the brain formed by nature to take in ideas properly, and if education is also poor all is lost. Teachers can convey only the impressions they themselves have received, and if those impressions are faulty, not "en proportion avec les objets," the pupil's powers of comparison will suffer (3:417-18).

Much like Locke in *Of the Conduct of the Understanding* as well as the *Essay* and *Some Thoughts on Education*, Montesquieu is actively on guard against the blindness of odd prejudicial habits of thought deriving from particular nations, professions, occupations, pastimes—and also delusive self-love. Vanity draws an author to favor his own writings, as does the way they reflect his customary ideas and pleasures. "Toutes nos idées se lient entre elles, & se lient à nous" ("All our ideas are attached to each other, and to us"): again something approaching the chain metaphor, suggesting an equivalent in the individual person of the secret, informing *principe* and *esprit général* of a state. We link our ideas to satisfy our prejudices: "Nous nous faisons l'esprit qui nous plaît, & nous en sommes les vrais artisans" (3:425; "We make for ourselves the mind which pleases us, and we are the true makers of it").

Much like Locke too, Montesquieu is not very optimistic about the individual person's capacity to rectify his own thoughts and feelings, yet as with Locke the impression given by the "Essai" is that the model of the mind it constructs may be of use to a person interested in assessing himself, and it is clear that opportunities for reevaluation and reformation of trains of ideas do present themselves to the alert person. Most appropriately in connection with the *Lettres persanes*, learning and travel can provide those opportunities: "Les voyages donnent . . . un très grande étendue à l'esprit: on sort due cercle des préjugés de son pays, & l'on n'est guère propre à se charger de ceux des étrangers" (3:424; "Traveling brings a great breadth to the mind: a person goes beyond the circle of his country's prejudices, and he is not very likely to burden himself with the prejudices of strangers"). Valid thought and feeling can thus be attained in a manner like that suggested by Locke and elaborated by his successors: through critical reconstruction of chains of thought and feeling, promoted by the perception of conflict between received associations of ideas and newly conceivable alternatives. Thus does the "Essai" illuminate the comment about the "generation and progress of their ideas" in the "Réflexions."

The indeterminacy of the *Lettres persanes*, especially before the final editing and the "Réflexions" of the 1750s, permitted it to change, as the Enlightenment proceeded, from being mainly a satirical anatomy to being mainly "a sort of novel," or a philosophical tale, as *Gulliver* is, though subject to unification more positive in two ways. First, as I shall argue in the next chapter, the main character grows intellectually as well as declines, does not simply parody growth. Second, a positive description of the process is available, from the "Réflexions" elaborated with the help of the *Lettres* and other, proximate writings of Montesquieu. As the center of gravity of the *Lettres persanes* shifted, it increasingly became a work of the constructive and not simply the critical Enlightenment, not so much attacking received ideas as presenting new ones, attractive ideas of natural causation affecting a human being's mental development, the mind *comme il va*—ideas which, as we shall see, the philosophical hero comes to be conscious of himself.

Thus the *Lettres persanes*, though first published before *Gulliver's Travels*, for crucial historical reasons should be considered afterwards; it remained a work in progress long after *Gulliver* was finished, even when changes in *Gulliver* after the first edition are taken into account. In my comparing and contrasting the two books, however, there may seem to remain a discrepancy of genre. *Gulliver* seems to differ greatly from Montesquieu's book, one a first-person narrative throughout, the other a collection of epistles from a good many different correspondents. That difference is apparent more than real. When the *Lettres persanes* is relatively fully understood, Usbek becomes unquestionably the main character and, virtually as much as Gulliver in the *Travels*, far and away the work's central consciousness. My particular reasons for saying this are best reserved for the next chapter, on Usbek. The general reason from which they flow belongs here as the conclusion to description of the book's evolving *esprit*.

There is a substratum of meaning in *Gulliver's Travels* and in the *Lettres persanes*, but that of the first is a cellar of trapdoors into the abyss of the impossibility of being human and being at all knowing and content at the same time. That says it mildly. Ideas the Enlightenment would embrace with a sense of hopefulness here dawn for an instant, twinkle, and plunge from sight. Perhaps the generous utilitarianism of the Brobdingnagian king slightly qualifies this assertion, in another country. It is less important than Gulliver's disparagement, in the same place, of the Pascalian book on the degeneracy of humankind even where there are giants upon the earth. Gulliver the enlightened scientist puts aside "the Quarrels we raise with Nature. . . . I believe upon a strict Enquiry, those Quarrels might be shewn as ill-grounded among us, as they are among that People."[30] Brave new Gulliver, foolish here for contesting the opinion, foolish later for adopting it, fool among knaves in part, finally revealed to be knavish enough himself despite (especially because of) his assurances to the contrary.

The substratum of meaning in the *Lettres persanes* differs; though it offers no paradise, the ground has solidity, and the solidity is that of desiderated accurate knowledge of natural causation. Like other books of the Enlightenment, it requires enlightenment of its readers. It may be compared to Bayle's *Dictionnaire*: like that tome, Montesquieu's apparent miscellany is one thing on the surface, something else underneath. Broadly speaking, the method famously continues in the *Encyclopédie*, especially via its subversive cross-references. An article of conventional, pious eulogy concludes with a mere hint directing the reader to another article, which when read turns the first to forceful satire: "A vile Encomium doubly ridicules." The trapdoors open further, though, to the Encyclopedists' utilitarian progressivism. Diderot boasts in the article "Encyclopédie" that the cross-references lead to articles presenting "vérités opposées" which destroy false systems of thought and belief and thus—quickly affecting the intelligent, acting covertly and infallibly upon ordinary minds—change "la façon commune de penser."[31] The work can operate, that is, in a manner "secrète et, en quelque façon, inconnue."

Yet no one could convince a reader that such triumphalism characterized Montesquieu's purposes. A somewhat closer, earlier parallel can be found in another collection of letters, Voltaire's *Lettres philosophiques*, which begins with a bouquet of liberal, not unappreciative chatter about the various religious sects tolerated in England—tolerant, generous Voltaire, writing about his experience in that country. Montesquieu's first editions of the *Lettres persanes* appeared before the period he himself spent there, and a decade before Voltaire's *Lettres* saw publication (and public burning) in France. Voltaire's book was in fact considerably less tolerant than it appears: the sixth letter concludes with a scene of secular revelation, showing the English who attend different churches all coming together at one, truly catholic stock market, the ecumenical motive self-interest proceeding from self-love.[32] I have mentioned the popularity among early eighteenth-century thinkers of the analogy between the Newtonian model of the universe and models of the mind. The analogy, with self-love half one term, concludes the third epistle of *An Essay on Man*:

> On their own Axis as the Planets run,
> Yet make at once their circle round the Sun:
> So two consistent motions act the Soul;
> And one regards Itself, and one the Whole.
>   Thus God and Nature link'd the gen'ral frame,
> And bade Self-love and Social be the same.

Maynard Mack cites earlier instances of this connection of ideas, including one in *Spectator* 588, and Margaret C. Jacob amply documents the reliance of prominent Anglican divines upon the Newtonian system to sanction inchoate capitalism.[33]

Elsewhere, drawing on René Pomeau, Jacob says Newtonianism "lay at the foundation of Voltaire's understanding of the world."[34] In the *Lettres philosophiques* Voltaire devotes more than three substantial, central letters to unreserved praise of Newton, the colossus of the collection. A reader open to the Enlightenment could not fail to sense a substratum of associated ideas unifying the ostensible miscellany, in the strongly implicit similitude between Newtonian attraction ("le grand ressort qui fait mouvoir toute la nature"—"the great principle which makes all of nature move," Voltaire calls this most fundamental principle)[35] and the self-love represented as essential to human activity. The *Lettres persanes* is similar in revealing a substratum of interest in natural human motivation—not, however, like Voltaire's in these letters, seemingly straight out of a fabliau; not so broadly, simply, and sanguinely comic. Montesquieu, as we shall see, even turns the analogy of the physical universe to this purpose, though he draws on the pre-Newtonian, Cartesian system. Thus in the *Lettres persanes*, as in the *Lettres philosophiques*, the *Encyclopédie*, and numerous other works of the time, the rhetorical surface exists to be penetrated. An anthology is discovered to harbor a sustained argument, though it need not be particulary doctrinaire. What is revealed may be, as in the *Lettres persanes*, simply a set of important "rapports" associated in and by human nature, that nature itself equivocal enough not to warrant special enthusiasm, though important enough to be taken very seriously, understood as well as possible for what it is, how it moves, the structural and historical principles of its spirit.

The *Lettres persanes* and other philosophical tales rely, distinctively, on characterization enlightened by genetic models of the natural process of becoming in the individual consciousness. Montesquieu was a founder of such realism not only in practicing it, as we shall see, but also, as we have seen, in calling attention to it and indicating how it might be defined.

CHAPTER SEVEN

The Generation and Progress of Usbek's Ideas in the *Lettres persanes*

L'homme, cet être flexible, se pliant dans la société aux pensées &
aux impressions des autres, est également capable de connoître sa
propre nature lorsqu'on la lui montre, & d'en perdre jusqu'au sentiment lorsqu'on la lui dérobe.

—Préface, *De l'esprit des lois*

*T*he chain of meaning in the *Lettres persanes* is to be traced by
readers as it was evidently traced by the author; but it is there
also to be investigated by the characters, especially the main
character, Usbek. One problem the book presents is that of determining the height of the relief in which various of the characters
stand. None stands very high if a reader comes to the book convinced beforehand that the fiction is definitely subordinate to the
ideas; that comprehension of the book is mainly a matter of iden-
tifying and classifying sources and analogues (Shaftesbury, Descartes); that it does not matter who *in* the book says what, when,
to whom. But if the underlying chain of chronology, coupled with
the dramatic potentialities of the epistolary form, is taken fully into
account, Usbek positively looms above the other characters. Next
to him in importance is Rica, the young man. Critics sometimes
write as if the two were about equally significant, versions of Heraclitus and Democritus. One might even think Rica more important, he takes everything so well in stride, whereas Usbek may bring
to mind Montesquieu's remark that having too few ideas causes

stupidity, having contradictory ideas causes folly, and having too many contradictory ideas causes insanity—the second of the three deficiencies being Usbek's. A man of intelligence, on the other hand, spontaneously sizes up a situation just as it is, responding only to its actual requirements; "il sait & il sent le juste rapport qui est entre les choses & lui."[1] That, seemingly, is Rica, whose quickness of parts enables him to see exactly where he stands.

To begin to discern the paramount importance of Usbek, somewhat veiled as it is by the superscriptions and signatures of the letters (there are so many letters and so many correspondents), one must note that while Rica writes 47 letters, Usbek writes 77. Still more important in an epistolary fiction, Rica receives but two letters whereas Usbek gets 46—only one fewer than Rica writes. Thus Usbek is a party, directly, to 123 letters, Rica to 49; in addition, more than Rica, Usbek is a person talked about in still other letters. Furthermore, Rica writes to Usbek 14 times, Usbek to Rica once, and while Usbek writes only four times to the single or multiple, anonymous "***"—in Letter 111, "****"—(who evidently writes, or write, no letters), Rica addresses 18 letters thus. Although all this musametric data largely speaks for itself, one or two interpretative comments may be useful. The letters I have mentioned last, to "***," like newspaper dispatches or even manuscripts put in bottles, are unilateral and disengaged in a way most of the other letters are not. Many of Rica's letters, especially but not only these, are simply *sui generis*, reflecting his freedom of circumstances as well as his liberality of mind. He is a free lance filing reports when the mood strikes him, from where his fancy has led; a letter from someone else seldom occasions one of his, and a letter from him seldom calls forth one from someone else. The "rapports" of Rica's letters concern chiefly his interests and the passing parade.

In sharp contrast, the relations made by Usbek's letters quickly become and remain plentiful, complicated, dense. If the *Lettres persanes* were an airline map of the Midwest, he would be Chicago, at the center of a web of long and short, different-colored strings. For much unlike Rica he figures in the work "comme homme, comme citoyen, comme père de famille";[2] one might add, "comme philosophe." Like Gulliver he is well-hostaged to fortune. And the epistolary form gathers itself about him. His writing so many letters is only the beginning; the form also, constantly, sends him letters to read, to react to, to interpret, to worry about, and to respond to—or to ignore; sometimes to be fooled by, especially when (like the misreader of this "espèce de roman" rebuked at the end of Montesquieu's "Réflexions") he wishes to fool himself, as he conspicuously does regarding his wives. Fancy motivates most of Rica's letters, but Usbek's are often the products of necessity: Rica about town, Usbek on the spot. The collection therefore not only focuses most attention on Usbek, often in dramatic circumstances; in frequently indicating his responses to well described stimuli, it also allows readers to take his measure, while Rica hovers and darts beyond assessment.

Where the generation and the progress of ideas are concerned, Usbek is the only richly interesting character the book provides, though that is providing a good deal, especially because Usbek goes beyond merely illustrating this process. In various inventive ways he exerts himself to understand his own mind. As a character in some degree reflective and self-conscious, he differs markedly from Gulliver because he achieves, as I shall argue here, a degree of valid self-assessment. He is several notches above Gulliver in verisimilitude, though obviously no Pamela in absorption of the reader; he is a tale hero, promoting the reader's sympathy *and* detachment, a combination of attitudes like Montesquieu's in *De l'esprit des lois*. On occasion Usbek can move as jerkily as Swift's hero, as when, after the rationalistic but highly intelligent series on the Troglodytes, a day later he writes obsequiously to a religious teacher expressing confidence that the latter, a mullah, if snagged by a hard passage in the Koran, will be promptly rescued by an angel (of course, an "autre ordre de sagesse" not applicable in a philosophical tale). That is, like Gulliver, Usbek can make abrupt turns, diminishing our sense of the integrity of Montesquieu's characterization, especially if we expect too much from tale characters. Yet even in the instance I have cited, Usbek is really not so implausibly inconsistent, for as other, comparable letters in the collection show, he is divided between traditional faith in Muslim teachers and a new, tentative reliance on his own perception and judgment. As in reading Swift, one must not be too hasty in accusing Montesquieu of "dropping the mask."

The fortunes of Usbek as he tries to cope with his divisions of mind are my general subject in this chapter, and my main point, as I have indicated, is that in a curious way he succeeds despite conspicuous failures, though in seeking to grasp and deal with his own mental processes he is not so remarkable as Candide and Rasselas. As with Gulliver and later philosophical heroes, as with eighteenth-century moral philosophy and the psychology it fostered, as with the eighteenth century itself in one of its tenderest, most important areas (the matter set forth in chapter 4 of the present book), the rub is especially the problems of self-love: recognizing it; assessing its obscure, powerful effects on personality, associations, behavior; seeking to deal with it and them; and seeking to acknowledge, temper, and legitimize it for purposes of self- and social government. Gulliver studies "how to run away"—Usbek too; yet Usbek's odyssey is from professed disinterest to confessed uninterest to recognition of the force of self-interest in others and in himself— to (in Adam Smith's phrase) the conception of social concords, not unisons. He labors to become the judicious magistrate of his own mind in the face of the difficulty Locke recognizes (and seeks to overcome): "It will be objected, That it is unreasonable for Men to be judges in their own Cases, that Self-Love will make Men partial to themselves and their Friends. And on the other side, that Ill Nature, Passion and Revenge will carry them too far in punishing others"[3]—a comment entirely applicable to the *Lettres persanes*.

But to perceive Usbek in pursuit of the questing beast of his own divided desires, the reader must first take into account the chain of chronology and implicit causation, versus the mere contiguity of the imperfectly chronological, somewhat conventionally rhetorical collection of letters as we have it (a distinction amplified in the preceding chapter). The reader must be sensitive to Usbek's dramatic prominence in the collection, as already argued here. The reader has to question Jean Starobinski's assertion, ventured in a superlative essay, that the text reverses itself.[4] And the reader has to consider doubting several other notions recurrent in commentaries on the *Lettres persanes*: that Rica is really important apart from his function as one of Usbek's characterizing foils; that the romantically named, colorful Roxane is as important as she may seem; and also that other of Usbek's wives, notably Zélis, are as unimportant or bourgeois as they may appear. It goes without saying by now that the reader cannot begin by assuming that the characters of Montesquieu's "espèce de roman" are, *a priori*, unworthy of consideration as fictional persons.[5] They are not real, or to be taken as such; they call realities to mind.

Like Imlac in *Rasselas*, not absolutely unlike a certain character from *Candide*, Usbek fancies himself a teacher. "Je t'ai souvent ouï dire que les hommes étaient nés pour être vertueux," says his cordial friend Mirza as early as Letter 10, "et que la justice est une qualité qui leur est aussi propre que l'existence. Explique-moi, je te prie, ce que tu veux dire" ("I have often heard you observe that men were born for virtue, and that justice is as natural to them as is existence. Kindly explain what you mean"). Mirza adds that he has sought wisdom from the mullahs in vain, for their passages from the Koran shed no light. He is a practical man who speaks not as a true believer but, in the phrases I have already employed from this letter, as a man, as a citizen, as a father. After a moment's polite deference, Usbek begins a series of letters—not abstract reasoning but a story, a fable—answering the question. The truths of morality, Usbek observes with Aristotelian sagacity, must be felt not merely known. The fable is of course that of the Troglodytes, pursued through four letters: how two members of that nation, having seen the others destroy each other by their pursuit of exclusive self-interest, reconstructed society and for a time attained utopia by devoting themselves to the common good.

This story, among other things a naturalistic recension of some Old Testament themes related to Samuel and Saul, has been commented on as much as any other part of the *Lettres persanes*, Montesquieu having become above all renowned as a political philosopher, the Troglodytes being foursquare in the tradition of social-contract theory. But what the fable tells about Usbek is my subject. Although tinged with foreboding—like the Israelites, the Troglodytes in the long run insist on having a king, though their Samuel advises otherwise, protesting that a king will contribute to their corruption because the citizens will then no longer take responsibility for themselves—the tale turns out to be extremely high-minded. So good-natured are the Troglodytes that they are motivated less by the common good than by extreme altruism.[6] Beginning a list of their generous deeds, having just said the nation thought of itself as one family, Usbek writes:

> Je ne saurais assez te parler de la vertu des Troglodytes. Un d'eux disait un jour: "Mon père doit demain labourer son champ; je me lèverai deux heures avant lui, et, quand il ira à son champ, il le trouvera tout labouré." (13)

> (I could hardly tell you enough about the virtue shown by the Troglodytes. One of them said one day: "My father must till his field tomorrow; I will get up two hours before him, and, when he arrives at his field, he will find the work done.")

Theirs is a diamond rather than a merely golden rule, and a platinum age. In theory, self-interest or self-love is important here, motivating devotion to the commonweal, but in practice self-interest is transcended just about thoroughly as Usbek warms to his favorite subject of virtue, in particular the virtue of justice, idealizing his fable, making the promised concrete abstract after all. Similarly he will expatiate later on glorious aspects of kingship (102), God (69), and various moral questions, as he has already preached virtue to his chief eunuch and, through him, to his wives (2). Usbek has a special fondness for "douceur" in government (80) and particularly disdains religious disputes (101). His most rhapsodic moment comes, perhaps, in Letter 83, when he contemplates justice, which he regards as more fundamental than God. Justice is an eternal, independent principle; we must believe it so, for the thought of its depending on human conventions would be too terrifying, since we are surrounded by men stronger than ourselves. "Quel repos pour nous de savoir qu'il y a dans le cœur de tous ces hommes un principe intérieur qui combat en notre faveur et nous met à couvert de leurs entreprises!" ("What comfort there is for us in the recognition of an intrinsic principle in all men's hearts which struggles for our good and shelters us from their scheming!") All in all, the doctrine is a variant of philosophical Optimism and foreshadows *Candide* in more ways than one, as does the teleological assertion that men "were born to be virtuous," introducing the Troglodytes.

Questions of motivation and self-interest arise in this letter, as throughout the *Lettres persanes* and the tradition of philosophical tales. Usbek's initial opinion of self-love is markedly negative:

> Les hommes peuvent faire des injustices, parce qu'ils ont intérêt de les commettre, et qu'ils préfèrent leur propre satisfaction à celle des autres. C'est toujours par un retour sur eux-mêmes qu'ils agissent: nul n'est mauvais gratuitement. Il faut qu'il y ait une raison qui détermine, et cette raison est toujours une raison d'intérêt.

> (Men have the capacity to commit injustices, because they have an interest in doing so and because they are partial to satisfying themselves. A person's actions always have reference to himself: nobody is gratuitously bad. There must be a reason which determines behavior, and that reason always involves self-interest.)

Justice, after all, is a "rapport de convenance" ("a proper relationship between persons")—sometimes hard to perceive even by those devoted to finding it. The good Troglodytes are exceptionally proficient in this regard, and very generous besides. Indeed their perceptions and Usbek's amount to the consolation of philosophy: "That Virtue only makes our Bliss below," as Pope would write in concluding *An Essay on Man*, but in Usbek's case without appreciation of Pope's next line, "And all our Knowledge is, ourselves to know." Usbek the teacher, like Johnson's Imlac, can attain quite comprehensive philosophical views and impressive self-assurance, liberating himself from the worries that afflict him and providing oracular assistance to his friends. (It may or may not be significant that after the letter which calls forth the series on the Troglodytes, Mirza does not write again.) Usbek's friend Rhédi, to whom the letters on population are sent, has a continuing part in the collection; before that series, in Letter 105, he will deplore the invention of gunpowder and declare chemistry a plague, to which Usbek will reply, as if more adventurous, progressive, optimistic, and sophisticated: "Ou tu ne penses pas ce que tu dis, ou bien tu fais mieux que tu ne penses" ("Either what you say is not what you think, or you comport yourself better than your thinking would make me expect"):

> Tu crains, dis-tu, que l'on n'invente quelque manière de destruction plus cruelle que celle qui est en usage. Non. Si une si fatale invention venait à se découvrir, elle serait bientôt prohibée par le droit des gens; et le consentement unanime des nations ensevelirait cette découverte. Il n'est point de l'intérêt des princes de faire des conquêtes par de pareilles voies: ils doivent chercher des sujets, et non pas des terres. (106)

> (You say you are afraid someone will invent a weapon more cruel than those now used. No. If so deadly an invention came to light, it would be promptly forbidden by the law of nations; and by unanimous agreement all nations would suppress that invention. It does not suit the interest of rulers to conquer by means of such devices; rulers need to seek subjects, not land.)

But the *Lettres persanes* is a book in which self-knowledge does not come easily. Usbek has lost no time in becoming suspect; his motives become intriguing at least as early as Letter 8. Although in the first letter of the collection he proclaims that he and Rica are perhaps the first Persians to have sought knowledge by forsaking their country and tranquillity, in the eighth, to the same correspondent, he confesses "le véritable motif de mon voyage": that he had to leave Persia to escape his enemies at court. And there is more. He had come to court when very young, and "Je le puis dire: mon cœur ne s'y corrompit point; je formai même un grand dessein, j'osai y être vertueux" ("I can declare it: my heart was not at all corrupted by the court; I even formed a grand ambition, I would risk being virtuous there"). He prefigures Voltaire's Memnon in the *conte* of that name, who resolved to be wise, and he outdoes him, for Usbek resolved aggressively to unmask vice. "Je portai la vérité jusques au pied du trône . . ." ("I brought truth as far as the base of the throne . . ."). Having quickly made enemies, he had retired from the corrupt court, pretended to be interested in learning and thus really became so, but finally had to flee. Thus by Letter 8 Usbek has put his left foot forward. It is Voltaire's narrator who informs us of Memnon's grand decision; by contrast, Usbek's design calls for more consideration, since he tells us about it himself, since he has been reluctant to admit it, since it is wooden, and since it has overtones of delusion (Gulliver too at the outset had possessed "too good a Conscience").

In a collection of letters by various hands, Montesquieu can underline Usbek's shortcomings immediately. The very next letter presents a more profound, sadder tale of origins for contrast with Usbek's, that of the first eunuch of his seraglio, who says he makes the wives think "je n'ai d'autre motif que leur propre intérêt, et un grand attachement pour elles" ("I have nothing in mind except the best interests of the women, and my considerable fondness for them"). Like Usbek's tale this concerns motives too; the wives, the eunuch thinks, regard him as something approaching a good Troglodyte. Yet he admits that he consoles himself for his harsh condition by the sense of power he feels in dominating the women, and he complains that every woman in the seraglio, though her hatred of him confirms his sense of power, has done and will do her best to vilify him when she is alone with Usbek. "J'ai autant d'ennemis dans son cœur, qui ne songent qu'à me perdre" (9; "I have as many enemies in his heart, who dream only of my destruction"). Thus was Usbek surrounded by enemies "dans une cour corrompue" (8; "in a corrupt court"), but the eunuch's court is Usbek's heart, and the eunuch, knowing his own heart, has a better sense of that court than Usbek does. The eunuch knows why he himself behaves as he does, recognizing the source of his own bad faith in severely promoting the virtue of Usbek's wives.

Usbek knows, as he has said in Letter 6, that he is sad to be away from home yet also, as he strongly implies, that he would be sad to be back there; he perplexedly and disconsolately confesses that he does not love his wives yet is anxious lest they and the eunuchs betray him. The eunuch, consciously motivated by the desire to dominate, at first seems a parody of Usbek. Upon reflection, however, the reader sees that Usbek, the prisoner maimed by jealousy he does not understand, is a parody of the more knowing eunuch, who declares, "Je n'ai jamais dans la bouche que les mots de devoir, de vertu, de pudeur, de modestie. Je les désespère en leur parlant sans cesse de la faiblesse de leur sexe et de l'autorité du maître" ("I having nothing but words of duty in my mouth—of virtue, of decorum, of modesty. I make them despair by speaking to them unceasingly about the frailty of their sex and about the master's authority"). The eunuch boasts of his hypocrisy; without comparable self-knowledge, Usbek feebly lectures to the wives as the eunuch does. Thus the book, by the ninth letter, has focused attention on motives. The reader and the eunuch know that a specific deprivation has motivated the eunuch's behavior and that Usbek's sense of his own desires is less clear than the eunuch's. Usbek's way of dealing with himself is by aspiration to an abstract ideal of virtue pursued through habituation (and, it seems, flight), not through an examination of his habits of thought.

The intermittency of the chain of events in the seraglio as the text sporadically reports it may be one reason why the chain hinted at in the "Réflexions" is so secret. Letters to and from Usbek, his wives, and the eunuchs are few and spaced: several at the very beginning (2–4, 7), then a little more than a dozen here and there before Letter 147, when the climactic series of fifteen begins; every ninth letter, on the average (I am not counting Letters 9, 15, and 22, to and by the eunuchs). Yet after Letter 65, in which Usbek delivers a stern warning to his wives, in response to what seems the first report of serious trouble, the given order of the volume provides only four letters to and from the seraglio in the next 81, only one of them from Usbek.

Before the exchange in Letters 64–65 the story becomes hard to follow for other reasons. In Letter 20 Usbek writes to his wife Zachi, rebuking her for having been found alone with the white eunuch Nadir; Zachi had written Letter 3 to Usbek, simply lamenting his absence. But in Letter 4 another wife, Zéphis, had protested to him that the black eunuch had unfairly accused her of intimacies with her slave Zélide. Now in Letter 20 Usbek scolds Zachi, not Zéphis, for that too, as if he were confused about which wife is which. (The confusion is possibly Montesquieu's but we sacrifice a good joke to think so—an understandable consequence of similar names and polygamy, especially on the part of a husband unhappy with his wives.)[7] Moreover, in Usbek's apparent confusion he seems to respond here to Zachi as well, after all, for she had written to him about her pride in being his favorite wife, and now in Letter 20 Usbek comes to a close by reassuring her, after a fashion: he says his love for a new wife, Roxane (it is the first time she is mentioned), does not affect his equal regard for Zachi's beauty, though her virtue is another matter.

Usbek writes that letter at the beginning of 1712 and sends an admonitory note to the chief white eunuch the same day. Two and a half years later, in mid-1714, the chief black eunuch writes to say the seraglio is in turmoil, the women at each others' throats, the eunuchs quarreling (64). In the meantime, Usbek has received three letters from his wives and answered none. Zachi sends news in Letter 47 of being reconciled to Zéphis (some acerb indirection here) and complains of the danger as well as inconvenience to which Persian women are subjected: she has nearly drowned when being ferried across a river while chastely enclosed in a traveling box. Another wife, Zélis, has written twice, more aggressively. In Letter 62, which recalls Zachi's complaint about being walled in, Zélis tells Usbek of the education of his seven-year-old daughter, soon to enter the seraglio so she will grow used to walls; women, Zélis says, must be forced to be submissive—a statement more potent than it looks. This is a rich letter, for Zélis alternates between imploring him to guard her closely, lest she think him indifferent, and musing tauntingly over the insight that his need to guard her shows he is more dependent on her than she on him.

Zélis deserves special attention.[8] In her earlier letter (53) she had written scornfully of the white eunuch Cosrou's intention of marrying her slave Zélide (Zéphis' complaints in Letter 4 that the black eunuch was about to deprive her of Zélide—evidently a lively woman—having been unavailing). Zélis is incredulous:

> Que veut-elle faire de cet infortuné, qui n'aura d'un mari que la jalousie, qui ne sortira de sa froideur que pour entrer dans un désespoir inutile; qui se rappellera toujours la mémoire de ce qu'il a été, pour la faire souvenir de ce qu'il n'est plus; qui, toujours prêt à se donner, et ne se donnant jamais, se trompera, la trompera sans

cesse et lui fera essuyer à chaque instant tous les malheurs de sa condition?

Et quoi? être toujours dans les images et dans les fantômes! ne vivre que pour imaginer! se trouver toujours auprès des plaisirs, et jamais dans les plaisirs!

(What does she want with that wretch, who will have none of a husband's traits but jealousy, who will take leave of his frigid condition only to encounter vain despair; who will constantly recall what he used to be, in order to make her remember what he no longer is; who, always ready to give himself, never giving himself, will endlessly fool himself, fool her, and make her absorb, at every moment, all the unhappiness of his condition?

To what end? To dwell always in illusions and fantasies! to live always for imaginings! to be forever on the verge of pleasures and never attain them!)

Although Zélis inserts a detail or two suggesting that she may really be talking about the impending misalliance, she obviously has her own marriage in mind, with Usbek parallel to Cosrou;[9] she proceeds:

Quel mépris ne doit-on pas avoir pour un homme de cette espèce, fait uniquement pour garder, et jamais pour posséder? Je cherche l'amour, et je ne le vois pas.

Je te parle librement, parce que tu aimes ma naïveté. . . .

(What contempt must one feel for someone of that sort, destined but to guard and not at all to possess. I look for love, and I do not find it.

I tell you my thoughts freely, because you enjoy my innocent candor. . . .)

Indeed. This is a Persian letter raised to the next power, in which subject matter familiar to the recipient is described from a new, foreign, revealing angle—if Usbek has eyes to read it.

Then at one point in her next letter, about the daughter's education (62), Zélis unobtrusively recalls the passage just quoted when seemingly introducing, a little irrelevantly in context, a favorable comparison of her own condition with Usbek's: "Cependant, Usbek, ne t'imagine pas que ta situation soit plus heureuse que la mienne: j'ai goûté ici mille plaisirs que tu ne connais pas; mon imagination a travaillé sans cesse à m'en faire connaître le prix; j'ai vécu, et tu n'as fait que languir" ("But Usbek, do not imagine your circumstances happier than mine; I have enjoyed a thousand pleasures here which are unknown to you; my imagination has labored without stop to make me appreciate the worth of them; I have been living while you only pine away"). In the larger context of Zélis' previous letter ("être toujours dans les images et dans les fantômes! ne vivre que pour imaginer!"), these new comments do not seem vague at all, especially when one recalls that Zélide's former mistress had been accused of irregularities with her (4). Perhaps Zélis is writing vaguely, or contradictorily out of simultaneous desire and hatred for the in-all-respects distant Usbek; perhaps, consciously or unconsciously, she is intent on fueling his jealousy ("Cosrou," the eunuch's name, suggests "coucou"); indirectly, but strongly, however, she is speaking to Usbek and to his condition. His jealousy is the largest consideration, for what is most important to the tale as a whole must be the implicit impact of letters such as this on him, the main character, and he has confessed as early as Letter 6, to Nessir, that his dominant feeling toward his wives is morbid jealousy. To the letters of Zachi and Zélis, Usbek does not reply, though he alludes to Zélis' second letter when responding to another of hers later (71). Having received the eunuch's news of dissension, he immediately tells the wives as a group that he does not want to be forced to adopt the eunuch's severe recommendations against them (65).

The eunuch had accused Usbek of being too tender-hearted. In a much earlier exchange Usbek had, against the eunuch's wishes, spared the threatened masculinity of a young slave named Pharan (41–43), closing with a mixture of congratulation for his own generosity and warnings to the youth about punishment should he take advantage of the acquittal. Here again is jealous Usbek ruling with what he would call "douceur." Far from Persia, early in the collection, he writes to that new wife, Roxane, telling her how fortunate she is to live in Persian innocence rather than Parisian shamelessness (26). He will later draw the same contrast without any evident ulterior purpose in corresponding with his friend Rhédi at Venice (48), and still later, to his friend Ibben, he will praise the temperateness of Persian love, compared with the French variety (56). How much is policy in these letters, how much sincerity, is not clear. Women are innately virtuous, he tells Roxane. He lingers over her initial shyness, as it seemed—the maidenly defense of her virginity that occasioned a two-month siege after their wedding. In the end, every reader of the book knows, when Usbek's dreams are shattered, Roxane proves the figure of Liberty at the Barricades, managing to be unfaithful despite Usbek's troop of guards, killing the eunuchs who killed her lover, killing herself, and, in her final moments, declaiming her hatred for her distant, deluded husband. Her last words revise Usbek's letter to her; she exclaims to him (161):

> Tu étais étonné de ne point trouver en moi les transports de l'amour. Si tu m'avais bien connue, tu y aurais trouvé toute la violence de la haine.
>
> Mais tu as eu longtemps l'avantage de croire qu'un cœur comme le mien t'était soumis. Nous étions tous deux heureux; tu me croyais trompée, et je te trompais.

> (You were amazed not to discover in me the raptures of love. If you had really known me, you would have discovered in me all the violence of hatred.
>
> For a long time, however, you have been privileged to believe that a heart like mine would submit to you. Both of us were happy; you thought me deceived, while I deceived you.)

This particular revision may truly come as a surprise to Usbek. Roxane does not write before the end, when it is too late. Usbek had no lines from her to read between, unless he had been able to read his own heart and to put himself in the place of someone else during the first two months of this marriage: Gulliverian forehead, Gulliverian brain. Roxane, that is, shows herself to be the fatefully fit match, counterpart, and nemesis for Usbek. Not until Letters 148, 150, and 153 had he fully displayed his anger to the wives. As late as Letter 151, Roxane is still described, by a eunuch, as dutiful and good. Wife as well as husband avoid confrontation as long as possible, then detonate—Roxane more sympathetic for the reader because enslaved and reacting; more natural too in having secretly enjoyed her lover while Usbek went on philosophizing.

But Roxane with her resonant literary name is a romantic heroine, and for a reader to stress her importance is, like stressing Rica's, to oversimplify the book. The philosophical heroine of the book is Zélis.[10] Given a less glamorous name than Roxane, confusable among the wives with their initial Z's, it is she who, unlike Roxane, unlike Usbek, has tried to speak up in due time. Roxane at the end boasts, "tu me croyais trompée, et je te trompais." Montesquieu in the final sentence of the "Réflexions" had said, "Certainement la nature et le dessein des *Lettres persanes* sont si à découvert qu'elles ne tromperont jamais que ceux qui voudront se tromper eux-mêmes." But in the text of the letters it is only Zélis who really tries to say this to benighted Usbek before it is too late, especially when, commenting on Cosrou and his intended bride, she says he "se trompera, la trompera sans cesse" (53). Roxane's secret rage breeds the poison tree, and she dies—excitingly, but really admirably?—exulting in her hatred.

Zélis, by contrast, in Letter 158, before stating that she renounces her love for Usbek, identifies his major practical lie, his preening himself abstractly upon his gentle government while, at a great distance, comfortably letting his ministers the eunuchs conduct business as usual at the expense of wives deprived of their only sanctioned solace and raison d'être. In the tone established by the *Lettres persanes*, not Roxane's tone halfway between Racine and Mascagni, Zélis passionately and analytically defines Usbek for himself: "Qu'un eunuque barbare porte sur moi ses viles mains, il agit par votre ordre. C'est le tyran qui m'outrage, et non pas celui qui exerce la tyrannie" ("When a barbaric eunuch puts his vile hands on me, he obeys your command. The tyrant is the one who affronts me, and not the mere instrument of that tyranny").

I turn from the wives to Rica with a sense of relief, initially; only initially, for he too will bring us back to Usbek and distress in the long run. Unlike the wives, who are closely bound up with Usbek, Rica starlike dwells apart. Not until the twenty-fourth letter does he write, the first letter in the collection to come from Paris, and it would not be an overstatement to say that Paris brings him into existence, though he has been mentioned earlier, in Letter 5. More than Usbek, Rica plays the part of clever misperceiver of foreign customs. He immediately, in Letter 24, classifies the king and the Pope as magicians who by fiat make the incredible true (resembling Peter in *A Tale of a Tub*). Next he visits a theater and regards what the audience is doing as the play (28); next he sees through the Inquisition (29). He is the entertaining, roving Citizen of the World, but his main function in the book is to be a foil for Usbek, youth to Usbek's middle age on the scale of the ages of man. Usbek observes, to Ibben, that he himself thinks much more slowly than Rica (25), and, to Nessir, that Rica is ebullient in spirit and body, Usbek's very opposite (27). Rica describes Paris, its streets, public places, and eccentrics, immediately upon arriving, and he draws comparisons with Persia only, as a rule, in afterthought; but Usbek must labor to think beyond the shock of contrast with what he is used to. Rica comes as a visiting socialite, Usbek as sociologist and moralist. Somber Usbek writes as if for the ages, Rica for the day, and his company seems to improve Usbek with time, somewhat softening but not obliterating these differences. By Letter 48, Usbek writes (to Rhédi):

> Tu ne le croirais pas peut-être, nous sommes reçus agréablement dans toutes les compagnies et dans toutes les sociétés; je crois devoir beaucoup à l'esprit vif et à la gaieté naturelle de Rica, qui fait qu'il recherche tout le monde, et qu'il en est également recherché.

> (Perhaps you will find it unbelievable: we are warmly accepted by all company, in all circles; I think I am much indebted to the lively mind and innate gaiety of Rica, which lead him to seek out all the world, and which cause him to be just as much sought after.)

This unusually long letter begins in the manner of Rica as Usbek describes a conversation with a Frenchman: Usbek has taken to him, and the new companion, referring to various persons at a party, gives a satirical cross section of the French. Yet when Usbek meets one of the party-goers, a rake who freely explains his tactics, the Persian reacts with horror, condemnation, and consoling ruminations on Persian innocence. At about this time something subtle but important happens; perhaps in the fit of disgust that concludes the letter under discussion, Usbek has evidently reached the limits of his endurance. Rica had first written to Usbek in Letter 45, during the autumn of 1713, nearly a year after their arrival in Paris. Rica writes because Usbek is staying at "***" for what seems to be a short visit to a place in the country outside the capital. But the visit appears permanent, a rustication. Every succeeding letter from Rica to Usbek, except the last (144), is addressed to him at, it appears, the same place; there are about eleven such letters through Letter 142, late in 1720, seven years afterwards! (Other correspondents write to Usbek "à Paris," from which their letters are presumably carried to him; Usbek writes "de Paris," except in the late, climactic letters 148 and 150, "de ***," when he may be too upset to bother with niceties.) We hear no more of Usbek and Rica together in Parisian society or of Usbek visiting identifiable, notable places in the capital, as he had visited Notre Dame (61). The single letter in the book from Usbek to Rica (74, spring 1715) registers disgust with the pride of a Parisian nobleman to whose home Usbek has been taken—a letter that until the posthumous edition of 1758 had been superscribed "Rica to Usbek," the change appropriate to Usbek's mood and not unsuitable to his apparent location. In the spring of 1714 (63), Rica had written to Usbek:

> Je crois que tu veux passer ta vie à la campagne: je ne te perdais au commencement que pour deux ou trois jours, et en voilà quinze que je ne t'ai vu. Il est vrai que tu es dans une maison charmante, que tu y trouves une société qui te convient, que tu y raisonnes tout à ton aise: il n'en faut pas davantage pour te faire oublier tout l'Univers.
>
> Pour moi, je mène à peu près la même vie que tu m'as vu mener: je me répands dans le monde, et je cherche à le connaître. Mon esprit perd insensiblement tout ce qui lui reste d'asiatique, et se plie sans effort aux mœurs européennes.

(I believe you want to spend all your life in the country: at first I went without you for merely two or three days, and now it is fifteen days that I have not seen you. True, you are at a charming house, you have company there that agrees with you, there you pursue your thoughts in comfort; you need no more to make you neglect the rest of the world.

As for me, I lead nearly the same life you have seen me live: I range about society, and I seek to understand it. My mind subtly loses what is left of its Asian quality, and adapts itself effortlessly to European ways.)

Versatile Rica slides easily into a new train of ideas. He proceeds with pleasure to describe the freedom of the sexes in France, contrasting French airiness with Persian rigor. The next two letters in the collection initiate the ascending action of the seraglio plot. Rica in succeeding letters, more to others than to Usbek, goes his own way, mingling with people, writing "characters," seizing the days. Usbek goes on to write about God, "douceur," justice, tolerance. In a country retreat permitting him to reason at his ease he has fled the world, the world to which he had fled earlier, and he has taken refuge in a placid seraglio of thought, though as before it is not clear who is keeping whom.[11] Even there life cannot be as serene as he would like, for bad news comes from the wives and innuendos come from his friends. Nargum, for example, writes in Letter 51 about the fondness of Russian women for being beaten by their husbands (recall Gulliver's women of Laputa). Meanwhile, Usbek's wives complain of neglect, Zélis having said in Letter 62 that the only thing she cannot bear is indifference. Ibben in Letter 67 tells the romantic tale of a young woman rescued from marriage to a eunuch. Rica writes to Usbek about how women fear growing old, and about the deceits they practice on themselves to escape the truth (52). Then (63), after bidding Usbek return to Paris, Rica says he has learned more about women in France than thirty years in a seraglio could have taught him. Indeed it is hard not to see that, indirectly, Rica repeatedly criticizes Usbek, in letters to him and to others—parodying a geometer's judgment of the arts (128), much earlier satirizing a man who thinks he knows everything (72; in the preceding letter Usbek has given judgment on tests for virginity), and, most to the point, still earlier, in Letter 59, to Usbek, exploring something like the Baconian Idols:

> Il me semble, Usbek, que nous ne jugeons jamais des choses que par un retour secret que nous faisons sur nous-mêmes. Je ne suis

pas surpris que les Nègres peignent le diable d'une blancheur
éblouissante et leurs dieux noirs comme du charbon; que la Vénus de
certains peuples ait des mamelles qui lui pendent jusques aux cuisses;
et qu'enfin tous les idolâtres aient représenté leurs dieux avec une
figure humaine et leur aient fait part de toutes leurs inclinations. On
a dit fort bien que, si les triangles faisaient un dieu, ils lui donneraient
trois côtés.

(It appears, Usbek, that we make no judgments about things without
secretly relating them to ourselves. It does not surprise me that
Blacks depict the devil as utterly white and their gods coal-black;
that the Venus of some peoples has breasts which hang to her
thighs; and in short that idolators have all portrayed their gods in
human form and given their own desires to them. The saying is
much to the point, that if triangles made a god it would have three
sides.)

Ten letters later, like clockwork, Usbek confidently describes
God, to Rhédi not Rica (69), having first confessed to being more
the metaphysician than ever (it is six letters since Rica's complaint
that Usbek sequesters himself). In trying to thread the wandering
maze of man's freedom versus God's power and foreknowledge,
Usbek has recourse to analogy:

Si l'on peut se servir d'une comparaison, dans une chose qui est au-
dessus des comparaisons: un monarque ignore ce que son ambas-
sadeur fera dans une affaire importante; s'il le veut savoir, il n'a qu'à
lui ordonner de se comporter d'une telle manière, et il pourra assurer
que la chose arrivera comme il la projette.

(If I may resort to comparison concerning something above comparisons: a king is ignorant of what his ambassador will do with
regard to an important decision; if the king wants to know, he need
only tell the ambassador to proceed in a particular manner, and he
can be certain that the matter will go forward as he wishes.)

One might think that analogies float free, to be used as the speaker
wishes, but the plot and design of the world of the *Lettres persanes*
make one wiser. This analogy or association of ideas, recalling the
world of triangles, has strings attached—or chains—implying Usbek's wishful sense of his own power as regards his monarchy in

the seraglio, and his comparably wishful sense of his "ambassador's" obedience and discretion, as if the resident supervisor of the seraglio had been separated from his own mind and will and anger during the qualifying operation. Four letters earlier, Usbek had overridden the head eunuch's plea to be allowed to rule harshly (64–65); the irony of the situation will become fully apparent only near the end when Usbek's first harsh letter to the seraglio (148) goes unopened, his second (150) is—perhaps intentionally—lost, and his third and last (153) brings about the unforeseen, tragic consequences.

Thus Rica seems to see through Usbek, like the eunuch—like Zélis too—understanding him better than Usbek understands himself, but, except in the early letter protesting Usbek's withdrawal, not criticizing him directly. Subsequently, Rica writes to Usbek only rarely, not at all between Letters 78 and 126 (when he expects Usbek "ici demain"), a three-and-a-half-year period, and Usbek does not write to him. Rica remains cordial, remarking in Letter 141 that he looks forward to visiting Usbek, and he writes twice more. Usbek, however, a year before those letters, in writing to Nessir (155)—the last time in the given sequence that he speaks to one of his friends—most strikingly laments:

> J'ai pressé mille fois Rica de quitter cette terre étrangère; mais il s'oppose à toutes mes résolutions: il m'attache ici par mille prétextes; il semble qu'il ait oublié sa patrie, ou plutôt il semble qu'il m'ait oublié moi-même, tant il est insensible à mes déplaisirs.

> (A thousand times have I pressed Rica to depart from this foreign land; but he has opposed all my efforts; he keeps me here on innumerable pretexts; it appears that he has forgotten his homeland, or more likely forgotten me, he is so indifferent to my feelings.)

In evident anguish Usbek wants Rica to treat him as a father, or a son—Rica who has been on his own for years, and whom Usbek has had very little to do with in all that time. Why cannot Usbek return to Persia without Rica? In this late letter the older man, cast down by anxiety about the seraglio, has gone beyond withdrawal and delusion to childishness. Rica, after all, more like Roxane than Zélis, has a limited interest in Usbek—to return, myself, to what

emerges as the main theme of the book, the recognition and reasonable assessment of personal desires, interests, and the views of
self and the world that derive from them.

This late, sad turn in Usbek is the more lamentable and interesting because, in the latter half of the collection, he has given
definite evidence of the positive progress of some of his ideas, but
ever so slowly, like a huge ship coming about in a river. The change
is quite evident by Letters 113-22, the series in which Usbek seeks
to describe the causes of the world's decline in population, a deplorable chain of events at a time when the maxim employed by
Swift was current: "People are the riches of a nation."[12] (Recall
Usbek's certainty that new and more devastating weapons would
be forbidden by princes, who want subjects not land.) This series
is twice as long as that of the Troglodytes, and more important
because less wishful. In a sense, those two radically good-natured
Troglodytes are Usbek and Rica, delivered from the corrupt Persian
court. Usbek's reflections in the letters on population are less self-
serving, more critical. Although the early fable finally depicts in-
cipient decline for the Troglodytes, who seek to evade responsibility
by choosing a king, supported no longer by their principled, customary virtue, they have mainly represented pronounced altruism.
The later survey of demography posits less exclusively moralistic
reasons for change, resting on less idealistic expectations from human
nature.

The limitations as well as the strengths of human beings are
here taken into account, by Usbek, in the most practical ways, and
in ways most directly applicable to the tale of the *Lettres persanes*.
As early as the second letter of the series, Usbek proclaims the
misery of the man who must satisfy numerous wives, then complains of the general misery and vicious sterility caused by Persian
domestic customs: unsatisfied wives as well as exhausted husbands,
slaves doomed to be childless, no children for most of the people,
few and sickly offspring for the rest (114). (Throughout the book
we hear of Usbek's at least five wives, yet of but one child, and
that a daughter—not, in the eighteenth century, a patriotic record.)
All the historical and sociological details brought together in the

series reflect Usbek's personal circumstances. For example, when generally arguing against colonization in Letter 121, he sums up his opinions in a metaphor: "On peut comparer les empires à un arbre dont les branches trop étendues ôtent tout le suc du tronc et ne servent qu'à faire de l'ombrage" ("We can compare empires to a tree with branches that extend too far, depriving the trunk of nourishment and producing nothing but shade"). Whether the colony is taken to be Usbek's ménage or Usbek himself, the effect is the same. Comparably, he argues in Letter 122 against dictatorial government whereby the king and his courtiers—by necessary analogy, Usbek and his eunuchs—have all the power and wealth, and the rest of the population is neglected. For (again a metaphor, recalling Bacon's georgics of the mind, a metaphor no more gratuitous than the last) "Les hommes sont comme les plantes, qui ne croissent jamais heureusement si elles ne sont bien cultivées" ("Men resemble plants, which never grow successfully if they are not cultivated well"); but Usbek is the very pattern of an absentee landlord as well as an overweening emperor. Grandly and comprehensively in these letters, Usbek describes a diametrical turn in his thinking, criticizing the social and political system that has given him so much misery—but doing so from a high scholarly and cosmic viewpoint, as if that huge ship, having been too much confined by the river, had ponderously risen to come about in the air, and had still to settle back in the water.

Yet it is too easy to concentrate on Usbek's ivory-tower futility and to find the *Lettres persanes* univocal against him, for he is an attractive character in several ways. Whatever the success of his practical efforts, his thought has progressed for the better. The letters on population promote his oft-expressed belief in governmental gentleness; in them, however, there is a new emphasis on something else related to it and more fundamental: the need of those who would flourish to have reason to seek to flourish, and to be able to see themselves as possibly flourishing. They will see no future for themselves if they regard themselves as slaves—to the state, to the church, or to an unloved spouse (115–117). A person's "tour dans son imagination" ("particular imaginative tendencies") may prevail for good or bad: the Jews want to procreate because

they believe a messiah will be born to them, whereas the Moham-
medans, considering themselves transients in the world, bound for
a better afterlife, neglect to work for themselves or their progeny
(119). In short, the angle of vision from which a person projects
his image of the world may be, one might remark, acute or obtuse,
and Usbek now is not, in his usual geometric way, merely opting
for a simple, rationalist's right angle, as when in Letter 75 he had
said he preferred Mohammedan consistency to Christian inconsistency. But beneath his willingness to consider various points of
view, and more important, is his imaginative concern for the point
of view of the governed: how they regard the governor, how they
regard themselves. Though Usbek is no radical in behavior, he has
changed radically in his thinking.

It seems he has done so, as a philosopher might, almost by
thinking about thought itself, and I would locate the event between
Letters 88 and 106, a series beginning in confusion. As if working
toward the series on population, Usbek tries to sort out what makes
different people satisfied and productive. In Persia the only nobles
are those who participate in government; in France the nobles do
not, and royal favor is entirely arbitrary (88). But the French are
active, devoted to seeking and maintaining "la gloire," because they,
unlike the Persians, are free (89). Yet "la gloire" sustains the socially
sanctioned, illegal, destructive practice of dueling (90). Usbek has
fruitlessly come full circle.

Then in Letters 94–95 he criticizes the disjunction between
national and international law, and in Letters 102–04 he takes up
the relation of a prince to his subjects, and in both the point of
view is mainly that of the ruled. In the former two letters stress
falls on the primacy of justice over domination; conquest confers
no rights (95). In the second set "douceur" rests upon something
other than noblesse oblige. Why, if all crimes bring heavy penalties,
as in Persia, will a subject inclined to a less grievous crime stop at
committing one that is worse (102)? Why, in Persia, where the ruler
is so distant from his people as to be invisible, will a dissatisfied
subject not kill him and take his place, sure that the unknown despot
will not be missed (103)? In Letter 104 Usbek, with a blend of
admiration and slyness, describes the curious English, who think

it justifiable to dethrone oppressive kings, as was done with every second seventeenth-century Stuart. The political theory resembles Locke's, the skepticism Hobbes's. The question remains unresolved. The point of view, though, remains that of the governed.

What becomes patent, underlined, is the application of all this to Usbek's own situation, where the point of view of the governed is not Usbek's but his wives'. For the English,

> il n'y a qu'un lien qui puisse attacher les hommes, qui est celui de la gratitude: un mari, une femme, un père et un fils ne sont liés entre eux que par l'amour qu'ils se portent, ou par les bienfaits qu'ils se procurent: et ces motifs divers de reconnaissance sont l'origine de tous les royaumes et de toutes les sociétés. (104)

> (there is but one tie which can attach people to each other, gratitude: husband, wife, father, son are attached to each other only through the love they feel, or the benefits they obtain; and from these different motives of gratitude originate all kingdoms and all societies.)

Usbek's mixed feelings about this idea are understandable because it resembles his earlier, idealistic notion of the Troglodytes, "une seule famille" (12), and because it touches directly on his main practical dilemma. The key matter in the series remains not the familial myth but the views of the governed, extended even to a hint of dialectical reversal in Letter 102: "Rien ne rapproche plus nos princes de la condition de leurs sujets, que cet immense pouvoir qu'ils exercent sur eux; rien ne les soumet plus aux revers et aux caprices de la fortune" ("Nothing draws our rulers nearer to the situation of their subjects than that immense power over them the rulers enjoy; nothing makes rulers more vulnerable to the turns and freaks of fortune"). The business of the prince, Usbek has come to believe, is to work on behalf of his people, to provide them with luxuries as well as necessities; it is in Letter 106, another anticipating the series on population, that Usbek has labored through his confusion about the motivation of human beings, at least regarding general political and social life:

> Paris est peut-être la ville du monde la plus sensuelle, et où l'on raffine le plus sur les plaisirs; mais c'est peut-être celle où l'on mène

une vie plus dure. Pour qu'un homme vive délicieusement, il faut que cent autres travaillent sans relâche. Une femme s'est mis dans la tête qu'elle devait paraître à une assemblée avec une certaine parure; il faut que, dès ce moment, cinquante artisans ne dorment plus et n'aient plus de loisir de boire et de manger: elle commande, et elle est obéie plus promptement que ne serait notre monarque, parce que l'intérêt est le plus grand monarque de la terre.

(Paris is perhaps the world's most sensuous city, and the city where people take the most care with their pleasures; but it is also, perhaps, the city where people live the hardest lives. For a man to live delightfully, a hundred other men must work without respite. A woman gets the idea that she must have a certain outfit for a party; from this moment, fifty workers sleep no more and have no chance to drink and eat; she commands, and she is obeyed more punctually than our king would be, for interest is the greatest monarch in the world.)

Not "douceur," not even justice; interest. Here Usbek stands at his farthest remove from Gulliver, who, trying to explain human motivation to his Houyhnhnm master, grumbled "that this whole Globe of Earth must be at least three Times gone round, before one of our better Female *Yahoos* could get her Breakfast, or a Cup to put it in."[13] The important discovery Usbek makes, in context, is not the legitimacy of luxury. For him, according to the traces I have been following, the crucial recognition is that of the importance of interest, everyone's interest or self-love, others' and Usbek's own; and not so much its legitimacy as its inevitable, universal existence in the concerns of everyone: it is a fact of life, neither to be celebrated nor to be ignored. Roxane will magniloquently proclaim in the last of the letters: "j'ai réformé tes lois sur celles de la Nature" ("I have corrected your laws by the pattern of nature's"). Yet Usbek had made his way to a new grasp of natural, general psychology long before and had based the population letters on it, letters far different from the Troglodyte series in realism of psychological assessment.[14]

I have noted the confusion in Letters 88–90 and the purposiveness of the brief series beginning with Letter 94, on law. Near these sets comes, unobtrusively, what may be the most eventful section of the *Lettres persanes*. Letter 92 stands out for the reader particularly interested in Montesquieu, or in the *Lettres* as a topical, satirical miscellany, because it announces the death of Louis XIV and the ascendancy of Philippe d'Orléans as Regent. For the reader mainly interested in Usbek, the letter is just as important because the Regent represents the ineffective, refractory head eunuch who also (the significance deepens) "a fait casser la disposition du monarque, qui, voulant se survivre à lui-même, semblait avoir prétendu régner encore après sa mort" ("has had the king's last will and testament broken; the king, wishing to survive himself, seemed to have meant to reign on after his death"). To drive home the parallel to readers, the head eunuch writes Letter 96, a perfect gem of false consciousness (or true eunuch consciousness). First he lingers over the way a new, beautiful wife can set the other wives against each other, making them more governable; then he complains of Usbek's absence: "Nous ne représentons que faiblement la moitié de toi-même: nous ne pouvons que leur montrer une odieuse sévérité. Toi, tu tempères la crainte par les espérances; plus absolu quand tu caresses, que tu ne l'es quand tu menaces." ("We stand weakly for but half of you: we can show the women only an odious severity. But you leaven their fear with hope, more authoritative when you fondle them than when you menace them"). The eunuch feels he represents yet another eunuch, whom he would have return to apply "douceur"; but Usbek knows somehow that with regard to the harem he is himself a eunuch, whether there or away, and he does not answer the letter or write to his wives—in both respects also behaving like a eunuch. The contrast between his newly fertile thought about politics and his feeble ties with his own subjects is emphasized by his commenting, a letter before (95, to Rhédi), that the weak can often equal the strong through the force of "désespoir"; the eunuch gloats that the newly arrived, beautiful wife forces the other wives to behave pleasingly despite their profound "désespoir" (96).

It is in the next letter, written not to the eunuch or the wives but to the dervish Hassein, that Usbek takes his major general stride as a thinker. He had ventured somewhat boldly in Letter 93 to explain evil spirits as nothing more than "nos passions . . .; ces monstres du cœur, ces illusions de l'esprit, ces vains fantômes de l'erreur et du mensonge" ("our passions . . .; these monsters engendered by the heart, these deceits of the mind, these figments of misunderstanding and duplicity"). Now in Letter 97 he declares that French philosophers have

> débrouillé le Chaos; et ont expliqué, par une mécanique simple, l'ordre de l'architecture divine. L'auteur de la nature a donné du mouvement à la matière: il n'en a pas fallu davantage pour produire cette prodigieuse variété d'effets que nous voyons dans l'Univers.

> (brought order to chaos; and have, by an uncomplicated mechanical system, explained the design of the divine architecture. The author of nature has given movement to matter; nothing more has been necessary to produce that prodigious diversity of effects visible in the universe.)

Then Usbek draws a contrast with human rulers: "Que les législateurs ordinaires nous proposent des lois pour régler les sociétés des hommes; des lois aussi sujettes au changement que l'esprit de ceux qui les proposent, et des peuples qui les observent!" ("Let ordinary legislators give us laws to regulate human societies, laws as changeable as the minds which propose them and the minds which obey them!")—again Usbek's new consciousness of the motivation of the governed, the spirit of the laws as expressed by law-abiders as well as law-givers. The French philosophers "ne nous parlent que des lois générales, immuables, éternelles, qui s'observent sans aucune exception avec un ordre, une régularité et une promptitude infinie, dans l'immensité des espaces" ("speak to us only of laws which are universal, changeless, eternal, which are followed without exception, in order, with regularity, and with an infinite punctuality in the immensity of all space"). Yet these laws, as drawn from Descartes, are simple:

> La première est que tout corps tend à décrire une ligne droite, à moins qu'il ne rencontre quelque obstacle qui l'en détourne; et la seconde, qui n'en est qu'une suite, c'est que tout corps qui tourne autour d'un centre tend à s'en éloigner; parce que, plus il en est loin, plus la ligne qu'il décrit approche de la ligne droite.

Voilà, sublime dervis, la clef de la nature: voilà des principes féconds, dont on tire des conséquences à perte de vue.

(The first is that all bodies tend to move in a straight line, so long as they are not deflected from it by meeting an obstacle; and the second, a law simply following from the first, is that all bodies circling round a center, tend to distance themselves from it, because the farther it is away, the more [they] pursue a straight line.

There it is, exalted dervish, the key to nature; these are the prolific axioms from which one may derive consequences past the extent of human vision.)

It is obviously the consequences of such axioms when applied analogically to political and social units and relations that Usbek has begun to grasp.

That his wives, and he himself, would have proclivities of their own, and a tendency to stray from an external center—tendencies intrinsic to their natures, to be taken into account, unwise to deny or ignore—he does not quite see, though he is a great many miles from home. But this new sort of thinking leads directly to the nearby letters on population and their central recognition of the indispensability of considering human, interested tendencies of a less rarefied kind than those celebrated in the Troglodytes. In the first of the letters on population Usbek implies the same comparison between physical and human causation (113):

La terre est soumise, comme les autres planètes, aux lois des mouvements; elle souffre au dedans d'elle un combat perpétuel de ses principes: la Mer et le Continent semblent être dans une guerre éternelle. . . .

Les hommes, dans une demeure si sujette aux changements, sont dans un état aussi incertain. . . .

(The earth is ruled, like the other planets, by the laws of motion; it endures within it an endless struggle of forces: the sea and the land seem locked in an endless war. . . .

Men, in a lodging so susceptible to changes, are in a condition as uncertain. . . .)

But in the case of mankind as in the case of planets, potent principles of order may be perceived beneath apparent chaos. The causes

Usbek will concentrate on in attempting to account for the vicissitudes of population are not physical, as he says at the end of this letter, the chief cause being, as he says at the beginning of the next, "celle qui est arrivée dans les mœurs" ("what has changed in morals and manners").[15] Human morals and manners also have laws of matter and motion. The analogy between the laws of nature and the laws of natural human behavior must be discovered.

My subject remains not Montesquieu the pioneer sociologist but Usbek the developing thinker and person whom Montesquieu learned to understand. Usbek, by forming this liberating analogy of nature's laws, has departed from the way he thought earlier, in form as well as content. Before, it seems, he worked always with pairs, forming comparisons and contrasts, especially between Persian and French manners. In the letters on population he has broken the fetters of binary thought (that trammeled Gulliver)—of setting one given against another, with no third possibility to reconcile them except wishfulness and withdrawal. Instead he has found a *tertium quid*, a third angle, to set against his habitual two, a new ground from which to observe and reason: the monarch interest and its laws.[16] The insight restores lost firmness to his stature. Ironically, the insight is the positive counterpart of a haunting earlier intuition recalled by the unappreciated Zélis (53).

> Je t'ai ouï dire mille fois [she had told him] que les eunuques goûtent avec les femmes une sorte de volupté qui nous est inconnue; que la nature se dédommage de ses pertes; qu'elle a des ressources qui réparent le désavantage de leur condition; qu'on peut bien cesser d'être homme, mais non pas d'être sensible; et que, dans cet état, on est comme dans un troisième sens, ou l'on ne fait, pour ainsi dire, que changer de plaisirs.

> (I have heard you say often that eunuchs feel a kind of sexual pleasure with women which is unknown to us; that nature compensates for eunuchs' losses; that she makes up for what they lack; that a man may cease to have his masculinity but does not lose his feelings; and that, in this condition, one exists in—as it were—a third state, where one only—so to speak—experiences a change of pleasures.)

The eunuch's point of view, which is Usbek's own by implication, which is also the wives' by reason of his absence and his jealous impotence, and which seems in so many ways to pervade the world east and west, has been partially understood and counteracted, at least by the progress of Usbek's thought.

Thus in his general thinking about the world—in his philosophy—does Usbek progress, developing a less rigoristic and abstract view of human motivation and ethics, based not upon comparatively selfless virtue but upon a practical, naturalistic attempt to reconcile virtue, self-love, and the individual's own perspective on them. At the same time, with regard to his own most personal concerns, and in some degree of consonance with his general thinking, he represents a "natural" progression of thought—"natural" because describable according to Montesquieu's notion of the generation and progress of an individual human being's ideas, the notion set forth in the "Essai sur les causes qui peuvent affecter les esprits & les caractères." The progress of Usbek's ideas emerges as the cause of the progress in his philosophical perceptions. Before examining that inner progress, however, we ought to take full note of its limitations, which have only partially been indicated here; both must be kept in mind since both are real, though they cannot be reconciled in a single, positive or negative, view of Usbek, who is both worse and better than he appears to the casual reader. Not unlike Gulliver adapting himself in arrears, Usbek takes his forward step while his world takes two, and the text of the *Lettres persanes* remains comparably unsynchronized, as if to emphasize the state of affairs in which the hero at last finds himself.

The placement of the final, sensational set of fifteen letters at the end is significantly anachronistic, some of the letters several years older than others preceding them in the collection. Restored to chronological order, the letters illuminate events in several ways. Usbek's harsh Letter 148, for example, was written two months after he finally discovered interest's monarchy (106), though hardly benefiting from that revelation, and his last bitter letters to the seraglio (153–54) are preceded, rather consistently, by his Letter 129, in which he applauds the legislative wisdom of allowing great scope to paternal power.[17] The dates of the letters turn out to be crucial, however, because they give quite a twist to the end of the book, a turn imperceptible to the reader who ignores them—as Montesquieu the "translator" does to some degree. The "Persian" calendar does not simplify matters. An excessively passive reader arrives at the last letter, Roxane's diatribe, and lifts the page to find Usbek's reaction, and—there is none, the book is finished. Poor Usbek must be thunderstruck, stopped in his tracks despite his positive progress toward an adequate sense of reality.[18] Letter 155, the last of his we have read, is a most personal lament to his friend Nessir about his loneliness, his alienation in Paris, his anxiety about his wives and his upset at not hearing from them, his more intense upset about what he may hear; his complaints of Rica's indifference; his horror of returning to Persia and to his enemies, and of administering illiberal punishment in the seraglio; his wishing his unhappy charges could feel *his* sorrow.

However, that is not how the story really ends.[19] The latest letters in the volume are written not by the wives but by Usbek, and they have appeared many pages before. His Letters 145 and 146, to "***" and Rhédi respectively, are dated during the moons of Chahban and Rhamazan, 1720 (October 22 and November 11). The final two sets of three letters from the seraglio, on the other hand, are dated respectively in the moons of Maharram and Rébiab I during the same year (156–58, all March 2; 159–61, all May 8). That is, the first set reporting acts of betrayal had been written to Usbek seven and a half months before his letter 145 and almost another month earlier than Letter 146. The second set, including Roxane's suicide letter, had been written five and a half months before Letter 145 and more than six months before Letter 146. Now from the beginning of the volume, letters to Usbek from the seraglio have only once taken more than six and a half months to reach him; most of the time they have taken less than six months, more than once less than five. In Letter 155 he complains that they sometimes take six months. Thus the first of the two final sets of letters from the seraglio certainly reached him before he wrote Letters 145–46, while the second of those sets certainly reached him before he wrote Letter 146 and probably before he wrote Letter 145 as well. The shock of any of the final seraglio letters had to be immense in any case, for he had heard nothing from that quarter between Letter

96, which he received by the fall of 1716, and Letter 147, which arrived early in 1718. His own letters in response to the first of the final reports went unopened or unreceived, as we have seen. Not until Letter 156, *written* to him in the spring of 1720, does he learn that one of his own letters has been received there, putting an end to his just about four years of suspense since he received Letter 96.

Usbek's inconspicuous Letters 145 and 146, then, must be read with the knowledge that, when writing them, Usbek is aware of the turmoil and probably of the bloodbath too.[20] Read in the given sequence of the volume the letters seem essays, items in the miscellany, but read in chronological order they are charged with personal significance regarding Usbek, and they provide a final view of him less becoming than did that silence after the pathetic personal lament to Nessir (155). Letter 145, about the musunderstanding and distrust encountered by the intellectual and the scholar, begins, "Un homme d'esprit est ordinairement difficile dans les sociétés; il choisit peu de personnes; il s'ennuie avec tout ce grand nombre de gens qu'il lui plaît appeler mauvaise compagnie; il est impossible qu'il ne fasse un peu sentir son dégoût. Autant d'ennemis!" ("A thinking man is usually troublesome in company; he is receptive to few others; he is bored with all the many people it suits him to regard as bad company; it cannot be but that he makes them feel his distaste. So many enemies!") He proceeds as if writing a formal essay, impersonally, but the person in the *Lettres persanes* who most neatly fits the description I have quoted is, without question, Usbek himself. Although other parallels between this letter and his situation could be set forth, the general point will suffice. The next-to-last glimpse of Usbek in the chronological order of the collection is the self-portrait of a man whose superiority has made him misunderstood and hated; who has more than a slight resemblance to the Usbek of the very early Letter 8, where he confided that he had fled Persia because "ma sincérité m'avait fait des ennemis"; and who seems intent on wresting an "espèce de roman" back into the ironical objectivity of a satirical anatomy

His last letter (146) is at least as telling—as impersonal on the surface, having much to do with what Usbek says he once witnessed in India (the fugitive impulse?); as personal in implication.[21] It is a discourse on the failing of, not husbands, not rulers, but ministers. The head eunuch Solim, before reporting Roxane's perfidy in the third-from-last letter of the volume, recalls, "J'ai commencé mon ministère par les châtiments . . ." ("I inaugurated my stewardship with punishments . . ."). In the next-to-last letter, that preceding Roxane's, he announces that he will now resume the policy. He had taken over from the incompetent Narsit, who had sensed no trouble (152), and who had himself just become chief eunuch upon the sudden and suspicious death of the veteran black eunuch (149). Usbek has perhaps not been served very well, but there is no evidence that he has been served dishonestly, and his expectations from the eunuchs, who find themselves in extraordinarily difficult circumstances of Usbek's making, have been perfectly unrealistic. As we know as early as Letter 2, Usbek expects from the chief eunuch complete loyalty, vigilance, and even gratitude: "Souviens-toi toujours du néant d'où je t'ai fait sortir . . ." ("Remember always from what nothingness I raised you . . ."). He has *made* the eunuch, as the King of France confers merit by his glance (37). Usbek at last fools himself, not the eunuchs or his wives. The chronological order of the letters underlines this failure.

Yet, it is clear, the reader cannot rest content with this image of a single-sided, tragically or tragicomically ironic, simply futile Usbek. The form of the book, laminated by combinations of ideas and of fiction, of rhetorical and chronological orders, will not permit full homogeneity of response. For Usbek is not simply a benighted tyrant. He is several things, quite good and quite bad; before the end, as we have seen, he becomes an enlightened political philosopher, thus achieving a new general, though insufficiently particular, understanding of himself. The subtle chronological order of the letters affirms this change as well as castigating his decline to folly. And the book takes leave of him without final resolution; that is, as is often the case in philosophical tales but not novels, his final or relatively final state of affairs remains unknown. Does he return to Persia? Does he simply brood, immobilized? Does he grow to yet another stage of consciousness? We do not know. What we know is that the *Lettres persanes*, on the positive side, finally reveals a brilliant symmetry. For Usbek, in the process of arriving at his genetic, empirical, consciously and thoughtfully analogical theory of human motives and associations of ideas, simultaneously develops as a character in a way that illustrates the same theory—Montesquieu's theory. In origin and progress, for worse and for better, Usbek's ideas and feelings have changed in stages understandable by means of Montesquieu's paradigm of natural, individual, human motivation and development, as set forth in the "Essai sur les causes . . . ," a paradigm comparable also, as I have suggested in the preceding chapter, to Montesquieu's notions of the stages leading to and sustaining or destroying the social contract, in *De l'esprit des lois* (ontogeny resembling phylogeny). With the application of these models to Usbek I shall close my case.

Usbek leaves Persia and enters the book professing and evidently believing that the ways of the Persians are good and satisfactory, despite the immoral treatment he says he has suffered at court. He feels a Gulliverian attachment to his homeland: Persian ways promote virtue. Usbek as governor of his wives wants them to know and feel this is true. He wants them to be as altruistic as the good Troglodytes, and he tells them so in letters—tells his friends as well. The combination of ideas "virtue equals Persian ways" leads to another, more complex combination, that whereby virtuous Persian ways are derived from the true religion, Mohammedanism, and so forth. As Montesquieu writes in the "Essai," the first idea a person receives is a cause of his acceptance of the next, and so on, because by the first he judges the second, and so forth; thus the first ideas that come to him seem "en quelque façon indestructibles."[22]

Yet though Usbek professes to find Persian ways admirable, something disturbs that placid, original train of ideas. He is secretly troubled; we meet him in flight. Although he has acquired ideas, he has not been able to proportion them "à la juste valeur des choses" or to the feelings he attaches to them—as Montesquieu, in the "Essai," says is necessary (3:415). For though it may suit Usbek to *govern* according to Persian ways (and it may not), it certainly does not suit him to be *governed*, himself, as he has been. He says he is in real jeopardy; his expedition to the West, he confesses belatedly, is motivated by the desire to remove himself from Persia. This seeming escape happens to be a luxury not permitted to the wives and eunuchs: Usbek's flight confirms his own eunuchdom, preserving his power in some respects and his impotence in others, helping him sustain, from afar, the system of governance that he cannot bear, much less enjoy. Yet he is not exactly a eunuch either, not so irremediably cast in one role, and not settled in the eunuchs' cynicism.

Montesquieu, tracing the progress of the individual's ideas, emphasizes the importance and especially the dangers of education. To the teacher a person brings his original train of ideas, often without benefiting from the transaction: merely absorbing faulty ideas from the teacher, who may weaken the pupil's powers of comparison. Then the student encounters a third condition, that presented by experience of the world beyond school (3.418). But it is interesting to note, in Usbek's case, that he gives little evidence of formal education, in fact says in Letter 8 that he retired to the country from the corrupt court and only then developed a taste for learning. He is mainly an autodidact. Such teachers as he has, it appears, are chiefly the mullahs, and he is in a state of indecision about the worth of their teaching from very near the beginning of the book. Fleeing to France, though, he finds no easy alternative system of life: some French ways appall him; some are in addition all too familiar. Louis XIV, for example, resembles "notre auguste sultan" (37). Every aspect of his new experience challenges rather than quiets that pivotal faculty of the mind, the faculty of comparison. And Usbek, by native disposition, is imaginative rather than otherwise, resembling—to cite Montesquieu's example from the "Essai"—the fictional hero who sees crystal walls and silver streams where another person would see only arid rocks.

His fertile imagination supplies the expedient he develops and clings to, that idealistic, innocent, transcendent, universal, and fabulous idea of virtue, especially the virtue of justice, illustrated by the good Troglodytes. The fable, proving the *Candide*-like point that men are born to be utterly virtuous, preserves Usbek's original notion of virtue, his first idea, while separating it from the sordid actualities of Persian and later Parisian life—prying loose the first idea from the others with which he had habitually associated it. For the good Troglodytes, forms of society, government, and religion are manifestly subordinate to practically selfless virtue. When Usbek has liberated himself from Persian and Parisian mores, his now isolated idea of virtue becomes his independent fulcrum of critical comparison and the fundamental idea of a new series.

In the first third of the collection, from the standpoint of ideal virtue, he variously criticizes the authoritarian and eccentric excesses of religion, Persian and French (Letters 16–17, 35, 46, 60; in Letter 61 he quotes a French priest to this effect). Perhaps the most significant (and, in the long run, most ironical) letter is the forty-sixth, wherein Usbek argues that the essential thing is less one's religious position than the quality of one's behavior as a citizen and as a father. Comparably and almost simultaneously, Usbek measures Oriental government by the standards of virtue, most prominently when in Letters 33 and 40 he deplores the intemperance of rulers.

But his task becomes more difficult as he takes up issues affecting women and the family; these issues concern him most directly, and he therefore finds abstraction less easy; he vacillates, now praising the vivacity of French women (e.g., Letter 34), now retreating from French licentiousness to comforting visions of Persian innocence (Letters 48, 56). The general, abstract idea of virtue, particularly the virtue of justice, only increases its sway over him. By Letter 69 Usbek is suggesting that justice is more fundamental than God's other attributes, and by Letter 83 that its existence is more necessary than the existence of God. The idea of altruistic virtue, of perfect justice, has become for Usbek the actual mainspring of the universe. There is a Gulliverian absoluteness in such abstraction from nations, history, other persons, concrete experience, ordinary human motives. Usbek, it should not be overlooked, now seems to live in the French countryside, far in spirit from Paris as well as Persia, in a Houyhnhnmland of solitary self-satisfaction.

Usbek is only a moment away from finding everyone out of step but himself and from becoming a declamatory satirist, like Gulliver. Like Gulliver he never accuses himself of any specific fault, and he would be perfect—perfectly virtuous, perfectly just,

perfectly selfless. The letter placing justice above God (83) closes
with direct expression of that wish:

> Quand un homme s'examine, quelle satisfaction pour lui de trouver
> qu'il a le cœur juste! Ce plaisir, tout sévère qu'il est, doit le ravir:
> il voit son être autant au-dessus de ceux qui ne l'ont pas, qu'il se
> voit au-dessus des tigres et des ours. Oui, Rhédi; si j'étais sûr de
> suivre toujours inviolablement cette équité que j'ai devant les yeux,
> je me croirais le premier des hommes.

> (When a man looks into himself, what satisfaction he finds in seeing
> that his heart is just. This pleasure, severe as it is, must ravish him:
> he esteems himself above those who lack this quality as much as he
> sees himself superior to tigers and bears. Yes, Rhédi, if I knew I
> would always pursue the ideal of fairness which shines before my
> eyes, I would believe myself to be the foremost of men.)

Montesquieu's captious critic the abbé Gaultier choked on this morsel, crying "Stulto placet qui sibi placet" ("He who pleases himself
pleases a fool")[23]—an early example of blind refusal to grasp the
drama of the book, as well as a rigorist reflex action, against self-
love.

It is in just such moments as this that the psychological significance of the philosophical tale becomes most evident: the character, seemingly philosophizing, is really seeking escape from himself. Nothing within *Gulliver's Travels* stops the headlong hero in
his tracks; the *Lettres persanes* puts up more resistance. The danger
of the sort impinging on solitary Usbek is a leitmotiv of the book,
expressed for example in Rica's memorable words, "Il me semble,
Usbek, que nous ne jugeons jamais des choses que par un retour
secret que nous faisons sur nous-mêmes" (59).[24] The triangle imagining a god with three sides, or the angry biped idealizing a quad-
ruped, might pause a moment and examine his motives—examine,
as well, the fundamental laws of nature which a conceptual edifice
is meant to serve, natural principles such as those set forth in *De
l'esprit des lois*, most baldly at the beginning of the brief first book.
There Montesquieu describes a mechanism of ideas and desires
common to all mankind, antecedent and basic to all diverse, particular social contracts, institutions, laws, and customs. A person's

absolutely basic desire to preserve his being leads to discovery of his wants. That discovery draws him to seek nourishment and then other satisfactions, those of the body and subsequently, through continued association with other persons, those of the spirit.

This program of phases is the essential, universal mechanism of human motivation and perception, rooted in individual self-interest yet susceptible to many refinements. It is, in Cassirer's sense, a genetic definition of the human being.[25] What is striking about Usbek is that he does not rest content with the idealized view of mankind projected on the Troglodytes from his wishful thinking about himself, an image different, as the choruses of eunuchs and wives show, from the reality of Usbek the concrete, social, political Persian and man.

It is exactly the problem with his wishful thinking about ideal justice that Usbek comes in some degree to recognize and to redress as he continues to ponder and write about the world from which he has sequestered himself yet which he seeks to comprehend. Having sought to evade consciousness of his own motives, he begins to give special prominence to the question of motivation—natural, not unusually selfless, motivation. This comparative realism about human desires succeeds the stage of his fit of abstraction, as that stage had succeeded his attempt to find virtue permeating Persian institutions. The question of reconciling virtue with natural human inclinations, or, substituting interest for virtue as the initial idea in his thinking, preoccupies him in at least the latter half of the book, culminating in the series on population—the most prominent counterpoise to the series on the Troglodytes. Perhaps the most notable evidence of this theme's ascent to prominence appears in Letters 76 and 80, which clear an entrance to admit Usbek's later thoughts about constructive social and political arrangements, those that make people flourish. How remarkable to hear him say, in the former letter, "Le prince veut-il que je sois son sujet quand je ne retire point les avantages de la sujétion?" ("Does the ruler want me to be his subject when being such does me no good?"). (The context is Usbek's academic defense of suicide, but I need not insist further on the importance of ironical analogies here.) How surprising in the second of these letters to hear him add that the most reasonable government is the one that leads its citizens in a way which best suits "leur penchant et . . . leur inclination"—this thought a seed of the *esprit général* in *De l'esprit des lois*.

What Usbek seeks to sustain—the Persian system—as governor of his wives, he cannot tolerate as a subject himself; it is so manifestly not in his interest. That is the contradiction, as I have said, which promotes his spurt of partial mental growth, whereby he begins to combine his fundamental idea of justice not with Persia, not with ideal selflessness, but with natural self-interest. But there is another mechanism of the progress of consciousness, derivable from *De l'esprit des lois*, which may further explain this transition. At the beginning of that work Montesquieu posits several phases of consciousness preceding man's entrance into society. First, struck by his own weakness, the individual encountering others imagines that he is weaker than they; then, with experience, he finds that the others also imagine themselves thus. It is only when society has been formed that men become belligerent, as if, for the first time, overvaluing themselves (Hobbes had declared such overvaluation, the tendency to be "glorious," characteristic of all men before the social contract).[26]

Regarding Usbek, there is every indication that while in Persia and an integral member of the Persian state he had overvalued himself, had thought himself a model citizen, courtier, and husband, while correspondingly he had undervalued everyone else, most of all his wives. It is only when he has left Persia far behind, and in a sense has left human society by remaining away from Paris as well, and has begun to probe the history of nations and population, that he begins to give serious consideration to the interests of other people—begins, that is, to moderate that overvaluation of himself and undervaluation of others. And travel, we recall from the "Essai," can help liberate a person from his prejudices (3:424). In a sense Usbek has managed to put himself in the state of nature, with an effect on his sense of himself and of others like the effect of the pre-social state as described in *De l'esprit des lois*. His flight to the state of nature, moreover, reverses the process of enchainment of ideas as explained in the "Essai": having experienced the wide world, he returns to the stage of initial combination or association so as to form new ideas and proportion them to the real nature of things. What he has admirably come to realize about the world, including himself, in general, he has not—or not yet—come to apply in particular to himself and those nearest him, his family and servants, when the wives rebel; he deserves only two cheers. Like *Gulliver's Travels*, the *Lettres persanes* satirizes ignorance of self while satirically anatomizing the world; in addition, Montesquieu's hero defines a relatively constructive as well as critical model of what the self-knower might come to know about the natural mechanisms of his own and others' motives and thought, promoting personal and social concords.

CHAPTER EIGHT

Candide: Structure and Motivation

Enlightenment is man's leaving his self-caused immaturity. Immaturity is the incapacity to use one's intelligence without the guidance
of another. . . . I do not have any need to think; if I can pay, others
will take over the tedious job for me.
—Kant, "What is Enlightenment?"[1]

*T*hat Candide the character is a marionette has become a commonplace in criticism of the tale, despite infrequent though recurrent statements to the contrary by some commentators.[2] Yet
the primary meaning of the famous, iterated final words is "his"
meaning, a matter of Candide's motives in speaking them. The
nature of human motivation, the inner counterpart of the "chain
of events" that increasingly occupied eighteenth-century thinkers,
had, by the time of *Candide,* become a central subject for writers
on ethics, politics, and the fledgling science of psychology. By mid-
century, too, there was a new, developmental sense of change in
embryology and physical cosmology.[3] Was there a comparable new
sense of the development of fictional characters?—of characters'
not simply being changed but changing themselves, and of their
doing so not *ex machina* but in relation to the tendencies, the inner
processes, that characterize them? If there was—and I believe there
was, as I have indicated with reference to the *Lettres persanes*—it
was likely to be tentative and subtle, since representation of self-
conscious development by characters would mark a distinct departure from the practices of romance writers and early novelists,
and from what is typical of the romance and novel as genres.

"Motivation" is also a technical term in formalist analysis of narrative, indicating the propulsion of a plot toward its conclusion (not to be confused with the comparatively arbitrary "human" motivation of fictional characters, which serves to disguise, and ease a reader's acceptance of, a plot's necessities).[4] A tale like *Candide*, however, presents problems to the formalist because the meaning of the ending is primarily a matter of what a character means to say, and the narrator does not tell us what that is; nor, definitively, does Candide. Those final words about the necessity of cultivating the garden are, according to Roman Jakobson's division, distinctly metonymical rather than metaphorical in their relation to the rest of Voltaire's tale, because Candide's statement differs considerably from, without directly contradicting, statements he has made earlier.[5] Most notably, Candide insists that an action is necessary; he has not spoken so peremptorily before. Less obviously, he sets himself apart from not only Pangloss' way of thinking but also that of everyone else, including Martin, as I intend to show. Moreover, the clause "il faut cultiver notre jardin" may itself be metaphorical: the necessary cultivation of that garden may stand for more than agriculture. But that possibility, especially when elaborated, will seem more evident to the historian of Voltaire's ideas than to the critic mainly concerned with *Candide* as an example of eighteenth-century narrative fiction. What Voltaire may have meant by the clause is one question; what the character Candide, who is not given to poetry or eloquence, may mean in addition to what he says explicitly, is quite another.[6]

A reading of the conclusion of the tale thus requires a reading of Candide's nature, to discover whether what he says there is linked to what he says earlier. But modern criticism, in its nearly relentlessly *a priori* emphasis on the difference between the philosophical tale (or apologue) and the nascent novel, has usually been unhistorically neat, too quickly ruling out possibilities of significant characterization in the tale, even though a tale like *Candide* is obviously less about philosophy itself than about the hero's peculiar use of it.[7]

Candide's character is not so uninterestingly or insignificantly simple as it seems. Perhaps the comparison with a marionette has itself become too simple. There were other eighteenth-century models of near humanity that a critic might draw upon. Although Voltaire enjoyed marionettes, he was interested too in automata, such as the celebrated flutist, drummer, and duck manufactured by Jacques Vaucanson ("rival de Prométhée," Voltaire called him in the *Discours en vers sur l'homme*).[8] Automata, it is true, only seem autonomous, though they manage to perform without visible strings, but there was still another, still more lifelike artificial Adam to converse about in the years just before *Candide*, the awakening statue which Condillac, in the *Traité des sensations* (1754), employed to demonstrate the conceivable derivation of thought from sense experience—an example put to similar use by Buffon and Charles Bonnet. The statue come to life presents additional evidence of the new, mid-eighteenth-century interest in self-conscious, although general, psychological development. But I mention this series of progressively more lifelike models mainly to suggest historical analogues for Candide other than the marionette, so as to promote reconsideration of him as a character, not to argue that Voltaire probably had one or more of these models in mind.

In reading a narrated philosophical tale one should be attentive to the character of the narrator, who himself may change in some important way, and whose comments are not necessarily more dependable than evidence drawn from what his characters say and do. Though Voltaire's narrator says in the first paragraph that Candide has the simplest of intellects, Candide's mind is certainly not so simple as it seems or as Candide himself regards it. When, in the wilds of South America, he kills the apes pursuing two naked girls, and before he learns from his companion Cacambo that the victims were the girls' chosen lovers, his first response is of delivery from guilt: "Dieu soit loué, . . . si j'ai commis un péché en tuant un inquisiteur et un jésuite, je l'ai bien réparé en sauvant la vie à deux filles" ("God be praised, . . . if I have sinned by killing an inquisitor and a Jesuit, I have made up for it well by saving the life of two girls"). Immediately, he has another thought: "Ce sont peut-être deux demoiselles de condition, et cette aventure nous peut procurer de très grands avantages dans le pays" ("These are perhaps two young ladies of quality, and this adventure can procure us very great advantages in the land").[9] The main chance does not escape him. At a later, prominent place in the book, the point of his decision to leave Eldorado, he seems swayed particularly by desire to rejoin Cunégonde, but the sentiment as he expresses it is again not single-minded:

> Si nous restons ici, nous n'y serons que comme les autres; au lieu que si nous retournons dans notre monde, seulement avec douze moutons chargés de cailloux d'Eldorado, nous serons plus riches que tous les rois ensemble, nous n'aurons plus d'inquisiteurs à craindre, et nous pourrons aisément reprendre mademoiselle Cunégonde.

> (If we remain here, we shall be only like the others; whereas if we go back to our world, with only twelve sheep bearing pebbles from Eldorado, we shall be wealthier than all kings put together, we shall not have any more inquisitors to fear, and we shall easily regain Mademoiselle Cunégonde.)

That Cunégonde figures as the bread and not the filling in this sandwich of motivation, the narrator insists in the one passage of the book that directly criticizes his hero: "on aime tant à courir, à se faire valoir chez les siens, à faire parade de ce qu'on a vu dans ses voyages, que les deux heureux résolurent de ne plus l'être, et de demander leur congé à Sa Majesté" (18; "people love so much to run around, to pride themselves among their friends, to make a show of what they have seen in their travels, that the two happy men decided to be happy no more and to ask his majesty for permission to go away").

The narrator generally speaks of Candide as an unfortunate innocent preyed upon by evildoers. Such is often the case, it seems, but Candide himself also seems eager to accept that explanation. In the ninth chapter, when surprised with Cunégonde by Don Issacar, who shares her with the Grand Inquisitor, Candide—"quoiqu'il eût les mœurs fort douces" ("although he had the gentlest manners"), the narrator says—slays the interloper. Minutes later, with the Inquisitor's entrance, the narrator records Candide's thinking "to the moment":

> Si ce saint homme appelle du secours, il me fera infailliblement
> brûler, il pourra en faire autant de Cunégonde; il m'a fait fouetter
> impitoyablement; il est mon rival; je suis en train de tuer, il n'y a
> pas à balancer.

> (If this holy man cries for help, he will unquestionably have me
> burned, he will be able to do as much to Cunégonde; he has had
> me whipped cruelly; he is my rival; I am already involved with
> killing, there is nothing to hesitate about.)

The selflessness he would think typical of himself is again mixed
with less rarefied motives. He runs the Inquisitor through. How
could he do it? exclaims Cunégonde, "vous qui êtes né si doux"
("you who were born so gentle"). Candide replies, "Ma belle de-
moiselle, . . . quand on est amoureux, jaloux, et fouetté par l'Inquisition, on ne se connaît plus" ("My sweet young lady, . . . when
a person is in love, jealous, and scourged by the Inquisition, he no
longer knows himself"). He does not readily acknowledge ordinary,
unedifying feelings, and his reluctance persists. Five chapters later,
he again looks down upon a man he has stabbed, again astonished
by himself: "Hélas mon Dieu! dit-il, j'ai tué mon ancien maître,
mon ami, mon beau-frère; je suis le meilleur homme du monde, et
voilà déjà trois hommes que je tue . . ." (15; "Oh, my God! he says;
I have dispatched my former master, friend, brother-in-law; I am
the best of men, and already there are three men I have killed . . .").

"Le meilleur homme du monde"—an epithet amusingly resonant in this tale about the best of worlds, chateaux, philosophers,
and so forth. It begins to appear that, if there were no Pangloss,
Candide would have to invent him. Invent him in a root sense,
Candide through much of the book wishes he could do: to find or
recover or resurrect him. It is a humorous obsession. Worlds burst;
still Candide yearns to know what Pangloss' explanation would be.
As late as the twenty-seventh chapter he is still insisting that Pangloss was right and that all is well. Candide the child keeps fathering
that man. And Candide's having saddled himself with Pangloss is
suggested also by the hero's manner of replacing him: Candide does
not fall in with Martin, his alternate Mentor, accidentally.

After encountering the wretched slave of Surinam, after being robbed of his last two Eldoradan sheep, after being cheated by the judge to whom he complained, Candide feels the deepest melancholy. "La méchanceté des hommes se présentait à son esprit dans toute sa laideur, il ne se nourrissait que d'idées tristes" ("The wickedness of men loomed in all its ugliness before his mind, he nurtured only sad ideas"). But he cannot sustain such ideas by himself; he needs assistance of the sort he is used to, so he sponsors an odd contest to select a traveling companion, advertising for someone "le plus dégoûté de son état et le plus malheureux de la province" (19; "the most revolted by his own condition and the most wretched man in the province"); if it were practical, he would undoubtedly seek the unhappiest person in the world. From the throng that replies, Candide chooses twenty and hears them out, with gratifying misery, thinking of how embarrassed Pangloss would be, until finally Martin is chosen, not because he particularly deserves the prize but because, besides professing to be miserable, he is a philosopher. The logic is bluntly Hegelian: if this is not the best of all possible worlds, it must be the worst. Candide still wishes to believe Pangloss, but if Martin can convince him of the truth of the opposite position, Candide may assent. One way or the other, he will arrive at the absolute truth of the matter. Although constantly regarding himself as indivisible in his sentiments, he is not.

The action of the next chapter, the twentieth, should be seen as an oblique but telling commentary upon the procedures of "le meilleur homme du monde." Candide is protesting to Martin that the world has some good when the noise of cannons interrupts them. They watch a naval engagement in which one ship suddenly sinks, all hands lost. Candide tends to agree with Martin that the event is diabolical—but, something red is floating in the water where a hundred men have just drowned, one of the Eldoradan sheep. Candide, we are told, "eut plus de joie de retrouver ce mouton, qu'il n'avait été affligé d'en perdre cent tous chargés de gros diamants d'Eldorado" ("was more delighted in regaining this sheep than he had been afflicted by the loss of a hundred sheep all carrying huge diamonds from Eldorado"). The drowned men, the lost sheep, the repetition of the number one hundred for them in so short a space, Candide's sympathy for the dead so quickly followed by joy at recovery of his treasure: he is rather more ordinary in his self-centeredness than he realizes.[10] He fondles his sheep and supposes that, since he has regained it, he may also regain Cunégonde.

The parallel is apt. Cunégonde, and indeed the women of the tale in general, unblushingly reveal an animality that Candide and Pangloss have also but rationalize away. (Candide of course does not notice it in the women either). Though beautiful at first, Cunégonde lacks other Petrarchan characteristics. It is she who takes the lead in Candide's first encounter with her, and later she eagerly receives him in the Grand Inquisitor's house, typically not wondering about their safety together. She tells her tale: a Bulgarian captain, having killed a soldier who was raping her, made her his slave; she adjusted herself to the situation, for "il me trouvait fort jolie, il faut l'avouer; et je ne nierai pas qu'il ne fût très bien fait, et qu'il n'eût la peau blanche et douce; d'ailleurs"—she is telling this to Candide—"peu d'esprit, peu de philosophie: on voyait bien qu'il n'avait pas été élevé par le docteur Pangloss" ("he thought me quite pretty, it must be said; and I shall not deny that he was very well put together, and that his skin was fair and smooth; otherwise, not much brain, not much philosophy; a person could see very well that he had not been taught by Doctor Pangloss"). Later, at the auto-da-fé, she saw Pangloss hanged and she fainted.

> A peine reprenais-je mes sens que je vous vis dépouillé tout nu; ce fut là le comble de l'horreur, de la consternation, de la douleur, du désespoir. Je vous dirai, avec vérité, que votre peau est encore plus blanche, et d'un incarnat plus parfait que celle de mon capitaine des Bulgares.
>
> (Hardly did I regain my senses when I saw you stripped entirely naked; that was the extremity of terror, vexation, sorrow, despair. I will say to you, truly, that your flesh is still whiter and of a finer rosiness, than my Bulgarian captain's.)

The flogging of Candide prompted her to recall all her misfortunes, which she summarizes in one of those pell-mell litanies of comically enchained events with which the book abounds—massacres, degradation, "et surtout [le] baiser que je vous avais donné derrière un paravent, le jour que je vous avais vu pour la dernière fois" ("and especially the kiss I had given you behind a screen, that day I saw you the last time"). "Vous devez avoir une faim dévorante," she concludes, no *non sequitur* for her; "j'ai grand appétit; commençons par souper" (8; "You must have a ferocious appetite; I am awfully hungry; let us start by supping").

The old woman has a similar history and personality, this once delectable daughter of a pope, beaten, robbed, mutilated, who wanted to kill herself a hundred times but still loved life (12). More resilient than Candide, the women have no need for a Pangloss or Martin. They have an amoral authority all their own because they claim no authority while simply doing as they like, as much as they can. They even readily fall in with the ways of the world that exploits them. Cunégonde resisted the first Bulgarian, she explains, because she did not know that "tout ce qui arrivait dans le château de mon père était une chose d'usage" (8; "everything that happened in my father's chateau was sanctioned by custom"). The old woman, stripped and probed by corsairs, was surprised, ignorant of the fact that everyone, even the Knights of Malta, acts that way; "C'est une loi du droit des gens à laquelle on n'a jamais dérogé" (11; "It is an article of international law from which no one has ever deviated"). Expostulating with cannibals, the somewhat comparably flexible Cacambo declares, "En effet le droit naturel nous enseigne à tuer notre prochain, et c'est ainsi qu'on en agit dans toute la terre" (16; "As a matter of fact, natural law instructs us to kill our neighbor, and it is thus that everyone behaves throughout the world").

Candide, who never voices complacent classifications of this kind, whose penchant is for acceptance of metaphysical cosmology rather than custom, seems to occupy a place like that of Man in Pope's *Essay*, between the assertive doctors, his light and dark angels, and the libidinal if not brutal women. Even in respect to his feelings for Cunégonde, however, he is less simple than the narrator says, not readily quixotic. He has not simply envisioned her as a lady of romance, nor has he given disinterested attention to philosophical Optimisim. He gave Pangloss his credence, the narrator says at the outset, "car il trouvait mademoiselle Cunégonde extrêmement belle." From the first, his motives are consistently double and mixed, his priorities transparent, to the narrator and the reader, not to him. "Il concluait qu'après le bonheur d'être né baron de Thunder-ten-tronckh, le second degré de bonheur était d'être mademoiselle Cunégonde, le troisième, de la voir tous les jours, et le quatrième, d'entendre maître Pangloss . . ." (1; "He determined that next to the good fortune of being born the Baron of Thunder-ten-tronckh, the second greatest sort of happiness lay in being Mlle Cunégonde, the third in gazing on her every day, and the fourth in understanding Master Pangloss . . .").

Though Candide would be the last to admit it, his love for Cunégonde and his faith in Pangloss have, consistently, much to do with his wish to be the best man in the best possible world: to be discovered, for example, to be the Baron's nephew, like that other obscure youth turned out of paradise, the romantic, more single-minded Tom Jones. That this is so seems still more probable when one considers Candide's final reason for marrying Cunégonde at the end. To reverse his set of priorities, checked off by events: fourth, Pangloss has become tedious to Candide; third and second, Cunégonde is ugly, poor, and abrasive, now neither companionable nor enviable; but, first, her baronial brother opposes the marriage as beneath her, so Candide, with but not determined by Cunégonde's solicitations, makes a point of going through with it (30).

Thus, repeatedly, though Candide thinks himself exceptional for his unselfishness, he acts upon self-regarding motives which he resists acknowledging, and he avoids such acknowledgment, systematically, either by displacing the object of his desires from one thing to another somehow associated with it (despite the fact that, after Locke, the main trend in psychology promoted critical consciousness of mental associations) or by attaching himself to an authority, such as Martin, and thus displacing the subject of his desires. Repeatedly it is shown that Candide's concern about whether the world is for the best or for the worst is displaced concern about how the world will deal with poor Candide. He is really more an automaton, brother to Vaucanson's duck—moved by a concealed drive wheel, concealed from himself—than he is a marionette. Once in a while Voltaire ties a string to him and jerks it, as when Candide, thinking he has killed the Jesuit, worries about what the *Journal de*

Trévoux will say (16). But most of the time Candide goes by his own spring, an adequately motivated comic character whose traits, while too thin for psychoanalysis, are not inhumanly mechanical. He moves the comedy, is not simply moved by it, and he does not simply carry about his favorite philosophical proposition; he embodies and enacts it. Odd as the statement may seem at first, Candide is, energetically, ingeniously on Voltaire's part, a trope.

Considered as a trope in the conventional sense, as a device of communication, as the equivalent of a figure of speech conceived by a rhetorician, Candide may seem a metaphor. His name would give that impression. But as I have tried to show, he is only partially *candide* (in one sense of the word), for he is not so with himself. He may be considered a figure of irony, and he is that much of the time, but he does not seem so definitely that when he speaks the concluding words. The other major tropes, besides metaphor and irony, are synecdoche and metonymy; and, broadly speaking, synecdoche is everywhere in the tale, but in saying that I use *synecdoche* not primarily in the common rhetorical sense, to indicate devices mediating between writer and reader. I use the term, rather, to indicate the way in which words are combined in sentences, ideas associated in the mind, by the characters and narrator. As we have seen, Cunégonde and other characters constantly explain (one might say *naturalize*) strange events by classifying them as species of general codes: custom, international law, natural law. The species-genus relation is especially synecdochic; the part-whole relation is usually regarded as synecdochic too. And, at least in the earlier sections of the tale, the narrator matches his characters in the production of broadly synecdochic associations, as in the particulars chosen to support faint praise of the Baron's chateau, exceptional in Westphalia: "son château avait une porte et des fenêtres" (1).

The grand architects of synecdoche in the tale, however, are the philosophical Optimists; "All are but parts of one stupendous whole," Pope had written.[11] Part-whole classification becomes Candide's main occupation. His esteem for Pangloss derives, as that name suggests, precisely from the philosopher's ability to identify the whole of which Candide is a part, thus establishing rootless Candide *as* a part, deducing his estimable character and expectations from that best whole. The philosophy of Optimism, as Kenneth Burke points out, is essentially synecdochic:

> The "noblest synecdoche," the perfect paradigm or prototype for all lesser usages, is found in metaphysical doctrines proclaiming the identity of "microcosm" and "macrocosm." In such doctrines, where the individual is treated as a replica of the universe, and vice versa, we have the ideal synecdoche, since microcosm is related to macrocosm as part to whole, and either the whole can represent the part or the part can represent the whole. (For "represent" we could substitute "be identified with.") One could thus look through the remotest astronomical distances to the "truth within," or could look within to learn the "truth of all the universe without." Leibniz' monadology is a good instance of synecdoche on this grand scale.[12]

It may be helpful to emphasize that the use of a trope by a metaphysician in this manner is not rhetorical but epistemological. Instead of employing the trope to illustrate a concept distinct from, antecedent to, the trope, he employs the trope to think. The metaphysics *is* a synecdoche. But statements about the philosophy are synecdochic in linguistic and rhetorical ways. In *Candide*, the various synecdochic associations constructed by the characters and the narrator have a splendid parodic symmetry. For the most part, the trope of irony persists rhetorically and dominates the epistemological and linguistic synecdoches, as in Cunégonde's unconsciously ironic recourse to custom, the narrator's deliberately ironic specification of door and windows, and mainly in comic transformations of Optimism.

A trope may have a mind of its own, like Alice's croquet mallet. Although in rhetoric *trope* means a turn or twist given to speech (one says "a sail" and means "a ship"), the figure may twist in one's hands, the resultant meaning not quite what one intended. The vitality of a trope may spring particularly from its instability as a compound, its tendency to be resolved in another trope—its tropism. A metaphor may reveal an implicit set of synecdoches. In Burke's example, initially the part is related to the whole; then it can be identified with it. But once the part has been so fully identified with the whole that it can stand for it, a curious turning occurs: the part tends to become the distinctive part of the whole, the really important part, even in a sense the *best* part. The trope of synecdoche, a kind of metaphor, tends to become pure metaphor by transforming the species that can stand for a genus, the part that can stand for a whole, into a new, more economical, higher genus or whole.

If, to return to *Candide*, the not so simple hero is categorized as a trope, his desires are seen to turn that way. Establishing himself as part of the best of all possible worlds, he would demonstrate that, far from being a nobody, he is not a microcosm but *the* microcosm: "le meilleur homme du monde." In the sense that Candide himself is synecdochic like Leibniz's noble synecdoche, the full title of the tale has its full significance: *Candide ou l'optimisme*, the philosophy and would-be philosopher are one.

But though synecdoche for the most part characterizes the hero and typifies much that the narrator says as well, the fundamental trope of the tale is metonymy, which, against some precedents, I should like to distinguish as much as possible from synecdoche as that term is usually understood.[13] Synecdoche may verge on the metaphorical, as in Burke and in what I have said thus far. But it may verge instead on the metonymical. Whereas metaphor works with items that have an intrinsic similarity to or identity with each other, metonymy works with items extrinsic to each other: relations of before and after, above and below, cause and effect; relations often temporal rather than spatial. Metonymy is often a trope of movement and change, of calculus rather than algebra. It is also the trope of otherness, for each trope implies a point of view, the condition of the knower in regard to what is to be known; but whereas metaphor and the more metaphorical sort of synecdoche, by their predication of whole or partial resemblance or identity in the items related, tend to identify the knower with the known, metonymy tends to keep them separate. Synecdoche verging on the metonymical rather than the metaphorical will suggest that any resemblance between the part and the whole is slight, or that any predication of identity between them, even partial identity, is arbitrary. A person should be wary about the adequacy of any theory of genus and species. A person sees that this accompanies that but remains in doubt about relations of identity between them, beyond the notion that they "go together." Hume's epistemology is thus fundamentally metonymical and extremely cautious: *post quod* is no more than that, and causes, important as they are to us, represent no more than the effects of one principle governing our association of ideas.[14]

It is into something like Hume's world that Voltaire has dropped Candide, arranging the tale so that it is from the basic, alienated point of view of epistemological metonymy that characters attempt to read the universe, that is, to associate events by general formulae. Throughout the tale Candide is assaulted by discrete, unassimilable, pressing events. He strains to read them metaphorically, to give them a teleology assimilating them to the grand pattern of a world deserving the qualification "best." His reasoning is always really practical, not speculative, but in person or in spirit there is always at his shoulder, by his choice, one of his mentors to keep him in the dark. Pangloss radiates obscurity. "Remarquez bien," he argues in the first chapter, "que les nez ont été faits pour porter des lunettes, aussi avons-nous des lunettes" ("Note well that noses were made to hold eyeglasses, so we have eyeglasses"). This reasoning, comically trivial on the surface, becomes sillier when looked into. In the first place, Pangloss has omitted the necessary middle term if the proposition that all is for the best is to make sense as philosophical Optimism, that term being the proviso of a perfect Creator, "Wisdom infinite" (*An Essay on Man* 1.44); it is because of God's nature that all must be for the best. Second, the given example begins to make sense only if employed to justify the existence of noses, but Pangloss wrenches the argument to justify what we do with our noses, anything we do.

It is not simply the position in which man has been placed that Pangloss is busy accepting; it is what man wants to do there, still clearer in a succeeding example: "les cochons étant faits pour être mangés, nous mangeons du porc toute l'année" ("pigs being made to be eaten, we eat pork all through the year"). Pangloss neatly, gratifyingly, confuses the theological and teleological sense of "end" with the personal and moral sense and thus can adduce the nature of the universe, implicitly the nature of God, to explain the rightness of whatever Pangloss wants to do. He attracts Candide by glossing everything, seeing resemblance in all that happens, and locating his desires in the nature of things rather than in himself. Through the whole argument there is a telling balance in the omission of the First Mover and the neglect of the human agent's motivation. Pangloss could seem rather cunning in all this, but he is not: though given to abstractions, he resembles the women of the tale in completely lacking critical self-consciousness.

It is in the nature of things, not of Pangloss, that he eats pork or gives Paquette a lesson in experimental physics. And Martin resembles him by similarly displacing motives, only shifting them to the devil's shoulders much of the time. Neither philosopher makes room for specifically human desires. And Candide, employing first one and then the other to think for him, establishes for himself the best of possible fools' paradises by successfully shifting judgment from his own shoulders onto theirs. Event follows event, detail is added to detail; the empirical relations are extrinsic, mere relations of contiguity. Why does event B follow event A? Will C, success, follow B? Yes, says Pangloss. No, says Martin. Such is the world, they say in chorus. Each thinks he is associating events by cause and effect when he is only, tacitly, correlating them with his own desires, and, like Candide, correlating his reasoning with a high opinion of himself. Each, to resolve the metonymy of experience, rashly makes the wrong tropic turn. Instead of inquiring into the relation between the whole of himself and the part constituted by his desires, he assumes he is a whole, all integrity, and concerns himself entirely with his relation to the whole universe.

However, metonymy forbids these flights and retaliates by promoting recognition of the most down-to-earth causes. In this respect the tale plays with the mechanistic explanation of human motives common in Swift. Cunégonde, spying Pangloss in the bushes with the chambermaid, "vit clairement la raison suffisante du docteur, les effets et les causes" (1; "clearly perceived the doctor's sufficient reason, the effects and the causes"). Descartes is being stood upon his head: men are machines, mechanically rationalizing animals. Given Cunégonde's regular animality, it follows that she would immediately find an opportunity for applying Pangloss' physics. Given Candide's innocence of natural rather than selfless human motives, he is particularly vulnerable to both manipulation and criticism in this mode.

Now it would seem that the tendency of metonymy is toward perception of chains of events as mechanical (the vogue of naturalistic fiction a century after *Candide* might seem the historical realization of that tendency, the empire of realism's metonymy). It would seem so, that is, if metonymy did not imply the point of view I have mentioned, that of extrinsicality. The would-be knower perceives one thing going with another; he may forge a causal link; but he does so, at his most self-conscious, with recognition that he has created the association, perhaps delusively.

There is definite movement in Voltaire's tale, in Samuel Johnson's *Rasselas* too, from the hero's expectation of full understanding of the world to fear that there can be no understanding of it, at least none warranting any contentment. At the beginning, Candide cheerfully accepts the notion that all is for the best with the implication that all shall be for his own personal good. Despite frustrations, he persists in seeking suitable evidence. "Isn't everyone happy?" he asks. Then, having discovered in the first third of the tale that everything European seems far from being for the best, and in the next third that the New World is little better, by chapter 19, Candide, near despair, hires Martin to prove that all is for the worst. Candide does not want to make that judgment, but his question has now become, "Isn't anyone happy?"—that wealthy, educated senator, or that seemingly jolly cleric with the girl on his arm? Martin's pessimism is repeatedly vindicated, and the metaphysical question falls to earth in the process. Martin seems an expert reader of this world's metonymies—until he ventures to ridicule Candide's faith in Cacambo: "Vous êtes bien simple, en vérité, de vous figurer qu'un valet métis, qui a cinq ou six millions dans ses poches, ira chercher votre maîtresse au bout du monde et vous l'amènera à Venise" (24; "You are really a simpleton to expect that a half-breed servant, with five or six million in his pockets, will go seeking your mistress to the end of the world and conduct her to you in Venice").

Candide could certainly profit from increased proficiency in reductive, mechanistic prediction of chains of human events, yet not in this instance, for of course his valet returns—without the money, it is true, but having acted in good faith and bringing news of Cunégonde's whereabouts. Martin's chain has broken. The tale moves inexorably toward an attitude of skepticism as explanation after explanation proves false, as metonymy outlasts noble synecdoches, yet there is no corresponding movement toward doctrinaire skepticism. The book moves toward skepticism conscious of and skeptical of itself. Explanations have failed but explanation itself has not been proven futile; what has, at most, been demonstrated is that explanation by unconscious wishful thinking is futile. Erich Auerbach's rather unsympathetic pages on *Candide* in *Mimesis*, summarized by the statement that "For Voltaire, it is a perfectly self-evident premise that no one in his senses can believe in . . . an inner justification for views,"[15] seem badly in need of qualification, the addition to the statement of "without first considering whether he is deluded about that inner justification." There the satirical stress falls; there Voltaire's ridicule comes to a point.

Candide may seem the helpless, passive object of a remarkable series of misfortunes. The misfortunes are remarkable, even an earthquake killing thousands, a natural disaster on a scale afflicting few fictional characters. The world seems Candide's nemesis. However, with the notable exception of that earthquake—which, for all its enormity, is an instance of natural evil virtually required in a work bearing on theodicy—the reader finds that Candide regularly, often actively, induces the world's nasty, morally evil reactions against him. As mimesis of probability in the objective world, the events loom unrealistically huge, frequent, and severe. Yet as mimesis of the probability of the world's responses to someone like Candide, the series of events comes to seem, at the least, less improbable; as mediated through a Candide the world takes on a different aspect. He invites misfortune at a rate very close to that of its occurrence, because, with Pangloss' spectacles on his nose, he insists upon secretly seeing "all things for my use," despite that warning about the wrong Optimistic turn in *An Essay on Man* (3.45).

It must be for the best when the Baron's daughter makes love to him, or when the Bulgarian press-gang attracts him by appealing eloquently to the same expectation. "Les hommes ne sont faits que pour se secourir les uns les autres" ("Men were made only so that each one could help out the others"), they say. Candide says that is just what Pangloss thinks. Even when Candide chooses to desert the army, he does so not out of a natural desire to be free and safe but out of the belief that "c'était un privilège de l'espèce humaine . . . de se servir de ses jambes à son plaisir" ("it was a right of human beings . . . for a man to have the benefit of using his own legs as he pleases"). Candide is a rigorist.

There is always, as Johnson said of Richardson's Clarissa, something which he prefers to truth, the truth of acknowledged desire. Given the choice of the gauntlet or the firing squad, he chooses by the divine gift of "*liberté*," and asking to be killed he is neither desperate nor angry but polite, requesting of the Bulgarians "qu'on voulût bien avoir la bonté de lui casser la tête" (2; "that someone would kindly be gracious enough to crush his head"). This comment nicely illustrates the positivity of Candide as a character; delivered in indirect discourse, it is obviously a sarcasm of the narrator's, yet the reader senses no sarcasm in what Candide seems to mean by it, and no improbability in *his* speaking this way. He has relative independence from his author. Having escaped, except mentally, Candide proceeds to deduce that the Dutch, being Christians, will take care of him, another Panglossian expectation to be frustrated, but he pays no attention to the anomaly presented by the kindness of the unbaptized Jacques; then, when Jacques is soon drowning, Candide allows himself to do nothing but look on, conveniently persuaded by Pangloss' assertion "que la rade de Lisbonne avait été formée exprès pour que cet anabaptiste s'y noyât" (5; "that the harbor of Lisbon had been shaped expressly for this Anabaptist to drown in"). And so forth; extremely unrealistic as Candide's credulity is, the chain of evil events, as significantly determined by his unrealistic longings, is not entirely without probability.

Although I have suggested in passing that Candide occupies a middle state between his doctors and the women, that vertical scale, that microcosmic Chain of Being, is illusory. Pangloss, Martin, Cunégonde, the old woman, all are in an important sense variations on the same theme. They think about different things, but the ways in which they think about them are fundamentally identical, for all these characters take the events they observe and mechanically reduce them to uniformity. To Pangloss they are all for the best; to Martin, for the worst; to Cunégonde, they are acceptable. (Belonging to a Bulgarian captain, or to Candide, or to a South American governor; it is all the same to her; at the end she does not recognize the change in her own appearance.) Each ancillary character processes experience as if by an assembly line. Each proceeds without introspection. Thus each, though enduring innumerable crises, inhabits a serenely uniform mental world, a world without change, all events linked by similarity. Toward such secure simplicity of world and mind, particularly as represented by the confident, authoritative philosophers, Candide is constantly propelled by his uneasy combination of self-esteem and self-regard. But at the end, whatever else he means by his closing remarks, he refuses to join his companions in continued mock-philosophizing.

In this late turn of events the hero is subtly but definitely seconded by the narrator (there is a parallel development in *Rasselas*). At the beginning of the tale the narrator had made himself prominent with continual, insistent irony, often sarcasm, but he plays a much subdued part as the tale progresses, particularly after the entrance of Martin in the nineteenth chapter. The narrator's earlier, extreme irony had made a witty, critical foil for the naive optimism of Pangloss and Candide, and for the complacency about cruelty and stupidity exhibited by most of the other characters. Martin, when he enters, is occasionally ironical (it is he who says, in chapter 23, that France and England "sont en guerre pour quelques arpents de neige vers le Canada"—"are at war for a plot of snow near Canada"), but in the main his is a direct critical voice, and he is in addition a pessimist. By contrast with this role, the narrator's, for much the most part toward the close of the tale, is that of an uneditorializing introducer of speakers and straightforward describer of actions. Directly or indirectly, the narrator of the latter part of the tale offers very few opinions, with the result that the irony lodged in his comments earlier now continues almost exclusively in the plot, and his earlier criticism is replaced by Martin's. Yet valid as Martin's criticism often is, he overreaches himself in his pessimism, which turns out to be similar in its affected omniscience about the chain of events, in kind if not in degree, to the optimism of Pangloss. When Cacambo defeats Martin's prediction by returning to Candide, the plot defeats Martin's philosophy too.

One rhetorical effect of the change whereby Martin takes on himself the judgmental responsibilities of the narrator is some attenuation of the tale's satire. The narrator's satirical reflections had worn the absoluteness and invulnerability of irony. Martin's criticism becomes vulnerable because based on a stated, then overstated doctrine; his point of view, unlike the narrator's, remains distinctly limited—formally, but also by consequences in the plot, by the limitations of his nature as fully revealed in the end, and perhaps even by one of the narrator's rare late judgments, the reference to Martin's "détestables principes" (30). That is, part of the satire which continues in the tale after the narrator steps down from the bench qualifies Martin's utterances. And the narrator, who at the outset had taken the reader into his confidence, offering him the absolute assurance that only an omniscient narrator can provide, an assurance like that which Candide sought from Pangloss and metaphysics, toward the end ranges himself less closely with the reader and more closely with Candide, whom the narrator resembles increasingly when Candide finally refrains from explanation, from commentary.

In the final pages, the hero, the narrator, and the tale resist commentary as misreading, likely to be the product of covert egotism, like the philosophies of Pangloss and Martin. In the last page or so Candide says, twice, "il faut cultiver notre jardin." The narrator, who had earlier made such a point of uncovering the true motives of his blind, compulsive hero, does not explain these declarative, in effect imperative statements, but presents them to the reader as final, seemingly discrete items in the series constituted by Candide's words, thoughts, and actions throughout the tale, presents them to be motivated in meaning by the reader. To be interpreted, Candide's final statements must be associated with his history, and virtually the only way *that* can be accomplished is to construe them as negation. As part of the tale, not as a historic statement by the historical Voltaire, the clause in context resists all but the most elementary commentary. So often duped by unexamined, grandiose, metaphorical habits of thought, Candide here speaks as unmetaphorically, as literally, as possible.

In the history of interpretation, it is true, the resistance of the text has often been resisted itself. The image of cultivating one's garden is so historically poetical, so pregnant with iconic potentiality—one may even find it in a passage Leibniz wrote about the necessity of universal progress[16]—that a scholar is hard put not to explode with learned associations. Surely, however, it ought to give an interpreter pause when he considers that the import of the remark in context, the final time Candide makes it, is precisely to rebuff Pangloss' Optimistic assimilation of events up to this moment;

> Tous les événements sont enchaînés dans le meilleur des mondes possibles, [Pangloss exclaims] car enfin, si vous n'aviez pas été chassé d'un beau château, à grands coups de pied dans le derrière . . .—Cela est bien dit, répondit Candide, mais il faut cultiver notre jardin.

> (All events are enchained in this best of possible worlds, for if you had not been turned out of a fine chateau with strong kicks in the rear. . . .—Well said, answered Candide, but it is necessary to care for our garden).

That *bien dit*, implying the gap between words and things: has Candide come full circle, finally emulating the narrator's former sarcasm? Pangloss' last speeches compose a brief grammar of facile interpretation, a Panglossary: philosophical, as in the comment just quoted; historical a paragraph before, as he enumerated unfortunate rulers, prompting Candide's first "il faut cultiver," prefaced by the suspect "Je sais aussi"; mythological and typological in Pangloss' reply, "Vous avez raison, dit Pangloss; car quand l'homme fut mis dans le jardin d'Eden, il y fut mis, *ut operaretur eum*, pour qu'il travaillât . . ." ("Correct, says Pangloss; for when man was placed in the Garden of Eden, he was placed in it *ut operaretur eum*, in order to work. . . ."). At this point Martin cannot forbear affirming, as he thinks, what Candide has said: "Travaillons sans raisonner"—without arguing, also without reasoning or even without rationalizing in the manner of Pangloss. Yet Martin, being Martin, also cannot resist interpreting and revising Candide's statement and giving a reason for not reasoning, yin for Pangloss' yang: "c'est le seul moyen de rendre la vie supportable" ("it is the only way to make living bearable"). Candide says nothing.

There is now in Candide a resistance to potentially delusive naturalization of decisions. He is, one might say colloquially, more realistic about the world and himself. But there is a way, though a quite special way, in which he is a rare example of literary realism in this respect. The two philosophers persist to the end in providing absolute reasons for life as they would have it. Candide seems to have learned something from the old Turk with a modest farm and isolationist views, but Candide does not seek to attach himself to that philosopher and he does not parrot his reasoning" ("le travail éloigne de nous trois grands maux, l'ennui, le vice et le besoin"— "work keeps three great evils away from us: boredom, vice, and want"), just as Candide does not echo Martin's reasoning. Candide's final words are most unusual for him in omitting concern for reasoning, while the motive for his behavior that the narrative suggests is, he has come to regard the metonymical from the point of view of metonymy; that is, with recognition that he perceives external events from the outside and that they remain in large measure unknowable except insofar as he can give them modest, motivated, metaphorical meaning, of desire and attainable object, by attending to his own desires instead of resisting acknowledgment of them.

Every effect has a cause, Voltaire would say in the *Dictionnaire philosophique* ("Chaîne des événements"), but every effect does not necessarily cause further effects.[17] In Candide's final words, he concentrates on causing rather than being caused.[18] The implication of his words is that, by possibly recognizing the automaton in himself, he may have enabled himself to be different, though what he may become we are not told. He does not grandly rouse himself and shake invincible locks. His repeated "il faut" could be more personal. This is no messianic (or Minervan) moment. But he would not abandon the habits of thought of his philosophical companions if he had not begun to cultivate his mind. In the garden he pauses; everything that has gone before in the tale indicates that he pauses to rid himself of disabling preconceptions, as Condillac's newly conscious statue stops to realize that he is not himself the scent of a rose that was his first sensation.[19]

Condillac's statue is meant to be taken as a fiction, a teaching model; but to understand it, the philosopher insists, we must share its point of view (as we must share Candide's). Condillac's prefatory "Avis important au lecteur" is urgent on the point: "J'avertis donc qu'il est très-important de se mettre exactement à la place de la statue que nous allons observer. Il faut commencer d'exister avec elle . . . : en un mot, il faut n'être que ce qu'elle est" (1:221; "I insist then that it is most important to place oneself exactly in the situation of the statue which we are going to observe. We must begin to exist with it . . . ; in a word, we must be only what it is"). Mental life being "une chaîne dont les anneaux sont tour à tour idées et desirs" ("a chain of which the links are by turns ideas and desires"), we have only to follow that chain "pour découvrir le progrès de toutes les connoissances de l'homme" (1:239; "to discover the progress of all the conceptions of man"). As in Locke, Gay, and others, a person must be very wary of, and curious about, the habits of thought he has formed, "Car, lorsqu'une fois nous avons contracté ces habitudes, nous agissons sans pouvoir observer les jugemens qui les accompagnent . . ." (1:298; "For once we have formed these habits, we act without being able to observe the judgments accompanying them . . ."). *Amour-propre* is the fundamental love felt by the statue (1:233); the mind has a certain natural bias, for example, whereby it tends to think that what pleases it intends to do so ("Elle pense donc que ce qui lui plaît, a en vue de lui plaire . . ."—(1:305). The mind is also very apt to imitate what it sees: "Nous sommes si fort portés à l'imitation, qu'un Descartes à sa place [in the condition of a wild child] n'apprendroit pas à marcher sur ses pieds: tout ce qu'il verroit suffiroit pour l'en détourner" (1:309; "We are so forcefully drawn to imitate that a Descartes in his condition would not learn to walk on his feet; everything he would see would tend to turn him away from doing so"). These hazards are to be avoided so that the statue, conscious of the chain of his thinking (1:310), may declare: "Instruite par l'expérience, j'examine, je délibère avant d'agir. Je n'obéis plus aveuglément à mes passions, je leur résiste, je me conduis d'après mes lumières, je suis libre . . ." (1:312; "Instructed by experience, I examine, I deliberate before acting. I no longer obey my passions blindly, I resist them, I go by my own lights, I am free . . .").[20]

The finally enlightened, liberated Candide is a rare and distinguished person in eighteenth-century fiction. A work such as *Candide*, or *Rasselas*, supports the seemingly paradoxical observation that the blatantly unrealistic philosophical tale tends to be more realistic, in what I have called realism of psychological assessment, than the "novel of worldliness" in France or the then-new English novel, because the tale promotes attention to the hero as assessor of his own sense of reality. In *Candide*, unlike most novels of the time, the hero is quite imperfect; there is considerable emphasis, as also in contemporary associationist philosophy, upon his preconceptions as obstacles to knowledge of himself and the "real" world; self-knowledge, including non-rigorist recognition of the hero's own desires, is requisite for whatever happiness may be found (marvelous coincidences finally solve no crucial problems for the hero); and the narrator, prominently and satirically distant from the hero at the beginning of the tale, has become unobtrusive by the end while his judgmental function has been assumed by a less authoritative person, Martin. The mentor or mentors engage the hero in productive exchanges of opinion, dialectic usually only said to be present in novels, and the ending thwarts novelistic absorption of the reader, rhetorical stress there remaining on the dangers of mindless idealization, not the allure of the ideal.

CHAPTER NINE

Conflict, Declamation, and Self-Assessment in *Rasselas*

... The first Years are usually imploy'd and diverted in looking abroad. Men's business in them is to acquaint themselves with what is to be found without; and so growing up in a constant attention to outward Sensations, seldom make any considerable Reflection on what passes within them, till they come to be of riper Years; and some scarce ever at all.
—*An Essay Concerning Human Understanding*, 2.1.8

"*I*t seems to me, said Imlac, that while you are making the choice of life, you neglect to live."[1] Readers of Samuel Johnson's *Rasselas* have tended to regard this reflection, from chapter 30, as just; have from time to time proceeded to remark that only when Pekuah is abducted in chapter 33 do the travelers cease to be mere spectators of life and begin to participate in it—although that harrowing degree of participation was not what Imlac had in mind three chapters before.[2] Indeed, so wise is Imlac, so often do his sayings correspond with those of the narrator, and with those uttered by Johnson elsewhere, that a reader has trouble sustaining disbelief that all three persons are not, for practical purposes, one. So natural is the trinitarian assumption that criticism, while alert to other possibilities of interpretation, has seemingly been restricted in its examination of them.[3] I hope to cast light on Imlac's relation to the narrator as well as to Rasselas, but first it will be necessary to question the validity of Imlac's "you neglect to live." Although the characters, it is true, have only tentatively involved themselves with complete strangers to this point more than midway through the tale, whether or not Imlac wishes to acknowledge it they have seriously become engaged—have participated—not just in life but also in conflict, with each other.[4] Although the book is not a novel, its account of the main characters' disagreement, resentment, and estrangement from each other deserves recognition.[5]

To emphasize the prominence of this chain of events, a chain linking together more than a third of the tale, I shall summarize the action before looking into it. By chapter 13, Rasselas is pleased to have found a friend in Imlac, who, while differing from him in the expectations they entertain about the world outside the Happy Valley, will help him escape. But by the twenty-third and twenty-fourth chapters, the prince and his sister, Nekayah, have come to distrust Imlac, to feel that he disapproves of their "search, lest we should in time find him mistaken." Imlac disappears for several chapters while brother and sister alone pursue the choice of life. By chapter 29, however, Rasselas and Nekayah have themselves fallen out, she tending to agree with Imlac and thinking Rasselas has now questioned *her* honesty: "I did not expect, answered the princess, to hear that imputed to falshood which is the consequence only of frailty" (28).

Then, after six or more chapters' absence, Imlac reenters to suggest living, specifically an instructive visit to the pyramids. Rasselas resists the suggestion but relents with—not eagerness but acceptance on principle: "I am willing, said the prince, to see all that can deserve my search" (30). Almost immediately, by denying the possible existence of ghosts, he provokes Imlac's stern disagreement, accompanied by a gratuitous slap at the doubts of some "single cavillers." And when news of Pekuah's abduction reaches the party, Imlac abruptly questions Rasselas' order for pursuit of the bandits. Rasselas does not respond, has difficulty controlling himself; he wants to accuse "them"—the Turkish guards, maybe others as well—of cowardice (33). Not until the end of the thirty-fifth chapter does the prince show any sign of willing cooperation with his mentor, when comforting Nekayah. It has been thirteen chapters since Rasselas' disaffection was announced to us, nearly a third of the book, and it will be longer still before Rasselas shows another sign of reconciliation. In chapter 37 Imlac refuses to let the prince accom-

pany him in ransoming Pekuah. Only in the fortieth chapter, with
fewer than ten chapters to go and very few episodes, mainly that
of the astronomer, is there evidence of renewed affection between
the younger man and the older.

But the nature of their conflict and of their means of resolving
it is more important than the fact of its existence, for the reader's
giving their competition its due weight will reveal new depth, almost a new dimension, in the meaning as well as the drama of the
tale, which has more fictional and rhetorical force than is usually
acknowledged. Its affinities with *Candide*, published the same year,
have often been noted.[6] Those affinities are extensive and deep,
and involve Jane Austen too, as I shall show when concluding this
book. *Rasselas* is a philosophical *tale*, not just philosophy superficially decorated by a story. The chain of events, faintly drawn as
it is in places, holds together; in part it is a chain of development
in the character of the prince and in his relationship with his mentor.

From Imlac, Rasselas wants help in choosing a station in life
attended by constant happiness. Yet within a chapter of what W.
K. Wimsatt calls Imlac's "curiously abrupt" entry into the book[7]—
that strangely inconspicuous entry, to which I shall return—Rasselas begins to be disappointed. As Imlac opens his autobiographical
account, he mentions his father's fear that the governors of the
province would take away his riches, and Rasselas is appalled that
his own father, the emperor, permits such villainy.

> "Sir, said Imlac, your ardour is the natural effect of vertue animated
> by youth: the time will come when you will acquit your father, and
> perhaps hear with less impatience of the governour. Oppression is,
> in the Abissinian dominions, neither frequent nor tolerated; but no
> form of government has been yet discovered, by which cruelty can
> be wholly prevented. Subordination supposes power on one part
> and subjection on the other; and if power be in the hands of men,
> it will sometimes be abused. The vigilance of the supreme magistrate
> may do much, but much will still remain undone. He can never
> know all the crimes that are committed, and can seldom punish all
> that he knows."

"This, said the prince, I do not understand, but I had rather hear thee than dispute. Continue thy narration."

(8)

Rasselas is inexperienced, Imlac wise, yet as the story continues Imlac shows a tendency to generalize about the world in a manner which, if not utterly disproved by the prince's later, disillusioning experience, is not wholly corroborated by it either. Imlac draws his contrasts too sharply, for example in these early words, from chapter 12: "The world, which you figure to yourself smooth and quiet as the lake in the valley, you will find a sea foaming with tempests, and boiling with whirlpools: you will be sometimes overwhelmed by the waves of violence, and sometimes dashed against the rocks of treachery. Amidst wrongs and frauds, competitions and anxieties, you will wish a thousand times for these seats of quiet, and willingly quit hope to be free from fear." The speech, like others in the book, is spoken not only about something but also to someone, with various potential intentions behind it.

Here Imlac may be fulfilling the role assigned to sages in the Happy Valley, who, as we are told in chapter 2, did everything possible to induce contentment in the pent sons and daughters of Abyssinia, including exaggerating the miseries and calamities of the world outside. That world, Rasselas will find, never becomes quite so malevolent as Imlac promises; the prince will later rebuke his sister for "producing, in a familiar disquisition, examples of national calamities, and scenes of extensive misery, which are found in books rather than in the world, and which, as they are horrid, are ordained to be rare" (28). In books like *Candide*, he might have said; in his own story, evil, though heard of, for the most part keeps its distance or enters in its Sunday clothes, as in the person of the kidnapper whose surface gentility almost rivals Imlac's. But to cite Imlac for exaggeration is to recognize not only that he is a sage of the Valley but also that he is human, and to understand that he speaks not in a vacuum but in the company of a young man with distressingly optimistic expectations. He is replying to Rasselas, evidently replying passionately, disturbed by his companion's attitude and exerting himself to change it by head-on verbal assault.

Ostensibly about civil government, what Imlac says in chapter 8 has broader application, and the subject will be pursued, discursively and dramatically, throughout the book. Nekayah, for example, will later remark: "If a kingdom be, as Imlac tells us, a great family, a family likewise is a little kingdom, torn with factions and exposed to revolutions" (26). The analogy is reminiscent of the *Lettres persanes*, with some comparable irony. Rather than addressing the subject of their own relationship, Imlac and Rasselas talk about their fathers—one of whom happens to be an emperor; but both fathers are governors of their children, and it begs no question to point out that Rasselas is seeking paternal guidance from Imlac. Indeed, Rasselas probably expects at first that Imlac, after listening to his complaints, will rummage through his own experience of the world and pick out just the choice of life to suit the young man's needs—Imlac, who has met with indifferent success in making his own choice. Would Imlac tell him if he could, or Rasselas heed him?

Again, later, Nekayah speaks to the purpose: "An unpractised observer expects the love of parents and children to be constant and equal, but this kindness seldom continues beyond the years of infancy: in a short time the children become rivals to their parents. Benefits are allayed by reproaches, and gratitude debased by envy" (26). She pursues her topic, that of the ages of man, in the manner of *Rambler* 151: there is, she says, a natural difference of perspective separating generations: "The opinions of children and parents, of the young and the old, are naturally opposite, by the contrary effects of hope and despondence, of expectation and experience, without crime or folly on either side." And, most appositely in so sententious a book as this, she adds, "Few parents act in such a manner as much to enforce their maxims by the credit of their lives. The old man trusts wholly to slow contrivance and gradual progression: the youth expects to force his way by genius, vigour, and precipitance." But despite her maxims and examples, the prince cannot agree with her. "Surely . . . you must have been unfortunate in your choice of acquaintance: I am unwilling to believe, that the most tender of all relations is thus impeded in its effects by natural necessity." In this obduracy he is not simply naive, as the book will show; he is not, finally, just Imlac's rival. (The reader might keep in mind a remark of Johnson's at an early meeting with Boswell: "Sir, a father and a son should part at a certain time of life. I never believed what my father said. I always thought that he spoke *ex officio*, as a priest does.")[8]

Nekayah's comment fits the case of Rasselas' relations with Imlac through the middle of the tale, fits it perfectly, although Rasselas may not notice. Rasselas has grown impatient with his mentor, especially it seems with Imlac's wanting to tell young people what to think, and to tell them at length. Wimsatt amusingly likens the Imlac of one passage to "a wound-up automaton, a speaking toy-philosopher."[9] As a poet of his own description, Imlac is not simply intolerant of youthful impetuosity; he yearns to play "the interpreter of nature, and the legislator of mankind"; he has maxims by the dozens, likes delivering them, has indulged himself in the fit of enthusiasm about poetry that culminates in chapter 11, is seldom without a string of universal opinions on any topic that arises. Soon Rasselas grows unwilling to raise any. Through the beginning of chapter 23 Imlac speaks a great deal, mostly to depress the prince's high expectations of happiness. "Do not seek to deter me from my purpose," Rasselas protests in chapter 12. After another exchange he exclaims, "surely happiness is somewhere to be found" (16).

When Imlac reappears after the seven chapters in which the two young people have conducted their search without him, his suggestion of a tour of the pyramids meets with a declamatory refusal from the prince.[10] "My curiosity, said Rasselas, does not very strongly lead me to survey piles of stone, or mounds of earth; my business is with man. I came hither not to measure fragments of temples, or trace choaked aqueducts, but to look upon the various scenes of the present world" (30). The princess, however, replies in a slightly different fashion. She too resists the suggestion, forcefully, but her statement ends with a question to Imlac about why · they ought to be concerned about old monuments, a question which, needless to say, Imlac is prepared to answer quite fully. Rasselas protests, then gives in; but Nekayah, albeit backhandedly, asks for information and gets it, to her satisfaction. "I, said the princess, shall rejoice to learn something of the manners of antiquity."

The distinction, though apparently small, is worth making because of what had occurred during the chapters just preceding this, in which Rasselas and Nekayah had searched alone, then had become disappointed with each other. They had fallen out over the question of marriage, Nekayah refusing to take its disadvantages lightly, Rasselas holding out for its advantages. The end of their debate naturally focuses on the relation of parents to children, that constant theme of the book. While Rasselas wants to believe in the possibility of some mediating bond between young and old, Nekayah insists that "those who marry late are best pleased with their children, and those who marry early with their partners." Says Rasselas: "The union of these two affections . . . would produce all that could be wished. Perhaps there is a time when marriage might unite them, a time neither too early for the father nor too late for the husband" (29). Still Rasselas dreams of a condition supplying "all that could be wished"! Still he resists the opinion that nothing sufficiently positive can be expected.

The princess not only disagrees, perhaps too forcibly; she also reassociates herself with the person whom she and her brother, in a happier moment, had allied themselves to evade. "Every hour . . . confirms my prejudice in favour of the position so often uttered by the mouth of Imlac, 'That nature sets her gifts on the right hand and on the left.'" And she amplifies the point as Rasselas' rejected mentor would. "Flatter not yourself with contrarieties of pleasure. Of the blessings set before you make your choice, and be content." These cryptic imperatives she confirms, like the poet's poet,[11] with "general and transcendental truths," truths decorated and emphasized by ideas drawn from the "awfully vast" and "elegantly little" in nature ("the plants of the garden" and so forth, as stipulated by Imlac in chapter 10). "No man," she says, probably feeling some "complacence in her own perspicacity" like that felt by Rasselas in chapter 2, "can taste the fruits of autumn while he is delighting his scent with the flowers of the spring: no man can, at the same time, fill his cup from the source and from the mouth of the Nile."[12] She

propounds her beliefs as if she possessed the wisdom of ages and
the tongue of an angel, and she leaves poor doubtful Rasselas to
pursue his increasingly forlorn search all by himself.

Her speech is pumped-up, insensitive. Everyone speaks with
relative formality in the book, but in different voices at different
times.[13] Imlac speaks *Rambler* essays, whenever he has the chance—
or so it seems up to this point. We know Imlac's ruling passion is
his love of speech poetic and authoritative, and we know, since
chapters 10–11, that it can run away with him. Moreover, he is
not the only major figure in the book with a tendency that way,
but I am not thinking now of Nekayah as she, on the occasion just
described, emits her master's voice. The other major figure with
an inclination for grandiloquence is, of course, the narrator, nowhere more so than in the first sentence of the book, the monitory
tones of which rumble as if they emanated from some primordial
chamber deep within the pyramids. "Ye who listen with credulity
to the whispers of fancy, and persue with eagerness the phantoms
of hope; who expect that age will perform the promises of youth,
and that the deficiencies of the present day will be supplied by the
morrow; attend to the history of Rasselas prince of Abissinia." Not
just chronologically does this voice have a place between those of
Milton's God and Blake's Nobodaddy, obliterating all distinction
between the assertive and the authoritarian as it holds forth about
"gates of iron, forged by the artificers of ancient days, so massy
that no man could, without the help of engines, open or shut them."
Some sort of "two-handed" engines no doubt.

To Rasselas' credit, he seldom speaks that way, doing so only
in the first half of the book, and only when complacent about his
perceptions or when about to be more directly opposed, as when
he futilely preaches sobriety to the Young Men of Spirit and Gaiety
(17). Rasselas grows quieter as the book progresses. His encounter
with the would-be Stoic in chapter 18 leaves him, we are told,
"convinced of the emptiness of rhetorical sound, and the inefficacy
of polished periods and studied sentences," a typical overreaction.
The next time he meets a sage of that sort, the advocate of a Life
Led According to Nature, he does not stay to haggle. "The prince
soon found that this was one of the sages whom he should under-

stand less as he heard him longer. He therefore bowed and was silent" (22). His debate with his sister provokes from him statements not free of the "errours of exaggeratory declamation" and "quer[u]lous eloquence" he finds in hers (28), but after the unhappy impasse with her, he says very little.

When he does speak between chapters 30 and 39, he continues to be at cross-purposes with Imlac. After consenting on principle to visit the pyramids, he is quiet for two chapters while Imlac discourses on the "hunger of imagination," until, hearing of Pekuah's misfortune, the prince announces his resolve to pursue the abductors, saber in hand. But Imlac quashes the idea with cool, or cold, common sense. (As Nekayah had said, "The old man trusts wholly to slow contrivance and gradual progression: the youth expects to force his way by genius, vigour, and precipitance.") Two chapters later we again hear something about Rasselas, that he has tried to console his sister, and after being quoted then he is not again heard from until, four chapters later, Pekuah is finishing the account of her adventure. Back in chapter 35, however, attempting to comfort Nekayah, he had reasoned in a spirit as appropriate to his condition as to hers: "At least, said the prince, do not despair before all remedies have been tried: the enquiry after the unfortunate lady is still continued, and shall be carried on with yet greater diligence, on condition that you will promise to wait a year for the event, without any unalterable resolution." Then the narrator gives us a highly significant piece of information, not sufficiently emphasized to strike the casual reader, that Rasselas had extracted this promise from his sister on Imlac's advice. Rasselas has once more turned to Imlac, accepted his guidance. How much time the prince had sat sulking in his tent—he has evidently been sulking—we are not told. His contention with Imlac, now active for thirteen chapters and more, is over.

When Rasselas speaks again, his sentences are not declamatory, are in fact seldom declarative; instead of asserting himself, he asks questions, his tone enquiring, reflective, his words beginning with "I could not" (47) or another comparably self-effacing phrase. His response to the astronomer's suggestion of a visit to the catacombs— "I know not, said Rasselas, what pleasure the sight of the catacombs can afford; but, since nothing else is offered, I am resolved to view them, and shall place this with many other things which I have done, because I would do something" (47)—this response, in contrast with his declamatory reply to Imlac regarding the pyramids, though tinged with plaintiveness, is not arrogant. That Rasselas' character has changed seems possible; another indication comes in the younger persons' various attitudes toward Imlac's account of the old, crazed astronomer, Rasselas' attitude more profound than the others'. "The prince heard this narration with very serious regard, but the princess smiled, and Pekuah convulsed herself with laughter." Imlac scolds the two women. "Rasselas," we are told, "more deeply affected, enquired of Imlac, whether he thought such maladies of the mind frequent, and how they were contracted" (43).[14] The young man's one outburst toward the end of the book is in temporarily successful opposition to the women's plan of deceiving the astronomer (46).

There is a plausible explanation for Rasselas' greater sympathy, inasmuch as he had induced Imlac to describe the astronomer by his own immature and enthusiastic declaration, at the start of chapter 40, that he meant to devote himself to a life of learning, a life like the astronomer's. Imlac's tale speaks directly to Rasselas' new fantasy. However, there is an indirect and deeper cause for the prince's sympathy. Alone among the young poeple in the book he seems to have experienced a change of mind affecting his whole sense of himself. Nekayah is recovered from solitary misery by an external, chance event, the return of Pekuah.[15] Rasselas, having broken with Imlac and then with his sister, himself moves—moves himself—toward recovery from potential solipsism.

I would not want to make too much of this reorientation: the book remains too schematic to be read as a psychological novel—yet at the same time is too provocative, psychologically, to be read as a set of philosophical propositions in disguise. Unobtrusively, consistently however, the change has occurred: the Rasselas who had professed to be an enquirer at the beginning of the book has begun to enquire in earnest, and has ceased to insist that the world conform to untested expectations: conform, that is, to what the philosopher John Gay called mental resting places and what Locke called associations of ideas.[16] Instead he will become more conscious of his preconceptions, most notably when, a few chapters later, he and Nekayah and Pekuah, as if members of an encounter group, confess their favorite daydreams. Rasselas' own "fantastick delight" has been "to image the possibility of a perfect government, by which all wrong should be restrained, all vice reformed, and all the subjects preserved in tranquility and innocence" (44).[17] That the world will not permit realization of that trope for state or family is the recognition he has been resisting throughout the book, since in the Happy Valley he began to differ with Imlac, refusing to accept the seemingly contradictory facts that there are some bad governors in Abyssinia and that his father is not to blame. Although entering the wide world, he has insisted on bringing the Happy Valley with him.

One could now introduce the twentieth-century psychological extrapolation that Rasselas' wish to make the world perfect, as his father has not, masks a wish to do away with his father and to rationalize and atone for parricide by excelling him in good works. But one need introduce nothing, for Johnson, with characteristic insight, has Rasselas both judge his utopian fantasy rightly, as "more dangerous" than his companions', and begin to understand it by approaching consciousness of his deep motives: ". . . I start, when I think with how little anguish I once supposed the death of my father and my brothers." This remarkable statement bears also on Rasselas' relations with Imlac, whose reply is a model of order and discretion. He selectively addresses himself not to Rasselas' surprising conclusion but to the general theme of all three young persons' confessions, and he has the grace to include himself in his generalization: "Such, says Imlac, are the effects of visionary schemes: when we first form them we know them to be absurd, but familiarize them by degrees, and in time lose sight of their folly."

The general subject of the chapter is the way in which solitary imaginings may begin to affect a person's actions, interfering with his perception of reality and his comportment of himself within it. Pekuah, Nekayah, and Rasselas all give instances of that tendency in their own past behavior; Pekuah, the servant, for example, in her desire for sovereignty—a desire paralleling and underlining Rasselas' desire for power—has at times nearly forgotten to be properly obedient to the princess. But only Rasselas begins to answer the consequent, disturbing question: what practical realization of the dream would entail. Although Pekuah's dream would possibly call for more havoc than his, and Nekayah's for evasion of a princess's responsibilities, the two women do not venture so far as to acknowledge these "side effects." Rasselas, to be sure, could go further. It is remarkable, however, that he has gone so far, so perceptively in the manner of eighteenth-century psychology.

The fact is that experience and Imlac have taught Rasselas a certain amount of psychology. Rasselas has come to understand some central truths about psychological mechanisms common to mankind, and about particular manifestations of them peculiar to himself. The beginning of chapter 44 gives the most important example of Imlac's instruction in this regard with respect to mankind in general. Very much like Locke at the outset of the chapter on the association of ideas, Imlac comments that

> Perhaps, if we speak with rigorous exactness, no human mind is in its right state. There is no man whose imagination does not sometimes predominate over his reason. . . . All power of fancy over reason is a degree of insanity; but while this power is such as we can controul and repress, it is not visible to others . . .: it is not pronounced madness but when it comes ungovernable, and apparently influences speech or action.

Imlac amplifies the point, citing the dangers of not only solitary speculation but, more fundamentally, of self-love, which commonly hungers and may grow wanton: "He who has nothing external that can divert him, must find pleasure in his own thoughts, and must conceive himself what he is not; for who is pleased with what he is?"[18] Motivated by desire, the imagination fixes itself on inaccessible objects and associates the ideas of them in "some particular train," which in time takes the mind captive. "By degrees the reign of fancy is confirmed; she grows first imperious, and in time despotick. Then fictions begin to operate as realities . . ."—

this last the peril Johnson had warned against, regarding novel reading, in *Rambler* 4: the power of fiction to take memory captive.

That Imlac the poet has chosen his words carefully becomes evident especially when we compare this analysis of the mind with that supplied by the unfortunate Stoic of chapter 18, an analysis which is similar but decidedly not the same. Like Imlac, the Stoic had recommended "government" of emotion and imagination. In context, however, it is clear that his word is a euphemism for something more severe than regulation; both imagination and emotion must be subjected to "conquest." The sage should be indifferent and impervious to them. Imlac, as we have seen, is equally wary of the ascendancy of these powers to a "reign" which at last becomes "despotick." On the other hand, though he speaks of the need to "repress" imagination, in the context of Imlac's teachings taken as a whole his prescription is appreciative of the value as well as the dangers of that faculty and of emotion. It is their power over reason, not their less presumptuous powers, that must be overcome. A despotism of reason such as the Stoic promotes is held to be inhuman.

Imlac's pupil Rasselas comes to know this well. Even before he begins to converse with Imlac, Rasselas, in the relative state of nature afforded by the Happy Valley, begins to recognize that he differs from the animals (in this awareness like Rousseau's primitive man)[19] and does so precisely because he has the imaginative power to envision circumstances other than those encompassing him. Comparably, it is only when Rasselas' imagination presents him with an object to desire—that is, when imagination and emotion combine to give him an enlivening curiosity about the world outside the Valley and about the "choice of life" to be made there—that he begins to taste any happiness. In word and deed, Imlac proves generally encouraging to him. Rasselas' conceptions of what life may offer are preconceptions, metaphors, associations of ideas, as he begins his search. Yet at root if not in branch they are necessary and valuable, for the direction, bases for comparison, activity, and pleasure they provide.

For Imlac, then, to "govern" the motivating powers of emotion and imagination is not to repress them in the sense of beating them down, except in cases of extreme disorder. It is generally to understand them and guide them so as to be nourished and enlightened by them, so that they may be free to seek, in Locke's terms, natural and right combinations of ideas rather than associations. When Nekayah, apparently depending on Imlac's wisdom, analyzes the common origins of love between the sexes, she illustrates the problem of such false associations:

> A youth and a maiden meeting by chance, or brought together by artifice, exchange glances, reciprocate civilities, go home, and dream of one another. Having little to divert attention, or diversify thought, they find themselves uneasy when they are apart, and therefore conclude they should be happy together. They marry, and discover what nothing but voluntary blindness had before concealed; they wear out life in altercations, and charge nature with cruelty.
>
> (29)

Though stern and sharpened by circumstances of debate, the insight is probing, especially with respect to what Nekayah calls "voluntary blindness," the effect of what Johnson elsewhere calls "voluntary delusion."[20] For Johnson, for Imlac, and in time for Rasselas, the function of reason when it seeks to govern imagination and emotion is fundamentally to discriminate between tendencies of the mind toward, on the one hand, reasonable satisfaction, and on the other, voluntary delusion.

Rasselas very much resembles Candide in harboring unacknowledged desires and in projecting what he imagines on himself and the world. Like Candide, he initially imagines the world to be perfectly good: "that every heart melted with benevolence" (16). He thinks his own heart as unexceptionable as everyone else's. In words that recall Gulliver's dream of becoming a sage and revered Struldbrugg, recall also Usbek's resolution to be perfectly virtuous and his dream of the Troglodytes, Rasselas rhapsodizes about what a fine member of society he will be, *comme homme, comme père de famille, comme citoyen*:

> I would injure no man, and should provoke no resentment: I would relieve every distress, and should enjoy the benedictions of gratitude.

I would choose my friends among the wise, and my wife among the virtuous; and therefore should be in no danger from treachery, or unkindness. My children should, by my care, be learned and pious, and would repay to my age what their childhood had received. What would dare to molest him who might call on every side to thousands enriched by his bounty, or assisted by his power? And why should not life glide quietly away in the soft reciprocation of protection and reverence? (12)

Rasselas, in short, like Candide, would be "le meilleur homme du monde," or would be a more successful Usbek, one whose resolution to be virtuous would win universal acclaim. Rasselas would also, it appears—appears not very subtly—glide imperceptibly into a position of great eminence and power, as would Gulliver, Usbek, and Candide. The ambitions expressed here most centrally explain Rasselas' resistance to Imlac, and Imlac's resistance to him: the chapters containing Imlac's autobiography refute Rasselas' illusions at every turn. And it should not be overlooked that, during early conversations with Imlac, Rasselas objects particularly to Imlac's finding dishonest "motives" in those travelers who cheated him in his youth (9). Comparably, Rasselas in chapter 17 can perceive no motive for the folly of the spirited young men. It is the shrewd reading of motives that, above all, Rasselas has to resist, for he refuses to look into his own and see the particular desire for power that lurks there, in conflict with his desire to be guiltless, indeed to be remarkably virtuous.

It is most important to observe that Rasselas, to acknowledge that particular desire for power, must be bravely honest with himself, for the desire is not simply a cause of illusion; in Rasselas' circumstances it is also, at least potentially, immoral. When he can admit to himself that he harbors a desire which conflicts with the interests and rightful claims of his father and his brothers, he has in a sense gone beyond Imlac's general views of psychology, or at least has applied them to a harder case then that presented by the astronomer, whose illusion was not at all so patently selfish. In seeing the particular tendency taken in himself by a mechanism general to mankind, Rasselas has become the psychologist of himself as well as, more generally, of man. In facing up to his morally dangerous desire, he has made himself capable of trying to regulate it.

Rasselas for a long time refuses to examine the train of his ideas. Like the beginning thinker described by Montesquieu, he is unknowingly chained in a system whereby he must judge the second idea only in comparison to the first, and so forth—until he is moved to confess his fantasy. What moves him is the sense he has acquired, from Imlac and from experience, that there is a mechanism of mind in everyone which, through desire and imagination, can produce either real satisfaction or maddening delusion, and possible wrongdoing. He has acquired a genetic model for conceiving of his own mind so as to govern it most fruitfully. As the book ends Rasselas is simultaneously aware that he desires a kingdom (a reminiscence perhaps of Sancho's dream of an island to govern); that the desire is always threatening to get out of hand ("he could never fix the limits of his dominion, and was always adding to the number of his subjects"—49); that any element of perfect altruism in the desire may mask a motive toward personal power and possible crime; that in whole or in part his "wishes" cannot be "obtained"; that having such wishes brings interest, activity, and pleasure to living; that preconceptions can be the raw material of true perception; that this mechanism is natural to mankind; that recognizing his own wishes is essential to self-assessment; and that his mind can be governed so as to promote whatever happiness is possible. In becoming thus enlightened, Rasselas becomes a realist of psychological self-assessment. He does not cease to form associations of ideas, figuring forth his desires and probing reality, but he has learned to do so with consciousness of the fact that that is what he is doing. Imlac may be seen as promoting such consciousness from early in the book, as in these words: "The world, which you *figure* to yourself smooth and quiet . . ." (12, my italics; the cognate *figurer* turns up in chapter 24 of *Candide* when Martin attacks the expectation that Cacambo will return with Cunégonde).

In the long run, Candide does not want Pangloss and Martin to think for him. Rasselas achieves still more, positive knowledge of his general and particular mental mechanisms, including a tendency toward illusion productive of evil—a tendency explained less fully by Imlac than by Johnson outside the tale. Near the end of *Rambler* 8, Johnson takes up the case of a person quite like Rasselas, a person seeking the same "fantastick delight" but farther along the road to delusion:

> It is easy to think on that which may be gained till at last we resolve to gain it, and to image the happiness of particular conditions till we can be easy in no other. We ought, at least, to let our desires fix upon nothing in another's power for the sake of our quiet, or in another's possession for the sake of our innocence. When a man finds himself led, though by a train of honest sentiments [compare Imlac's "some particular train," above], to a wish for that to which he has no right, he should start back as from a pitfal covered with flowers. He that fancies he should benefit the publick more in a great station than the man that fills it, will in time imagine it an act of virtue to supplant him; and, as opposition readily kindles into hatred, his eagerness to do that good, to which he is not called, will betray him to crimes, which in his original scheme were never purposed.

What should the person in such a case do? Johnson proceeds: the man must "govern his actions," but to do so he must first "regulate his thoughts by those of reason," and to do that he must "remember that the pleasures of fancy, and the emotions of desire are more dangerous as they are more hidden"—why? because they "escape the awe of observation."[21] In the end, Rasselas, a most extraordinary hero of fiction, has gained the ability to observe and rectify them. To describe his accomplishment in the spirit of *Rambler* 4, Rasselas is equipped to live—or to read novels—without losing sight of what a person may realistically hope for and perform. More particularly, he is equipped to live without blindly making himself the prey of his rooted, conflicting desires for virtue and power.

Time, experience, solitude, suffering, and the instruction of Imlac have brought about the change in Rasselas, although it is difficult to specify what each has exactly contributed. What Imlac has certainly not done is give in to Rasselas' opinions, despite the prince's opposition and withdrawal. Imlac has, however, not withdrawn himself, and events have drawn the two of them back together—chiefly, the event of Rasselas' change in attitude. But a still more subtle trait distinguishes Imlac's behavior toward the prince, the gist of which a reader may discern in what Imlac says to Nekayah when she blames herself for not having commanded Pekuah to enter the pyramid, out of real harm's way: ". . . Do not reproach yourself for your virtue, or consider that as blameable by which evil has accidentally been caused. Your tenderness for the timidity of Pekuah was generous and kind" (34). He labors the point, but not beyond recognition; and the respect for Pekuah he praises in Nekayah is a general attitude toward others which Imlac himself, in action if not in every word, always maintains. (By contrast, Nekayah in the next chapter will summon Imlac to attend her against his will.) Imlac's conduct unflaggingly exemplifies a point made by Rasselas in the marriage debate: "We will not endeavour to modify the motions of the elements, or to fix the destiny of kingdoms"— again the fantasies of Rasselas and the astronomer. "It is our business to consider what beings like us may perform; each labouring for his own happiness, by promoting within his circle, however narrow, the happiness of others" (28).[22]

From the beginning, Imlac tends to behave as if he has seen it all and wants to save Rasselas the trouble, assuming that the prince will in the long run come to see everything as his mentor already does. But in the course of the book Imlac tempers this attitude somewhat, complementing the change in Rasselas. With time Imlac tends to adopt a tone less of pronouncement than of statement—statement, moreover, in which he ranges himself with rather than above or against his young companions. The tonal contrast is sharp in chapter 30, for Rasselas ("rather pretentiously," according to Walter Jackson Bate)[23] has just delivered himself of a pronouncement himself, the "My business is with man" passage, and his sister has asked, not entirely in the tone of someone seeking an answer, "What have I to do with the heroes or the monuments of ancient times?" Here is Imlac's reply.

> To know any thing . . . we must know its effects; to see men we must see their works, that we may learn what reason has dictated, or passion has incited, and find what are the most powerful motives of action. To judge rightly of the present we must oppose it to the past; for all judgment is comparative, and of the future nothing can

be known. The truth is that no mind is much employed upon the present: recollection and anticipation fill up almost all our moments. Our passions are joy and grief, love and hatred, hope and fear.

To the young persons' reactive first-person singulars, Imlac answers in the first-person plural. Like the narrator with his "Ye," Imlac has tended to speak as if he belonged to a species outside and above the condition occupied by the prince and his sister, as if the sage had access to "un autre ordre de sagesse," but here he pointedly speaks otherwise. And although there is a "we" which flatters or coerces, and a neutral editorial "we," Imlac's in this passage is arguably neither aggressive nor toneless but conciliatory, for he is speaking not of the limitations peculiar to the young or remotely affecting abstract mankind, heretofore his usual, sometimes fruitless topic, but of the limitations he, Imlac, shares with his companions. In the first-person plural he is speaking directly about the force and burdensomeness of his own as well as others' emotions. He does so again, poignantly, in response to the prince's startling confession involving the death of his father and his brothers (44).

Not that, in the latter part of the book, Imlac holds this position unfailingly; he is too much drawn to the declamatory, as we have seen, and, before quitting the pyramid, he will make it reverberate with—it has been noted[24]—an echo of the narrator's first sentence: "Whoever thou art, that, not content with a moderate condition, imaginest happiness in royal magnificence, and dreamest that command or riches"—and so on (32). But this apostrophe, at this point, relates only quite indirectly to any of his companions, and after his tempered tone has brought him somewhat closer to them, near the end of the book, there comes a chapter in which he joins their search not simply as philosopher and friend but because he shares their longings. Like a guide passing the boundary of the tract he knows, the older man becomes an explorer again, in his suggestion that the party question a very old man, "that we may know whether youth alone is to struggle with vexation, and whether any better hope remains for the latter part of life" (45).

For Imlac the questions are not purely speculative. Like Rasselas on so many previous occasions, he resists the old man's despondency. He even tries to place in the old man's mouth the words he himself needs to hear: "You may at least recreate yourself, said Imlac, with the recollection of an honourable and useful life, and enjoy the praise which all agree to give you." (This statement closely resembles a consolation of old age mentioned approvingly in the *Rambler* paper on "the climactericks of the mind": "At length weariness succeeds to labour, and the mind lies at ease in the contemplation of her own attainments. . . .")[25] In vain; the old man goes on to summarize "The Vanity of Human Wishes." The narrator for the first time in the book draws all the travelers together in a single reaction to an intellectual experience, commenting that the old man left "his audience not much elated with the hope of long life." This episode and the evening end with each of the young people's finding a characteristic defense against the old man's unpalatable words—Rasselas showing less resistance than the others.[26] Imlac, who has already bared his feelings, does not declaim; he, "who had no desire to see them depressed, smiled at the comforts which they could so readily procure to themselves, and remembered, that at the same age, he was equally confident of unmingled prosperity and equally fertile of consolatory expedients. He forbore to force upon them unwelcome knowledge, which time itself would too soon impress."

There are so many dichotomies in *Rasselas*, so many cases of things set either on the right hand or on the left, that one may come away from the book with a sobering sense of the unalterable discreteness, if not the downright contrariety, of everything and everyone. Yet to emphasize this point may be to miss another, equally important, that exists in a state of constant tension with it. For the contrariety of persons, at any rate, a contrariety which becomes emphatic midway through the book, does not sum up their relationship, nor does discreteness, important as it is. Had Pekuah not been restored to Nekayah, it is doubtful whether the princess would have recovered fully from her loss. Rasselas is a more stable, less expressive figure, never as close to despair as his sister can be and evidently immune to her degree of novelistic or romantic attachment. The book may seem without any sort of mediation between the terms of its dichotomies, yet that is too one-sided a view. There *is* mediation, or a measure of it; there is, in fact, a mediator, namely Imlac, who does something to join past, present, future, and other discrete entities, including Rasselas and himself. He does not fuse them; he cannot, nor can any mediator, at least in nature as the book presents it and as Johnson evidently saw it—at best concords not unisons. But through trial and error, error and trial, Imlac, with increasing cooperation from Rasselas, seems to guide his pupil and himself to a state of self-knowledge and mutual understanding that—the action of the tale implies—people do not find readymade even by traveling from China to Peru.

Back in chapter 13, Rasselas, upon coming to know Imlac, had "thought that even the *happy valley* might be endured with such a companion, and that, if they could range the world together, he should have nothing further to desire"; he expected too much, as usual, but—also as usual—there was something to be said for his expectations when tempered. Less ardently drawn to the "choice of eternity" than his sister, Rasselas is relatively at home in the world by the end of the tale, like Imlac; from a high level of generalization, Harold E. Pagliaro nicely describes the "illusion that Imlac-Rasselas exists eternally."[27] Unlike the exemplary personages of "The Vanity of Human Wishes," Rasselas and Imlac seem capable of making, in some degree, the happiness they "do not find." Moreover, through participating from near the beginning of the tale in what seems a heuristic, educational process for himself as well as Rasselas (who is not merely Imlac's pupil), the older man helps the prince acquire not a new sort of dependency but the capacity to make, independently, his own moderate contentment beyond the illusions of blind desire. Something is concluded, I think readers will agree, at the famously inconclusive conclusion of the tale: Rasselas' pressing need for Imlac's guidance.

The main characters readjust themselves, and so—very subtly, yet at one point very awkwardly—does the book as a whole. First the subtle readjustment: I have described the way in which the hortatory, declamatory, even accusatory tone which Imlac sometimes favors resembles that taken by the narrator at the outset of the tale. The narrator of *Rasselas* speaks as if omniscient in the fullest sense, not only as if privy to everything in the world, including the workings of the characters' minds, but also privy to what is finally right and wrong in the world. The narrator is omniscient in the conventional narrative sense of the word, and in the theological sense as well, an energetically judgmental narrator, a pantocratic overseer. As such, the condition of the narrator could be said to realize the deepest desires of Rasselas, perhaps of Imlac the poet as well. The Stoic of chapter 18 seemed at first, in Rasselas' enthusiastic words, "a man who can teach all that is necessary to be known, who, from the unshaken throne of rational fortitude, looks down on the scenes of life changing beneath him." Only such a person could accomplish the perfect choice of life, or perfectly legislate for mankind.

The narrator, however, is not so formidable as he seems to be; he seems more judgmental than he is because he is so much so at the beginning of the book, with his booming exordium, his so formal setting of the scene, his propensity for dry maxims ("But pleasures never can be so multiplied or continued, as not to leave much of life unemployed") and valetudinarian wisdom ("But in the decline of life shame and grief are of short duration"—4), and his ironies against Rasselas' gropings, in which the initial thunder may seem more forceful for being held in check. With his "but's" and his palpable assurance, he is more overbearing than Imlac in his emphasis on human limitations, particularly because he seems subject to none himself. He enjoys totalitarian freedom.

Until Imlac enters the book. With Imlac's awkward entrance, the narrator subtly changes his tone, even his ironies almost entirely vanishing. He settles down to being omniscient only in the conventional narrator's way, and the burden of judgment is assumed by Imlac, much as, in *Candide*, it is assumed by Martin. From then on in *Rasselas*, the narrator describes, Imlac prescribes. To the prince, Imlac's burdensome prescriptions must seem utterly, oppressively weighty, heavier than the reader finds them; after hearing the narrator's voice of doom, the acute reader cannot help but find less authority in Imlac's voice, no matter how imposing his declamation. The effect is that judgment itself becomes emphasized as limited and non-transcendent, a matter of exertion and expression by specific, limited persons under a mute sky, and any potential agreement now appears to be a matter not of unilateral submission, although it seems so to Rasselas and will continue to seem so for some time, but of common understanding insofar as it can be established and maintained.

The change in the posture of the narrator turns the universe of the book inside out: from a place where everyone seems required to know absolutely everything (as does Imlac's poet and, by implication, the poet Imlac), it changes to a place where everyone must learn to tolerate vast reaches of uncertainty. The change parallels Rasselas' experience of his quest, as he goes from imagining he need only choose the best of all possible lives, to wondering gloomily whether a suitable choice exists anywhere, to acknowledging and sustaining his desire and simultaneously expecting that it could not "be obtained" (49). The tale—generically resembling *Candide* in these various ways—with fallible, human Imlac unobtrusively taking over the judgmental function of the superhuman narrator, enacts for the reader the fall into reality and relativity that Rasselas endures.

In closing, I return to the question of Imlac's strange entrance— the awkward readjustment of the book. Unlike the unnamed sage of chapter 2 or the also unnamed would-be aviator of chapter 6, unlike Rasselas too, Imlac first turns up (in chapter 7, "The Prince Finds a Man of Learning") unheralded by any description of his character, as if he had already been introduced, and by name. New readers must commonly pause and glance back at the preceding chapters, like the woman rebuked by Tristram Shandy, to see if they have somehow overlooked his introduction. It seems, though, that he is already known to us in some manner, being the dramatic, diminished, earthbound surrogate of the sublime narrator, who remains above and out of the hearing of prince, mentor, and, in life, the grown-up reader, who here must reenact the experience of his own leap from the nest of absolutely valid guidance. "The transition from the protection of others to our own conduct," wrote Johnson in a letter which Paul Fussell has brought to bear upon *Rasselas*, "is a very awful point of human experience."[28]

"Highly episodic," superficially exotic, *Rasselas* nevertheless "refuses" to be fully an Oriental tale.[29] It remains a philosophical tale, however. Its plot is decidely not that of a *Bildungsroman* as later writers would develop the form. Yet the tale is much more than a staged philosophical disquisition. It is also, in large measure, a serious representation of human life, bringing realities to mind, memorably sensitive to its characters and their chain of mental becoming, perhaps unsurpassed by any fiction in its relatively full development of the theme of realistic psychological self-assessment.

PART III

*The Philosophical Tale,
Jane Austen, and the Novel*

CHAPTER TEN

Self-Assessment
in *Les Liaisons dangereuses*
and *Northanger Abbey*

The Honourable Mr. Listless. Tea, late dinners, and the French Revolution. I cannot exactly see the connection of ideas.
Mr. Flosky. I should be sorry if you could; I pity the man who can see the connection of his own ideas. Still more do I pity him, the connection of whose ideas any other person can see. Sir, the great evil is that there is too much commonplace light in our moral and political literature; and light is a great enemy to mystery, and mystery is a great friend to enthusiasm.

—*Nightmare Abbey*, ch. 6

*C*hoderlos de Laclos and Jane Austen make an odd pair, not noted for affinities, yet affinities there are, illuminating ones. Austen's very short novel *Lady Susan* bears a resemblance to Laclos' *Les Liaisons dangereuses* in being a collection of letters, even more so in presenting a major character who is shrewd and manipulative—the woman of Austen's title and Laclos' Mme de Merteuil.[1] Both novels too are very economical in construction, as the traditional epistolary novel is decidedly not. But in their almost schematic economy, these two novels resemble not only each other but also the philosophical tale, a resemblance fortified by the presence in both authors of the theme that, as I have argued in this book, makes the philosophical tale "philosophical": that is, the theme of the importance of realism of psychological self-assessment. Although *Lady Susan* is not so fully developed as a fiction to sustain this thesis, the rest of Austen's canon does so strongly, especially the early *Northanger Abbey*. That short novel may usefully be seen as a link between the philosophical tale and the novel in general as Austen shaped it: not a surprising link, I trust, given Austen's widely recognized admiration for Samuel Johnson. The resemblance of her fiction to Johnson's and her development of the theme of the philosophical tale, a development with a new and interesting twist, deserve study.[2] But first I should like to raise certain points and questions about *Les Liaisons dangereuses* from the perspective of the philosophical tale, in a manner introductory to Austen.

More than any other eighteenth-century fiction, *Les Liaisons* presents, in Mme de Merteuil, a character who recommends self-study as the key to everything one knows and is. The crucial section of the book is the long eighty-first letter, wherein—proceeding from a sympathy-inducing explanation of the disadvantages women suffer thanks to society's double standard, disadvantages also prominent in Austen, sharpening heroines' sensitivity—Mme de Merteuil explains her own mental development, so different from that of other women, who feel but do not think. Rather, she says, she has reflected deeply and strenuously, as a Lockean might and should, on the principles of her own thought, feelings, and behavior, transcending blind habit.

> Mais moi, qu'ai-je de commun avec ces femmes inconsidérées? quand m'avez-vous vue m'écarter des règles que je me suis prescrites, et manquer à mes principes? je dis mes principes, et je le dis à dessein: car ils ne sont pas, comme ceux des autres femmes, donnés au hasard, reçus sans examen et suivis par habitude, ils sont le fruit de mes profondes réflexions; je les ai créés."

> (But I, what do I have in common with these unthinking women? When have you seen me break the rules which I have set for myself, and fall short of my principles? I say my principles, and I say it advisedly, because they are not, like other women's, gained haphazardly. received without examination, and followed by rote; they are the offspring of my deep reflections; I have created them).

Her next statement is astonishing—"et je puis dire que je suis mon ouvrage ("and I can say that I am the product of my own workmanship").[3] It is the fulfillment of the grandest dream of historical self-assessment (and also foreshadows the project of Dr. Frankenstein), but the reader must be careful to understand it as it is qualified by the context. The rules of behavior and the fundamental principles from which they follow have been *created* only in the sense that they represent an original formulation on Mme de Merteuil's part in response to empirical analysis of herself and her society. Her *principes* therefore correspond to those that Montesquieu the sociologist had half-discovered, half-devised in attempting to determine what motivates a given people's peculiar laws and customs. Furthermore, the fact that the broader context is an epistolary novel alerts a reader to the possibility that the chief function of this letter may be rhetorical rather than descriptive; the effects on Mme de Merteuil's correspondent, rather than the true history of her own origins, may be her overriding concern.

Even regarded with appropriate wariness, however, the chain of events as traced in this letter constitutes an extraordinary performance, more remarkable still than the comparable autobiography at the beginning of Fielding's *Amelia* employed by Miss Matthews to seduce the hero. As Mme de Merteuil explains, before the onset of adult sexuality she became devoted to knowledge instead of love ("je ne désirais pas de jouir, je voulais savoir"—p. 201) and manifested a thorough detachment from herself: her wedding night, "dont on se fait pour l'ordinaire une idée si cruelle ou si douce, ne me présentait qu'une occasion d'expérience: douleur et plaisir, j'observai tout exactement, et ne voyais dans ces diverses sensations, que des faits à recueiller et à méditer" (p. 202; "of which one ordinarily forms an idea so harsh or so sweet, gave me only an opportunity to experiment; sorrow and pleasure, I observed all precisely, and saw in these diverse sensations only facts to collect and think about")—Locke in the boudoir, attentive to the experience of sensations, avoiding the customary association of ideas.

That the marriage has been arranged eases this detachment, which is not without its own gratifications. Taking to her studies, Mme de Merteuil finds ways of diversifying them among the peasants of her husband's estate, her search for "bonheur" (attended by no troubles of conscience) eventuating in the discovery of the principle that "l'amour que l'on nous vante comme la cause de nos plaisirs, n'en est au plus que le prétexte" (pp. 203, 202; "love, which people celebrate as the cause of our pleasures, is no more than the pretext for them"). She will devote herself to the pursuit of varied erotic pleasure and the subjection of lovers and society at large, always, however, with reference to analysis of her own mind and motives: "Descendue dans mon cœur, j'y ai étudié celui des autres" (p. 204; "Having descended into my heart, I there studied the hearts of others"). Satisfaction, for her, lies in knowing herself as well as the world, perfectly, as a result of the intricate, methodical process of study and experiment which she records here, the extent of which, in its various stages, I have only suggested. She professes herself not merely a heroine of worldliness but also a philosophical heroine; she exemplifies, in principle, a fulfillment of the quests of Gulliver, Usbek, Candide, and Rasselas. She claims to know herself in the generation and development of her ideas and feelings, their history here so originally written. She has created herself and finds herself—not good, of course, but good *at:* very satisfying.

If the dream of reason (as opposed to that of sleep) ever produced a monster, however, that monster is Mme de Merteuil—though she is simply the most horrid in the book's society of horrors. What is more, the book insinuates a monstrous love story, that of Mme de Merteuil and the Vicomte de Valmont, her almost as fascinating counterpart in the successful erotic manipulation and destruction of others. Valmont is ultimately defeated by that love affair. In order to prove his strength to himself when challenged by Mme de Merteuil, he sacrifices a comparatively good and innocent woman he has come to care for against his rakish principles and his triangular love and self-love.

But having won this battle, Mme de Merteuil quickly loses all. Valmont's last deed is to reveal her correspondence to the world, which ostracizes her. And that is not all: in rapid succession, Mme de Merteuil disastrously loses a legal suit and then, as if this were Thebes in the old days, sees her beauty succumb to smallpox. Overkill, to be sure. Mme de Merteuil's last letter (159) is a ringing threat of revenge upon Valmont. After that, she is only spoken about, almost like Clarissa when she makes her more ceremonious exit; so we do not know, from Mme de Merteuil, what her final reflections on it all are. The resolution of her story is more external than the book had been up to that point, the ending not economical in events but riddled with superfluity. Indeed, so gratuitous is two-thirds of the punishment, or all of it (the society from which she is banished is such that exile has overtones of blessing), that the reader may find himself more sympathetic to Mme de Merteuil, at the end and beyond, than might have been the case. There was, after all, something positive about her vaunted self-knowledge—so probing, so heroic in some respects, and so understandable, given those initial, severe disadvantages.

The resolution of the plot suggests, indeed, that Laclos mis-understood the drive of his own book, though one ventures that possible opinion with some hesitation since there is so much evidence of the author's consummate understanding. Perhaps, given the book's virtually incomparable efflorescence of evil, he wanted to make sure his readers' need for poetic justice was amply satisfied. But I need not pursue this issue, well covered by Laclos' modern critics.[4] It is more appropriate here to note that grounds for a satisfactory, coherent, and economical resolution, in keeping with the tale-like clarity of direction Laclos had brought to the epistolary novel, are laid very well in the letter to which I have called special attention. For as Mme de Merteuil boasts of her powers in the eighty-first letter, addressed to Valmont, she fatally reveals her weakness, without recognizing that she is doing so. Her safety, she declares, depends upon her careful practice of never writing letters that may be used in evidence against her (pp. 200, 204), and upon her binding those to whom she confides by the most secure ties of confidentiality: her correspondents' own fears of exposure in turn. This she has done with her maidservant as well as Valmont (p. 206). With Valmont she enjoys a thrilling intimacy of a sort whereby they make love to each other by sharing details of their false intimacy with third parties.

It never occurs to Mme de Merteuil that Valmont, out of love for one of those parties, and anger—and perhaps having an off day with the duelling sword—would suddenly spring himself, as he does, into both eternity and the divulgence of her secrets. Valmont calls forth the autobiographical letter with the supercilious warning "l'esprit ne suffit pas" (p. 194; "the mind by itself is not enough"). Yet the adequacy of careful calculation, in the context of the book, is not so patent. For in the midst of Mme de Merteuil's singularly impressive self-analysis, in that eighty-first letter, she is heedless of the satisfaction she takes in having a Valmont to confide in, to admire her if not to love her. The woman's wondrous intelligence does not suffice, because she has deluded herself into belief in her own complete self-sufficiency—while belying it in correspondence. There the reader senses a combination of ideas, a dangerous *liaison des idées* in Condillac's Lockean terminology, which she has failed to examine. In the solitude she cannot tolerate the book places her at last. But this plight goes unnoticed by those still vocal in the society, who remark instead the trivializing impositions of what might be taken as cosmic retribution.

Her custom-tailored hell might have been foreseen and avoided by Mme de Merteuil had she known herself as profoundly as she says she does. Her central perception about herself is revealed in that assertion about love, only a pretext for pleasure. The perception occurs after her husband has removed her from Parisian society for a time; in the country, like one of Rousseau's characters, she comes to her version of wisdom. Yet what the actual cause of pleasure in her view is, she does not say. The reader imagines her to think it sensuality or, more likely, power—a combination of the two; her fuzziness about her deepest motives suggests a comparable lack of focus in her largest purposes.

With her husband's death she returns to the country, to complete her studies. She reads the novelists, the philosophers, the moralists, not to know herself but to know what appearances to preserve in society as camouflage for her machinations (pp. 202–03). In such a removal from Paris to the country she may seem to be proceeding from the state of society to the state of nature: returning to a locus of elemental human nature so as to get true bearings, like those sought by Montesquieu's Usbek—seeking to fathom the essentials of the human condition rather than suffer the impression of society's prejudices. Yet she only parodies such a process, much as she may think otherwise. Inequality, which she declaims

against at the beginning of the autobiographical letter, is too much
her preoccupation, even her obsession. The selfish duplicity of society that Rousseau depicted as the final stage of evolution in the
second *Discours* has formed her fundamentally;[5] *it* has created her,
her desires, her imagination. Her claim to have assessed herself,
like Gulliver's, emphasizes the fact that she has not, though Swift
makes Gulliver's failure in precisely this respect more salient than
Laclos makes Mme de Merteuil's.

Among reasons why Laclos's novel is fine, however, is the
historic criticism it implies of the unconcern about introspection
central to the novel of worldliness. And the English novel does not
go unscathed either: the woman whom Valmont, Lovelace-like,
destroys, like Clarissa prefers some things to truth, having more
vanity than she cares to know. Before Valmont succeeds in his plot
to make her "une nouvelle Clarisse" (p. 286), she gives evidence of
having read Richardson's novel, but only the first volume (p. 279).

Still more than Laclos, Austen boldly brings the genre of the
novel into close juxtaposition with that of the tale and its characteristic theme of realism of psychological self-assessment, doing so
in several novels, with distinctly imaginative results. It has not been
recognized how much her novels are formed by the philosophical
tale. The best evidence for this provenance, my main example in
the pages that follow, is *Northanger Abbey*, a sister of *Rasselas* and
Candide in form, meaning, and conceptual framework: that of eighteenth-century psychology. Although *Northanger Abbey's* exact historical place in the canon is open to some dispute, the book is generally held to be the first of the extant novels to have been completed.
It was sold to a publisher in 1803 but not published, and was later
revised, evidently in a minor way; publication together with *Persuasion* occurred in 1817, after Austen's death.[6]

There is a sense, then, in which *Northanger Abbey* historically
encapsulates the Austen canon, alpha and—with *Persuasion*—omega.
In form and theme *Northanger Abbey* and *Persuasion* do so as well,
as I argue here and in my final chapter, with some attention to
Mansfield Park. It is in these three novels that the formal and thematic matters characteristic of the philosophical tale are most im-

portant. They are less prominent in Austen's other three full-size novels, which bear a sharper resemblance to the eighteenth-century novel; my reasons for saying this I shall give in a moment, briefly. Before straying too far from Laclos, I should explain that Austen's greater boldness lies in her peculiar modification of the emphasis of the philosophical tale, so as to take into account exactly what Mme de Merteuil cannot: human incompleteness, vulnerability, and dependency—all potential obstacles to self-love—recognized as compatible with strength and empirical insight. The "female" dis-advantages that Mme de Merteuil confronts by attempted domi-nation of others are in one sense human disadvantages threatening everyone, though historically more adverse to women. Austen re-peatedly shows this by revealing most of her heroes, at the end of the novels in which they figure, to be much less self-assured than they had appeared. I shall return to this special quality of Austen's fiction.

I cannot study all her novels here. To emphasize that point I advisedly give *Sense and Sensibility*, *Pride and Prejudice*, and *Emma* the shortest possible shrift. They differ significantly from the oth-ers, to some extent and in varying degree—resembling the eight-eenth-century novel more, the tale less—especially because, like *Tom Jones*, when Squire Western is introduced to play the part of Sophia's desires, these three novels tend to allegorize the heroine's mental conflict instead of locating it exclusively within her mind. Putting the matter a little too bluntly (but these novels are not my subject): the heroes Darcy and Knightley represent their heroines' faculty of judgment, in *Pride and Prejudice* and *Emma*, respectively, while in *Sense and Sensibility* we have, from this point of view, a heroine representing that faculty, Elinor, and a sister, Marianne, to bring out Elinor's feelings. In all three of these novels, more-over—a point following from the last—the resolution of the plot depends heavily on a revelation or several to set an erring heroine straight, comparatively external revelations—news unexpected by the heroine. An attractive young man is revealed to be a bounder, or to be an eligible suitor.[7]

In *Northanger Abbey*, *Mansfield Park*, and *Persuasion* on the other hand, though there are elements of plot and character comparable to these, they are subtly but distinctly, significantly, superfluous. The emphasis, shifted, is on the heroine's resources for assessment, of self and other, that make external revelations less crucial, as I seek to prove in the following pages. This necessarily cryptic paragraph will make more sense when I have finished the chapter, and I ask readers, in the meantime, to attend to the applicability of my argument to the works I write about, rather than those I pass over. Emma's indirectly rendered exclamation "What blindness, what madness, had led her on!"[8] is directly to the point; had the statement ended in a question mark, or had her novel as a whole implied interest in such a question, she would be important to this chapter.

Realism of psychological self-assessment is a concept sufficiently uncommon to warrant reiterated explanation; I have explained it most pointedly when concluding chapter 4. What it resembles but is not is what C. S. Lewis defines as "the hardness— at least the firmness—of Jane Austen's thought" whereby "great abstract nouns of the classical English moralists are unblushingly and uncompromisingly used; *good sense, courage, contentment, fortitude,* 'some duty neglected, some failing indulged,' *impropriety, indelicacy, generous candour, blamable distrust, just humiliation, vanity, folly, ignorance, reason.* These are the concepts by which Jane Austen grasps the world. In her we still breathe the air of the *Rambler* and *Idler.* All is hard, clear, definable; by some modern standards, even naïvely so."[9]

This list of terms is too exclusively moral, really moralistic; nearly all denote conceptions of religious, civil, and social virtue, and one element in the air of the *Rambler*, the oxygen one may think, is ignored. Other terms, deriving from the natural history of the mind as established by seventeenth- and eighteenth-century philosophers, should be added to the list and should perhaps come first. They are *idea* and *image, associations, understanding, memory, conscious, development, natural, motives, reflection, observation, voluntary delusion, habit* (especially habits *of thought*), *imposition* (especially, *on oneself*), *prejudice* (note its psychological shading, as contrasted to the morality of *pride*), *preconception, insanity* (especially through perversion of *imagination,* or poor *government* of it, not necessarily the same as repression), and the series *age, situation, and probable habits of life.* These terms indicate the presence in Austen's fiction of a stratum of discourse from empirical psychology. The psychology is not irreconcilable with the morality; to the extent that the psychology is Johnsonian, however, it can be more fundamental.[10] It is certainly distinct from the morality. As a reference point for study of Austen's fiction it has the advantage of requiring no apology for any real or apparent naivety.

The early pages of *Northanger Abbey* develop as if Austen had just reread *Rambler* 4, so much are they pointed against the expectations of readers of romantic novels. The narrator introduces the main character, Catherine Morland as—if there can be such a thing— singularly ordinary, not as someone to be idealized at all.[11] There is a Gulliverian plainness about Catherine: a middle child in a family with ten children, born in the middle of England, at fifteen "almost pretty," at seventeen still unnoticed by any nobleman or lesser hero.[12] As in the opening pages of *Candide* and *Rasselas*, the narrator is incomparably more prominent and forceful than the main character and keeps the reader as well as the heroine at a definite distance, with a multitude of sly remarks. The narrator, freely discursive, will even digress into essayistic, arch commentary, such as that on the propriety of a young woman's feeling love before the man in question has declared himself, or that on the merits of the novel as a form, versus the more respectable and duller *Spectator* (1.3.29–30; 1.5.37–38). The narrator, moreover, has the air of authority, of virtually absolute authority, that I have noticed in the narrators of Voltaire and Johnson: being very positive, often with the special force of irony, against the follies of the world, of the reader, and of most or all of the characters. The very naive Catherine, the narrator repeatedly calls a "heroine," emphasizing the loose fit of any such mantle upon her. The narrator's irony, however, may also hang loosely about Catherine, for she gives few signs of any heroic aspirations.

And as in the philosophical tale, the main character is vulnerable to preconceptions, which the tale will disabuse her of; and the psychological basis of those preconceptions, and the need for realism of self-analysis, will be given prominence in the process.

The most striking and best known instance of preconception on Catherine's part, indicated in the book's title, is her imposing Gothic mystery on Northanger Abbey and conferring Gothic guilt on the Abbey's proprietor, General Tilney. (She has earlier begun to take quixotic delight in Gothic novels.) Brought to the Abbey with the General's daughter, Eleanor, and his son Henry, both of whom Catherine dearly loves, she sees the place as supernaturally threatening. An "immense heavy" old chest in her Abbey room fascinates her, but Catherine is still more impressed, with embarrassment, when Eleanor unexpectedly enters just as the heroine has succeeded in opening it (to find a mere counterpane inside). A blushing Catherine forms "wise resolutions" (2.6.163–65). Yet this mortifying episode is followed almost immediately by another quite like it: her discovery in the same room of a mysterious-seeming black cabinet which, until Catherine has opened it, gives her no rest, though all it contains is tradesmen's bills. Again, shame: "She felt humbled to the dust. Could not the adventure of the chest have taught her wisdom? . . . How could she have so imposed on herself?" Just as with associations in Locke, Catherine's ideas prove extremely resistant to being detached from each other, and the affliction continues, driving her "away as soon as possible from a room in which her conduct produced such unpleasant reflections" (2.7.173). This aversion is Lockean too, like the case Locke describes of the man repelled by the idea of the physician who had hurt him in the process of curing him.[13] Soon Catherine comes to regard the strange, unpleasing General as a veritable Montoni (the gruesome villain of Ann Radcliffe's Gothic novel *The Mysteries of Udolpho*), who has doubtless murdered his wife or sealed her up in some forgotten chamber.

What is said of Arabella, the "Female Quixote" described in Charlotte Lennox's novel of that title (1752), suits Catherine's case up to a point. The grand figures of seventeenth-century French romances haunt, intoxicate Arabella in precisely the Lockean way: "Heroism, romantick Heroism, was deeply rooted in her Heart; it was her Habit of thinking, a Principle imbib'd from Education. She could not separate her Ideas of Glory, Virtue, Courage, Generosity, and Honour, from the false Representations of them in the Actions of *Oroondates, Juba, Artaxerxes*, and the rest of the imaginary Heroes."[14]

Catherine, like Arabella, is a victim of association, and it is only when Catherine is discovered, by her beloved, respected Henry, to harbor the most offensive thoughts about his father—this discovery the worst shock of her life—that she is snapped out of her delusive habits and traces them to some of their historical causes: ". . . It had been all a voluntary, self-created delusion, each trifling circumstance receiving importance from an imagination resolved on alarm, and every thing forced to bend to one purpose by a mind which, before she entered the Abbey, had been craving to be frightened. She remembered with what feelings she had prepared for a knowledge of Northanger. She saw that the infatuation had been created, the mischief settled long before her quitting Bath, and it seemed as if the whole might be traced to the influence of that sort of reading which she had there indulged" (2.10.199–200). These sentences are strikingly of a piece with eighteenth-century psychology, especially the reference to "voluntary . . . delusion"—a Lockean concept and term that, as Paul Alkon observes, is central to Johnson's thought.[15] We should not underestimate Catherine's intelligence—a matter to which I shall return. Her reflections on her thinking are actually more penetrating than the often-quoted passage in which Henry summons her to reason by reminding her of what is probable in Christian England, though he concludes by asking "Dearest Miss Morland, what ideas have you been admitting?" (2.9.198).

The Lockean note sounds again later when Catherine reflects on the way the Abbey has changed its character in her eyes, "no more to her now than any other house. The painful remembrance of the folly it had helped to nourish and perfect, was the only emotion which could spring from a consideration of the building. What a revolution in her ideas!" (2.11.212). The broad relevance to Austen's canon of such practical concern with the relations of ideas is suggested by Mary Lascelles when, seeking to define the special comedy of the novels, she generalizes about its involving "the interaction of idiosyncrasy and life" and its affecting all the characters, the wise as well as the foolish, all "peering through mists of prejudice": "Indeed, I do not think it too much to say that *counterfeit connexion* symbolizes this distinctive quality . . ."[16] The italics are mine, calling attention to a Lockean concept in non-Lockean terminology, here deftly recognized as fundamental to Austen and her characters. It may be said in addition that, like Johnson and other of Locke's successors in psychology, Austen probes more deeply than Locke into the perilous question of how a delusive association of ideas may be voluntary.

Lennox's female Quixote is finally (at very long last) liberated from her associations when a clergyman, in debate with her—the chapter has sometimes been thought to have been written by Johnson—forces her to compare the morals of her bloodthirsty and licentious heroes and heroines with those that she herself holds. That is, in the manner of an eighteenth-century comic novel, the clergyman acts as the heroine's critical, judging faculty, and in response fanciful Arabella must repudiate her idols and with them her associations; her heroes have been murderers, her heroines . . . ("*Arabella's* Blushes now hinder'd him from proceeding as he had intended").[17] Henry Tilney similarly asks Catherine to compare her perception of the General with her estimation of what degree of villainy one is likely to find in central England. As in the case of Arabella, Catherine is not asked by Henry to address the deeper question of what motivated the delusive association of ideas in the first place. But later, in different circumstances less directly troubling to Catherine, he does pose this sort of question. When Catherine expresses puzzlement about her feelings toward her friend Isabella Thorpe, who in throwing over Catherine's brother has disappointed and grieved her—puzzlement that she is not more offended than she feels—Henry invites her to reflect more deeply on her motives: "Such feelings ought to be investigated, that they may know themselves" (2.10.207).

Henry's *not* asking Catherine to investigate her feelings about the General is a sign of Austen's injecting into the novel that thematic realism of self-assessment which I have derived from the philosophical tale. The tales constantly confront the main character with other characters to assess, as does the novel, but the tales typically—and Austen—also simultaneously exploit the opportunities for self-assessment afforded by every encounter. Austen's secondary characters, in *Northanger Abbey* and elsewhere, are invariably significant for resemblances to and differences from the main characters. Thus the supporting characters have a rhetorical function, defining the characteristics of the heroine in the reader's eye. But the secondary characters—everyone other than the heroine, in fact—may serve an additional, distinct purpose in Austen: they may be employed also by the heroine herself, as touchstones to self-knowledge, the more so as the heroine grows stronger. (A consequence is that the concept of the association of ideas regains some of its initial, Lockean metaphorical meaning, for ideas are embodied by characters, and one aspect of the question is whether associations between characters are natural and right or not; to the heroine the search for truly amiable others is an aspect of the quest for self-knowledge and self-love worth having.) More handicapped by naivety than most of Austen's leading women, Catherine slowly, reluctantly learns to assess herself while assessing others, and the additional elements of the novel provide appropriate orchestral accompaniment. The overall pattern, entailing the heroine, the narrator, and the reader, is that of the philosophical tale as I have described it with regard to *Rasselas* and *Candide*.

For approximately the first half of the novel, before Catherine goes to the Abbey—and except for her experience of some very pleasant, refined moments with Henry and Eleanor—Catherine is besieged by grotesques: the crudely selfish Isabella Thorpe (a character "emptied and flattened"),[18] who befriends Catherine once she arrives in Bath, and the still cruder John, Isabella's brother. The Thorpes regularly, and even forcibly, keep Catherine away from the Tilneys. John especially is such a blowhard that his place in a novel, rather than in a non-realistic philosophical tale, is questionable, while Isabella could almost stand in for Cunégonde, so energetic, duplicitous, and transparent are her professions and rationalizations, to the reader if not to Catherine—who is pleased when her brother James becomes engaged to Isabella, and who is also surprised by this event, though James has broadly signaled his feelings. Catherine would have noticed, the narrator says, "had she been more expert in the developement of other people's feelings, and less simply engrossed by her own" (1.7.45).

The narrator, we have seen, is a forceful presence; but chiefly in the first half of the book, while Catherine is learning to distrust and resist the Thorpes, if not to understand them. Yet the narrator's satirical reflections spare the Tilneys, not surprisingly, since Henry happens to be the person in the book whose shrewd, bantering remarks most resemble those of the narrator. The inexperienced Catherine is repeatedly, ironically called a "heroine" by the narrator, each time at the expense of Catherine's stature as anything even remotely deserving that (in this book sentimental) honorific. In Book 1, chapter 8, for example, having been asked to dance by John Thorpe, who keeps her waiting among the wallflowers, Catherine must share "with the scores of other young ladies still sitting down all the discredit of wanting a partner. To be disgraced in the eye of the world, to wear the appearance of infamy while her heart is all purity, her actions all innocence, and the misconduct of another the true source of her debasement, is one of those circumstances which peculiarly belong to the heroine's life . . ." (1.8.53).

However, as General Tilney begins to be more prominent as a character, and as a puzzle, the narrator's tone and tenor change. As in *Candide* and *Rasselas* at a certain point, the narrator who had presided so judgmentally over the text becomes less conspicuous. The main character grows in awareness while the narrator points out less and less. Moreover, just as Imlac and Martin take the place of the narrator in those philosophical tales—that is, take over the narrator's function as commentator and judge—so too does a character here, the person to whom the heroine is most attracted in a manner resembling (though significantly not the same as) Rasselas' being drawn to Imlac, Candide to Martin. The character in question, the chosen mentor, is as I have already suggested Henry Tilney. Mary Lascelles succinctly notes this development: ". . . The authoress hands over to the newly arrived hero her own office of interpreter: it is he, from now on, who will remind Catherine of her duties as heroine, and point the difference between her situation as it should develop under the laws of fiction, and as it is actually developing." The device, however, is not so pronounced a "piece of ingenuity"[19] as it is made out to be, since it had been exploited by Voltaire and Johnson.

There is even, I believe, a slight wavering in the text, a juggling of the baton, as the transition occurs, though not so noticeable as the omission from *Rasselas* of an introduction for Imlac. While Catherine, Henry,. and Eleanor are chatting about literature and other topics in Book 1, chapter 14—the first considerable conversation they have had the chance to enjoy—Catherine suddenly feels shame at her ignorance of the picturesque, and the narrator enlarges on the pointlessness of her shame, proceeding to wry comments not only on how endearing ignorance can be to the vanity of would-be instructors but also on the relative merits of ignorance versus imbecility in women (1.14.110–11). This passage is the last excursus by the narrator for a hundred pages, and with very minor modification it could have been placed in the mouth of Henry, who will be the conversational, opinionated speaker through the pages to come, and who, in this chapter, holds forth in similarly ironical strains, teasingly, to the two young women. Here Henry supersedes the narrator; we will find Henry, not the narrator, saying of the discredited Isabella Thorpe, "—Open, candid, artless, guileless, with affections strong but simple, forming no pretensions, and knowing no disguise" (2.10.206)—heroine-ing her with a vengeance. Upon the narrator's retirement as commentator, the reader must try to understand General Tilney with only the help afforded Catherine by Henry. As in *Rasselas* and *Candide*, however, the instruction rendered to one character by another is not so full and authoritative as the commentary of a narrator. Henry, even Henry, like Imlac or Martin, must be taken with a grain of salt, or must be supplemented somehow.

To be sure, Henry is wise and good, like Imlac particularly, and he can be instructive, in his bantering way as well as in those more sober tones subsequent to his discovery of Catherine's suspicions against the General. There occurs an excellent instance of Henry's wisdom when Catherine says Henry's brother Frederick wants to dance with Isabella (now engaged to James) only because he does not wish her to have to sit by the wall.

Henry smiled, and said, "How very little trouble it can give you to understand the motive of other people's actions."

"Why?—What do you mean?"

"With you, it is not, How is such a one likely to be influenced? What is the inducement most likely to act upon such a person's feelings, age, situation, and probable habits of life considered?—but, how should *I* be influenced, what would be *my* inducement in acting so and so?"

(2.1.132)

It is sufficiently time-honored wisdom. In *Spectator* 399 Addison had observed, "A wise Man will suspect those Actions to which he is directed by something besides Reason, and always apprehend some concealed Evil in every Resolution that is of a disputable Nature, when it is conformable to his particular Temper, his Age, or Way of Life, or when it favours his Pleasure or his Profit."[20]

Henry's comments recall the narrator's early remark that Catherine is inexpert "in the developement of other people's feelings." When Catherine has to try to understand General Tilney, as she must toward the middle of the book and afterward, she is up against a harder case than that presented by the young Thorpes, since he does not advertise his motives to the extent they do and since there is a gap of years, as well as of ignorance on Catherine's part, separating him from her mind. In their repeated meetings before the General abruptly and inexplicably turns Catherine out of the Abbey, he proves extremely attentive and courteous to her; yet Catherine notices that his presence casts a pall over his children. The moments when they are together are moments of strain. It is the chasm between these facts that Catherine later tries to bridge with her Gothic fantasy.[21] Beforehand, "It puzzled her to account for all this. It could not be General Tilney's fault. That he was perfectly agreeable and good-natured, and altogether a very charming man, did not admit of a doubt, for he was tall and handsome, and Henry's father" (2.1.129). The explanation reads like a textbook account of the forming of false associations, and recalls the comedy of another young person's motives for admiring the philosopher of Thunder-ten-tronckh: "Candide écoutait attentivement, et croyait innocemment; car il trouvait mademoiselle Cunégonde extrêmement belle . . ."

("Candide listened closely and believed innocently, for he thought Mlle Cunégonde quite beautiful . . .").[22]

It turns out the General had been under the impression that Catherine was rich, thus in his eyes a match worth cultivating for Henry. (Resembling Gulliver the potential naval hero of Lilliput, Catherine does not think to wonder why the General is being so very cordial.) When the General learns the truth of her modest means, he rages not at his own error but at poor Catherine—mystifying her, because in some respects she is as "ignorant and uninformed" as the narrator had said when beginning the second chapter of the novel; particularly because she is ignorant in the way Henry specifies with his reference to feelings, "age, situation, and probable habits of life considered." Another, quite formal way of diagnosing this weakness would be to say that Catherine has no genetic theory of natural mental development such as Montesquieu described in the "Essai sur les causes qui peuvent affecter les esprits & les caractères" or, to cite an example nearer Jane Austen, such as Johnson pursues in *Rambler* 151, on "the climactericks of the mind."[23] Katrin Ristkok Burlin draws attention to that *Rambler* essay, accounting for Catherine's youthful love of novelty.[24] It is a trait that some reading in Johnson might have made Catherine conscious of in herself. Henry is a little too generous when he says that Catherine always imagines how *she* might be influenced, what inducements she would have to act in a certain way; she at first does so only spontaneously and limitedly, without natural-historical perspective on herself of the kind that Johnson labored to make available. But Catherine's ignorance in this respect is brought out more clearly with regard to her imaginings about the General.

It cannot occur to her that a man who recurrently shows himself anxious to impress her with an idea of his wealth (his estate, his china) might be concerned about hers—particularly at his age— even though, as nearby as the *Rambler* essay, she might have learned that in middle years a person's attention is "transferred from pleasure to interest" and that "Nothing now dances before the eyes but wealth and power" (p. 41). The General, in fact, is a counterpart of Catherine, so inclined to voluntary delusion that he takes the word of that "rattle" John Thorpe about Catherine's supposed fortune and persists in his opinion without other evidence. As Johnson had written, in later life "the opinions are settled, and the avenues of apprehension shut against any new intelligence." So stiff in ill-formed opinion is the General that he has a tantrum upon the discovery of his error and peremptorily sends Catherine away; to an old man, Johnson adds, "nothing is . . . so odious as opposition" (p. 40). The eighteenth-century psychologist, adapting the theme of the ages of man, could write a useful natural history of the mind, a guide to be employed with discretion as a supplement to the new shrewdness about connections of ideas in the individual's history. General Tilney does not have to be the typical corrupt old man, of course; if he is not to be, however, this stereotype is something he must set about recognizing and avoiding. Comparably, placing him in the ages scheme would not be the same for Catherine as really knowing him, but it would get her started, sensibly. Here the studiously unphilosophical nature of Catherine's reading actually handicaps her; the narrator's disparagement of her ignorance proves an amusing comment with more meaning than at first appears.

Concluding *The Rise of the Novel*, Ian Watt suggests that the "full maturity" of the novel as a genre could perhaps come only when a reconciliation had been achieved between the different methods of Richardson and Fielding—between, respectively, "realism of presentation and realism of assessment, of the internal and of the external approaches to character"—a reconciliation Watt discerns in Austen.[25] Extending Watt's insight, Ronald Paulson says that "The important element in Austen's amalgam . . . is the theme of self-discovery, . . . best seen in her use of point of view." Paulson continues:

> Austen begins with the Fielding narrator and a character and then brings the two points of view together. Fielding never allows this (except perhaps in *Amelia*). In his novels the omniscient narrator and the characters are always radically separate, and so the self-discovery is only in the reader or, in a sense, in the narrator—the only person in the fiction who, by the end, knows the whole truth. Neither Clarissa nor Tom makes as definitive a discovery about himself as the reader's. But in *Pride and Prejudice*, where the narrator's aware-

ness is in general close to the protagonist's, the protagonist comes to self-knowledge: the crucial truth is in a character's realization instead of the reader's. When Elizabeth, after reading Darcy's letter, recognizes the truth about the character of Darcy and Wickham, she sees the truth about herself: "till this moment," she cries, "I never knew myself."[26]

Elsewhere, Paulson writes probingly about Fielding's playing his characters against stereotypes, so as to define the characters but also to intensify readers' feelings that the characters are real, for the stereotypes finally do not account for the characters. Joseph Andrews in one sense resembles the victim in the parable of the Good Samaritan, in other senses recalls Telemachus, Hector, and Achilles. The comparisons illustrate Joseph's character; his character, however, transcends any and all of those figures, being defined against them as well as by them.[27]

In *Northanger Abbey* and the novels I have said resemble it, Austen attributes a technique of this kind not simply, in rhetorical fashion, to the narrator but to the heroine. Avrom Fleishman calls attention to the way Catherine Morland, after discovering the true motives of the General, with new sophistication "employs her reading to provide a metaphoric construct, rather than a literal description, of his behavior: 'Catherine, at any rate, heard enough to feel that, in suspecting General Tilney of either murdering or shutting up his wife, she had scarcely sinned against his character, or magnified his cruelty.'" Fleishman explains, "When the heroine becomes aware that a literary convention does not predict or determine the behavior of those to whom it superficially applies—and yet that it may be taken as a useful metaphoric construct by which to shape one's response to them, as Catherine does with regard to General Tilney—she has arrived at a peak of cultural self-consciousness, in which one both sees through the artificiality of all cultural symbols and yet remains an active and skillful participant in their processes."[28] In other words, she has not ceased to think figuratively, to associate ideas; but now, emulating Rasselas, she has begun to be aware of her associating them. *Northanger Abbey* is a tale more than it is a novel; befitting the book's status as a philosophical tale, it emphasizes the combination and association of ideas. Locke, though he might bemoan the limitations of Catherine's reading, would smile approvingly at her new ability to bring critical comparison to bear upon the resemblances and differences between her initial and later ideas of that "substance" General Tilney, between early association and subsequent, right connection. The combination of the heroine's and the narrator's demonstrating the indispensability as well as the danger of preconception is directly in the tradition of *Rasselas*.

But, just as importantly, the matter of General Tilney raises questions about the wisdom of Catherine's mentor, not merely about the value of her Gothic maxims. On the subject of his father—the most crucial subject—Henry is most limited, leaving Catherine's judgment on its own. Hence it is the revelations Catherine comes to, rather than those which Henry provides, that are most important in the book. The subject actually in play when Henry delivers his wise comment about the ages of man is whether his brother Frederick can be paying court to a woman engaged to someone else—Frederick, who is old enough and rich enough to have been married for some years yet remains a handsome bachelor and (worse) an army officer. The idealized Henry "must know best" (2.4.153). But when it comes to informing Catherine about the deficiencies of his brother's moral character, not to mention his father's failings, Henry can be thoroughly reticent and even evasive—successfully of course with Catherine.[29] And though his evasiveness may be explained as the filial and fraternal duty of a good man, even the charity and discretion of a clergyman, which Henry is, such explanation does not persuade, for—at least in the more important case of his attitude toward his father—Henry clearly stands in awe and fear of the irascible older man. The "filial disobedience" committed by Henry in the long run, when he declares to the General an intention of seeking Catherine's hand, is filial in only the most oppressive sense of the term. As the narrator summarizes Henry's account of that confrontation,

> The conversation between them at Northanger had been of the most unfriendly kind. Henry's indignation on hearing how Catherine had been treated, on comprehending his father's views, and being ordered to acquiesce in them, had been open and bold. The General,

accustomed on every ordinary occasion to give the law in his family, prepared for no reluctance but of feeling, no opposing desire that should dare to clothe itself in words, could ill brook the opposition of his son, steady as the sanction of reason and the dictate of conscience could make it. But, in such a cause, his anger, though it must shock, could not intimidate Henry, who was sustained in his purpose by a conviction of its justice. He felt himself bound as much in honour as in affection to Miss Morland, and believing that heart to be his own which he had been directed to gain, no unworthy retraction of a tacit consent, no reversing decree of unjustifiable anger, could shake his fidelity, or influence the resolutions it prompted.

(2.15.247)

Henry publicly rests his case for marrying Catherine on the rigorist, selfless claims of reason, conscience, justice, and the precedent of his father's encouragement. His feelings—including what the eighteenth century would call self-love in the philosophical sense, his regard for his own well-being and happiness—really do not enter into account; the General does not expect that they would, and he is right. A reader wonders whether Henry, if his feelings for Catherine were the only issue, would himself have thought them significant enough to dare clothe them in words. It is not only heroines who cannot bring themselves to be forthright about what they want. (The elder Tilney's being a general may momentarily remind us of Voltaire's observation that the severe Great Chain of Being appeals to those who enjoy contemplating the ecclesiastical hierarchy.) From this point of view, the clergyman son whom Catherine idealizes appears less strong and wise, and it appears that his talent for pleasing chat can conceal as well as ornament him.[30]

Young Henry and younger Catherine will marry and move to Henry's parsonage, "within twenty miles of the wicked General's Abbey" (as Darrel Mansell remarks),[31] where they can no doubt look forward to years of visiting back and forth with the quotidian monster until an apoplexy someday carries him off. I hope I will not seem tendentious if I suggest that, this considered, the bower to which Henry and Catherine repair has subtle overtones of Candide's tarnished little compound near Constantinople. *Northanger Abbey* does nothing to diminish a reader's sense of the General's unlikeableness, while the narrator—who in the last few chapters becomes prominent again, with reason—bustles in to tell us that hero and heroine are now "hastening together to perfect felicity" and in the same paragraph conveys the General's "forgiveness" of his son, the blessing being permission "to be a fool if he liked it!" (2.16.250). "To begin perfect happiness at the respective ages of twenty-six and eighteen, is to do pretty well," the narrator's last sentence opens; to see the conclusion of the book as initiating "perfect happiness" is of course to see it in a long authorial perspective, softening some realities and calling attention to that softening. It is a final irony at the expense of extreme romance expectations. The world of *Northanger Abbey*, like that of philosophical tales, at best permits only concords, not unisons, and endings that imply both happiness and unhappiness afterward. Austen's book mingles elements of formal, novelistic realism with the pattern of the tale, but closes firmly in the key of the latter.

Like Imlac, Henry is wise, helpful, and imperfect. Like Rasselas, however, imperfect Catherine is abler than she may appear. Pages before Henry advises her to investigate her feelings, she has demonstrated a relatively independent capacity to imagine that recourse and act on it, regarding her associations about the General. Reviewing the subject after her painful confrontation with Henry, Catherine does not rest content with his mild inquiries into whether it is probable that an Englishman could be so utterly evil as she has imagined his father to be. She goes beyond Henry's shocked question about "what ideas" she "had been admitting." His being shocked she can hardly bear (". . . Could he ever forgive it?"— 2.10.199). It is true that she reflects on the confrontation during an evening when Henry behaves very kindly toward her; his solicitude greatly helps her come to terms with herself. But his assistance should not distract us from appreciating the degree of independent insight marking her own efforts. The scene of her reflections resembles that in which Rasselas, with Imlac's support but also by reason of his own intelligence and candor, comes to recognize and begin to understand his own fantastic bent of mind.

Catherine's meditative evening should be seen as presenting a dangerous new opportunity for self-deception. A coarser person might now concentrate on what could be considered the political mistake of her disclosing those suspicions to Henry. A weaker person might have run away from him, in one manner or another, or might have lost herself in a new, distracting train of thought; more than ever before, Catherine is in a position to seek the delusion prompted by a person's feeling displeased, as Imlac said, "with what he is." We are told that Catherine "hated herself more than she could express" (2.10.199). Henry, a formidable judge, had been shocked by her thoughts; a more rigid, ethically rigoristic person than Catherine might have been immobilized by horror at the evil summoned up in her heretofore chaste imagination. But instead of finding self-deceptive refuge, Catherine assesses herself historically, delves into what caused her to apply those Gothic ideas to the General, and, as we have seen, in good Lockean fashion, traces the association of ideas to her reading habits and subsequent, Johnsonian "voluntary . . . delusion." This last, we are told, proceeded from a "craving to be frightened," a trait of youth that may need no commentary, but her reflections do not stop at that. They go on to clarify what was voluntary—her train of thought amusingly in character, hardly unsubjective, self-protective in part, yet really probing.

Her point of departure, only that, is Henry's cue about what is probable in England as contrasted with the settings of Gothic novels. The narrator gives us Catherine's subsequent train of thought:

> Among the Alps and Pyrenees, perhaps, there were no mixed characters. There, such as were not as spotless as an angel, might have the dispositions of a fiend. But in England it was not so; among the English, she believed, in their hearts and habits, there was a general though unequal mixture of good and bad. Upon this conviction, she would not be surprised if even in Henry and Eleanor Tilney, some slight imperfection might hereafter appear; and upon this conviction she need not fear to acknowledge some actual specks in the character of their father, who, though cleared from the grossly injurious suspicions which she must ever blush to have entertained, she did believe, upon serious consideration, to be not perfectly amiable.
> Her mind made up on these several points, and her resolution formed, of always judging and acting in future with the greatest good sense, she had nothing to do but to forgive herself and be

happier than ever; and the lenient hand of time did much for her by insensible gradations in the course of another day. Henry's astonishing generosity and nobleness of conduct, in never alluding in the slightest way to what had passed, was of the greatest assistance to her. . . .

(2.10.200–01)

This train of thought is shrewd, first of all, in pursuing the association of the General with Montoni beyond the simple, mechanistic explanation provided by the idea of habit, pursuing it to the issue of motivation, beyond the directly observable. The habit was "voluntary"—how, why? Catherine's thoughts probe past the matter of what is likely in England to the commonplace about the universality of mixed characters. The commonplace is news to her; a Candide, she has constantly perceived almost no evil in anyone, others or herself, having felt none, or almost none—and never having been able to bring herself to feel any, unquestionably for fear that doing so would reveal in her a certain nastiness of mind. Earlier in the book, she could not have been slower to acknowledge to herself that she dislikes John Thorpe, flagrantly and comically obnoxious as he repeatedly proves himself. Only his active interference with her desire to accompany the Tilneys finally forces her to think him "quite disagreeable" (1.9.69). She had endured a comparable inner battle when beginning to contemplate the General—a battle still more upsetting because of his central importance as Henry's father. "Catherine," we had then been told, as she hit on the idea that he had mistreated his wife, "attempted no longer to hide from herself the nature of the feelings which, in spite of all his attentions, he had previously excited . . ." (2.7.181). She has had to imagine the General as a Gothic villain to justify to herself the aversion to him which she feels, and she has had to justify her aversion so she could acknowledge that she feels it.

Now, on the evening following her confrontation with Henry, she tries to accept the fact that, almost unintentionally, she has done wrong, to face the fact with psychological integrity by attempting to see what moved her to do it. Her train of thought could be more sophisticated. She could see and describe the episode as provoked by a crisis of self-love, her rigoristic self-esteem requiring her to invent a vision of the General which made her negative feelings tolerable to her. But in effect she does just that, or goes forward as if she had. To find herself bearable she proceeds to find everyone else fallible, even her idealized Henry (no harm in that), and maintains her sense of there being something amiss in his father (rightfully so). Hesitant as her train of thought is in some respects, in others it is strong and may even have overtones of profundity. Her imaginative vision of the General, the vision which Avrom Fleishman describes as a promising if unbalanced application of literary experience to life, has, even at the outset, a shadowy complement: that fiction also casts the imaginer, Catherine—belatedly—as a would-be heroine after all, who wishes to be perfectly virtuous in word and thought yet is also ambitious enough to want to withstand an extreme villain and marry a hero. Thus, in realizing how she has willfully typecast the General, and in facing the fact that she has done it, Catherine implicitly discovers the facts of her own mixed desires and particular mental processes, almost as fully as Rasselas discovers his.

As earlier, Henry helps, the representative of conscience but also an exemplar for Catherine's acceptance of herself; that is, her restoration to self-love based, as is so commonly the case, on adoption of non-angelic (and non-diabolical) standards, a new order of *sagesse*. ("There, such as were not as spotless as an angel, might have the dispositions of a fiend, but in England . . .") Henry could be still more helpful: he might have suggested, at the time of the confrontation, that she explain how she has come by her suspicions. But the issue of his father's openness to suspicion is a subject he prefers to avoid, and in circumventing it he gives Catherine the opportunity to show that she is not entirely dependent on his tutelage. A philosophical heroine, Catherine comes to be able to think for herself, well, about her own mode of thinking. Nowhere must Lennox's female Quixote go so deep.

In representing Catherine's reflections, Austen gives serious attention to the theme of self-love, present in the philosophical tale but never greatly elaborated there, though closely related to the theme of psychological self-awareness, indeed indispensable to it, as Austen sees. Not that the issue of self-love is neglected in the philosophical tale, far from it. Time and again in the tales, the greatest obstacle to self-knowledge is misplaced self-love, ill-assessed pride: loving oneself for qualities one does not possess, fearing to examine oneself lest one make that discovery. Complementarily, it is often true self-knowledge that, by its presence or palpable absence, is identified as the requisite foundation for durable love of self and others. The philosophical tales, with one or another degree of emphasis, all touch on the quest for sound self-love as well as for self-assessment. But the obstacles to the latter, including unsound varieties of self-love, command main attention. Usbek's new appreciation of the motive of interest, Candide's setting his own sights for a change, are less significant than these characters' freeing themselves from presuppositions. Only *Rasselas* gives prominent attention to both issues, self-love central to Imlac's question "for who is pleased with what he is?" and to that part of the tale's action which radiates from it.[32]

It is an overarching premise of the present study that a major problem after the age of absolutism in religion and politics had passed, was the general, new need of the individual human being for a strengthened combination of, and means to, self-knowledge and self-love, so that people carrying an increased burden of choice could govern themselves with hope of reasonable success. This broad consideration reveals in Jane Austen a depth of political sense oddly in contrast to her usual reputation of having kept her head securely beneath the sands of her Napoleonic and reactionary times, for she especially concentrates on the legitimization of self-love in the philosophical sense of the term, appropriately in historical conditions of widened individualism of choice, individualism affective and cognitive.

In *Northanger Abbey*, unpolished, provincial Catherine comes close to seeming a *tabula rasa* upon which, at a critical time, destiny has inscribed the characters of the Gothic and little else. But the error of this assessment is clear, and possibly clearest when we consider Henry's love for her, which Austen explains near the end rather self-consciously, in a playful manner that may prevent us from looking hard at what is said: ". . . I must confess that his affection originated in nothing better than gratitude, or, in other words, that a persuasion of her partiality for him had been the only cause of giving her a serious thought. It is a new circumstance in romance, I acknowledge, and dreadfully derogatory of an heroine's dignity; but if it be as new in common life, the credit of a wild imagination will at least be all my own" (2.15.243). Is the explanation surprising? Or is it only surprising to discover, in a work of some formal realism, such an excursion into the plausible and ungodlike? The explanation itself may surprise, at first, Henry has presented himself so debonairly from his first entrance, so resembling the narrator in easy self-assurance, even when Catherine touches on the sore point of his brother's conduct with Isabella. Yet upon consideration the reader sees the narrator is right: that given Henry's circumstances, simple affection from someone other than his sister may be as new to him as it is necessary, especially after the long experience of his father's hostility to feeling. In the long run it is the simplicity of the narrator's account, not of Henry's motive, that remains surprising, a simplicity against the grain of the novelistic but befitting a tale.

It is in an aspect like this that Catherine, another simple tale character, though ignorant and uninformed, is strong from the beginning, is something of a blank page but with a certain radiance, "her heart . . . affectionate" (1.2.18). On the occasion of Catherine's naive explanation of Frederick Tilney's asking Isabella to dance, after Henry comments cannily on what Catherine does not know he proceeds—sensibly, in character, and in a manner consistent with Austen's final, surprising account of his motives—to compliment her: "Well then, I only meant that your attributing my brother's wish of dancing with Miss Thorpe to good-nature alone, convinced me of your being superior in good-nature yourself to all the rest of the world." The comment, in context, has a number of purposes, among them probably that of distracting Catherine from the issue of Frederick's motives, and the tone of the comment is not entirely one of good faith, is manipulative.

However, there remains truth as well as deception in Henry's strong compliment; though Catherine "blushed and disclaimed," she found "something . . . in his words which repaid her for the pain of confusion" (2.1.133); and the evidence is that she is not motivated so strongly by simple gratitude as Henry, in his love for her, turns out to be. Though protected from the knowledge of gross evil, and though realistically influenced by rigorist ethics, she has from the first a sense of her being imperfect, especially in manners, yet lovable nevertheless. Henry at the end defies his father and seeks Catherine out, comes to rescue her. In this heroic deed, however, he has been anticipated—one might suggest, he has been shown the way—by the artlessly affectionate Catherine, who in modest defiance of conventional ladylike heroism has repeatedly extended herself to be on good terms with him, as in the conversation preceded by these irresistible sentences, ". . . She could almost have run round to the box in which he sat, and forced him to hear her explanation. Feelings rather natural than heroic possessed her . . ." (1.12.93).

The issue of self-love underlies one or two of the narrator's most salient opinions early in the book and thus summons special attention. The narrator cannot tell whether Catherine dreamed of Henry after their first meeting, and hopes she did not, ". . . for if it be true, as a celebrated writer has maintained, that no young lady can be justified in falling in love before the gentleman's love is declared, it must be very improper that a young lady should dream of a gentleman before the gentleman is first known to have dreamed of her" (1.3.29–30). The celebrated writer a footnote identifies as Richardson, in *Rambler* 97, where—besides making the point mentioned—the author of *Clarissa* extols the young woman who "is all resignation to her parents. Charming resignation, which inclination opposes not."[33] Catherine, however, like Candide, unlike Pope's friend who "always thinks the very thing he ought," is too interested in her own happiness to let propriety delude her into thinking she is not.

Appreciative of the historical evolution of characters, Austen has provided Catherine with a family whence a reader can easily derive her blend of affection for, and detachment from, herself—a point that need not be pursued here. Ethereal, a "heroine," she is not; sane she unshakably is, though susceptible to intervals of another state of mind like the human beings described by Locke and Johnson. That characteristic sanity is the product of Catherine's modest, preliminary affection for herself, which leads her to feel affection for others. She and Mme de Merteuil can say together, "Descendue dans mon cœur, j'y ai étudié celui des autres," indicating for Catherine a source of strength as well as weakness. Having never known real meanness in herself, Catherine must fall in her attempt to comprehend General Tilney and soar too high in her unqualified esteem for his son; she has been "free from the apprehension of evil as from the knowledge of it" (2.14.237). Yet it would be very inept, with most of Austen's novels, to lay emphasis on the Fall in any grand manner, or to lay too much stress on the determining effects of the main characters' upbringing. These conditions are simply part of the mix of desire, experience, and reflection which the characters must encounter and make their way through.

The posture recommended in *Northanger Abbey* and elsewhere in Austen is constantly one of alertness about the association of ideas and motives in the past and present, bearing on the future—an assertion I shall substantiate further in my final chapter. More than the novels represent life, they represent the need for that alertness, but as important is Austen's emphasis on the need for fundamental self-loving interest in one's own well-being and happiness. It is said that Austen amused herself by making up stories of her characters' lives beyond the end of the books,[34] as well she might have, for unlike many novelists she created characters capable of living on, conclusions in which everything is not concluded, as in *Rasselas* and *Candide*. Catherine's final view of the General is promising in feeling and thought: as Henry tells her of his father's motives for turning her out, "her feelings soon hardened into even a triumphant delight" (2.15.244). She may yet be a match for her father-in-law. The final paragraph of the book indicates that the General's opposition has possibly been useful, "improving" the lovers' "knowledge of each other, and adding strength to their attachment"—a process not complete but firmly begun. Thus is love, including self-love, reconciled with understanding, including self-assessment. Had Catherine become more expert about Henry within the covers of the book, the narrator would not have needed to become so conspicuously playful again in the final chapters. However, like Voltaire's and Johnson's narrators, this narrator has changed, especially in warming to Catherine as she has grown. The frequent designation "heroine" of the earlier part of the book becomes, toward the end, "my heroine."

The foregoing account of *Northanger Abbey*, as of the major philosophical tales, depends on the axiom that not only all the characters, whatever their apparent moral authority, but also the narrator and the reader, no matter how authoritative the narrator may sound, can conceivably stand in some degree of dramatic conflict with each other. That this axiom may be correct is a possibility not sufficiently taken into account by most commentators on Austen as well as those on the philosophical tales. Among critics of Austen who closely approach the issue, Graham Hough flatly denies that axiom in generalities attached to an analysis of *Emma*. Distinguishing between the voices to be heard in Austen novels, he includes among them a narrative voice "talking on behalf of society or Dr. Johnson or God" (I cannot imagine comparisons better suited to my purposes) and another voice: "that of the narrator as an individual woman, . . . sensible, sometimes tart and frequently amused." The second of these narrative voices, moreover, "is just as reliable as the voice of the graver passages; the sparkle of satire or irony does not lead into error. . . ." With incisive consistency and a measure of truth, Hough adds somewhat later: "The narrator is permitted to be sharp and lively and also right; but when the characters are sharp and lively they are most often slightly wrong."[35]

But the possibility must be considered that neither narrative voice is *a priori* perfectly reliable, indeed that the very, very authoritative voice, as in *Candide* and *Rasselas*, can entrap the authoritarian, unenlightened reader, and that the second, more human narrative voice may have a comparable function for readers prejudiced in other ways. The degree to which Austen anticipates the drama of Henry James's narration does not seem widely enough appreciated despite useful studies to that effect by critics such as Irène Simon and A. Walton Litz.[36] Trust the tale, as Lawrence says.

The power of *Emma*, I would add, is perhaps not fully taken

in if, like Hough and others, one sees Mr. Knightley as "never wrong."
Hough gratifyingly makes just the comparison again that I would
make: Mr. Knightley maintains the grave "Johnsonian" style of commentary "more consistently than anyone else" in *Emma*. "He is
everywhere a pricker of bubbles, the foe of unregulated fancy. The
acutest passages of moral and psychological analysis are accorded
to him. In his presence conversation is always lifted from the familiar and the anecdotal to the level of general reflection; the characters become types; and the actual persons around him assume the
air of personae in a moral apologue."[37] The problem with such a
judgment about this apt comparison is, as I have argued throughout
the present book, that it is based on too restricted a view of the
best-known apologues, the best philosophical tales. If Mr. Knightley is the Imlac of *Emma*, he may deserve no more reverence than
Rasselas accords Imlac. I need not qualify and elaborate; but to the
extent that Emma and *Emma* idealize Mr. Knightley, the novel may
ironically subvert Emma and her readers.

I have sought to show that *Northanger Abbey* plays on and against
the authority of the narrator. Like Imlac and *Candide*'s Martin, Henry
is a comparatively realistic surrogate for the omniscient, judgmental
narrator; that is, he is fallible, not omniscient, though generally
wise; and the contrast between him and the narrator bears decisively
on the reader's feelings about the tale as a whole. Henry's recitative
echoes the narrator's early arias, with the only possibly helpful
authority of a mortal mentor as it may be useful to a heroine not
without some authority herself. In the combination of wisdom and
weakness characteristic of Henry and Catherine, there is the kind
of authority that, unlike the narrator's absoluteness, brings realities
to mind. Upon the narrator's late return to witty conspicuousness
in what she calls the "tell-tale compression" of the ending (2.16.250),
we may view her at a certain distance, suitable to the genre of the
tale.

CHAPTER ELEVEN

"Delicious Consciousness" in *Persuasion*, via *Mansfield Park*

Very few can boast of hearts which they dare lay open to themselves,
and of which, by whatever accident exposed, they do not shun a
distinct and continued view.

—Johnson, *Life of Pope*

*I*n her last complete novel, *Persuasion*, published posthumously
with *Northanger Abbey*, Jane Austen consolidates her original
development of the theme and pattern of the philosophical tale,
concentrating on the relation of self-love to self-knowledge. The
fundamental issue of the tale, the importance of attention to the
chain of mental events depending from initial association, could
not be more prominent or more splendidly comprehended and represented. Though there are secondary characters in the book who
may seem cast in the mentorial role, the heroine's lack of any really
useful mentor lifts to the highest relief her responsibility and capacity for individual, personal assessment of self and other; allegorical representation of the heroine's faculties by other characters,
representation unbeknownst to her—a device found elsewhere in
the Austen canon—hardly matters here. Instead, more even than
in *Northanger Abbey*, there is rich use of the eighteenth-century psychological vocabulary to describe perception, conflict, and resolution within a single mind.

Two imaginative fictional devices, in addition to employment of that vocabulary, enhance the prominence of the mind of the heroine, Anne Elliot, and compensate for the absence of an effective mentor. (I have introduced discussion of these two devices in the preceding chapter.) First, when news comes concerning the wickedness of a potential suitor, that device important to the resolution of *Sense and Sensibility, Pride and Prejudice,* and *Emma,* it comes so late as to be unrevealing—*this* device pointing to the mental resources of the heroine which have made the revelation superfluous.[1] Second, the dramatic function of the taleteller, the narrator, has been emphasized to promote readers' trust in the tale of the heroine's consciousness. To some extent these observations of mine also fit Austen's *Mansfield Park* (1814), a novel less satisfactory from the vantage point of the philosophical tale, yet illuminated as a novel when seen thus. I begin by saying why.

But first I wish to note that the critic who has most closely approached perception of the resemblance between Austen's fiction and the philosophical tale is Darrel Mansell, whose work has eased mine. He comments that when Catherine, in *Northanger Abbey,* has to choose between the values of the young Thorpes and Tilneys, a reader may sense "something . . . not far from the aggressive intellectual purposefulness of *Rasselas.*" His main point, "Austen's use of her fictional material to further a rather brittle plan for the psychological reformation of her heroine," broadly resembles my argument. By "brittle" Mansell means that Austen's "overriding intellectual scheme" of reformation results in diminished realism of presentation and plot—particularly "implausible" events serving that scheme, events involving the subject matter of surprising revelations to the heroines.[2] I do not agree with Mansell about the function of those revelations, at least in *Persuasion* and *Mansfield Park,* where, as I have said, the revelations are significantly superfluous. Nor, of course, would I describe the philosophical-tale manner, given its peculiar combination of realism and nonrealism, as "brittle" (if Mansell intends that extended application of the word). I suggest recognition in *Persuasion* of a tale-manner in felicitous combination with elements of formal, novelistic realism, and in *Mansfield Park* an attempt at that combination.

Mansfield Park is a painful novel, as a deeply realistic philosophical tale might be. The chessboard of Austen's fictional conventions permits many strategies with the same or similar sets of
pieces. The chief modification of *Northanger*'s Catherine-figure in
Mansfield Park makes the heroine, Fanny Price, almost entirely unloved, virtually unnoticed: a product not of a large, "happy" family
but of scarcely remitted indifference, and worse.[3] Her uncle, Sir
Thomas Bertram, takes her into his stately home of Mansfield Park
when she is ten, so as to relieve her large, overburdened, impe-
cunious family at Portsmouth. But at Mansfield she is ignored,
condescended to, or more aggressively mistreated by all the family
except Sir Thomas' son Edmund, who becomes the child's mentor
and, as she enters womanhood, her love. (In recalling details of the
novel I make no attempt to convey a full sense of its imposing
richness but mention only what my argument requires, an argument directed mainly toward understanding of *Persuasion*.) Before
long, Edmund can no longer be the mentor he was, because to
Fanny's sorrow he has fallen in love with the beautiful, somewhat
reckless Mary Crawford. Mary's comparably attractive brother Henry
later begins to court Fanny, and when she proves unresponsive the
severe Sir Thomas sends her back to Portsmouth to see if so pre-
cipitous a descent from the high life of Mansfield will bring her to
reason.

Now occurs the revelation: a newspaper informs Fanny that
Henry has run off with one of Sir Thomas' daughters, Maria, who
for six months has been Mrs. Rushworth. Fanny cannot marry
Henry now. But whether she would ever have done so was always,
to say the least, unclear, given the set of her mind. Thus the news
is superfluous or comparatively beside the point. Yet at the end of
the book the narrator says Fanny would have married Henry had
he behaved "uprightly,"[4] had he persisted in his suit, and had Edmund married Mary (he does not). The triple set of conditions is
important. Not only does Fanny find Henry difficult to trust; she
does not love him; and she does love Edmund. She is pre-engaged
by her affection for him, secretly, unknown to Edmund or anyone
else. The triple set of conditions complicates understanding of Fanny

and her probable behavior yet generously repays the effort to understand, by the precision with which it defines her circumscribed, defensive strength and weakness and her very considerable power as a literary, novelistic character.

Austen endows Fanny with a particular, twofold capacity of mind, represented clearly in psychological discourse. Fanny proves quite alert to her thoughts and feelings (increasingly so, a point not necessary to my argument). In a manner not unlike that of the later *Rasselas*, she guards herself against wishful thinking while maintaining consciousness of what she wishes. Fanny, Bacon-like, knows the mind's tendency to believe what it wants to believe and, as in the case of Johnson's astronomer, to lose its grip on itself and its world. What Catherine in *Northanger Abbey* has to discover, Fanny knows very early, as in this reflection on her feelings toward Edmund, halfway through the novel: "To think of him as Miss Crawford might be justified in thinking, would in her be insanity. To her, he could be nothing under any circumstances—nothing dearer than a friend. Why did such an idea occur to her even enough to be reprobated and forbidden? It ought not to have touched on the confines of her imagination" (2.9.264–65). Reading these sentences we find ourselves on the most familiar ground: Lockean and Johnsonian fear of voluntary delusion, that is, of an association of that "idea" which, through dangerous "imagination," could bring "insanity."

The narrator immediately seasons the fortitude of Fanny's consequent "good resolutions on the side of self-government" with a dash of skepticism, not omitting wise reference to the "ages" ("the feelings of youth and nature"), as the narrator of *Northanger Abbey* responds to Catherine's comparable thoughts. In *Mansfield Park*, though, the ironic, humorous qualification is not so convincing. For the second strength of Fanny's doubly potent mind, second to her alertness in exposition here but I think primary in importance, even shading into weakness because of its insufficiently balanced power over her, is in her memory—a memory, according to Locke's division, both retentive and quick, respectively Gulliverian and un-Gulliverian. There is a powerful moment in *Les Liaisons dangereuses* when the young, unsuspecting Cécile catches her supposed mentor Mme de Merteuil in a contradiction, but so unctuously overpowering is the older woman that Cécile doubts her own memory rather than doubt her instructress. There could never be such a moment with Fanny. The quasi-orphan Fanny is a daughter of Mnemosyne; at one point, most unusually for so reticent a heroine, she rhapsodizes in public about the force, mystery, and importance of the faculty of memory (2.4.208–9).

This is a Book of Memory: following the passage just cited, Fanny delights in the emblematic evergreen. Elsewhere she blanches at the thought of anyone's cutting down the avenue of trees at Sotherton (1.6.56), and she expresses disappointment at the newness of the estate's chapel (1.9.85–86). Mansfield Park by contrast is a monument, and the East room, for Fanny, her room of mementos for hours of "musing," everything having "an interesting remembrance connected with it" (1.16.151–52)—that is, associated with it in a positive sense, as Locke employs *connection*. (This room quite the opposite of one at Northanger.) The necklace Fanny receives with unwillingness from Mary is to be a "remembrancer" of Henry (2.8.259), and the witch Aunt Norris certifies the excellence of Fanny's memory by disparaging it early in the novel (1.2.19). One could dwell long on the charm and irony bound up in this theme, but for my purposes it is more important to examine how Fanny puts her memory to use. She squanders none of her experience; she carefully links day to day, event to event to event, in the interest of self-knowledge and knowledge of others; and the others—many of them—are explicitly described as lacking in self-knowledge (e.g., 1.2.19, 1.9.91, 1.12.114–15, 3.16.459).

In contrast to most of her fellow characters, Fanny is represented as having no important delusion or illusion to overcome, though she has things to learn. When she returns from Mansfield to her immediate family's disorderly Portsmouth home, she feels the household is worse, and she unhappier in it, than she thought would be the case. (Here occurs the well-known reference to *Rasselas*: "In a review of the two houses, as they appeared to her before the end of a week, Fanny was tempted to apply to them Dr. Johnson's celebrated judgment as to matrimony and celibacy, and say, that though Mansfield Park might have some pains, Portsmouth could have no pleasures"—3.8.392.)[5]

Mansell, taking a contrary view, that Fanny has illusions to overcome, says she must face two tests, that of participating in the play *Lovers' Vows* and that presented by Henry's courtship. It is his theory that she reveals a propensity for romantic illusions in her disappointment at Sotherton Chapel.[6] But he retreats from an earlier assertion that Fanny "begins to drift into the play," so that she was only "on the verge of being drawn," and on the more significant topic of her feelings for Henry, Mansell gives the wrong impression with his similar remark, that "She seems now on the verge of yielding to Henry" when news comes of the elopement. "Now the 'truth' rushes on Fanny. She begins to perceive the 'horrible evil', the 'gross . . . complication of evil' that Henry is capable of perpetrating. It is now a fact that Henry is not what Fanny has always supposed: a mixture in which evil has merely its part. He has now been shown to be evil itself."[7] If we review the scene, the context of the quoted parts of this passage (3.15.440–41), we find—emphatically—no evidence to support the idea that Fanny awakens from, or ever entertained, an illusion amorous or otherwise about Henry. She is shocked, but by the evil Henry and Mrs. Rushworth have done together—done not to herself, as she conceives it, but to the Bertrams; Fanny considers the impact of the news on most of them in turn, especially Edmund, whose life and sanity she fears for. The supposed blow to herself, to her personal wishes, is first given direct attention by Edmund, later, in a letter recalling Fanny to Mansfield and thereby putting her "in the greatest danger of being exquisitely happy, while so many were miserable" (3.15.442–43).

Although the extent of the wrongdoing on this occasion surpasses Fanny's idea of the probable, she is not surprised that Henry would do ill, for she has kept the beam of memory steadily trained on his record, the good and the bad. When Henry has attempted to buy her affection by arranging promotion for a dear brother of hers in the navy, she has found the deed "like himself, and entirely of a piece with what she had seen before . . . —But such were his habits, that he could do nothing without a mixture of evil" (2.13.301–

2). The judgment goes much beyond Catherine Morland's recognition of the universality of mixed characters, and Fanny labels and files it in the East room of her mind, for reference when needed. Again, defending her disapproval of Henry in a conversation with Edmund, she is ready with her cumulative record, here especially the fact of Henry's flirting with the engaged Maria Bertram (no need for Edmund to speak to Fanny about the inducements of "age, situation, and probable habits of life"): "At the time of the play, I received an impression which will never be got over" (3.4.349). Sir Thomas, scolding Fanny for not accepting Henry, tells her to "take in the whole of the past" (3.1.313); the uncle could scarcely be more ill-informed about his niece's mind. She is the antithesis of Pamela, and cannot judge except "by events." As in the theorizing of an eighteenth-century philosopher, memory seems to give Fanny her personal identity, her lifeline. She protects her memory jealously, as her first and last border of support and defense.

But among the household smells of Mansfield, even in the airy East room, there is a slight trace of herring. Suppose Edmund had married Mary. Suppose, against probability, that Henry had reformed his mind, had become an Edmund, gentle and good-natured. Given these changes, the narrator says, Fanny would have married Henry, and in fact would have done so "very voluntarily." Once married, Fanny would have benefited both from Henry's affection and from "her conscience in subduing her first inclination" (3.17.467)—that is, her love for Edmund, the reference subtle here. The issue was emphasized by the narrator when Henry began to court Fanny, in a chatty, personal narrative tone untypical of the book, reminiscent of the early and late *Northanger* style. Mary learns of Henry's plan and

> left Fanny to her fate—a fate which, had not Fanny's heart been guarded in a way unsuspected by Miss Crawford, might have been a little harder than she deserved; for although there doubtless are such unconquerable young ladies of eighteen (or one should not read about them) as are never to be persuaded into love against their judgment by all that talent, manner, attention, and flattery can do, I have no inclination to believe Fanny one of them, or to think that with so much tenderness of disposition, and so much taste as be-

longed to her, she could have escaped heart-whole from the courtship (though the courtship only of a fortnight) of such a man as Crawford, in spite of there being some previous ill-opinion of him to be overcome, had not her affection been engaged elsewhere. With all the security which love of another and disesteem of him could give to the peace of mind he was attacking, his continued attentions—continued, but not obtrusive, and adapting themselves more and more to the gentleness and delicacy of her character,—obliged her very soon to dislike him less than formerly. She had by no means forgotten the past, and she thought as ill of him as ever; but she felt his powers.

(2.6.231–32)

This strange paragraph is certainly more dramatic and expressive than analytical and expository. The *Northanger* blitheness fades out quickly, supplanted by what can best be described as a rhetorical shell game, in which the hard nut of Fanny's prepossession in favor of Edmund is repeatedly displayed and just as frequently concealed. The two long central sentences insist on the insuperable fact of pre-engagement and then effectively obliterate it, giving prominence instead to what the paragraph explicitly says is a non-issue, whether Fanny can love Henry. The next twelve chapters, well over a hundred pages, subject Fanny to wave upon wave of Henry's advances, direct and vicarious, with no mention of Fanny's prepossession until the reader is suddenly told that she "escaped . . . without detection. Her secret was still her own" (3.5.365). Only a reader whose eye was deliberately in search of the prepossession issue would, I think, immediately know what the narrator is talking about. The curiously parallel issue of Fanny's "previous ill opinion" of Henry has long and thoroughly dominated the field. If the narrator has not forgotten the other issue, and of course the narrator has not, she has buried it.

And well she might. For all the evidence suggests that even if Henry could become *an* Edmund, Fanny could love only *the* Edmund. The book is much too particular about the interaction of Fanny's peculiar mind and the influences upon it to permit the conception of Fanny's loving anyone but Edmund, who at the end is about to marry Fanny sooner or later, when he gets over his lingering feelings for Mary. It is again James Morland's project of forgetting Isabella Thorpe, hardly noticed at the end of *Northanger Abbey* but in *Mansfield Park* thrust into complete prominence; like Isabella, Mary cannot reconcile herself to a clergyman's modest income and tastes, but that similarity does not begin to do justice to Mary's power over Edmund and readers. Here are concords not unisons indeed. Fanny, however, is not discontented: Edmund is all she wants, more than she has ever expected, all she can imagine—the final index to her humble goodness and to the extent of her deprivation and resultant weakness.

Fanny hangs on the cousin who has given her the only particular, generous, sympathetic attention and affection she has ever received, except from her almost always far-off brother William. "Children of the same family, the same blood, with the same first associations and habits, have some means of enjoyment in their power, which no subsequent connections can supply" (2.6.235). Thus the narrator on the psychological ground of Fanny and William's affection— a technical explanation immediately preceded by the statement that the pleasure of shared memories is "a strengthener of love, in which even the conjugal tie is beneath the fraternal." It is but a hair's breadth away to account in the same manner for Fanny's love of Edmund, going back to his finding her weeping on the staircase as a child. Another young woman could have found Henry worth a struggle. Not Fanny. As Norman Page says, "Some of Fanny's critics seem to have been surprised that she should not have had the temperament of an Emma Woodhouse, when her situation in fact more closely resembles that of Oliver Twist."[8] The idea of a husband and the idea of Edmund make an original association in Fanny's mind which she has not the strength to examine; much less can she imagine alternatives. Her devotion to Edmund is the pathetic counterpart of Henry Tilney's gratitude to Catherine, and its particular power in *Mansfield Park* is profound, troubling, appropriately unforgettable. For Fanny, beginning to end, self-love has too small a foundation. She leans heavily for her strength upon moral self-esteem. Like Sir Thomas the novel is severe.

And how does the narrator cope with these sobering realities?—in the end, by too forcibly seeking to wrest *Mansfield Park* into the nonrealism of a tale[9]—by thrusting an obtrusive tale narrator into this extremely transparent, realistic narrative, where there had been few such obtrusions before (e.g., 3.10.402, 3.13.425, and the *Northanger* passage of 2.6.231). "Let other pens dwell on guilt and misery," the concluding chapter notably begins. "I quit such odious subjects as soon as I can, impatient to restore every body, not greatly in fault themselves, to tolerable comfort, and to have done with all the rest" (3.17.461).[10] Was it a tale after all, its pages subjectable to "tell-tale compression"? "My Fanny indeed . . . ," the text continues, recalling "my heroine" late in *Northanger Abbey*. And Edmund—

> Scarcely had he done regretting Mary Crawford, and observing to Fanny how impossible it was that he should ever meet with such another woman, before it began to strike him whether a very different kind of woman might not do just as well—or a great deal better. . . .
>
> I purposely abstain from dates on this occasion, that every one may be at liberty to fix their own, aware that the cure of unconquerable passions, and the transfer of unchanging attachments, must vary much as to time in different people.—I only intreat every body to believe that exactly at the time when it was quite natural that it should be so, and not a week earlier, Edmund did cease to care about Miss Crawford, and became as anxious to marry Fanny, as Fanny herself could desire.
>
> (3.17.470)

Once hardships so potent as those touched on in this book have been presented in absorbing formal realism, it may not be possible simply to "bring them to mind" again. The tone of this passage, which would have served very well for the faint case of James Morland and Arabella Thorpe, is a betrayal of the book.[11] In fact, it is a tone like that of no one in *Mansfield Park* so much as it is like Mary Crawford's, as in the postscript to one of her letters, meant to finesse and cajole Fanny—just what the narrator of *Mansfield Park* is not above attempting with the reader. Mary writes, "I had almost forgot (it was Edmund's fault, he gets into my head more than does me good), one very material thing. . . . My dear little creature, do not stay at Portsmouth to lose your pretty looks. . . .

Only keep your cousin Edmund from me at such a time, I should not like to be tempted. What a long letter!—one word more," and so on. As the plainer narrator of the earlier part of the book comments, in a way not inapplicable to the narrator's own performance at the end, Mary's "was a letter to be run through eagerly, to be read deliberately, to supply matter for much reflection, and to leave every thing in greater suspense than ever" (3.12.416–17). The narrator, like Mary, reveals a defect of feeling.

There is something of a precedent for the concluding mis-marriage of tone and substance in a philosophical tale I have not examined in this book, one in which the genre of the tale is set against that of the novel, Voltaire's *L'Ingénu*—he once said it was better than *Candide* because "infiniment plus vraisemblable."[12] But it is thus only in part, an odd hybrid of competing genres. *L'Ingénu* matches a tale hero, supposedly an American Indian and certainly a paragon of self-love, whose exploits are narrated with suitable nonrealism in the first half of the book, with a novel heroine, whose sufferings are represented comparatively realistically in the remainder. She gives herself sexually to an official holding the hero in prison, so as to secure his release, then dies because she cannot imagine that he will forgive her—dies, that is, of an insufficiency of self-love. A lugubrious conclusion reverses the expectations raised by the beginning; less joltingly, however, than the narrator's final tone affects a reader of *Mansfield Park*.

Fanny's behavior, then, is more cogent than the narrator's theory of it, or the narrator's feelings about it. The narrator's opinion (to anticipate *Persuasion* for a moment) is "good or bad only as the event decides," and the chain of events is against it. Perhaps sensing the danger that Fanny's romantic love may be too appealing to readers, the narrator denies its importance—denies what the novelist has so passionately and persuasively established. The narrator fails to sense, except perhaps dimly and disturbingly, that Fanny's overwhelming love for Edmund alone is a symptom of weakness, and moreover, of exactly the weakness to which the heritage of eighteenth-century psychology, of the philosophical tale, and of *Northanger Abbey*, particularly calls attention: the importance of original associations, bearing on self-knowledge and self-love. The narrator cannot look at Fanny whole, from her origins, as Fanny cannot, and the narrator tries to keep us from doing so on our own, as we may wish to do, especially if we are attentive to the philosophical-tale pattern.

Trying to fathom the problem presented by Fanny and the narrator, we may go deeper. Free of significant illusions, Fanny walks on the brink of actual, serious delusion, or past it—Edmund, fortunately, is a good enough young man—and *Mansfield Park*, dense in imagined, highly particularized representation of life, is finally too particular for eighteenth-century psychology. The motive of Fanny's love is a rooted, terrible sorrow. Not Northanger but Mansfield is the haunted house, the narrator haunted too. Like a patient on a couch, a patient suddenly impaled upon too accurate a question, the narrator becomes incoherent or strangely jocular when the issue of prepossession arises. The narrator's story of Fanny's possibly loving Henry is a fantasy of the gravest kind. Yet Fanny, who cannot minister to herself in the manner promoted by the philosophical tale, uncannily rhapsodizes about memory, including consideration of its inconsistency, its tyranny, and its mystery, itself "past finding out" (2.4.209)—as if she found herself compelled to "change the subject." Hers is truly and evocatively a telltale heart. And while the philosophical tale, compared to such a fiction as *Mansfield Park*, may seem thin, and unrealistic even psychologically about what can be the abyss of self-knowing, a wise reader might lament that the form did not maintain its identity and strength after the eighteenth century, because the considerations central to the tale so usefully supplement the concerns of the novel and of novel readers.

Persuasion—in a sense a reworked *Mansfield Park*—is by contrast a novel which profits at every turn from the theme and pattern of the philosophical tale, with Austen's special emphasis on self-love as well as self-knowledge, an emphasis achieved by various devices now familiar to us: mitigation of novelistic realism (the brevity of the book one aspect), dependence on a central mind represented with the aid of eighteenth-century psychological discourse, careful attention to the chain and chaining of events, the heroine's recognition of herself in encounters with others, attention to the conflict of self-love against rigorist self-esteem, a significantly superfluous revelation, and a dramatic narrator. Take a heroine at least as perceptive as Fanny Price and give her half a chance. Surround her too with a ménage of selfish, unloving, unappreciative relatives, but give her the experience of having been warmly loved— by her mother and, after her mother's death, by her godmother, Lady Russell; more strikingly, by an ardent young naval officer, Frederick Wentworth. Then deprive her of his attentions for eight years, after the event of Lady Russell's persuading her not to marry him when his fortune was still to be made; deprive her too of special physical attractiveness—the penalty she has paid for those hard years. Then bring her again into proximity with her lost suitor, who behaves as though he no longer has or can have any interest in her. He is not a relative; there is, however, a cousin ready to receive her, Mr. Elliot. The two men represent variations of Fanny Price's connection with cousin Edmund, naval brother William, and dashing newcomer Henry.

Yet make this book much shorter than *Mansfield Park*, less realistic in presentation: not so encompassing of secondary characters' feelings, less absorbing in fullness of event and detail, less enclosing of the reader's sense of possibility. Add an enlivening grotesque: a James Thorpe, old as General Tilney, in *Persuasion* the heroine's fantastically conceived father, Sir Walter. Begin the book by dwelling as acerbly as possible on his folly, through the narrator's sharp eyes. Keep the tone of the novel in closer touch than *Mansfield Park* with the tone of a tale. If the heroine is in danger of disabling self-pity, make sure that at the critical moment she will be introduced to a minor character who specializes in that failing, so she may be seen to recognize it in herself as well as in him, thus remaining sufficiently conscious of herself to steer a difficult course.

The heroine is Anne Elliot and this acquaintance Captain Benwick, whose plight compares with Anne's to the extent that he has lost his intended wife, but by death, and only some months before. "He was evidently a young man of considerable taste in reading, though principally in poetry; and besides the persuasion of having given him at least an evening's indulgence in the discussion of subjects, which his usual companions had probably no concern in, she had the hope of being of real use to him in some suggestions as to the duty and benefit of struggling against affliction, which had naturally grown out of their conversation."[13] (It is noteworthy that Anne here acts on a "persuasion," the main thematic word in the book.)[14] "Feeling in herself the right of seniority of mind," like Imlac's in seeking to comfort Nekayah after the abduction of Pekuah, Anne exerts herself against Benwick's tendency (in Imlac's words) to "increase the burden of life by a voluntary accumulation of misery."[15]

It is clear to the reader, from the delicate satire of the narrator against Benwick's reading, his taste, and his authenticity (he pauses to wonder "how the *Giaour* was to be pronounced"), that Anne is more alarmed for him than he deserves; before long she will realize her mistake, as Rasselas does after pursuing some would-be teachers. Still unenlightened about Benwick, Anne recommends, rather sternly—befitting the gravity of her feelings—that he read less poetry and more prose, mentioning "works of our best moralists" (unquestionably Johnson among them) "calculated to rouse and fortify the mind by the highest precepts, and the strongest examples of moral and religious endurances." Her alarm for Benwick occasions the prescription of strong, idealistic medicine, laying stress on the need for brave virtue rather than self-investigation of the sort promoted by the end of *Rambler* 4 (e.g., "vice is the natural consequence of narrow thoughts, . . . begins in mistake, and ends in ignominy").[16] Wrong about the quality of Benwick's feelings, projecting her own feelings upon him, she overlooks pertinent psychological questions.

More importantly, however, Anne proves lucid in the application of the episode to her own condition, recognizing her own extraordinary, self-expressive interest in the young man's sorrow and putting herself properly on guard against the illusory association she is courting: "When the evening was over, Anne could not but be amused at the idea of her coming . . . to preach patience and resignation to a young man whom she had never seen before; nor could she help fearing, on more serious reflection, that, like many other great moralists and preachers, she had been eloquent

on a point in which her own conduct would ill bear examination"
(3.11.101). For a parallel to this scene of the main character's empirical, psychological self-assessment, we would look in vain at the
novel before Jane Austen and look long at the novel afterward. We
would find the equivalent, however, in *Rasselas*, not fully when
Imlac comforts Nekayah but quite so, within a single mind, when
the prince responds to Imlac's account of the astronomer's mental
aberration flowing from his "narrow thoughts." Imlac discourses
on the perils of association: "some particular train of ideas fixes the
attention . . . false opinions fasten upon the mind." That Rasselas
responds first by according Imlac's story much more "serious regard" than do his sister and her maid, and second by confessing
his own secret, dangerous "fantastick delight,"[17] shows—dramatically, subordinating the ideas to the fiction while releasing the hero
from subordination to his fixed ideas—that he has relatively independently sensed the application of the astronomer's case to his
own mental tendencies. On one side, Anne Elliot is Rasselas' daughter, comparable in positive self-consciousness.

The main choice of life the book holds out to her before the
end, apart from despondency, is the opportunity to marry her
cousin Mr. Elliot. Quite unlike Imlac, Lady Russell urges her on,
painting the similitude between Anne, restored to the family home
which Mr. Elliot has inherited, and her beloved, dead mother who
once presided there. Anne falters, her attention fixed: "For a few
moments her imagination and her heart were bewitched. The idea of
becoming what her mother had been; of having the precious name
of 'Lady Elliot' first revived in herself; of being restored to Kellynch, calling it her home again, her home for ever, was a charm
which she could not immediately resist." All she must do is connect
this "idea" with that of Mr. Elliot as comparably charming. "The
. . . image of Mr. Elliot . . . brought Anne to composure again.
The charm of Kellynch and of 'Lady Elliot' all faded away. She
never could accept him. And it was not only that her feelings were
still adverse to any man save one; her judgment, on a serious consideration of the possibilities of such a case, was against Mr. Elliot"
(4.5.160). How unpleasant to wed Mr. Elliot—a topic I shall return
to, with consideration of the revived Fanny-Price question of pre-

possession. In this passage just quoted we see a train of associations form and accelerate only to be stopped very suddenly. Anne is too perceptive about the workings of her own mind, her "judgment" too alert, to associate all these ideas in a voluntary delusion.[18]

Persuasion equips Anne with no active mentor, no Henry Tilney to learn from, to idealize, and, in time, to distinguish herself from. There has been: Lady Russell, who persuaded Anne not to marry Wentworth years before. There could still be, for Lady Russell remains ready with advice. There have actually been two mentors in *Persuasion*; Wentworth had long ago done his utmost to turn Anne away from Lady Russell's influence. At that time Anne had, Candide-like, been torn between two mentors. Neither of them could be an infallible guide: Lady Russell is swayed by considerations of wealth, and Wentworth does not seem extremely perceptive; he cannot understand Anne's motives for rejecting him, and he misses signs in other ways, for example, in taking Benwick at face value long after Anne has stopped. *Persuasion*, one could say, therefore begins at what was the middle of *Rasselas*, the point at which the main character perceives that his point of view is not quite the same as anyone else's.

If Anne is to have a mentor, she must be her own, being spectator of as well as participant in her life, as Adam Smith had recommended. We have begun to see how remarkably skilled she is. It helps that she apparently—unlike Candide and Rasselas, Catherine Morland and Fanny Price—has no original association of ideas to unmake, that she is not laboring under any notable illusion or delusion. In this respect she may differ from both Lady Russell and Captain Wentworth, but I need not go into that aspect of things. Instead of having to perform archeology upon herself, she has to be the historian of current events, of present associations in the perspective of memory. More than any fictional heroine or hero I can think of, Anne Elliot shows herself, in the ongoing present, as "someone upon whom nothing is lost." In the manner of eighteenth-century psychology, Anne proves alert to every possible valid and invalid association of ideas in and around her.

This extraordinarily receptive presence of mind the narrator forcefully intimates, from Anne's point of view, as soon as she and Wentworth begin to be regularly in the same company again.

> Whether former feelings were to be renewed, must be brought to the proof; former times must undoubtedly be brought to the recollection of each; *they* could not but be reverted to; the year of their engagement could not but be named by him, in the little narratives or descriptions which conversation called forth. His profession qualified him, his disposition led him, to talk; and '*That* was in the year six;' '*That* happened before I went to sea in the year six,' occurred in the course of the first evening they spent together: and though his voice did not falter, and though she had no reason to suppose his eye wandering towards her while he spoke, Anne felt the utter impossibility, from her knowledge of his mind, that he could be unvisited by remembrance any more than herself. There must be the same immediate association of thought, though she was very far from conceiving it to be of equal pain.

> (3.8.63)

Howard S. Babb has excellent pages on what he calls Anne's "intuition" regarding Wentworth and others.[19] That power becomes still more intelligible when explained by reference to associationism, in keeping with the narrator's own terminology, and such explanation can only promote suitable alertness and wariness in the reader.

During the conversation introduced by the paragraph I have just quoted, Wentworth quickly turns to so remote a topic as his first command, the ship *Asp*, superannuated and depreciated as such by one of the present group. But Wentworth exclaims, "Ah! she was a dear old Asp to me. She did all that I wanted. I knew she would.—I knew that we should either go to the bottom together, or that she would be the making of me . . ." (3.8.65–66). The narrator does not comment on these words, only a few of those he speaks that could bear commentary, but Anne too is feminine, dear, dependable, and "old." Wentworth does not see the analogies he is raising. Had he and Anne married years before there would have been the risk and the promise he goes on about. But Anne, we may be sure, sees in Wentworth's words what she loves about him, the thinking and feeling principle beyond appearances that enforces his affection for the old ship. Unrecognized by anyone else present, this is a moment of exquisite love and suffering for her. The dramatic power of the scene could be elaborated; it picks up themes of dependency, faithfulness, danger and death, marriage as a ship, the image of the affectionate and sound old nautical couple the Crofts, the November of life, and surely more. The point I wish to make, however, is mainly Anne's power to take all this in, consciously. The scene also indicates why she cannot conceivably love Mr. Elliot, though, as she will think, his appearance is pleasing, and his manners are as excellent as Wentworth's (4.3.143). For with Anne's fine perspicacity she is aware that, thoroughly unlike Wentworth, Mr. Elliot never gives himself away. Beyond appearances in his case there is nothing, or evil. There should be signals, intimations; there are none. The inner transmitter seems dead.

Mr. Elliot has returned to Anne's family after affronting her sister years before. How can Anne know he has changed for the better? It is the question, based on the chain of events, that Pamela will not face and that Fanny, regarding Henry Crawford, only seems to take seriously. Anne faces it squarely: ". . . Though he might now think very differently, who could answer for the true sentiments of a clever, cautious man, grown old enough to appreciate a fair character?" (4.5.161). His cold ambition for social standing to add to his wealth, a motive about which Anne will later be informed by her friend Mrs. Smith, is approached closely enough in this conception of possibility. More happily, Anne's sensors take in "ideas" from Wentworth's comments, signals of a particular "consciousness" in him, that immediately, unintendedly disclose the return of his love for her and the beginning of his being jealous of Mr. Elliot—to Anne "the only intelligible motive" for an abrupt departure (4.8.184,183,186,190). It is as if Anne were reading for us. When late in the book she hurries to the White Hart, "to see again the friends and companions of the last autumn, with an eagerness of good will which many associations contributed to form" (4.10.220), the word *associations* designates Anne's element, social and mental. It is just the receptiveness to consciousness of *rapports* characterizing Anne which Montesquieu broadly promotes in representing the empirical achievements and failures of the hero of the

Lettres persanes, the search into relations between professions and likely interests.

Varieties of the word *conscious* turn up time and again through *Persuasion* (also 3.8.72, 4.12.248), illuminating scenes between Anne and Wentworth—notably the reference to "a delicious consciousness" felt by Anne after he has declared his love (4.11.246). As Jean H. Hagstrum shows, *conscious* had been an especially potent word in the eighteenth century, when (distinctly echoing the struggle of self-love against rigorism) it meant "a kind of self-approving awareness that attends good behavior," thus was related to *conscience*, but increasingly carried strong overtones of sensual pleasure.[20] The second meaning is not inappropriate here at the end of the novel, when we find Anne at last "glowing and lovely in sensibility and happiness" (4.11.245; "sensibility" another sexually active word).[21] Wentworth darts a "conscious look" at Anne after overhearing a third character speak of engagements of marriage in a way that recalls Wentworth's own disappointment years before (4.11.231). The word had its present-day meaning then, being aware of something or concentrating on it. There was also, however, what the *OED* labels an obsolete sense that is valuable for talking of Anne. The word once meant sharing knowledge of something with another person, and more, being privy to something with someone, the case with Anne when she is deliciously conscious in an unsuspecting crowd. (In *Mansfield Park* the word turns up with this meaning to describe a moment involving Edmund and Mary—2.4.214). But as Anne observes Wentworth through the novel, her talent for understanding his mind extends the obsolete meaning so as to take in having access to someone's thoughts without that person's knowing it. Anne is a powerful character.

Persuasion also has a strong narrator, especially (as in the major philosophical tales) at the beginning: a penetrating narrator who sums up people devastatingly right and left. I have said that Catherine Morland's preliminary judgment of General Tilney, who must be good-natured because handsome and Henry's father, resembles Candide's first judgment of Pangloss, credible because listened to by the desirable Cunégonde. The narrator of *Persuasion* sees Anne's father, Sir Walter, as similarly mechanized by associated ideas: "He considered the blessing of beauty as inferior only to the blessing of a baronetcy; and the Sir Walter Elliot, who united these gifts, was the constant object of his warmest respect and devotion" (3.1.4). Elizabeth, his eldest daughter, comparably likes Mr. Elliot, her cousin, "for himself, and still more for being her father's heir" (3.1.8). But the strongest statement by the narrator comes somewhat later, the shockingly blunt appraisal of the dead son of Mrs. Musgrove ("a very troublesome, hopeless son; . . . the good fortune to lose him before he reached his twentieth year," and more—3.6.50). This is a voice not unreminiscent of the omniscient, authoritative, judgmental narrators of the beginning of *Rasselas* and *Candide*: the narrator whose earthbound surrogate is the fallible mentor who succeeds him in the chair of judgment.

That surrogate in *Persuasion* is Anne, her own mentor. And true to philosophical tale form, there is a dramatic difference between Anne's mind and the narrator's. What the narrator sharply observes about foppish Sir Walter and worthless "Dick" Musgrove would not be news to Anne: she sees these things very well, too well for her comfort. But she is too conscious also of the ramifications of circumstances, and the limitations as well as strengths of individual points of view, to indulge herself in satirically simple summings-up. Hence it would not be going too far to say that the narrator's strong persuasion of seeing all has ironical analogues in Lady Russell's positiveness against Wentworth, or in that hardness of resolution which Wentworth for a while admires in Louisa Musgrove. Wentworth himself displays a richer consciousness than the narrator's in the scene of the *Asp*. He had been Dick's commander; sentimental Mrs. Musgrove wants Wentworth to sympathize with her. He generously, not indiscriminately however, "entered into conversation with her, in a low voice, about her son, doing it with so much sympathy and natural grace, as shewed the kindest consideration for all that was real and unabsurd in the parent's feelings" (3.8.67–68). There is a fine counterpoint here between Wentworth's Smithian, concordant response, which is undoubtedly understood and appreciated by Anne, and what seems the narrator's refusal to give in so easily. The narrator subjoins a paragraph and more about the ungainliness of Mrs. Musgrove's "large fat sighings"—a passage that manages to sound not unlike "silly, conceited" Sir Walter Elliot.

The narrator, that is, has a dramatic role to play, against Anne, as if grasping the other characters more fully than she does her heroine, as if Anne's heart were not entirely within the comprehension of the narrator's more detached rationality. When Anne's friend Mrs. Smith reveals the nasty facts about Mr. Elliot, the narrator injects a short paragraph about Anne's shuddering at the thought that Lady Russell might have persuaded her to marry him (4.9.211). But the notion that Anne could have married a man whom her heart has come to be so perceptively set against is unconvincing except as a wholly expressive false surmise on Anne's part.

Again, as in the graver parallel case of whether Fanny Price could love Henry Crawford, comparison with Darrel Mansell's opinion will clarify mine. Urging the idea that Anne suffers from illusions, Mansell argues for her susceptibility to Mr. Elliot, finding Joseph Wiesenfarth "in error when he says that before Mrs. Smith reveals Mr. Elliot's true character Anne 'has decided against' him. She has almost decided against him, but not quite." Mansell explains that, with Mrs. Smith's revelation, "For Anne 'the charm was broken'—the same words that had signalled Edmund Bertram's disenchantment" with Mary Crawford in *Mansfield Park*. Anne "has been saved from what she now admits was at least the possibility 'that she might have been persuaded by Lady Russell' to marry Mr. Elliot. It remains only for Anne 'to retrace . . . the few steps of unnecessary intimacy she had been gradually led along.'"[22] Again, problems. First, the statement about the charm's being broken has, in Austen's context, no direct bearing on Anne, since it occurs as one of Mr. Elliot's thoughts when he suddenly, the first time he speaks with her after the revelation, finds her cool to him (4.10.214). Second, the words here about Anne's retracing "the few steps of unnecessary intimacy" simply mean, in context, that with the evidence she now has about Mr. Elliot's baseness she will no longer be sociable with him as she had been when she could conceive of an alternate possible trope for his character—the notion of his being simply a hollow man. Two genetic models had been plausible; with the new, substantial testimony from Mrs. Smith, one of them collapses. The steps of intimacy have been few in any event, and Anne has been "gradually led along" in them by Mr. Elliot, who has taken petty advantage of his close social relation with Anne to insinuate something closer, in ways too conceivably ambiguous for her to resist them. Henceforth she will be less tolerant; that is all the statement means.

Third, and most important, there is the matter of what the narrator says Anne admits, the passage as follows: "Anne could just acknowledge within herself such a possibility of having been induced to marry him, as made her shudder at the idea of the misery which must have followed. It was just possible that she might have been persuaded by Lady Russell!" (4.9.211) The fragility of the "idea," the slimness of the possibility, is emphasized by the repeated "just," and that slimness shrinks to invisibility when the reader contemplates all that precedes this scene. The fourth chapter of the book proclaims Anne's regret that Lady Russell had persuaded her to refuse Wentworth's proposal more than seven years before, and mentions Anne's having refused to marry Charles Musgrove three years after that, though Lady Russell approved the match (3.4.28). Lady Russell has persuaded Anne about nothing of real importance since Wentworth's proposal. Anne is too intelligent and sane to let herself be manipulated again by the same or any other hand.

Moreover, if this evidence will not suffice, there remains the clearcut declaration on the subject that I have already quoted, from one of the chapters before this scene: "She could never accept" Mr. Elliot, "And it was not only that her feelings were still adverse to any man save one; her judgment, on a serious consideration of the possibilities of such a case, was against Mr. Elliot" (4.5.160). The defense rests. A reader must minimize the importance of that statement to maximize the possibility of a second persuasion by Lady Russell, and the accumulated force of Anne's character is decisively against doing any such thing. In other words, the narrator, in sanctioning the implausible, has cast herself loose from the events of the narrative. The authority of the narrator must be judged accordingly; must be deprived, that is, of any privileged position we may have accorded it in comparison with the authority of Anne.

Thus the mentor—Anne, for herself—takes over the narrator's judgmental function, according to the tale pattern of *Rasselas* and *Candide*.

Perceiving the dramatic part of the narrator clarifies the part played by Mrs. Smith, the physically disabled, longtime friend of Anne introduced late in the book who testifies against Mr. Elliot. Here is the superfluous revelation that gives emphasis to the heroine's independent powers of mind (a second such revelation being Wentworth's later announcement of revived love for Anne, in keeping with her well established consciousness of his motives). Besides being the witness for the prosecution who arrives after the fact of conviction, the forceful Mrs. Smith also functions in the book as vestigial, superfluous mentor to Anne, thus also increasing our sense of Anne's strength. And somewhat like Anne and the narrator, Mrs. Smith has what she praises in her nurse, "a line for seeing human nature," the knack of collecting information from social intercourse "that makes one know one's species better" (4.5.155). But unlike Anne, yet like the narrator, Mrs. Smith can be very sharp-tongued, revealing what the narrator finally describes as glowing spirits in contrast to Anne's tender "warmth of . . . heart" (4.12.252). The presence of the distinctly flawed Mrs. Smith—who, unlike her news, is not superfluous—helps a reader distinguish the narrator from Anne, as, less satisfactorily in literary effect, the presence of Mary Crawford in *Mansfield Park* helps define the false tone of the narrator.

There is another instance of the narrator of *Persuasion*'s overshooting the mark, after the passages about Mr. Elliot. Anne has just been described as most pleasurably walking along, with her head full of thoughts of Wentworth, "and be the conclusion of the present suspense good or bad, her affection would be his forever. Their union, she believed, could not divide her more from other men than their final separation." The narrator comments, "Prettier musings of high-wrought love and eternal constancy, could never have passed along the streets of Bath, than Anne was sporting with from Camden-place to Westgate-buildings. It was almost enough to spread purification and perfume all the way" (4.9.192). Susan Morgan explicates the latter sentences by reference to Austen's general distrust of unalterable first attachments and thereby distinguishes an excess of enthusiasm in Anne's thoughts on this occasion.[23] Yet there is something slightly egregious about, particularly, the sentence on purification and perfume.[24] Anne has in fact painfully felt her love a long time, is hardly likely to drop it quickly, and, most important, will shortly suggest a middle position perfectly suited to her circumstances and her delicate, firm feelings, that of "loving longest, . . . when hope is gone" (4.11.235).

In contrast to Anne's judgments, those of the narrator tend to seem one-sided. The omniscient, judgmental point of view which tale heroes at first immaturely covet is here, as there, seen to be shallow or, in Adam Smith's term, dissonant. But as I have suggested, slightly off-center comments by a narrator are not necessarily pointless, for they may have the virtue of defining the centrality of the main character's distinct responses. In this respect *Persuasion*, unlike *Mansfield Park*—and Fielding's *Amelia*, which at grim moments can also emit an oddly toned, seemingly desperate, obtrusive passage by the narrator[25]—remains securely under control. The proof is in the fact that the narrator, at the end of *Persuasion*, unlike the narrators of *Mansfield Park* and (for a different reason) *Northanger Abbey*, does not call much attention to herself. This is in keeping with the philosophical-tale economy of *Candide* and *Rasselas*. Since—unlike Catherine Morland to some extent, and, in the last analysis, unlike Fanny, but like Voltaire's and Johnson's heroes—Anne can be fully the mentor of herself, maintaining both sympathy and detachment with respect to all the elements of her world, the narrator—like Voltaire's and Johnson's—need not make a flamboyant final appearance for purposes of distancing the fiction from us. In fact, the narrator has significantly disqualified herself for so high-handed a part.

In Jane Austen the cardinal sin, or tragic flaw, or besetting or besotting folly is to claim to know what one does not. "I know you better than you know yourself," prates Isabella Thorpe in *Northanger Abbey* (1.10.71). Emma Woodhouse knows what is best for everyone—the matter for further examples abounds, including matter from the narrators' commentary. Pervasive in Austen is a firm, unpretentious, relative secularity of vision, in her most admirable characters and in her novels taken entirely, and this quality may indicate her deepest affinity with the spirit of the philosophical tale, which is philosophical not only in emphasizing the psychological dimension of knowledge but also in the consequent epistemology. I have said most about this when commenting on *Candide*: dropped as he is into Hume's world, learning in the long run not to impose causality on the merely similar or contiguous, or to be wary when doing so—being critical as well as constructive about the enchainment of events, events in the world, events in the mind: connections and associations of ideas.

In *Rasselas* it is noteworthy that the "choice of eternity," transcendent wisdom, means more to the middle-aged Imlac and to Nekayah than it does to Rasselas, who is chiefly intent on learning to live well. What Johnson probably objected to above all in the new, formally realistic comedies of romance, was their tendency to become oracular about the full meaning of life, in a way not reconcilable with the empirical standpoint of the genre: realism becoming naturalism—genetic models of the conceivable being transformed into assertedly final truth that rules out better possibilities. *Rambler* 4 contains a reasoned attack on such a notion, the theory "that certain virtues have their correspondent faults, and therefore that to exhibit either apart is to deviate from probability"; for example (in what Johnson contemptuously calls "this sagacious maxim"), the idea that men are "grateful in the same degree as they are resentful" (3:23).

The heritage of the philosophical tale embracing *Northanger Abbey* and *Persuasion* preserves and defends a plainer, more fully human point of view than the one Johnson attacks, promoting imperfect but helpful clarification of that human point of view, probing it without exaggerating either its real powers or its real perils. That heritage brings realities to mind while making an effort to insure that other realities are not ignored. Its disposition, encountering an originally sad case like that of Fanny Price in *Mansfield Park*, a case sealed up in novelistic circumstantiality, is rebuffed. Encountering less claustral a set of circumstances, Anne's in *Persuasion*, it can go forward to the end with typical, modest honesty, leaving us with the vision of happy lovers who have lost eight years, who on Anne's side have "no family to receive and estimate" Wentworth "properly; nothing of respectability, of harmony, of goodwill" (the near-Northanger life), and who, attached to the navy, have enough to worry about, as the last sentences of the book make plain: "His profession was all that could ever make her friends wish that tenderness less; the dread of a future war all that could dim her sunshine. She gloried in being a sailor's wife, but she must pay the tax of a quick alarm for belonging to that profession which is, if possible, more distinguished in its domestic virtues than in its national importance" (4.12.251–52).

Here at the end is a properly tale-like concord not unison, happily and unhappily ever after, both important, neither to be underrated. Anne has been fortunate, ungratuitously, while Wentworth at the end has to forego the satisfaction he takes in "believing myself to earn every blessing that I enjoyed. . . . I must learn to brook being happier than I deserve" (4.11.247). The final, terrestrial consolation of the perspective of the philosophical tale is that in intelligently holding some dear and vexing things certain yet in allowing sufficient room for the truly unknown—in preserving a limited and positive, not smuggling in the overarching, point of view—that perspective does not rule out the possibility of consequences better than might reasonably be expected.

But in attempting to define Anne Elliot's formidable powers of consciousness, I have thus far said too little about the issue of self-love, another subject of consciousness and hardly the least important. Austen's pointed attention to it, I have suggested, signals her most original development and extension of the theme and pattern of the philosophical tale. Wentworth's words just quoted are to the point: the notion of earning every blessing indicates, to say the least, an unexamined ordering of man and the world, and constitutes an unreliable prop for self-love. Character after character in *Persuasion* is shown to have distorted the world and himself in seeking unrealistic self-satisfaction, and Anne is not inhumanly above that tendency. But as we are told in a cardinal passage, "Her early impressions were incurable. She prized the frank, the openhearted, the eager character beyond all others. Warmth and enthusiasm did captivate her still" (4.5.161). Here Anne is thinking about what Mr. Elliot lacks, and the "early impressions" may refer simply to her impressions of him—I do not think so. The application of the phrase is as much to the succeeding sentence as to the rest of the context, and defines the original, most fundamental genetic principle of Anne's character: what she herself potentially (certainly not always actually) is and would be, as much as her circumstances allow. Anne's being so much on her own, having to make her way in the condition of individualism (which she and the book do not celebrate but make the best of), and her being so acute of mind, permit Austen to concentrate on the issue of Anne's self-love in addition to her self-knowledge. As the book begins, that knowledge must be sustained, but that love must be increased, against odds.

What the quest for self-knowledge is to *Rasselas*, Anne's quest for restored self-love is to *Persuasion*. Both objects are essential elements in realism of psychological self-assessment. As long as Anne loves Wentworth, marriage to him remains indispensable for her happiness; just as important, however, is her love of herself, interdependent with love of him so long as it lasts. Yet her refusal of Wentworth, while doing nothing to abate her feelings for him, has dealt her feelings for herself a grievous blow, with a wound signified by the recurrently mentioned "early loss of bloom" (3.4.28). The indifference of others to her feelings—of Wentworth above all but not alone—is a burden she can scarcely bear, and nearly everyone conspicuously takes her for granted. *Persuasion* comes closest to *Mansfield Park* and Anne most nearly approaches "self-delusion" (3.6.42) under the pressure of this frustration—an extreme case of Imlac's "For who is pleased with what he is?" It hurts her, far more than a comparable remark hurts Elizabeth Bennet, to hear Wentworth's low opinion upon seeing her again: "so altered he should not have known you" (3.7.60). It marks Austen's strength that Anne can be stoical only for a moment and that, despite her shrewdness, she is unable to entertain the possibility that Wentworth may be expressing in the remark only his undiminished anger, fueled by continued love.

A passage in Hume illuminates this chain of events in Wentworth as well as Anne, and Anne's capacity when less upset to recognize it. Complementing the association of ideas, Hume discerns a *"second* property . . . in the human mind" which he terms "a like association of impressions. All resembling impressions are connected together, and no sooner one arises than the rest immediately follow. Grief and disappointment give rise to anger, anger to envy, envy to malice, and malice to grief again, till the whole circle be compleated."[26] Thus in human nature there is a natural undercurrent of association of feelings affecting the association of ideas. With minor modification, the sequence in Hume's example could be used to plot the genetic, mechanical curve of Wentworth's feelings through much of the book, "grief and disappointment" proceeding to anger, then malice, then jealousy. (Anne's feelings would move much like those but for her greater sensitivity and self-discipline.) Malice leads Wentworth to remark that Anne has changed so. Anne in time perceives his motive. The blissful, late, complementary passage is that in which Wentworth, having forgotten his remark, tells her that "to my eye you could never alter." Anne smiles and says nothing, displaying her Humean insight into human, affective causality. "It was too pleasing a blunder for a reproach. It is something for a woman to be assured, in her eight-and-twentieth year, that she has not lost one charm of earlier youth: but the value of such homage was inexpressibly increased to Anne, by comparing it with former words, and feeling it to be the result, not the cause of a revival of his warm attachment" (4.11.243).

Long before this, in wishing she were still lovely, Anne testifies to the demands of her self-love—to the natural human desire to be thought attractive which her father has so perverted (suggesting Austen's purpose in equipping him with exactly that flaw). The cultural (and novelistic) bias against self-love is an obstacle much in evidence—as it should be, so imposing an obstacle was it in Austen's time, before, and after. When Anne discovers Wentworth free of an attachment to another woman, "She had some feelings which she was ashamed to investigate. They were too much like joy, senseless joy!" (4.6.167–68) There is no sense in the joy mainly because by rigorist conventions a person, especially a woman, ought not to have personal, non-altruistic desires. Anne must comparably steel herself to accept the happiness of discovering Wentworth still loves her: ". . . She re-entered the house so happy as to be obliged to find an alloy in some momentary apprehensions of its being impossible to last. An interval of meditation, serious and grateful, was the best corrective of every thing dangerous in such high-wrought felicity; and she went to her room, and grew steadfast and fearless in the thankfulness of her enjoyment" (4.11.245). For a Christian like Anne to be grateful to God for providential success and happiness is as one might expect, but that is not the case here. Her uneasiness about being happy compels her to think vague propitiatory thoughts; something like the Great impersonal or malevolent Chain, the nemesis of self-love, hangs overhead. And a particular symptom of Anne's regrettable discomfort with the most elementary and innocent self-love is the adjective "high-wrought," a mock-sentimental term (used by the narrator in that dissonant passage about purification and perfume) here quite out of place, Anne's sentiments deserving no disparagement.

But it would be easy to misread Anne's and Jane Austen's responses on these occasions. As much as they show Anne to be inhibited by the real cultural bias against self-love, they show Anne straining, realistically, against that bias. A novelist less intrepid about the realities of the mind than Austen would not have included the statements I have quoted; instead, Anne would have been represented as the ineffably mindless maiden. Austen's candor on the difficult subject of self-love is admirable even in these passages, and manifestly so elsewhere, the claims of self more generously entertained. In one such scene Anne is in a shop, knows Wentworth is approaching it, and looks outside—pretending to see if it is raining. "Why was she to suspect herself of another motive? Captain Wentworth must be out of sight. She left her seat, she would go, one half of her should not be always so much wiser than the other half, or always suspecting the other of being worse than it was. She would see if it rained" (4.7.175). Anne's half-deluding herself here so as to disarm the bias against self-love suits her most attractive warmth of heart.

But the issue of self-love is not simple: self-love itself can be dangerously biased. Like Bacon, Anne cries, "What wild imaginations one forms, where dear self is concerned!" (4.9.201). And she is in some danger. Before meeting the plaintive Benwick, Anne reveals a desire to indulge in poetic despondency herself. She summons up thoughts of the ages of man—the ages of Anne—on the analogy of autumn, "the declining year, with declining happiness, and the images of youth and hope, and spring, all gone together." She is slow to emulate the farmer "meaning to have spring again" (3.10.85). Yet she tries to practice a georgics of the mind. She has a genetic model, related to the ages of man, with which to conceive of herself: "She had been forced into prudence in her youth, she learned romance as she grew older—the natural sequel of an unnatural beginning" (3.4.30); and, "Anne hoped she had outlived the age of blushing; but the age of emotion she certainly had not" (3.6.49). She does not merely stand and wait for Wentworth to revive his love for her. She actively perseveres in living, counteracting despondent feelings with conscious analysis and moral and epistemological discipline; unlike the astronomer in *Rasselas*, avoiding seclusion; refusing to impose an unhappy ending. She does not venture to accord Wentworth a final summing-up, as fear or anger might lead her to do. She does bestir herself to take an interest in others, to please and be pleased, unpromising as her companions may be—yet she does not pretend that she is really contented. Even when thinking she has lost Wentworth forever, she can be temporarily "delighted" by a useful deed she has performed for her hypochondriacal, querulous sister Mary (4.1.122). The tincture of rigoristic self-approbation here—perhaps at its worst in her regrettable reflection on Mr. Elliot's "Sunday-travelling" (4.5.161)—is in keeping with her character, but hardly represents the whole of it.

The central movement of self-love, the restoration of Anne's bloom, could not be more felicitously rendered, befitting the delicate interplay of Anne's own efforts in behalf of her spirits, the effects of the sea air at Lyme, her being thought useful in the emergency that occurs there, and several instances of refreshing admiration that others begin to accord her. The stranger who will turn out to be her cousin Mr. Elliot gives evidence of thinking her attractive, and when she next meets Lady Russell, "either Anne was improved in plumpness and looks, or Lady Russell fancied her so; and Anne, in receiving her compliments on the occasion, had the amusement of connecting them with the silent admiration of her cousin, and of hoping that she was to be blessed with a second spring of youth and beauty" (4.1.124). The connection of these ideas in Anne's consciousness produces something much superior to despondency, no doubt enhancing her beauty still further.

The process of simultaneous perception and creation suits Anne's nice balance of vulnerability and strength, dependence and independence. On the one hand, she never deludes herself into thinking, with Mme de Merteuil, that her rationality does away with her need to be loved. Regarding that need, late in the book, she confesses herself "not wise yet" (4.7.178). She knows some important things are beyond her control, and that sometimes the most she can accomplish is not to work against her own interest in regard to them—as she might by indulging anger against Wentworth or herself. Because she knows enough to contribute, within her power, to the writing of a reasonably happy ending, and not to invite an unhappy one by adopting willful associations, she does what a philosophical heroine can do to bring satisfaction about: not everything but something.[27]

On the other hand, that something can be very substantial, suited to the most positive self-love. She never hides her love for Wentworth from herself. Yet when she thinks him unavailable to her, she can become definitely interested in the question of whether she could love Mr. Elliot, and pursues the subject with, at first, encouraging results (3.2.136, 3.3.143–44)—thus neatly distinguishing herself from the morbidly dependent Fanny Price. Anne proves herself to be generally active and honest in forming and preserving helpful contingent conceptions: imagined ideas which forward her understanding, which help her to know. That is, she knowingly entertains hopeful, figurative quasi-preconceptions, flowing from her own desires accurately assessed, about other characters' motives and about various possible means of happiness for herself. (Recall Rasselas' lingering desire for a kingdom.)

She forms and acts on more than one such idea, not merely the idea of marriage to Wentworth. And when she learns that he is still interested in her and wrongly thinks her attracted to Mr. Elliot, she is soon ready to bestir herself: "How was such jealousy to be quieted? How was the truth to reach him? How, in all the peculiar disadvantages of their respective situations, would he ever learn her real sentiments?" (4.8.191). Though for the moment this may be mere verbal hand-wringing, she soon strains decorum to deliver her message, declaring to a company including Wentworth that she would rather attend the theater, in a group of which he will be one, than attend another gathering where Elliot is to be present. Further, in conversation with Wentworth, she asserts she is "not yet so much changed" (4.10.224–25). And there is more: Anne's perhaps unconsciously letting her voice rise to an eager cry as she concludes a passionate defense of women's love, in a long discussion with a friend of Wentworth, Wentworth himself sitting nearby—within hearing, it turns out; and then Anne's maneuvering to have a moment alone with him (4.11.235, 238–39). And finally, "delicious consciousness." Despite realistic inhibitions realistically presented, Anne with tale-like clarity proclaims herself a heroine of self-love. "Feelings rather natural" move her.

This tale-like novel even concludes with an extra, subtly tale-like twist. It takes Wentworth aback that Anne, at the end, despite suffering so much so long, maintains she was right in letting herself be persuaded against him eight years before. This declaration also surprises the first-time reader and may remain unpalatable in later readings. Anne explains that she would have suffered still more, "because I should have suffered in my conscience," had she rejected the persuasion of her mentor of the time, Lady Russell, who "was in the place of a parent." Yet Anne's motive was not merely the "strong sense of duty" she mentions (4.11.246). Her decision represented no cold exercise of obedience, but was rather her response to an experienced and devoted woman "whom she had always loved and relied on" (3.4.27) and whom she has continued to love. In other words, however frigid, misdirected, and even deluded Lady Russell's prudence, Anne's in being guided by it was otherwise: her docility proceeded from the fund of affection and reasonableness upon which Wentworth also draws and, we are certain, can continue to rely. Anne, years earlier, at that early phase of the ages of man, could not have done otherwise and remained herself. She acted as she thought best accorded with her actual motives and unforced expectations, and in doing what she did "imagined herself consulting his good, even more than her own" (3.4.28). The reader may wince, but may feel less inclined to do so if the fundamental logic of Anne's position is given its due. To the extent that there had been any voluntary delusion in all of this, and the force of Anne's comments is to insist there was not, it had clearly been risked by her so as to avoid another, seemingly more likely voluntary delusion.

It may help readers to accept Anne's speech if they consider the possibility that it completes the novel's philosophical-tale pattern. There was an early association of ideas. The event of that persuasion is the counterpart of the Gothic association which Catherine Morland must disassemble and of the link with Edmund which Fanny Price cannot bear to examine—not to reiterate the particular preconceptions of Gulliver, Usbek, Candide, and Rasselas. What Anne concludes about the event is that her being persuaded represented a valid connection of ideas on her part, though the act of persuading, on Lady Russell's part, proceeded from a false association (". . . Captain Wentworth's manners had not suited her own ideas . . ."—2.12.249). Too much influenced by respect for established power and wealth, Lady Russell had overestimated their importance while underestimating Wentworth's spirit and ability. Anne has examined the event from the time it occurred, assessed it carefully, and discovered that it was not so irrational on her part as might have been supposed, or as Wentworth views it. Anne's self-love, her sustained, modest willingness to think well of herself while probing her thought and motives, completes the pattern of realistic self-assessment. Seen from the standpoint of the philosophical tale, *Persuasion* thus concludes with the unsurprising yet unconventional thought that just as a person may look to the future for something better than expected, especially if one comports oneself so as to leave room for it, there is the possibility that one may find in the past, in one's chain of becoming, something more positive than one fears.

Notes

1. The Philosophical Tale and the Novel

1. Sheldon Sacks, *Fiction and the Shape of Belief: A Study of Henry Fielding with Glances at Swift, Johnson and Richardson* (1964; rpt. Berkeley and Los Angeles: University of California Press, 1967), p. 57. Parenthetical references in my text are to this edition.

2. *The Autobiography of Benjamin Franklin*, Leonard W. Labaree et al., eds. (New Haven and London: Yale University Press, 1964), p. 72.

3. *The Early Diary of Frances Burney, 1768–1778*, Annie Raine Ellis, ed. (London: George Bell, 1889), 1:14–15, quoted in part by William Kenney, "Johnson's *Rasselas* after Two Centuries," *Boston University Studies in English* (1957), 3:89.

4. Commenting on late-eighteenth-century reviewers, Ioan Williams says that "while they often stated that the romances of Mrs. Radcliffe were in a different class from the novels of Fielding, the basis of their distinction was merely the degree to which either writer imitated nature, a criterion which had been used so often, in so many contexts throughout the century, that it had lost its precision and usefulness." *Novel and Romance 1700–1800: A Documentary Record* (New York: Barnes & Noble, 1970), p. 23; my epigraph for chapter 1 is from pp. 193–94. To what extent does *Rasselas* imitate real life? Bernard L. Einbond comments that "*Rasselas* criticism is far more allegorical than *Rasselas*" and that the characters are "individuals or types, not metaphors." *Samuel Johnson's Allegory* (The Hague and Paris: Mouton, 1971), pp. 83–84. He proceeds to take a position like A. R. Humphreys'—that "to overstress the general and abstract would be misleading. . . . The tale chooses a middle ground between abstract and concrete, on which morality can be embodied as an impression of real life adequately but not obtrusively maintained." "Johnson," *From Dryden to Johnson*, vol. 4 of *The Pelican Guide to English Literature*, Boris Ford, ed. (Harmondsworth, Middlesex: Penguin, 1957), p. 412.

5. Daniel Defoe, *The Life and Strange Surprizing Adventures of Robinson Crusoe*, J. Donald Crowley, ed. (London: Oxford University Press, 1972), p. 273. Regarding the boat, see pp. 126–28 and Harry F. Robins, "How Smart Was Robinson Crusoe?" *PMLA* (1952), 67:782–89.

6. James Burnett, Lord Monboddo, *The Origin and Progress of Language* (1776); James Beattie, *On Fable and Romance* (1783): excerpts in *Novel and Romance 1700–1800*, pp. 292, 316.

7. René Pomeau, ed., *Candide* (Paris: Nizet, 1959), pp. 53, 56 (Introd.).

8. Frederick W. Hilles, "*Rasselas*, an 'Uninstructive Tale,'" *Johnson, Boswell and Their Circle: Essays Presented to Lawrence Fitzroy Powell* (Oxford: Clarendon, 1965), p. 114. W. K. Wimsatt, "In Praise of *Rasselas*: Four Notes (Converging)," in Maynard Mack and Ian Gregor,

eds., *Imagined Worlds: Essays on Some English Novels and Novelists in Honour of John Butt* (London: Methuen, 1968), p. 124.

9. G. B. Hill, ed., *Rasselas* (Oxford: Clarendon, 1887), pp. 31, 29 (Introd.).

10. Douglas A. Bonneville, *Voltaire and the Form of the Novel*, *Studies on Voltaire* (1976), 158:13–16. Bonneville aptly considers the *Lettres persanes* in the context of the philosophical tale, pp. 101–13. Robert Shackleton explores the relations between Voltaire and Montesquieu in "Allies and Enemies: Voltaire and Montesquieu," *Essays by Divers Hands* (1977), N.S. 39:126–45. Yvon Belaval writes magisterially about the genre in "Le Conte philosophique," in W. H. Barber et al., eds., *The Age of Enlightenment: Studies Presented to Theodore Besterman* (Edinburgh and London: Oliver and Boyd, 1967), pp. 308–17, esp. 313–14. Other useful recent studies of the genre include Nicole Gueunier, "Pour une définition du conte," *Roman et lumières au XVIIIe siècle* (Paris: Éditions Sociales, 1970), pp. 422–36, and Henri Coulet, "La Distanciation dans le roman et le conte philosophiques," *ibid.*, pp. 438–47. Martha Pike Conant's *The Oriental Tale in England in the Eighteenth Century* (New York: Columbia University Press, 1908) should not go unmentioned, nor should I omit mention of Dorothy Madeleine McGhee's books: *Voltairian Narrative Devices as Considered in the Author's contes philosophiques* (1933; rpt. New York: Russell & Russell, 1973), *Fortunes of a Tale: The Philosophic Tale in France,—Bridging the Eighteenth and Nineteenth Centuries* (Menasha, Wis.: George Banta, 1954).

11. Arthur Sherbo, ed., *Johnson on Shakespeare*, in John H. Middendorf, ed., *The Yale Edition of the Works of Samuel Johnson*, vol. 7 (New Haven and London: Yale University Press, 1968), pp. 78–79.

12. Samuel Johnson, *The Rambler*, W. J. Bate and Albrecht B. Strauss, eds., in Middendorf, ed., *ibid.*, vol. 3 (1969), p. 11. Parenthetical references to the *Rambler* are to this edition. Jacques Barchilon remarks that Voltaire's *contes* observe "one of the laws of the fairy tale (and of all good fiction) so succinctly stated by mlle Bernard in 1696: 'Que les aventures fussent toujours contre la vray-semblance & les sentimens toujours naturels.'" "Uses of the Fairy Tale in the Eighteenth Century," *Studies on Voltaire* (1963), 24:127.

13. Frank Brady, "Vexations and Diversions: Three Problems in *Gulliver's Travels*," *Modern Philology* (1978), 75:351.

14. Georges May, *Le Dilemme du roman au XVIIIe siècle: Étude sur les rapports du roman et de la critique (1715–1761)* (New Haven: Yale University Press; Paris: Presses Universitaires de France, 1963).

15. Paul Kent Alkon concentrates on the import of this phrase of Johnson's (from *Rambler* 146) in *Samuel Johnson and Moral Discipline* (Evanston: Northwestern University Press, 1967), ch. 4.

16. Ian Watt, *The Rise of the Novel: Studies in Defoe, Richardson and Fielding* (1957; rpt. Berkeley and Los Angeles: University of California Press, 1959), p. 32 and ch. 1 passim.

17. *Ibid.*, pp. 288, 297. The broad opposition between satire and the novel elegantly exploited by John Lawlor in "Radical Satire and the Realistic Novel," *Essays and Studies* (1955), N.S. 8:58–75, is, I believe, too broad to accommodate the philosophical tales and Jane Austen.

18. Watt explains that his treatment of "realism of assessment" was originally lengthy but had to be cut to bring *The Rise of the Novel* to a reasonable size. "Serious Reflections on *The Rise of the Novel*," *Novel: A Forum on Fiction* (1968), 1:207. My label "realism of psychological assessment" is not Watt's, precisely, but I trust represents legitimate particularization of his "realism of assessment," distinguishing psychological from sociological and moral matters—an operation which may be safely performed upon his statement, from this article,

that in *Pamela* and *Tom Jones* "the as-yet-undifferentiated ego of the protagonist is brought into contact with the various psychological, moral, and social norms of the author and his period. The very form of their basic plots enacts their normative assessment . . ." (p. 215). Cf. Ronald Paulson's comments on Fielding and Richardson's respective realisms in *Satire and the Novel in Eighteenth-Century England* (New Haven and London: Yale University Press, 1967), p. 106.

    19. Watt, *The Rise of the Novel*, p. 30.

    20. Peter Brooks, *The Novel of Worldliness: Crébillon, Marivaux, Laclos, Stendhal* (Princeton: Princeton University Press, 1969).

2. The Chain of Being, the Chain of Events, and the Chain of Becoming

    1. Arthur Sherbo, ed., *Johnson on Shakespeare*, in John H. Middendorf, ed., *The Yale Edition of the Works of Samuel Johnson*, vol. 7 (New Haven and London: Yale University Press, 1968), p. 88.

    2. John Locke, *An Essay Concerning Human Understanding*, Peter H. Nidditch, ed. (Oxford: Clarendon, 1975), p. 44.

    3. Donald Greene, *The Age of Exuberance: Backgrounds to Eighteenth-Century English Literature* (New York: Random House, 1970), p. 126.

    4. Pope, *The Dunciad* 4.643–44, James Sutherland, ed., in John Butt, ed., *The Twickenham Edition of the Poems of Alexander Pope*, 3d ed., vol. 5 (London: Methuen; New Haven: Yale University Press, 1963), p. 408.

    5. Arthur O. Lovejoy, ch. 9, "The Temporalizing of the Chain of Being," *The Great Chain of Being: A Study in the History of an Idea* (1936; rpt. New York: Harper, 1960), pp. 242–87. The chain of events is mentioned briefly p. 363*n*.

    6. David Hume, "An Enquiry Concerning Human Understanding," *Philosophical Works*, T. H. Green and T. H. Grose, eds. (1882; rpt. Aalen: Scientia, 1964), 4:19*n*. This "Enquiry" was first published in 1748 and was reprinted numerous times (with revisions) before the posthumous edition of 1777, in which the passage I quote was omitted; see *Enquiries Concerning Human Understanding and Concerning the Principles of Morals*, L. A. Selby-Bigge, ed., 3d ed., rev. P. H. Nidditch (Oxford: Clarendon, 1975), pp. 358 (*n*. 24.25), 350.

    7. Henry Fielding, *Amelia*, Everyman's Library, 2 vols. in 1 (London: Dent; New York: Dutton, 1974), 2:269; 1:4.

    8. Agnes G. Raymond, "Encore quelques réflexions sur la 'chaîne secrète' des *Lettres persanes*," *Studies on Voltaire* (1972), 89:1338. Diderot explains the word *encyclopédie* in the article of that title as meaning "enchaînement des sciences." *Œuvres complètes*, vol. 14, J. Assézat, ed. (Paris: Garnier, 1876), pp. 414–15.

    9. Jean Le Rond d'Alembert, "Discours préliminaire de l'Encyclopédie," *Œuvres complètes* (1821; rpt. Genève: Slatkine, 1967), 1:32, 33, 17, 28. Cf. Georges Poulet's comment that in d'Holbach's terms (from the *Système de la nature*) the universe may be described as "une chaîne immense de causes et d'effets." *Études sur le temps humain* (Edinburgh: Edinburgh University Press, 1949), p. 26.

    10. Denis Diderot, *Lettres à Sophie Volland*, André Babelon, ed. (Paris: Gallimard, 1938), 1:155 (Oct. 20, 1760).

11. Jean-Jacques Rousseau, "Discours sur l'origine . . . de l'inégalité," *Œuvres complètes*, Bernard Gagnebin and Marcel Raymond, eds., Pléiade Ed., vol. 3 (n.p.: Gallimard, 1964), p. 132; "Confessions," *ibid.*, vol. 1 (1959), p. 278.

12. Julien Offray de La Mettrie, *La Mettrie's L'Homme machine: A Study in the Origins of an Idea*, Aram Vartanian, ed. (Princeton: Princeton University Press, 1960), p. 167.

13. Étienne Bonnot de Condillac, "Traité des sensations," *Œuvres philosophiques*, Georges Le Roy, ed. (Paris: Presses Universitaires de France, 1947), 1:239.

14. Hume, "An Enquiry . . .," p. 20*n*. *A Treatise of Human Nature*, L. A. Selby-Bigge, ed., 2d ed., rev. P. H. Nidditch (Oxford, Clarendon, 1978), p. 262.

15. *The Idler* and *The Adventurer*, W. J. Bate, John M. Bullitt, and L. F. Powell, eds., in John H. Middendorf, ed., *The Yale Edition of the Works of Samuel Johnson*, vol. 2 (New Haven and London: Yale University Press, 1963), p. 441.

16. Laurence Sterne, *Works*, James P. Brown, ed., vol. 3 (London: Bickers, 1873), p. 38. My attention was drawn to this sermon by Michael V. DePorte, *Nightmares and Hobbyhorses: Swift, Sterne, and the Augustan Idea of Madness* (San Marino, Calif.: Huntington Library, 1974), p. 120.

17. Edward Gibbon, *Memoirs of My Life*, Georges A. Bonnard, ed. (New York: Funk & Wagnalls, 1969), p. 17.

18. Giambattista Vico, *The New Science*, Thomas Goddard Bergin and Max Harold Fisch, trans., rev. ed. (Ithaca, N.Y.: Cornell University Press, 1968), p. 122. For the chain of events in Stoicism, see F. H. Sandbach, *The Stoics* (New York: Norton, 1975), pp. 81–82.

19. Charles-Louis de Secondat, baron de Montesquieu, *Lettres persanes*, Paul Vernière, ed. (Paris: Garnier, 1975), p. 5. For Montesquieu's use of the metaphor see Raymond, pp. 1339–40, and Jean Starobinski, *Montesquieu par lui-même* (Paris: Éditions du Seuil, 1953), pp. 38–40.

20. Ernst Cassirer, *The Philosophy of the Enlightenment*, Fritz C. A. Koelln and James P. Pettegrove, trans. (Princeton: Princeton University Press, 1951), pp. 253–54.

21. *An Essay on Man* 1. 290, 164, Maynard Mack, ed., in John Butt, ed., *The Twickenham Edition of the Poems of Alexander Pope*, vol. 3–1 (London: Methuen; New Haven: Yale University Press, 1950), pp. 50, 35.

22. Voltaire, "Zadig ou la destinée," *Romans et contes*, Henri Bénac, ed. (Paris: Garnier, 1960), p. 56; cf. the similar passage from the late *conte* "Les Oreilles du comte de Chesterfield," p. 558.

23. Hume, *A Treatise of Human Nature*, p. 662.

24. Ian Ross, "Philosophy and Fiction. The Challenge of David Hume," *Hume and the Enlightenment: Essays Presented to Ernest Campbell Mossner* (Edinburgh: Edinburgh University Press; Austin: University of Texas Humanities Research Center, 1974), p. 70.

25. James Long, *An Enquiry into the Origin of the Human Appetites and Affections* (1747), in Paul McReynolds, ed., *Four Early Works on Motivation* (Gainesville, Fla.: Scholars' Facsimiles and Reprints, 1969), p. 457.

26. Eric Rothstein's *Systems of Order and Inquiry in Later Eighteenth-Century Fiction* (Berkeley, Los Angeles, and London: University of California Press, 1975) is sensitive to eighteenth-century epistemology entailing analogy and association (see pp. 13–14), but concentrates on the organization of works of fiction to control readers' responses, not on the process of thought in the main characters. Cf. his dismissal of Rasselas' "growth in wisdom" (p. 37) with my chapter on that book.

27. Although the main line of associationism is generally understood to proceed from Hobbes and, especially, Locke, through various British philosophers, before entering active French thought in Condillac during the 1740s, there had been precedent (besides Aristotle) for such analysis in Continental philosophy before Condillac, notably in Descartes and Malebranche—see Howard C. Warren, *A History of the Association Psychology* (1921; rpt. New York and London: Johnson Reprint, 1967), pp. 32–33, 181–82—and in Spinoza and Leibniz—see David Rapaport, *The History of the Concept of Association of Ideas* (New York: International Universities Press, 1974), pp. 48–65, 86–106, and passim. Useful summaries of the history of associationism appear in the *Encyclopaedia Britannica*, 11th ed. (1911), 2:784–86, and, by Robert M. Young, in *Dictionary of the History of Ideas*, Philip P. Weiner, ed. (New York: Scribner's, n.d.), 1:111–18. Martin Kallich's *The Association of Ideas and Critical Theory in Eighteenth-Century England: A History of a Psychological Method in English Criticism* (The Hague and Paris: Mouton, 1970) has early chapters on the philosophical and psychological background, giving due attention to Hobbes (as eighteenth-century philosophers usually did not).

28. Locke, p. 395.

29. David Hartley, *Observations on Man, His Frame, His Duty, and His Expectations* (1749; rpt. New York: Garland, 1971), 1:402–3. "It was only during the last quarter of the eighteenth century that psychiatrists generally adopted this form of presentation." Richard A. Hunter and Ida Macalpine, *Three Hundred Years of Psychiatry 1535–1860: A History Presented in Selected English Texts* (London: Oxford University Press, 1963), p. 338.

30. As Hartley says, 1:[v].

31. William King, *An Essay on the Origin of Evil*, Edmund Law, ed. and trans. (London: W. Thurlbourn, 1731). Maynard Mack points out that the date of publication was actually 1730 (*The Twickenham Edition of the Poems of Alexander Pope*, vol. 3–1, p. xxvii*n*). Gay's "Dissertation" occupies pp. xi–xxxiii of King; parenthetical references in my text are to this edition. The "Dissertation" is conveniently reprinted in Edwin A. Burtt, ed., *The English Philosophers from Bacon to Mill* (New York: Modern Library, 1939), pp. 767–85 and (abridged) in D. D. Raphael, ed., *The British Moralists 1650–1800* (Oxford: Clarendon, 1969), 1:409–21.

32. King, pp. 208–11.

33. Long, pp. 440–41. Hartley, 1:81; Hartley's passage is quoted by Basil Willey, with reference to Wordsworth, in *The Eighteenth-Century Background: Studies on the Idea of Nature in the Thought of the Period* (London: Chatto & Windus, 1946), pp. 144–45. In Hartley's psychology, as in the psychology of some other eighteenth-century proponents of necessity—Willey notes (p. 228)—" . . . Nothing could have been otherwise, yet we both can and must make it otherwise!" Condillac's phrase about the mind's chain of ideas and desires (at note 13 above) continues "et qu'il suffit de suivre, pour découvrir le progrès de toutes les connoissances de l'homme" (1:239). Locke anticipates Long's use of *trace* in this connection, pp. 560–61; precedent for Gay's axioms or resting places can be found in Locke on "habitual Knowledge," pp. 528–30.

34. Francis Bacon, "Novum Organum," *Works*, James Spedding et al., eds., vol. 4 (London: Longmans, 1883), p. 54.

35. *Ibid.*, "The Advancement of Learning," vol. 3 (1876), pp. 468–69.

36. Samuel Johnson, *The Rambler*, W. J. Bate and Albrecht B. Strauss, eds., in John H. Middendorf, ed., *The Yale Edition of the Works of Samuel Johnson*, vols. 3–5 (New Haven and London: Yale University Press, 1969), 3:21. On the close relation of *image* to *idea* in

Johnson's thought and usage see Donald J. Greene, "'Pictures to the Mind': Johnson and Imagery," *Johnson, Boswell and Their Circle: Essays Presented to Lawrence Fitzroy Powell* (Oxford: Clarendon, 1965), p. 153.

37. Samuel Richardson, *Pamela; or, Virtue Rewarded*, Shakespeare Head Ed. (Oxford: Basil Blackwell, 1929), 2:14, 27, 14. The verses are cited by Lovejoy, p. 207.

38. Voltaire to Charles Augustin Feriol, comte d'Argental, May 16, 1767, D14179, *Complete Works*, vol. 116, Theodore Besterman et al., eds. (Banbury: Voltaire Foundation, 1974), pp. 111–12. Ahmad Gunny surveys Voltaire's attitudes toward prose fiction and English authors (including Swift, whom he greatly admired) in *Voltaire and English Literature: A Study of English Literary Influences on Voltaire, Studies on Voltaire* (1979), 177:234–82.

39. Samuel Richardson, *Clarissa; or, The History of a Young Lady*, Shakespeare Head Ed. (Oxford: Basil Blackwell, 1930), 7:43.

40. Denis Diderot, *Œuvres complètes*, vol. 5, J. Assézat, ed. (Paris: Garnier, 1875), 213.

41. Johnson, *The Rambler*, No. 97, 4:153. *Boswell's Life of Johnson*, George Birkbeck Hill, ed., rev. L. F. Powell (1934; rpt. Oxford: Clarendon, 1971), 2:49. Cf. Locke's remarks, regarding our understanding of individual persons, on the knowledge of "the famous Clock at *Strasburg*" possessed by the horologist as contrasted with that possessed by the casual observer (p. 440).

42. Marie-Madeleine de La Fayette, *La Princesse de Clèves*, Émile Magne, ed. (Paris: Droz, 1946), p. 192.

43. Claude Crébillon, *Les Égarements du cœur et de l'esprit*, René Etiemble, ed. (Paris: Armand Colin, 1961), p. 6.

3. Self-Assessment: Two Heads or One

1. Ronald Paulson, *The Fictions of Satire* (Baltimore: Johns Hopkins University Press, 1967), p. 171.

2. John Gay, "A Dissertation Concerning the Fundamental Principle and Immediate Criterion of Virtue . . . ," in William King, *An Essay on the Origin of Evil*, Edmund Law, ed. and trans. (London: W. Thurlbourn, 1731), p. xxxiii.

3. René Girard, *Deceit, Desire, and the Novel: Self and Other in Literary Structure*, Yvonne Freccero, trans. (Baltimore and London: Johns Hopkins University Press, 1966), pp. 5, 17.

4. Jacques Barzun, "The Novel Turns Tale," *Mosaic* (1971), 4:33–34.

5. François de Salignac de la Mothe-Fénelon, *Les Aventures de Télémaque*, Albert Cahen, ed., 2 vols. (Paris: Hachette, 1920), 1:287.

6. *Ibid.*, 2:555.

7. Francis Bacon, "Essays," *Works*, James Spedding et al., eds., vol. 6 (London: Longmans, 1890), p. 392; "The Advancement of Learning," *ibid.*, vol. 3 (1876), p. 419.

8. David Hume, *A Treatise of Human Nature*, L. A. Selby-Bigge, ed., 2d ed., rev. P. H. Nidditch (Oxford: Clarendon, 1978), p. 401.

9. As Roland Barthes comments in *S/Z*, Richard Miller, trans. (New York: Hill and Wang, 1974), p. 206. Extensive, fertile commentary on the topos of the ages of man may be found in Samuel C. Chew, *The Pilgrimage of Life* (New Haven and London: Yale University Press, 1962), pp. 144–73; Philippe Ariès, *Centuries of Childhood: A Social History of Family Life*, Robert Baldick, trans. (New York: Vintage, n.d.), esp. pp. 18–32; and Arthur Beatty, *William Wordsworth: His Doctrine and Art in Their Historical Relations* (3d ed.; Madison: Uni-

versity of Wisconsin Press, 1960), pp. 69–96, 136–49. Martin C. Battestin and other critics have employed the topos in analysis of Fielding; see Battestin, *The Providence of Wit: Aspects of Form in Augustan Literature and the Arts* (Oxford: Clarendon, 1974), pp. 189–90, 300*n*.

10. *An Essay on Man* 2. 275–82, Maynard Mack, ed., in John Butt, ed., *The Twickenham Edition of the Poems of Alexander Pope*, vol. 3–1 (London: Methuen; New Haven: Yale University Press, 1950), p. 88.

11. *Rhetoric*, bk. 2, chs. 12–14—the quoted words from the Loeb Classical Library edition, *The "Art" of Rhetoric*, John Henry Freese, trans. (London: William Heinemann; Cambridge, Mass.: Harvard University Press, 1926), p. 247.

12. George-Louis Leclerc, comte de Buffon, "Histoire naturelle générale et particulière," *Œuvres philosophiques*, Jean Piveteau et al., eds. (Paris: Presses Universitaires de France, 1954), pp. 309–12; Charles Bonnet, *Essai analytique sur les facultés de l'âme, Œuvres d'histoire naturelle et de philosophie*, vol. 6 (Neuchatel: Samuel Fauche, 1782), cited by Isobel F. Knight, *The Geometric Spirit: The Abbé de Condillac and the French Enlightenment* (New Haven and London: Yale University Press, 1968), p. 83. Knight also mentions, but dismisses as "unjust," Grimm's charge that Condillac had stolen the statue-man idea from Diderot's *Lettre sur les sourds et muets*. Bonnet, who says he finished writing the *Essai* in 1759 (*Essai*, p. 407)—the year of *Candide* and *Rasselas*—refers repeatedly to the statue as an "automate" (pp. 43, 275, 396). I return to the eighteenth-century concern with automatons later in the present book, especially in chapter 8, regarding *Candide*. (Rousseau's "scène lyrique" *Pygmalion* should not go unmentioned here.)

13. To J. H. Reynolds, May 3, 1818, *The Letters of John Keats*, Hyder Edward Rollins, ed. (Cambridge: Harvard University Press, 1958), 1:280–82.

14. Francis Hutcheson, *An Essay on the Nature and Conduct of the Passions and Affections*, 3d ed. (1742), introd. Paul McReynolds (rpt. Gainesville, Fla.: Scholars' Facsimiles and Reprints, 1969), p. 132.

15. *The Rambler*, W. J. Bate and Albrecht B. Strauss, eds., in John H. Middendorf, ed., *The Yale Edition of the Works of Samuel Johnson*, vols. 3–5 (New Haven and London: Yale University Press, 1969), 5:38. Parenthetical references in my text are to this edition. *Rambler* 49 (3:263–68) quite comparably traces the development of the natural and "adsciticious" (or artificial) passions.

16. *Boswell's London Journal 1762–1763*, Frederick A. Pottle, ed. (New York, London, Toronto: McGraw-Hill, 1950), p. 62.

17. Jerome Hamilton Buckley, *Season of Youth: The Bildungsroman from Dickens to Golding* (Cambridge: Harvard University Press, 1974), p. 17.

18. *Ibid.*, pp. 19, 20, 18.

19. Adam Smith, *The Theory of Moral Sentiments* (1759; rpt. New York: Garland, 1971), p. 38.

20. Jean Ehrard, *Littérature française: Le XVIIIe siècle*, vol. 1 (Paris: Arthaud, 1974), p. 124.

21. Smith, p. 391. Usbek and Rica variously prefigure the hero and his nephew, respectively, of Smollett's *Humphry Clinker*, an epistolary travel novel (remarkably synoptic in form and content) that is explicable in other ways by reference to the philosophical tale.

22. Ronald Paulson, *Popular and Polite Art in the Age of Hogarth and Fielding* (Notre Dame, Ind., and London: University of Notre Dame Press, 1979), pp. 163–70.

23. *Clarissa; or, The History of a Young Lady*, Shakespeare Head Ed. (Oxford: Basil Blackwell, 1930), 3:318; *Pamela; or, Virtue Rewarded*, Shakespeare Head Ed. (Oxford: Basil Blackwell, 1929), 2:55. Richardson published a translation of *Télémaque* in 1728. See T. C. Duncan

Eaves and Ben D. Kimpel, *Samuel Richardson: A Biography* (Oxford: Clarendon, 1971), p. 37. Marivaux's *Le Télémaque travesti* is also worth mentioning here.

24. Henry Fielding, *Joseph Andrews*, Martin C. Battestin, ed., *The Wesleyan Edition of the Works of Henry Fielding* (Middletown, Conn.: Wesleyan University Press, 1967), pp. 212–13 (bk. 3, ch. 3); parenthetical references in my text are to this edition, giving book, chapter, and page numbers respectively.

25. Dick Taylor, Jr., "Joseph as Hero in *Joseph Andrews*," *Tulane Studies in English* (1957), 7:109.

26. Henry Fielding, *The History of Tom Jones a Foundling*, Fredson Bowers, ed., introd. Martin C. Battestin, *The Wesleyan Edition of the Works of Henry Fielding*, 2 vols. (Middletown, Conn.: Wesleyan University Press, 1975), 1:227 (bk. 5, ch. 5); parenthetical references in my text are to this edition, giving book, chapter, volume, and page numbers respectively. See note 33 below.

27. C. J. Rawson, *Henry Fielding and the Augustan Ideal Under Stress: "Nature's Dance of Death" and Other Studies* (London and Boston: Routledge & Kegan Paul, 1972). See, for example, regarding *Amelia*, pp. 95–97.

28. Henry Fielding, *Amelia*, Everyman's Library, 2 vols. in 1 (London: Dent; New York: Dutton, 1974), 1:114 (bk. 3, ch. 5); parenthetical references in my text are to this edition, which in the passages quoted corresponds, with insignificant differences, to the Shakespeare Head Ed., 3 vols. (Oxford: Basil Blackwell, 1926); book and chapter numbers precede volume and page numbers.

29. Henry Fielding, *The Life of Mr Jonathan Wild the Great*, Shakespeare Head Ed. (Oxford: Basil Blackwell, 1926), p. 29. Fielding's "An Essay on the Knowledge of the Characters of Men" is (as is typical of him) about how to understand others, not oneself: *Miscellanies by Henry Fielding, Esq; Volume One*, Henry Knight Miller, ed. (Middletown, Conn.: Wesleyan University Press, 1972), pp. 153–78.

30. Hume, p. 415. Martin C. Battestin argues that Booth's opinions are derived from Hume. See "The Problem of *Amelia*: Hume, Barrow, and the Conversion of Captain Booth," *ELH* (1974), 4:613–48.

31. *An Essay on Man* 2. 163, p. 74.

32. Hume, p. 608.

33. For an account of this scene as it is framed by the tradition of comic romance see Henry Knight Miller, *Henry Fielding's* Tom Jones *and the Romance Tradition* (Victoria: English Literary Studies, Monograph No. 6, 1976), p. 69. Miller's chapter 4, "*People/*The Characters," provides a useful analysis of characterization based on *being* rather than *becoming*; regarding Tom Jones's reformation see also p. 19.

34. Frances Burney, *Evelina or the History of a Young Lady's Entrance into the World*, Edward A. Bloom, ed. (London: Oxford University Press, 1968), p. 404.

35. David Hartley, *Observations on Man, His Frame, His Duty, and His Expectations* (1749; rpt. New York: Garland, 1971), 1:465.

4. The Rub of Self-Love

1. Francis Bacon, "Novum Organum," *Works*, James Spedding et al., eds., vol. 4 (London: Longmans, 1883), p. 60—"held in suspicion" but not therefore ignored or avoided,

since, according to Jeffrey Barnouw, for Bacon "real knowledge of the world" presupposes the rejection of Stoicism and involves "a specifically modern sense of Enlightenment in which self-knowledge is inseparable from knowledge of the world." Barnouw, "Active Experience vs. Wish Fulfilment in Francis Bacon's Moral Psychology of Science," *The Philosophical Forum* (1979), 9:86 and passim.

2. Henry Fielding, *Amelia*, Everyman's Library, 2 vols. in 1 (London: Dent; New York: Dutton, 1974), 1:7.

3. David Hume, *A Treatise of Human Nature*, L. A. Selby-Bigge, ed., 2d ed., rev. P. H. Nidditch (Oxford: Clarendon, 1978), pp. 12–13: the association of ideas "a kind of ATTRACTION, which in the mental world will be found to have as extraordinary effects as in the natural." Peter Gay, *The Enlightenment: An Interpretation*, vol. 2, *The Science of Freedom* (New York: Knopf, 1969), pp. 174–87. Earlier, Basil Willey noted the popularity of Newtonian comparisons among psychologists in Hume's time. See *The Eighteenth Century Background: Studies on the Idea of Nature in the Thought of the Period* (London: Chatto & Windus, 1946), pp. 111–12.

4. Voltaire, *Dictionnaire philosophique*, Julien Benda and Raymond Naves, eds., rev. ed. (Paris: Garnier, 1967), p. 22.

5. D. H. Lawrence, "A Propos of *Lady Chatterley's Lover*," in Harry T. Moore, ed., *Sex, Literature, and Censorship* (New York: Viking, 1959), p. 109. The lines on Knox are from *The Collected Poetry of Dorothy Parker* (New York: Modern Library, n.d.), p. 94.

6. Adam Smith, *The Theory of Moral Sentiments* (1759; rpt. New York: Garland, 1971); parenthetical references in my text are to this edition.

7. John Gay, "A Dissertation Concerning the Fundamental Principle and Immediate Criterion of Virtue . . .," in William King, *An Essay on the Origin of Evil* (London: W. Thurlbourn, 1731), p. xxxii. Parenthetical references in my text are to this edition.

8. F. B. Kaye, ed., *The Fable of the Bees*, by Bernard Mandeville, 2 vols. (Oxford: Clarendon, 1924), 1:xlviii, lxxiv–lxxv and *n*.

9. *Ibid.*, 1:xlviii and *n*.

10. Bernard Harrison, *Henry Fielding's* Tom Jones: *The Novelist as Moral Philosopher* (London: Chatto & Windus, for Sussex University Press, 1975), pp. 110–12.

11. *Ibid.*, pp. 99–100n.

12. Paul Kent Alkon, *Samuel Johnson and Moral Discipline* (Evanston, Ill.: Northwestern University Press, 1967), pp. 130, 131, 133, 132. Here and elsewhere I am deeply indebted to Alkon's book, which lucidly argues for the fundamental importance of empirical psychology in Johnson's writings on morality (see esp. pp. 26, 86, 97). Alkon begins (p. 8), as I do, with the quotation from Johnson's *Preface to Shakespeare* about sounding "the depths of the heart for the motives of action" and concludes with attention to the Baconian heritage of "the culture of the mind" (p. 209).

13. Samuel Johnson, *Rasselas, Poems, and Selected Prose*, Bertrand H. Bronson, ed., 3d ed. (New York: Holt, Rinehart and Winston, 1971), p. 694. *The Idler* and *The Adventurer*, W. J. Bate et al., eds., in John H. Middendorf, ed., *The Yale Edition of the Works of Samuel Johnson*, vol. 2 (New Haven and London: Yale University Press, 1963), p. 262.

14. Edward Young, *Conjectures on Original Composition*, Edith J. Morley, ed. (Manchester: University Press; London: Longmans, Green, 1918), pp. 23–24. Young later cites Bacon on men's fancying "their abilities less, than they really are" (p. 31). Alan D. McKillop suggests that Richardson persuaded Young to include what he had to say about moral genius within the *Conjectures* by commenting on Addison's death. "Richardson, Young and the *Conjectures*," *Modern Philology* (1925), 22:391–404.

15. Jean-Jacques Rousseau, "Discours sur l'origine . . . de l'inégalité," *Œuvres complètes*, Bernard Gagnebin and Marcel Raymond, eds., Pléiade Ed., vol. 3 (n.p.: Gallimard, 1964), pp. 219–20. Basil Willey calls the issue of self-love versus social love "the classic problem of eighteenth century ethics" (p. 87). The closest any critic has come to full-scale study of the significance of self-love in eighteenth-century fiction is Lester G. Crocker's chapter "Human Nature in the Novel" in *An Age of Crisis: Man and World in Eighteenth Century French Thought* (Baltimore and London: Johns Hopkins University Press, 1959), pp. 404–46, which is devoted to French novelists and especially to the manner in which they forwarded the decay of morality in the West that Crocker perceives as deriving from the Enlightenment. He sees the novels of Marivaux, for example, as "connected to that phase of eighteenth-century ethical and psychological exploration which emphasized self-deception and the prostitution of reason by the deeper vitalities: a line of thought which was to culminate, though only after a leap, in the work of Sade" (pp. 422–23).

16. Leslie Stephen, *History of English Thought in the Eighteenth Century* (1876; rpt. New York: Harcourt, Brace & World, 1962), 2:41–42.

17. Douglas H. White, *Pope and the Context of Controversy: The Manipulation of Ideas in An Essay on Man* (Chicago and London: University of Chicago Press, 1970), pp. 174–75.

18. Anthony Ashley Cooper, 3d earl of Shaftesbury, "*Sensus Communis*; An Essay on the Freedom of Wit and Humour," *Characteristics*, John M. Robertson, ed. (1900; rpt. Indianapolis and New York: Bobbs-Merrill, 1964), 1:80. Mandeville suggests the term "Self-liking" to cover the more prideful aspect of self-love, and Kaye's note to the passage suggests he does so to answer Butler (Kaye, 2:129–31).

19. William Hazlitt, "Self-Love and Benevolence" (1828), *Complete Works*, P. P. Howe, ed., vol. 20 (London and Toronto: J. M. Dent, 1934), pp. 166, 170.

20. Arthur O. Lovejoy, *Reflections on Human Nature* (Baltimore: Johns Hopkins University Press, 1961), p. 129 and passim. The passion I have called love of "praise" is complicated (see pp. 88–89).

21. Hume, *A Treatise of Human Nature*, pp. 297–98.

22. David Hume, *Enquiries Concerning Human Understanding and Concerning the Principles of Morals*, L. A. Selby-Bigge, ed., 3d ed., rev. P. H. Nidditch (Oxford: Clarendon, 1975), pp. 215–19, 295–302.

23. Jeremy Bentham, *A Table of the Springs of Action* (dated 1815, pub. 1817), in Paul McReynolds, ed., *Four Early Works on Motivation* (Gainesville, Fla.: Scholars' Facsimiles and Reprints, 1969), pp. 477–512; see esp. the attempt to provide the "neutral" term "self-regarding interest," p. 504. Cf. Bentham's similar remarks in J. H. Burns and H. L. A. Hart, eds., *An Introduction to the Principles of Morals and Legislation* (London: Athlone Press, 1970), pp. 101–2.

24. Francis Hutcheson, *An Essay on the Nature and Conduct of the Passions and Affections*, 3d ed. (1742), introd. Paul McReynolds (rpt. Gainesville, Fla.: Scholars' Facsimiles and Reprints, 1969), p. ix (Introd.).

25. McReynolds, *Four Early Works on Motivation*, p. xxix (Introd.).

26. Hutcheson, p. 109.

27. Joseph Butler, *Works*, W. E. Gladstone, ed. (Oxford: Clarendon, 1897), 2:22.

28. Archibald Campbell, . . . *An Enquiry into the Original of Moral Virtue* (Westminister: B. Creake, 1728), pp. 40, xxxvii.

29. Gay, p. xxv; cited by White, p. 179*n*.

30. Étienne Bonnot de Condillac, "Traité des sensations," *Œuvres philosophiques*, Georges Le Roy, ed. (Paris: Presses Universitaires de France, 1947), 1:233.

31. Hume, *A Treatise of Human Nature*, pp. 340, 354–55, 486–87. Long derives social love from enlightened self-love (p. 94).

32. David Hartley, *Observations on Man, His Frame, His Duty, and His Expections* (1749; rpt. New York: Garland, 1971), 1:458–70.

33. Albert O. Hirschman, *The Passions and the Interests: Political Arguments for Capitalism Before Its Triumph* (Princeton: Princeton University Press, 1977), pp. 32–33.

34. *Ibid.*, pp. 22, 58. Alkon, ch. 5. *Boswell's Life of Johnson*, George Birkbeck Hill, ed., rev. L. F. Powell (1934, rpt. Oxford: Clarendon, 1971), 2:323. For comments on this quip and Johnson's attitude toward self-love, see Robert Voitle, *Samuel Johnson the Moralist* (Cambridge, Mass.: Harvard University Press, 1961), pp. 97, 56–58.

35. John Donne, "Satyre III," *Poems*, Herbert J. C. Grierson, ed. (1912; rpt. London: Oxford University Press, 1968), 1:157. The array of works focusing on religious choice includes Sir Thomas Browne's *Religio Medici*, Dryden's *Religio Laici*, and Pope's *Essay on Man*.

36. For a potent statement to this effect in Locke, see *An Essay Concerning Human Understanding*, Peter H. Nidditch, ed. (Oxford: Clarendon, 1975), pp. 659–61. See also Paul Delaney's remarks, regarding the rise of autobiography, on the thesis that "unprecedented general social mobility" was "the spur to increased self-awareness among seventeenth-century Englishmen," so that "it was by the end of the period normal for an intelligent, introspective man to enquire into the sociological or psychological origins of his own and others' beliefs, and to see himself and his class, in Lukacs' phrase, 'both as an object and a subject in the social process.'" Delaney, *British Autobiography in the Seventeenth Century* (London: Routledge & Kegan Paul; New York: Columbia University Press, 1969), pp. 19–20. Delaney observes that it did not become "normal for an educated man to choose his own philosophy" as distinguished from his religion until the late eighteenth century—this, however, a generality about a broad social class, not true of Hobbes and other notable thinkers (p. 173). The issue of personal affection as a basis for marriage has been given extensive study by Lawrence Stone in *The Family, Sex, and Marriage in England, 1500–1800* (New York: Harper & Row, 1977).

37. White, p. 183.

38. Voltaire, *Lettres philosophiques*, Gustave Lanson, ed., 2d ed. (Paris: Hachette, 1915–1917), 2:197. It is Voltaire on self-love, not on Pascal, that concerns me. There were textual problems afflicting the text of the *Pensées* available to Voltaire, as Mara Vamos shows (in a study to which Otis Fellows kindly called my attention): *Pascal's Pensées and the Enlightenment: The Roots of a Misunderstanding, Studies on Voltaire*, vol. 97 (1972).

39. Voltaire, *Lettres philosophiques*, 2:222.

40. Arthur O. Lovejoy, *The Great Chain of Being: A Study in the History of an Idea* (1936; rpt. New York: Harper, 1960), pp. 252–53, on Voltaire's scientific objections. On his moral objections, see Peter Gay, *Voltaire's Politics: The Poet as Realist* (Princeton: Princeton University Press, 1959), pp. 21*n*–22*n*.

41. Voltaire, *Dictionnaire philosophique*, p. 101.

42. Voltaire to Elie Bertrand, February 18, 1756, D6738, *Complete Works*, vol. 101, Theodore Besterman et al., eds. (Banbury: Voltaire Foundation, 1971), p. 73 (from the same page: "On a besoin d'un dieu qui parle au genre humain").

43. Lovejoy, *The Great Chain of Being*, pp. 184, 252–55.

44. A facsimile of Johnson's review, from the *Literary Magazine* (1757), is given as an appendix to Richard Schwartz's *Samuel Johnson and the Problem of Evil* (Madison: University of Wisconsin Press, 1975), pp. 97–112. My quotations in this paragraph are from pp. 108, 106.

45. Voltaire, *Lettres philosophiques*, 2:186.

46. David Hume, *The Natural History of Religion and Dialogues Concerning Natural Religion*, A. Wayne Colver and John Valdimir Price, eds. (Oxford: Clarendon, 1976), p. 222. The reference to King is on p. 221 and the comment about metaphysicians on p. 219.

47. Samuel Richardson, *Pamela; or, Virtue Rewarded*, Shakespeare Head Ed. (Oxford: Basil Blackwell, 1929), 4:354. Pamela's reference to Locke: *The Educational Writings of John Locke*, James L. Axtell, ed. (Cambridge: Cambridge University Press, 1968), p. 245. Margaret Anne Doody calls attention to a letter in which Richardson speaks of his own youthful "sheepishness." *A Natural Passion: A Study of the Novels of Samuel Richardson* (Oxford: Clarendon, 1974), p. 7.

48. George Meredith, *The Egoist* (New York: Modern Library, 1951), p. 314.

49. Mark Kinkead-Weekes, *Samuel Richardson Dramatic Novelist* (Ithaca, N.Y.: Cornell University Press, 1973), p. 365. The eighteenth-century English novel heroine, it must be acknowledged, is better at knowing what she does *not* want—this repulsive suitor or that one. Julia Prewitt Brown sensibly asserts that the heroines are heroines because of their efforts to be free to choose whom they will marry. *Jane Austen's Novels: Social Change and Literary Form* (Cambridge, Mass., and London: Harvard University Press, 1979), p. 20.

50. Robert Mauzi, *L'Idée du bonheur dans la littérature et la pensée françaises au XVIIIᵉ siècle*, 4th ed. (Paris: Armand Colin, 1969), pp. 636–37, 641–42; Crocker, pp. 256–324 and passim; the subject is investigated further in his *Nature and Culture: Ethical Thought in the French Enlightenment* (Baltimore: Johns Hopkins University Press, 1963). Like Crocker (*An Age of Crisis*, pp. 279–80), Jean Starobinski, in his notes to the "Discours sur . . . l'inégalité" (*Œuvres complètes*, 3:1,376), cites several precedents for Rousseau's distinction between *amour-propre* and *amour de soi*, emphasizing that set by Vauvenargues, which Rousseau knew; Starobinski also calls attention to Marcel Raymond's pointed article "Du Jansénisme à la morale de l'intérêt," *Mercure de France* (1957), No. 1126:238–55, which gives Nicole a pivotal position in the radical change from seventeenth-century distrust of self-love to eighteenth-century reliance on it. Further light on the intricate history of *amour-propre* is provided by: Anthony Levi, S.J., *French Moralists: The Theory of the Passions* (Oxford: Clarendon, 1964), esp. pp. 174, 225–33; A. J. Krailsheimer, *Studies in Self-Interest from Descartes to La Bruyère* (Oxford: Clarendon, 1962); and Paul Zweig, *The Heresy of Self-Love: A Study of Subversive Individualism* (1968; rpt. Princeton: Princeton University Press, 1980), esp. pp. 134–41, on Spinoza and Leibniz.

51. Jean A. Perkins, *The Concept of the Self in the French Enlightenment* (Genève: Droz, 1969), pp. 77, 81.

52. Ronald C. Rosbottom, *Marivaux's Novels: Theme and Function in Early Eighteenth-Century Narrative* (Rutherford, N.J.: Fairleigh Dickinson University Press, 1974), pp. 157, 169–70, 164. For the extent to which the narrator criticizes her younger self, the heroine, see Leo Spitzer, "A propos de la *Vie de Marianne*," *Romanic Review* (1953), 44:119, and Patrick Brady, *Structuralist Perspectives in Criticism of Fiction: Essays on* Manon Lescaut *and* La Vie de Marianne (Bern: Lang, 1978), pp. 68, 71, 125.

53. Henry James, "Nana," *Documents of Modern Literary Realism*, George J. Becker, ed. (Princeton: Princeton University Press, 1963), pp. 243, 241–42.

54. *The Life and Opinions of Tristram Shandy, Gentleman*, Melvyn New and Joan New, eds., *The Florida Edition of the Works of Laurence Sterne* (Gainesville: University Presses of Florida, 1978), 1:42 (vol. 1, ch. 14).

55. *Ibid.*, 1:258 (vol. 3, ch. 31). Association does not thoroughly control Tristram's mind, as Arthur H. Cash explains in "The Lockean Psychology of *Tristram Shandy*," *ELH*

(1955), 22:125–35, but that judgment is based in part on the strictest possible construction of Locke's theory. Cf. Helene Moglen, *The Philosophical Irony of Laurence Sterne* (Gainesville: University Presses of Florida, 1975), p. 15 and passim. There is no need for me to go further, here, into the intricate scholarly debate over Sterne's relation to Locke, which has been summarized by Lodwick Hartley in *Laurence Sterne in the Twentieth Century: An Essay and a Bibliography of Sternean Studies 1900–1965* (Chapel Hill: University of North Carolina Press, 1966), pp. 23–28, and more recently by Martin C. Battestin, *The Providence of Wit: Aspects of Form in Augustan Literature and the Arts* (Oxford: Clarendon, 1974), pp. 313–14. Jonathan Lamb suggests a link between Sterne and Hartley in "Language and Hartleian Associationism in *A Sentimental Journey*," *Eighteenth-Century Studies* (1980), 13:285–312.

56. Notable comparative studies of the two novels appear in Alice Green Fredman, *Diderot and Sterne* (New York: Columbia University Press, 1955) and Robert Alter, *Partial Magic: The Novel as Self-Conscious Genre* (Berkeley, Los Angeles, and London: University of California Press, 1975), pp. 30–83.

57. See Carol Blum's comments on the self-knowledge Diderot promotes in readers of *Jacques*, in *Diderot: The Virtue of a Philosopher* (New York: Viking, 1974), pp. 129–39. On Diderot's attention to the association of ideas, see John Robert Loy, *Diderot's Determined Fatalist: A Critical Appreciation of Jacques le Fataliste* (New York: King's Crown Press, 1950), pp. 105–06.

58. Denis Diderot, *Jacques le fataliste et son maître*, Simone Lecointre and Jean Le Galliot, eds. (Genève: Droz, 1976), p. 296. Parenthetical references in my text are to this edition.

5. Gulliver's Habits and Prejudices

1. Dick Taylor, Jr., "Gulliver's Pleasing Visions: Self-Deception as Major Theme in *Gulliver's Travels*," *Tulane Studies in English* (1962), 12:47, 9–10. An older, Jamesian essay on Gulliver poses a question still salutary: whether the "kind of observation made in the last book demands the kind of observer Gulliver is, and the kind of observer he is demands the motivation of the first three books." Joe Horrell, "What Gulliver Knew," *Sewanee Review* (1943), 51:496–97.

2. W. B. Carnochan, *Lemuel Gulliver's Mirror for Man* (Berkeley and Los Angeles: University of California Press, 1968), pp. 134–35.

3. Denis Donoghue, *Jonathan Swift: A Critical Introduction* (Cambridge: Cambridge University Press, 1969), pp. 19–20. Donoghue also says that "what happens is far more important in its own right than the fact that it happens to Gulliver"—a comment I would not disagree with. It seems clear, from statements later on, that Donoghue (not unreasonably since articles and books continue to appear in which the *Travels* is called a "novel") is somewhat overstating the case against the importance of Gulliver as a character because it is essential that he not be taken too solemnly. "If the reader tries to gratify himself by completing Gulliver, tries to add intimations of character, soul, feeling, depth, then he convicts himself; he is a sentimentalist, Swift's favourite butt" (pp. 162–63). Refusal to take Gulliver as a *novel* character is necessary if the reader is to take in the vexing wit of tone and implication illuminated by such critics as: C. J. Rawson, *Gulliver and the Gentle Reader: Studies in Swift and Our Time* (London and Boston: Routledge and Kegan Paul, 1973); William Bowman Piper, "The Sense of *Gulliver's Travels*," *Rice University Studies* (1975), 61:75–106; Jenny Mezciems, "The Unity of Swift's 'Voyage to Laputa': Structure as Meaning in Utopian Fiction," *Modern Language*

Review (1977), 72:1–21; and Frank Brady, "Vexations and Diversions: Three Problems in *Gulliver's Travels," Modern Philology* (1978), 75:346–67. Gulliver must be taken as a *tale* character, as I have explained that category in the first chapter of this book.

4. As the present book went to press a book was published which appositely reads Swift against the empiricist tradition: Frances Deutsch Louis, *Swift's Anatomy of Misunderstanding: A Study of Swift's Epistemological Imagination in* A Tale of a Tub *and* Gulliver's Travels (Totowa, N.J.: Barnes & Noble, 1981). Louis documents the parallels between the "psychology of error" (p. 136) manifest in some of Swift's spokesmen and that warned against by Bacon, Hobbes, Locke, and their successors. Though she concentrates on *A Tale of a Tub*, she makes several observations about Gulliver's thinking which anticipate mine, for example her sustained emphasis on his egotism and her particular reference to, and application of, Locke's comment on the insularity of the Marian islanders (p. 150), cited by me at note 27 below. On the other hand, she does not investigate Gulliver's philosophical terminology and associations as I do here.

5. Jonathan Swift, *Gulliver's Travels, Prose Works*, Herbert Davis, ed., vol. 11, rev. ed. (1959; rpt. Oxford: Basil Blackwell, 1965), pp. 133–35 (bk. 2, ch. 1). All references are to this edition, parenthetical citations in my text giving, respectively, the book, chapter, and page numbers.

6. John Locke, *An Essay Concerning Human Understanding*, Peter H. Nidditch, ed. (Oxford: Clarendon, 1975), p. 47 and *n*. Henceforth *ECHU*.

7. Ricardo Quintana, *Two Augustans: John Locke, Jonathan Swift* (Madison: University of Wisconsin Press, 1978), p. 77. The passage is from "Remarks upon a Book, Intitled, The Rights of the Christian Church," *Prose Works*, Herbert Davis, ed., vol. 2 (Oxford: Basil Blackwell, 1957), p. 97. Kenneth MacLean had earlier said, "An unacknowledged influence of Locke's *Essay* is most apparent in Swift's writings." *John Locke and English Literature of the Eighteenth Century* (1936; rpt. New York: Russell & Russell, 1962), p. 9.

8. Piper, p. 79.

9. Thomas Hobbes, *Leviathan, English Works*, Sir William Molesworth, Bart., ed. (1839; rpt. Aalen: Scientia, 1962), 3:12.

10. *ECHU*, pp. 395–96.

11. *Ibid.*, pp. 398, 401. For passages taking a less pessimistic view, see pp. 553, 560, 682.

12. See *ante*, ch. 2.

13. Peter H. Nidditch, Introduction, *ECHU*, p. xxviii.

14. *Locke's Conduct of the Understanding*, Thomas Fowler, ed., 2d ed. (1882; rpt. New York: Burt Franklin, 1971), pp. 87–88. Ernest Lee Tuveson notes Locke's pessimism about undoing associations but does not comment on this exceptional statement. Tuveson says that Locke's "emphasis on environmental influences rather than on the inner will in the shaping of the self places him in the modern line. To 'take care' of the association of ideas, we find, is a matter of seeing to it that the mind receives the right impressions, under the right circumstances; that is primarily a task for education. . . ." Tuveson adds, "It would seem almost inevitable that, after reaching this point, Locke should suggest that much could be done by way of fishing the associations out of the recesses beyond the immediate awareness, and subjecting them to the kind of historical reconstruction he makes in the case of the man who fears the dark [*ECHU*, pp. 397–98]." This remedy, Tuveson concludes, would remain unavailable for another two hundred years. *The Imagination as a Means of Grace: Locke and the Aesthetics of Romanticism* (Berkeley and Los Angeles: University of California Press, 1960), p. 36. Yet Locke, as the passage just quoted in my text shows, does indicate the possibility of

tracing, recognizing, and disconnecting associations. (What he does not indicate is the modern distinction between his merely habitual, unrecognized associations and "unconscious" associations caused by repression.) Locke reiterates his positive view later in *Of the Conduct*: Teachers should provide students with a rule "to be their guide in the whole course of their lives and studies, viz. that they never suffer any ideas to be joined in their understandings in any other or stronger combination than what their own nature and correspondence give them; and that they often examine those that they find linked together in their minds, whether this association of ideas be from the visible agreement that is in the ideas themselves, or from the habitual and prevailing custom of the mind joining them thus together in thinking. "This is for caution against this evil, before it be thoroughly riveted by custom in the understanding: but he that would cure it, when habit has established it, must nicely observe the very quick and almost imperceptible motions of the mind in its habitual actions" (p. 89).

15. See Carnochan's apt quotation from Swift's verse, and accompanying comments, p. 132; MacLean demonstrates the near ubiquity of Locke's influence on the century (passim).

16. Stanley Eugene Fish, *Surprised by Sin: The Reader in Paradise Lost* (1967; rpt. Berkeley, Los Angeles and London: University of California Press, 1971), p. 51.

17. Michael V. DePorte, *Nightmares and Hobbyhorses: Swift, Sterne, and Augustan Ideas of Madness* (San Marino, Calif.: Huntington Library, 1974), pp. 23–24. Cf. Helene Moglen's description of the wider implications of Locke's account of association, implications drawn from statements of his which indicate that associations may be caused, actively, by the mind's "private inclinations . . . and interests." *The Philosophical Irony of Laurence Sterne* (Gainesville: University Presses of Florida, 1975), p. 15.

18. See, for example, Louis L. Martz's chapter "Self-Knowledge: The Spiritual Combat," *The Poetry of Meditation: A Study in English Religious Literature of the Seventeenth Century*, Yale Studies in English, 125 (New Haven: Yale University Press, 1954), pp. 118–52.

19. *ECHU*, p. 394.

20. Louis Landa, in his introduction to the sermons, says circumstances "do not permit confident rejection or acceptance" of this sermon as by Swift. *Prose Works*, Herbert Davis, ed., vol. 9 (Oxford: Basil Blackwell, 1948), p. 106.

21. *Ibid.*, p. 359.

22. *Ibid.*, pp. 361–62.

23. *Ibid.*, p. 357.

24. *Ibid.*, p. 358. A blend of Lockean interest in a person's unwitting formation of wrong habits of thought and of more traditional interest in "excessive self-esteem" may be found in a later tract, John Mason's *Self-Knowledge* (1745; rpt. London: Gale, Curtis, and Fenner, 1814), ch. 9 (my quotation from p. 68).

25. *Minor Poems*, Normal Ault and John Butt, eds., *The Twickenham Edition of the Poems of Alexander Pope*, vol. 6 (London: Methuen; New Haven: Yale University Press, 1964), p. 273. Regarding the authorship and provenance of the "Verses on *Gulliver's Travels*" see pp. 266–67 and George Sherburn, "The 'Copies of Verses' about Gulliver," *Texas Studies in Literature and Language* (1961), 3:3–7.

26. *Minor Poems*, pp. 276–77.

27. *Locke's Conduct of the Understanding*, pp. 8–9.

28. *Minor Poems*, p. 280.

29. *Locke's Conduct of the Understanding*, pp. 37, 48, 50.

30. Taylor, pp. 15, 46–47, explained with reference to Gulliver's excessive self-love. Ila Dawson Traldi comments on his "egotism" in leaving Laputa. "Gulliver the 'Educated Fool': Unity in the Voyage to Laputa," *Papers on Language and Literature* (1968), 4:39. Ac-

cording to Charles Peake, Swift's nonsatirical writings indicate a tolerant, measured attitude towards self-love, resembling Pope's. "Like Pope, Swift believed that all the human passions could be seen as 'Modes of Self-love', and that it was impossible to call self-love good or bad since all good came from the proper control of this great passion by reason and all bad from an improper relationship between them." "Swift and the Passions," *Modern Language Review* (1960), 55:170.

    31. John Middleton Murry, *Jonathan Swift: A Critical Biography* (1955; rpt. New York: Farrar, Straus, and Giroux, 1967), p. 336; John B. Radner (who cites Murry), "The Struldbruggs, the Houyhnhnms, and the Good Life," *Studies in English Literature* (1977), 17:420.

    32. *ECHU*, p. 507.

    33. *Ibid.*, p. 445. Some other passages illustrating the quandary: pp. 502, 517, 572, 577, 666, 709. Clive T. Probyn, building upon the work of R. S. Crane and Rosalie L. Colie, explores the philosophical and linguistic background of the problem in "Swift and Linguistics: The Context Behind Lagado and Around the Fourth Voyage," *Neophilologus* (1974), 58:425–39.

    34. *ECHU*, p. 546. For "wary Reasoning from Analogy" see p. 666.

    35. A. E. Dyson says the Houyhnhnms "insinuate into Gulliver's mind a vision of himself that becomes increasingly more repellent." "Swift: The Metamorphosis of Irony," *Essays and Studies* (1958), N.S. 11:61. Yet Gulliver has already given evidence of finding himself repellent.

    36. Arthur E. Case says, "Gradually, in the course of the conversations with his master which occupy the fourth, fifth, sixth, and seventh chapters, Gulliver falls into the habit of referring to Europeans as yahoos, partly for convenience. . . ." *Four Essays on Gulliver's Travels* (1945, rpt. Gloucester, Mass: Peter Smith, 1958), p. 118. The Lockean framework of association, habit, and prejudice clarifies this process, which, as we have seen, is not gradual. Locke writes, "It is visible that men's prejudices and inclinations . . . impose often upon themselves . . . Inclination suggests and slides into their discourse favourable terms, which introduce favourable ideas, till at last, by this means, that is concluded clear and evident, thus dressed up, which taken in its native state, by making use of none but the precise determined ideas, would find no admittance at all." *Locke's Conduct of the Understanding*, p. 91. Harold D. Kelling reminds us that Gulliver is speaking "in the Houyhnhnm tongue, which contains no words for evil except what the Houyhnhnms 'borrow from the deformities or ill qualities of a Yahoo.'" "*Gulliver's Travels*: A Comedy of Humours," *The University of Toronto Quarterly* (1952), 21:372. This is a complementary consideration but I think less striking than Gulliver's resorting to "Similitudes." I cannot agree with Robert M. Philmus' assertion "that the language forces Gulliver to use the word *Yahoo* to designate men." "Swift, Gulliver, and 'The Thing Which Was Not,' " *ELH* (1971), 38:68.

    37. *ECHU*, pp. 394, 400.

    38. On this general trait of Swift's style: Maurice J. Quinlan, "Swift's Use of Literalization as a Rhetorical Device," *PMLA* (1967), 82:516–21.

    39. *ECHU*, p. 395.

    40. Rawson observes regarding Gulliver's behavior to Captain Mendez, ". . . We should note that he has not learnt such bad manners (or his later hysterical tone) from the Houyhnhnms' example" (p. 28).

    41. *ECHU*, p. 153.

    42. For a different interpretation of this episode see Kathleen Williams, *Jonathan Swift and the Age of Compromise* (Lawrence: University of Kansas Press, 1958), pp. 175–76.

    43. Cf. Locke on the way "Custom and Education" affect the Roman Catholic: ". . .

How is he prepared easily to swallow, not only against all Probability, but even the clear Evidence of his Senses, the Doctrine of *Transubstantiation?* This Principle has such an influence on his Mind that he will believe that to be Flesh, which he sees to be Bread" (*ECHU*, pp. 712–13). The *swallow* is particularly Swiftian.

44. Robert C. Elliott has provided an excellent Jamesian analysis of Gulliver's narrative points of view, the *ingénu* becoming the misanthrope—with, Elliott says, small lapses, including passages inexplicable unless Gulliver is speaking ironically (which, I agree, is unlikely). "Clearly, Gulliver as character holds, simultaneously, two completely incompatible attitudes toward human experience." But I find myself disagreeing with Elliott's view that Swift "does not exploit artistically any such psychological split in Gulliver's character"— "Gulliver as Literary Artist," *ELH* (1952), 19:58—because there is comical and satirical force in eruptions of the secret inner Gulliver and in his efforts to cover them; the tale character devised by the Dean resembles the vicar invented by Monty Python.

45. Cf. the passage from Locke quoted above, at note 14; an extended quotation is given as the epigraph to my ch. 3.

46. Alexander Campbell Fraser, ed., *An Essay Concerning Human Understanding* (1894; rpt. New York: Dover, 1959), 1:304*n*.

6. The Spirit of the *Lettres persanes*, and of Enlightened Characterization

1. Northrop Frye, *Anatomy of Criticism* (Princeton: Princeton University Press, 1957), p. 365 (Glossary); also pp. 308–14.

2. Jonathan Swift, *Gulliver's Travels, Prose Works*, Herbert Davis, ed., vol. 11, rev. ed. (1959; rpt. Oxford: Basil Blackwell, 1965), pp. 49, 19. Charles-Louis de Secondat, baron de Montesquieu, *Lettres persanes*, Paul Vernière, ed. (Paris: Garnier, 1975), Lettres 24, 104; because the letters are typically very short, I give only letter numbers in my text and notes.

3. Benjamin Motte to Swift, July 31, 1735, *The Correspondence of Jonathan Swift*, Harold Williams, ed., vol. 4 (Oxford: Clarendon, 1965), p. 372. Elsewhere Harold Williams remarks that the *Lettres persanes* was not among the books Swift is known to have possessed. *Dean Swift's Library* (Cambridge: Cambridge University Press, 1932), p. 93. Bolingbroke's periodical *The Craftsman* published several Persian letters—not by Montesquieu, of course. Number 150 (May 17, 1729) presents a letter from Rica to Usbek describing an interview with Gulliver; reprinted in *Gulliveriana*, introd. Jeanne K. Welcher and George E. Bush, Jr., vol. 5 (Delmar, N.Y.: Scholars' Facsimiles & Reprints, 1974), pp. 92–97.

4. Samuel H. Monk, "The Pride of Lemuel Gulliver," in James L. Clifford, ed., *Eighteenth-Century English Literature: Modern Essays in Criticism* (New York: Oxford University Press, 1959), p. 117. Cf. James L. Clifford, "Gulliver's Fourth Voyage: 'Hard' and 'Soft' Schools of Interpretation," in Larry S. Champion, ed., *Quick Springs of Sense: Studies in the Eighteenth Century* (Athens: University of Georgia Press, 1974), pp. 33–49.

5. Jonathan Swift, *Journal to Stella*, Harold Williams, ed. (Oxford: Clarendon, 1948), 1:254–55.

6. Frederick C. Green, *Literary Ideas in 18th Century France and England* (1935, entitled *Minuet*; rpt. New York: Frederick Ungar, 1966), p. 399; Henri Coulet, *Le Roman jusqu'à la Révolution* (Paris: A. Colin, 1967), pp. 392–93.

7. Roger Laufer, "La Réussité romanesque et la signification des 'Lettres persanes' de

Montesquieu," *Revue d'Histoire Littéraire de la France* (1961), 61:188–203; Roger Mercier, "Le Roman dans les *Lettres persanes*: structure et signification," *Revue des Sciences Humaines* (1962), 107:345–56. The way of reading initiated in these articles—though there is an important precedent in Roger B. Oake's "Polygamy in the *Lettres persanes*," *Romanic Review* (1941) 32:56–62—has been emulated and extended by other commentators including Aram Vartanian, "Eroticism and Politics in the *Lettres persanes*," *Romanic Review* (1969), 60:23–33.

8. J. Robert Loy remarks that Montesquieu's "Quelques réflexions sur les Lettres persanes," a brief commentary of 1754 to which I shall turn later in this chapter, "bear the cachet of surprise of the man who has only later realized what he managed to write some thirty years earlier." *Montesquieu* (New York: Twayne, 1968), p. 49. Scholars have nevertheless disagreed about Montesquieu's late attitude toward the book—a question much too complicated for anything but glancing review here. One element of the question, the very intricate history of the text, involving numerous editions and manuscripts, is summarized by Vernière (*Lettres persanes*, pp. xxxv–xlii). When reconsidering the *Lettres*, the elderly author (who would die in 1755) was much upset by sectarian attacks on the book and *De l'esprit des lois*. In various statements and emendations he sought to decrease the critical and satirical force of the *Lettres*. Yet the weight of the evidence is on the side of his continued pleasure in the book, if not in its susceptibility to attack. (The signs of haste and disorder Vernière perceives in the fact that the 1754 edition adds letters in a supplement—p. xxxvii—could very well be a contrived show of casualness.) Montesquieu's continued satisfaction with the book is indicated by: the extensiveness of his revisions in the early 1750s, not all of them prudent (p. xl); his amplifying the text as well as preserving additional material not included (e.g., the further history of the Troglodytes, pp. 336–38); his claims that the book contributed to the establishment of the epistolary novel (pp. 3, 373); and, above all, the extent to which the book is unquestionably the germ of his life's work. See Robert Shackleton, *Montesquieu: A Critical Biography* (London: Oxford University Press, 1961), p. 45; Oake, p. 62; Alan M. Boase, "The Interpretation of *Les Lettres persanes*," in Will Moore et al., eds., *The French Mind: Studies in Honour of Gustave Rudler* (Oxford: Clarendon, 1952), pp. 152–59; Ira O. Wade, *The Structure and Forms of the French Enlightenment* (Princeton: Princeton University Press, 1977), 1:350, where it is suggested, after F. Brunetière, that *De l'esprit des lois* may possibly have originated as a satirical "continuation" of the *Lettres*. That Montesquieu, despite his protestations to the contrary, did not ignore the *Lettres* during the thirty years before republication is clearest from Elisabeth Carayol's discovery, in an Amsterdam periodical (1745), of eight Persian letters first published by Montesquieu in the edition of 1754. He probably gave them to the editor of the periodical before 1740, possibly as early as 1730. "Des Lettres persanes oubliées," *Revue d'Histoire Littéraire de la France* (1965), 65:18.

9. Briefly, the two editions of 1721 (designated *A* and *B* by scholars) had 150 and 140 letters, respectively. The 1754 edition (*C*), with its supplement, had 161, as did the 1758 edition (*D*). Vernière records the many variations in the text from edition to edition (*Lettres persanes*, pp. 373–410). Keeping track of the letters' numbers, dates, etc., is no mean feat; errors of citation are not uncommon in the commentators.

10. Robert Shackleton, "The Moslem Chronology of the *Lettres Persanes*," *French Studies* (1954), 8:17–27.

11. Pauline Kra concentrates on classification of Montesquieu's ideas yet notes that "if the chronological order had been preserved the influence of the eunuchs, the reign of terror and the rebellion would reflect political situations discussed in what would be adjacent letters." "The Invisible Chain of the *Lettres persanes*," *Studies on Voltaire* (1963), 23:51n.

12. *Lettres persanes*, p. 3. The term *roman* as employed by Mercier and others, although

at first useful to emphasize the neglected fictional aspect of the work, is ultimately unsatisfactory. Some of the questions raised by Jean-Marie Goulemot deftly make this point: should the book really be considered a novel if, as is the case, it was for so long refused that classification by critics, if the text taken as a whole may not warrant it, and if the author himself only belatedly saw the book that way? "Questions sur la signification politique des 'Lettres persanes,'" *Approches des lumières: Mélanges offerts à Jean Fabre* (Paris: Klincksieck, 1974), p. 223. Comparison of the *Lettres persanes* with philosophical tales is more useful since it encourages measured appreciation of the novelistic element without aesthetic confusion. Georges Benrekassa, after investigating Montesquieu's mixed feelings about the genre of *roman* (there were few examples in his library, which included *Gulliver's Travels*), nicely observes that Montesquieu knew his works did not fit in the standard genres and, Benrekassa believes, felt a secret satisfaction in the fact that they did not. "Montesquieu et le roman comme genre littéraire," *Roman et lumières au XVIIIe siècle* (Paris: Éditions Sociales, 1970), pp. 28, 30.

13. Shackleton, *Montesquieu*, p. 27.

14. Ronald Grimsley, *From Montesquieu to Laclos: Studies on the French Enlightenment* (Genève: Droz, 1974), p. 14.

15. "De l'esprit des loix," *Œuvres complètes*, André Masson, ed., 3 vols. (Paris: Nagel, 1950), 1:5–6 (the first series of numbered pages). Henceforth *OC*.

16. *The Spectator*, Donald F. Bond, ed. (Oxford: Clarendon, 1965), 1:215.

17. *OC*, 1:200–230.

18. *Montesquieu*, p. 45. Cf. p. 42.

19. Robert F. O'Reilly, "The Structure and Meaning of the *Lettres persanes*," *Studies on Voltaire* (1969), 67:96–97.

20. *Lettres persanes*, p. 8.

21. O'Reilly, p. 96.

22. This and subsequent passages of the "Réflexions" are from *Lettres persanes*, pp. 3–5.

23. *OC*, 1:lxii.

24. I must underscore the inadequacy of viewing Montesquieu's insistence on the dramatic character of the Persians' remarks as no more than a ruse to foil hostile critics (see Vernière's comments, *Lettres persanes*, pp. xxxvii–xxxviii). Sympathetic comprehension of the logic and worth of points of view other than one's own is absolutely central to his thought; see *OC*, 1:lix–lx.

25. D'Alembert makes a comparable point sharply in a passage of the "Discours préliminaire" owing much to Montesquieu: the student of politics must not forget that "la loi naturelle, antérieure à toutes les conventions particulières, est aussi la première loi des peuples, . . . et pour être homme d'État, on ne doit point cesser d'être homme" ("the natural law, anterior to all particular contracts, is also the basic law of humanity, . . . and in order to be a statesman one must not cease to be a man"). Jean Le Rond d'Alembert, *Œuvres complètes* (1821; rpt. Genève: Slatkine, 1967), 1:37. Kra calls attention to the relevant Letter 30 in which Rica "passes unnoticed in the streets of Paris as soon as he wears European clothes" (p. 32).

26. D'Alembert, pp. 18–19.

27. *OC*, 3:412. Parenthetical references to the "Essai" in my text employ this edition. The "Essai" is "of cardinal importance" in Montesquieu's thought, according to Shackleton, who assigns its composition to the years 1736–1743 (*Montesquieu*, p. 314) and relates it to the development of the idea of the *esprit général* (p. 316). Montesquieu also composed a

"Discours sur la formation et le progrès des idées" (ca. 1734) and, much earlier, a "Discours sur le système des idées" (1716) and a paper "De la différence des génies" (1717), all lost (pp. 405, 400–1).

28. The only commentator on the *Lettres persanes* to have expressed interest in the generation and progress of the characters' ideas refers appropriately to Locke, and to Montesquieu on self-love, but does so in passing: Mark Hulliung, *Montesquieu and the Old Regime* (Berkeley, Los Angeles, and London: University of California Press, 1976), pp. 117, 120, 128.

29. René Hubert, "La Notion du devenir historique dans la philosophie de Montesquieu," *Revue de Métaphysique et de Morale* (1939), 46:587–88, 609.

30. *Prose Works*, 11:121–22.

31. Denis Diderot, *Œuvres complètes*, vol. 14, J. Assézat, ed. (Paris: Garnier, 1876), p. 463.

32. Voltaire, *Lettres philosophiques*, Gustave Lanson, ed., 2d ed. (Paris: Hachette, 1915–1917), 1:74.

33. *An Essay on Man* 3:313–18, Maynard Mack, ed., in John Butt, ed., *The Twickenham Edition of the Poems of Alexander Pope*, vol. 3–1 (London: Methuen; New Haven: Yale University Press, 1950), p. 126. Margaret C. Jacob, *The Newtonians and the English Revolution 1689–1720* (Ithaca: Cornell University Press, 1976).

34. Margaret C. Jacob, *The Radical Enlightenment: Pantheists, Freemasons and Republicans* (London, Boston, Sydney: George Allen & Unwin, 1981), p. 105, citing René Pomeau, *La Religion de Voltaire* (Paris: Nizet, 1956), pp. 119–84.

35. *Lettres philosophiques*, 2:26.

7. The Generation and Progress of Usbek's Ideas in the *Lettres persanes*

1. Charles-Louis de Secondat, baron de Montesquieu, "Essai sur les causes qui peuvent affecter les esprits & les caractères," *Œuvres complètes*, André Masson, ed., 3 vols. (Paris: Nagel, 1950), 3:418. Henceforth *OC*.

2. Charles-Louis de Secondat, baron de Montesquieu, *Lettres persanes*, Paul Vernière, ed. (Paris: Garnier, 1975), Letter 10; because the letters are typically very short, I give only letter numbers in my text and notes.

3. John Locke, *Two Treatises of Government*, Peter Laslett, ed., 2d ed. (London: Cambridge University Press, 1967), p. 293.

4. Jean Starobinski, "Les 'Lettres persanes': Apparence et essence," *Neohelicon* (1974), 2:105–6. All is reversed because on a second reading our knowledge of the book's startling conclusion inverts our estimate of Usbek: he now appears blind.

5. Cf. F. C. Green's unexplained judgment against Montesquieu as a writer of fiction: "extremely deficient in psychological penetration." "Montesquieu the Novelist and Imitations of the 'Lettres persanes,'" *Modern Language Review* (1925), 20:34. A *pensée* of Montesquieu (*OC*, 2:647; no. 2157) quoted by Georges Benrekassa is much to the point: Montesquieu contrasts the blind fatality determining the lives of characters in Oriental fiction with the thinking of the West whereby good fortune is the consequence of prudence and wisdom. "Montesquieu et le roman comme genre littéraire," *Roman et lumières au XVIIIᵉ siècle* (Paris: Éditions Sociales, 1970), p. 33.

6. In a valuable article on the intellectual background of the *Lettres persanes*, Allessandro

S. Crisafulli nevertheless exemplifies too literal, undramatic reading for "the ideas" when he argues that, in Montesquieu's opinion, virtue is natural and effortless for mankind and finds the opinion borne out by the example of the good Troglodytes and other letters including Letter 26, in which Usbek arrogantly preaches the point to Roxane. "Montesquieu's Story of the Troglodytes: Its Background, Meaning, and Significance," *PMLA* (1943), 58:382. Crisafulli touches on the Old Testament parallel regarding the Troglodytes (p. 373*n*).

7. Antoine Adam employs the confusion about the wives to argue that the book is not fully a *roman*. *Lettres persanes* (Genève: Droz, 1954), pp. xviii–xix. Roger Mercier holds that Zéphis, last mentioned in Letter 47, and Zélis, first mentioned in Letter 53, are—inadvertently—the same woman. "Le Roman dans les *Lettres persanes*: structure et signification," *Revue des Sciences Humaines* (1962), 107:345–46. Adam also suggests a belated impulse in Montesquieu to create consistency in these characters, an impulse that would reinforce my point about the way the book changed in Montesquieu's eyes. It is notable in this respect that Letters 157 and 158, from Zachi and Zélis respectively, finishing their stories, were added to the book in 1754, as was Solim's Letter 160, and that, in 1758, the reference to Zachi in Solim's Letter 159 was changed to Zélis, so as to be consistent with Usbek's reference to Zélis in Letter 148. In an appendix, Vernière prints a letter never included in the collection, which Usbek writes protesting Zélis' attempt to secure a legal separation from him (*Lettres persanes*, pp. 344–45). Had Montesquieu inserted the letter in the text at the proper chronological place, the letter would be the third that Usbek writes after 104, in which he considers the English practice of dismissing unsatisfactory kings.

8. Zélis has received close attention from Jeannette Geffriaud Rosso, who comments on this wife's very active disposition and notes that, according to Letters 151–52, she has by the end apparently joined forces with Roxane in cuckolding Usbek. *Montesquieu et la fémininité* (Pise: Goliardica; Paris: Nizet, 1977), pp. 322–26.

9. Mary M. Crumpacker, among other commentators, notes the resemblance between Usbek and the eunuchs. "The Secret Chain of the *Lettres persanes*, and the Mystery of the B Edition," *Studies on Voltaire* (1973), 102:134.

10. Robert F. O'Reilly calls Zélis "the most perceptive and most mature of Usbek's wives." "The Structure and Meaning of the *Lettres persanes*," *Studies on Voltaire* (1969), 67:116.

11. Pierre Testud says that Usbek goes to the country retreat at first for brief stays, then for longer periods. "Les 'Lettres persanes', roman épistolaire," *Revue d'Histoire Littéraire de la France* (1966), 66:654. But apart from Letter 74, in which Usbek says he has just visited a house in Paris (and he could do so from the country), there is no evidence, in his letters succeeding Rica's complaint, that Usbek is ever in the city. He repeatedly speaks of being told about French events, as a person in the country would be (e.g., 89, 101, etc.). Rica on the other hand speaks of visiting a cafe (132), a library (133)—and of having seen Louis XV (107). Usbek, by contrast, mentions a Persian, not himself, who has seen Louis XIV (91). And the letter I have cited as exceptional (74), in which Usbek mentions visiting a house in Paris, is somewhat problematical in attribution, having been assigned to Rica until the 1758 edition. There is still another letter from Rica to Usbek, dated in 1717, beginning, "Tu restes à la campagne, et moi, je suis dans le tumulte de Paris" ("You remain in the country, and I, I am in the whirl of Paris"), among the materials not published by Montesquieu, printed by Vernière, pp. 345–46.

12. Swift, "Maxims Controlled in Ireland," *Prose Works*, Herbert Davis, ed., vol. 12 (Oxford: Basil Blackwell, 1964), p. 135.

13. *Prose Works*, Herbert Davis, ed., vol. 11, rev. ed. (1959; rpt. Oxford: Basil Blackwell, 1965), pp. 251–52.

14. The passage on interest governing the world, with its appreciation of the effects of luxury, is the exact reverse of the absolute scorn for luxury felt by the inhabitants of Fénelon's Bétique. François de Salignac de la Mothe-Fénelon, *Les Aventures de Télémaque*, Albert Cahen, ed., 2 vols. (Paris: Hachette, 1920), 1:327–31. Bétique was an important model for the utopia of the Troglodytes, according to Crisafulli, pp. 375–77. There is no question that Montesquieu, like Usbek, could sometimes write very idealistically about virtue, in *De l'esprit des lois* and elsewhere. See Robert Shackleton, *Montesquieu: A Critical Biography* (London: Oxford University Press, 1961), pp. 272–77. But he could write very practically about self-interest too, and the key question, at least in ordinary circumstances, has to do with reconciliation of these elements, not the choice of one to the utter or virtual exclusion of the other.

15. A comparable transition from physical to moral causes is to be found in the "Essai sur les causes . . ." (*OC*, 3:413).

16. Starobinski's essay concludes with the comment that Montesquieu, despite Usbek's failures, makes us face a problem we have yet to learn how to solve: how to make our deeds as well as our words accord with libertarian sentiments (p. 112). It is because Usbek as well as Montesquieu comes to a general understanding of this problem and how it may be fruitfully addressed—even though Usbek fails to put his principles into practice with his own wives and slaves—that all is not reversed in the *Lettres persanes*.

17. Pierre Testud's rich article is particularly good on the significance of the chronological order. Of Letter 129, for example, he comments that it is the only philosophical letter Usbek writes in 1719, and it is very severe: explicitly supporting obedience to bad laws and the unrestricted authority of the *paterfamilias*, implicitly supporting despotism—after the liberal letters on population. Testud explains (pp. 652–53) that between those letters and the severe Letter 129 Usbek had received the unsettling letter from the seraglio that announces the death of the chief eunuch (149). It should be noted, too, that the writer, Narsit, blandly and most vexingly says he has not opened Usbek's crucial letter of instructions to the deceased eunuch about how to deal with the seraglio crisis. (Before the 1758 edition, Letter 129 had not been given the significance described here, being dated more than three years earlier.)

18. Cf. Roger Laufer, "La Réussité romanesque et la signification des 'Lettres persanes' de Montesquieu," *Revue d'Histoire Littéraire de la France* (1961), 61:203.

19. Patrick Brady comments, "The chronology of the letters shows Usbek silent towards the harem from 1714 . . . to 1718 . . ., which locates the end of his indifference earlier than does the serial order of the letters." "The *Lettres persanes*—Rococo or Neo-Classical?" *Studies on Voltaire* (1967), 53:74.

20. Robert C. Frautschi notes that Letter 146 is deflated in tone because Usbek has just received the dreadful concluding Letters 159–61. "The Would-Be Invisible Chain in *Les Lettres persanes*," *French Review* (1967), 40:609. See also Jean Ehrard, "La Signification politique des *Lettres persanes*," *Archives des Lettres Modernes*, No. 116 (1970), p. 48. Letters 145 and 146 bore earlier dates in one of the 1721 editions, thus lacking the significance described in my text and confirmed by the 1754 and 1758 editions. For alternate views of the meaning of Letter 145 see Crumpacker, pp. 140–41; Frautschi, p. 611; my reading complements Testud's, p. 653.

21. Testud comments only that the satire is against the financier Law (p. 653), but the fugitive impulse, as motive, deserves consideration. We have not been told that Usbek has visited India; his saying so now resembles Gulliver's late revelation of the sojourn in Tribnia (p. 191), also delivered in a time of emotional stress.

22. *OC*, 3:416. Subsequent parenthetical references in my text are to this edition.

23. *Lettres persanes*, p. 176*n*.

24. Vernière (*ibid.*, p. 124*n*) cites precedents for this attack on anthropomorphism in Spinoza, Marana, and possibly Fontenelle. Bernard Mandeville (drawing on Montaigne and, through him, Xenophanes) similarly observes, ". . . If Brutes were to paint the Deity, they would all draw him of their own Species." *The Fable of the Bees*, F. B. Kaye, ed. (Oxford: Clarendon, 1924), 2:131.

25. *OC*, 1:5–6. Ernst Cassirer, *The Philosophy of the Enlightenment*, Fritz C. A. Koelln and James P. Pettegrove, trans. (Princeton: Princeton University Press, 1951), pp. 253–54.

26. *OC*, 1:7. Thomas Hobbes, *Leviathan*, *English Works*, Sir William Molesworth, Bart., ed. (1839; rpt. Aalen: Scientia, 1962), 3:112.

8. *Candide:* Structure and Motivation

1. *The Philosophy of Kant*, Carl J. Friedrich, ed. and trans. (New York: Modern Library, 1949), pp. 132–33.

2. Much of the history of this question is conveniently summarized in William F. Bottiglia, *Voltaire's* Candide: *Analysis of a Classic*, 2d. ed., *Studies on Voltaire* (1964), 7A; esp. p. 70. For Bottiglia the characters are suddenly and mysteriously transformed into human beings at the end (p. 197). Critics tend to waver somewhat about how to take the characters, as I have indicated in chapter 1. Such wavering, however, is preferable to insensitive deductions about the characters based on heavy-handed preliminary classification of a mercurial work. Among critics who have paid serious attention to the characters, Henri Coulet makes several very useful observations, including the statement that Pangloss' doctrine was made for Candide. "La Candeur de Candide," *Annales de la Faculté des Lettres et Sciences Humaines d'Aix* (1960), 34:87. And Jacques Van den Heuvel, taking Candide very seriously, says the tale is a sketch of a *Bildungsroman*, Candide coming to think more and more deeply. *Voltaire dans ses contes: de "Micromégas" à "L'Ingénu"* (Paris: Armand Colin, 1967), pp. 289, 290.

3. A. O. Lovejoy writes, "One of the principal happenings in eighteenth-century thought was the temporalizing of the Chain of Being. The *plenum formarum* came to be conceived by some, not as the inventory but as the program of nature, which is being carried out gradually and exceedingly slowly in the cosmic history." *The Great Chain of Being: A Study in the History of an Idea* (1936; New York: Harper, 1960), p. 244. Chapter 9, "The Temporalizing of the Chain of Being," explains Kant's early theory of cosmic evolution and refers in passing (p. 268) to the "evolutionistic" biological transformism of Diderot and Maupertuis, which Lovejoy had described in "Some Eighteenth Century Evolutionists," *Popular Science Monthly* (1904), 65:238–51, 323–40.

4. See Gérard Genette, "Vraisemblance et motivation," *Figures: Essais*, vol. 2 (Paris: Éditions du Seuil, 1966), pp. 96–99.

5. Metaphorical relations, for Jakobson, are based predominantly on "similarity," metonymical relations on "contiguity." See his "Two Aspects of Language and Two Types of Aphasic Disturbances," in Roman Jakobson and Morris Halle, *Fundamentals of Language* (The Hague: Mouton, 1956), pp. 81–82. For a recent scholarly evaluation of Jakobson's theory, see David Lodge, *The Modes of Modern Writing: Metaphor, Metonymy, and the Typology of Modern Literature* (Ithaca, N.Y.: Cornell University Press, 1977), pp. 73–124, and my review essay, "The Metonymic and the Poetic," *Essays in Criticism* (1979), 29:254–63.

6. Roy S. Wolper, at the conclusion of an illuminating exchange with Lester G. Crocker on the subject of an article by Wolper, urges that narrative point of view be given more attention by students of *Candide*. "Forum," *Eighteenth-Century Studies* (1971), 5:152.

7. See my chapter 1. Jean Sareil comments that, in the *conte philosophique*, the ideas are quite sufficiently subordinated to, and a vehicle for, the fiction. *Essai sur Candide* (Genève: Droz, 1967), p. 40. Ira O. Wade's account of Voltaire's complicated attitude toward Leibniz, in *Voltaire and "Candide": A Study in the Fusion of History, Art, and Philosophy* (Princeton: Princeton University Press, 1959), pp. 50–61, prevents a reader from taking the tale's philosophy too literally.

8. André Doyon and Lucien Liaigre, *Jacques Vaucanson, mécanicien de génie* (Paris: Presses Universitaires de France, 1966), p. 56. Bottiglia gives evidence of Voltaire's interest in puppets and the like (pp. 81–95). Hugh Kenner's *The Counterfeiters: An Historical Comedy* (Bloomington: Indiana University Press, 1968) proceeds by way of Vaucanson to consideration of Turing's Game, which hinges on the problem of proving the difference between a human being and a computer (oddly, there is no mention of La Mettrie).

9. Quotations are from Voltaire, *Candide*, René Pomeau, ed., *Complete Works*, vol. 48, William Barber et al., eds. (Oxford: Voltaire Foundation, 1980). Because the chapters are short I give only chapter numbers in my parenthetical citations—here chapter 16.

10. Douglas A. Bonneville has noted Candide's initial selfishness. *Voltaire and the Form of the Novel, Studies on Voltaire* (1976), 158:48–50.

11. *An Essay on Man* 1. 267, Maynard Mack, ed., in John Butt, ed., *The Twickenham Edition of the Poems of Alexander Pope*, vol. 3–1 (London: Methuen; New Haven: Yale University Press, 1950), p. 47. Parenthetical references are to this edition.

12. Kenneth Burke, "Four Master Tropes," *A Grammar of Motives* (1945; rpt. Berkeley: University of California Press, 1969), p. 508. See also Hayden White, *Metahistory: The Historical Imagination in Nineteenth-Century Europe* (Baltimore and London: Johns Hopkins University Press, 1973), pp. 31–38.

13. Dumarsais' rhetorical definition is similar to mine: of synecdoche he comments that "il est facile de confondre cette figure avec la métonymie, . . . mais la relation qu'il y a entre les objets, dans la métonymie, est de telle sorte, que l'objet dont on emprunte le nom, subsiste indépendament de celui dont il réveille l'idée, et ne forme point un ensemble avec lui. Tel est le raport qui se trouve entre la *cause* et l'*éfet*, entre l'auteur et son ouvrage, entre Cerès et le blé, entre le *contenant* et le *contenu*, come entre la bouteille et le vin, au lieu que la liaison qui se trouve entre les objets, dans la synecdoque, suppose que ces objets forment un ensemble come le *tout* et la *partie*; leur union n'est point un simple raport" ("It is easy to confuse this figure with metonymy, . . . but in metonymy the relation between the objects is such that the object which is named exists independently of the object implied and does not make a whole with it. Such is the relation found between a cause and an effect, between an author and his book, between Ceres and grain, between a container and what it contains—as for example between a bottle and wine. In synecdoche, on the other hand, the relation between objects requires that they make one object, like the whole and the part; the union of the objects does not depend on merely one strand of relationship"). *Les Tropes de Dumarsais avec un commentaire raisonné . . . par M. Fontanier*, introd. Gérard Genette (Genève: Slatkine Reprints, 1967), 1:130–31.

14. Hume's insistence that the mind associates ideas by only three principles, "RESEMBLANCE, CONTIGUITY in time or place, and CAUSE and EFFECT," the third being utterly questionable—*A Treatise of Human Nature*, L. A. Selby-Bigge, ed., 2d ed., rev. P. H. Nidditch (Oxford: Clarendon, 1978), p. 11—anticipates Jakobson's two polar linguistic relations,

that based on similarity and that based on contiguity. See note 5, above. Nowhere should I be understood as claiming that Hume influenced *Candide*—only that the tale is written with informed sensitivity about empirical psychology in the tradition of Locke, whom Voltaire gives substantial praise in the *Lettres philosophiques*, Gustave Lanson, ed., 2d ed., 2 vols. (Paris: Hachette, 1915–1917), Lettre 13 (see my epigraph to ch. 2); at the end of "Micromégas," *Romans et contes*, Henri Bénac, ed. (Paris: Garnier, 1960), p. 112; and elsewhere. The Lockean tradition of course includes Condillac; cf. note 19, below.

15. Erich Auerbach, *Mimesis: The Representation of Reality in Western Literature* (1953; rpt. Garden City, N.Y.: Doubleday Anchor, 1957), p. 360. Pierre Haffter, in an article that takes its origin from Auerbach's comments, notes that Voltaire's most trustworthy characters tend to be those who speak succinctly. "L'Usage satirique des causales dans les contes de Voltaire," *Studies on Voltaire* (1967), 53:27.

16. See Lovejoy, *The Great Chain of Being*, p. 257, for the quotation from *De rerum originatione radicali* (1697), about the progress "of the universe as a whole . . . just as a great part of our earth is already subject to cultivation and will hereafter be so more and more."

17. Voltaire, *Dictionnaire philosophique*, Julien Benda and Raymond Naves, eds., rev. ed. (Paris: Garnier, 1967), p. 104. Jean Starobinski quotes from this passage while pursuing a point similar to, but not the same as, mine. "Candide et la question de l'autorité," *Essays on the Age of Enlightenment in Honor of Ira O. Wade*, Jean Macary, ed. (Genève: Droz, 1977), p. 309. Cf. his remarks about Martin on the same page.

18. Explaining the "conative or drive-directed" aspect of Enlightenment thought proceeding from Bacon and Hobbes, Jeffrey Barnouw provides a comment exactly applicable to Candide's final orientation as I have described it: "The rationality of the New Science depends on the certainty of knowledge to be achieved where we are not left simply to infer or conjecture causes from apparent effects or phenomena but can know possible effects from causes in our own control." "Active Experience vs. Wish-Fulfilment in Francis Bacon's Moral Psychology of Science," *The Philosophical Forum* (1979), 9:93.

19. Étienne Bonnot de Condillac, "Traité des sensations," *Œuvres philosophiques*, Georges Le Roy, ed. (Paris: Presses Universitaires de France, 1947), 1:225. Parenthetical references in the next paragraph of my text are to this edition. As I have said, I do not claim that *Candide* was written with Condillac in mind, though the resemblance of the two names is tempting. Pomeau notes an uncommon word used by Voltaire with respect to both his hero and the philosopher (p. 29). In the *Correspondence* Voltaire speaks highly of Condillac, especially in a letter of 1756 inviting him to stay and work at Voltaire's home: "Il me semble que personne ne pense ni avec tant de profondeur, ni avec tant de justesse que vous" ("It seems to me that no one thinks so very profoundly and justly as you do"). Voltaire imaginatively elaborates the invitation in a manner that calls to mind the little philosophical circle in Westphalia: ". . . Vous seriez le maître chez moi comme chez vous; je serais votre vieux disciple; vous en auriez un plus jeune dans mad. Denis, et nous verrions tous trois ensemble ce que c'est que l'âme" (". . . You would be the teacher in my home as in yours; I would be your elderly pupil, and you would have a younger one in Mme Denis, and we would, all three together, investigate what the soul is")—D6998, *Complete Works*, vol. 101, Theodore Besterman et al., eds. (Banbury: Voltaire Foundation, 1971), pp. 319, 320; other references: D7603 (1758), vol. 102 (1971), p. 392; D12234 and D12288 (1765), vol. 92 (1973), pp. 239, 299; D15418 (1769), vol. 118 (1974), p. 236.

20. Drawing on Hannah Arendt, Ronald Paulson usefully distinguishes between *liberation* and *freedom*, the former indicating a release from constrictions, the latter "creation of a new order from the bottom up." "Burke's Sublime and the Representation of Revolution,"

Culture and Politics from Puritanism to the Enlightenment, Perez Zagorin, ed. (Berkeley, Los Angeles, London: University of California Press, 1980), 259. When Voltaire's book ends, Candide has achieved liberation and is in the process of seeking freedom.

9. Conflict, Declamation, and Self-Assessment in *Rasselas*

1. All quotations of *Rasselas* are from Samuel Johnson, *Rasselas, Poems, and Selected Prose*, Bertrand H. Bronson, ed., 3d ed., enl. (San Francisco: Rinehart, 1971), pp. 607–709. Because the chapters are short, I give only chapter numbers in my parenthetical citations.

2. Gwin J. Kolb, in an important early critical study of the tale, qualifies that opinion, saying that the characters "become more active participants by taking a trip to the pyramids." "The Structure of *Rasselas*," *PMLA* (1951), 66:710. But such qualification is rare. Frederick W. Hilles says "the observers become participants" with Pekuah's abduction and the consequent suffering of her friends. "*Rasselas*, an 'Uninstructive Tale,'" *Johnson, Boswell, and Their Circle: Essays Presented to Lawrence Fitzroy Powell* (Oxford: Clarendon, 1965), p. 113. Alvin Whitley remarks, "Up to this point we have been viewing a pure comedy of ideas; now we are faced with a comedy of emotion and behavior as well." "The Comedy of *Rasselas*," *ELH* (1956), 23:63. According to Carey McIntosh, "Quite suddenly the travelers are living in earnest, transformed from observers to participants. In the first half of *Rasselas* they had examined the actions and sufferings of others; now they act and suffer themselves." *The Choice of Life: Samuel Johnson and the World of Fiction* (New Haven and London: Yale University Press, 1973), p. 190. Emrys Jones says, more simply, that with the abduction the travelers become "actively involved with other men," but does not comment on their prior emotional involvement with each other. "The Artistic Form of *Rasselas*," *Review of English Studies* (1967), 18:397. The list of such statements could be lengthened. At issue, really, is the generic classification of the tale, and especially the question of how seriously the characters should be taken, a question I have considered in chapter 1. W. Jackson Bate, explaining the inadequacy of classifying *Rasselas* simply as a satire (a difficulty that applies, I think, to all the major philosophical tales), sensitively observes that "Johnson was just as strongly identified with the naive expectations of Rasselas as the mournful wisdom of Imlac." For Johnson "could not simply watch. He had to participate; and his own willing participation sets a bar to satire." "Johnson and Satire Manqué," W. H. Bond, ed., *Eighteenth-Century Studies in Honor of Donald F. Hyde* (New York: Grolier Club, 1970), pp. 159, 150. The latter sentence gives the neck of the spectator-participant canard a deft twist, and Jeffrey Barnouw gives it another while addressing himself to the question of generic classification, at the start of a searching review of *Rasselas* criticism: "If Johnson's *Rasselas* has generally been taken as a rather obvious exemplification of the dubious notion of the vanity of human wishes, this is because it has been approached as a text whose meaning is already known, a story in no need of the reader's active participation." "Readings of *Rasselas*: 'Its Most Obvious Moral' and the Moral Role of Literature," *Enlightenment Essays* (1976), 7:17.

3. Earlier studies took Imlac as Johnson's spokesman, or at least as the complete spokesman for the message of the work, until C. R. Tracy's comic interpretation, "Democritus Arise! A Study of Dr. Johnson's Humor," *Yale Review* (1949), 39:306–9. Agostino Lombardo singles Imlac out as Johnson's hero, adding that Imlac's "essays interpolated into the body of the novel are . . . justified also in relation to narrative structure, in that they are phases in the development of Rasselas, the means by which his *éducation sentimentale* is achieved."

"The Importance of Imlac," in Magdi Wahba, ed., *Bicentenary Essays on* Rasselas, *Supplement to Cairo Studies in English* (1959), p. 39. But (leaving aside the allusion to Flaubert) the particular stages of that development and education are not enumerated, nor is the conflict between Rasselas and Imlac recognized, beyond Imlac's function as a destroyer of Rasselas' illusions. J. P. Hardy, defending Rasselas as Johnson's hero, cites the aimlessness of Imlac's final disposition in the book. *The History of Rasselas Prince of Abissinia* (Oxford: Oxford University Press, 1968), p. xxiv. Howard D. Weinbrot has carefully distinguished Imlac's theory of poetry from Johnson's, in "The Reader, the General, and the Particular: Johnson and Imlac in Chapter Ten of *Rasselas*," *Eighteenth-Century Studies* (1971), 5:80–96; see also the rejoinder by Donald T. Siebert, Jr., "The Reliability of Imlac," *ibid.* (1974), 7:350–52.

4. McIntosh, more than any other commentator, has noticed the way in which "Chapters 23–29 develop in a mounting atmosphere of doubt and distrust" (p. 190). Lombardo, taking Imlac as the author's spokesman, in sketching the action of the book repeatedly skips over the crucial chapters 19–29 (pp. 40–41, 44–45).

5. That, as Hilles says, "We do not read *Rasselas* for the story" (p. 114) is an axiom of most *Rasselas* criticism, expressed earlier by Bronson in a postscript dated 1958 (p. xx). But, as I have indicated in my notes to chapter 1, Wimsatt discerns in Hilles "a warmer affection for the story (character and plot)" than may be found in Kolb—W. K. Wimsatt, "In Praise of *Rasselas*: Four Notes (Coverging)," Maynard Mack and Ian Gregor, eds., *Imagined Worlds: Essays on Some English Novels and Novelists in Honour of John Butt* (London: Methuen, 1968), p. 124—though Kolb too remarks that "the prince and his companions have definite characters" and their actions have "at least a superficial resemblance to the parts of a real story" (p. 714). Jones, noting that "Critics of *Rasselas* have tended to stress the philosophy at the expense of the fiction," broadly describes one meaning inherent in the story: "Rasselas loses his insularity, his state of innocent isolation from ordinary living . . ." (pp. 392, 397). Despite the axiomatic unimportance of the story, readers have continually responded to it as if the characters were interesting persons; I give examples in my text and subsequent notes, as well as in chapter 1.

6. Johnson said *Candide* "had more power in it than any thing that *Voltaire* had written"; Voltaire found *Rasselas* "d'une philosophie aimable, et très-bien écrit"—see *Boswell's Life of Johnson*, George Birkbeck Hill, rev. L. F. Powell, eds., vol. 3 (1934; rpt. Oxford: Clarendon, 1971), pp. 356, 500. See also James L. Clifford, "Some Remarks on *Candide* and *Rasselas*," *Bicentenary Essays on* Rasselas," pp. 7–14, and Donald Greene, "Voltaire and Johnson," *Enlightenment Studies in Honour of Lester G. Crocker* (Oxford: Voltaire Foundation, 1979), pp. 111–31.

7. Wimsatt, p. 131.

8. *Boswell's London Journal, 1762–1763*, Frederick A. Pottle, ed. (New York, London, Toronto: McGraw-Hill, 1950), p. 284.

9. Wimsatt, p. 127.

10. "Declamation" and cognate words, as employed here, in my title, and elsewhere in this chapter, are meant to convey the sense set forth by Johnson not only in the *Dictionary* ("A discourse addressed to the passions; a harangue; a set speech; a piece of rhetoric"—1st ed.) but also, quite pejoratively, in *Ramblers* 172 and 202 and the "Preface to Shakespeare": "His declamations or set speeches are commonly cold and weak, for his power was the power of nature; when he endeavoured, like other tragick writers, to catch opportunities of amplification, and instead of enquiring what the occasion demanded, to show how much his stores of knowledge could supply, he seldom escapes without the pity or resentment of his reader." Arthur Sherbo, ed., *Johnson on Shakespeare*, in John H. Middendorf, ed., *The Yale*

Edition of the Works of Samuel Johnson, vol. 7 (New Haven and London: Yale University Press, 1968), p. 73. Cf. Johnson on the chief disease afflicting eighteenth-century tragedy: "From Bard, to Bard, the frigid Caution crept,/Till Declamation roar'd, while Passion slept" ("Prologue Spoken by Mr. Garrick . . . 1747"), and note that the canting stoic of *Rasselas*, ch. 28, who suffers the sharpest reversal of the book, is discovered in a "hall or school of declamation."

11. Hugo M. Reichard, "The Pessimist's Helpers in *Rasselas*," *Texas Studies in Literature and Language* (1968), 10:60. This essay is remarkably severe about the intellectual shortcomings of the characters, who are called "boobies" (p. 63). Truly flat characters would provoke neither hot disdain nor, as is more customary in critics of *Rasselas*, positive affection.

12. See the informative and provocative study by Earl R. Wasserman, "Johnson's *Rasselas*: Implicit Contexts," *Journal of English and Germanic Philology* (1975), 74:1–25. I note the essay here rather than earlier—like the critics mentioned in note 2, Wasserman upholds the spectator-participant distinction (p. 23)—because, in order to deny the possibility of any stable "mean between extremes" in the tale, he cites the speech by Nekayah which I have just quoted, insisting that it be seen in the context of the tale's numerous comments on the stream-like nature of life, comments including Imlac's description of the world outside the valley as "a sea foaming with tempests," etc. (pp. 10–12). But if, as I am arguing, Nekayah seems to be imitating Imlac, too hastily making up her mind, and if Imlac seems to be exaggerating the world's normal perils, then explicatory recourse to allusion—Wasserman here sees negative allusion to the familiar eighteenth-century concept of *concordia discors*—must commence with more attention to equivocal elements in Johnson's text.

13. Many commentators have noted the presence of, in Hilles' words, the "Grand Style" (p. 113). McIntosh, particularly usefully, observes that the "sublime and majestic gloom" of the "pseudo-oriental sage," echoed by Imlac and other of the characters, is subverted by the events of the tale, while the less overbearing voice of the "confident teacher of true pessimism" is not; he distinguishes other voices as well (pp. 168–74, 186).

14. "His nature is deeper than his sister's," wrote G. B. Hill in his edition of *Rasselas* (Oxford: Clarendon, 1887), p. 29. Elsewhere Hill faults Johnson's characterization of Nekayah, who is "sometimes Rasselas, sometimes Imlac, sometimes undisguised Johnson" (p. 31), but there is good reason to suppose that Hill has discovered Nekayah's problem rather than Johnson's mistake.

15. Sheridan Baker's comment, in "*Rasselas*: Psychological Irony and Romance," *Philological Quarterly* (1966), 45:258, that time cures Nekayah's grief is overstated. Time lessens it, but at the end of the crucial chapter (36) she says she will "henceforward fear to yield my heart to excellence, however bright, or to fondness, however tender, lest I should lose again what I have lost in Pekuah."

16. "Johnson surely knew Gay's work," in the opinion of Richard B. Schwartz, "Johnson's Philosopher of Nature: *Rasselas*, Chapter 22," *Modern Philology* (1976), 74:198.

17. Both Reichard (p. 63) and Whitley (pp. 69–70) cite Rasselas' continued longing for a kingdom as evidence of his unteachability, as if once a person had learned not to expect something he would necessarily stop desiring it.

18. On this speech of Imlac's, with reference to Locke on madness, see Paul Kent Alkon, *Samuel Johnson and Moral Discipline* (Evanston: Northwestern University Press, 1967), pp. 90–100, especially his comment that Johnson departs somewhat from Locke in stressing the deranging effects of "solitude acting in conjunction with self-dissatisfaction" (p. 100). On Johnson's considering dissatisfaction with oneself a root cause of error, immorality, and

delusion, see W. Jackson Bate, *Samuel Johnson* (New York and London: Harcourt, Brace, Jovanovich, n.d.), pp. 296–317.

19. Jean-Jacques Rousseau, "Discours sur l'origine . . . de l'inégalité," *Œuvres complètes*, Bernard Gagnebin and Marcel Raymond, eds., Pléiade Ed., vol. 3 (n.p.: Gallimard, 1964), p. 165.

20. *The Rambler*, No. 146, W. J. Bate and Albrecht B. Strauss, eds., in John H. Middendorf, ed., *The Yale Edition of the Works of Samuel Johnson*, vols. 3–5 (New Haven and London: Yale University Press, 1969), 5:15. Alkon devotes ch. 4 to the subject of such delusion.

21. *The Rambler*, 3:45–46.

22. Martin Price's opinion that Imlac participates in Rasselas' search "as if being the spectator to another's desire were a palliative to the absence of his own"—*To the Palace of Wisdom: Studies in Order and Energy from Dryden to Blake* (Garden City, N.Y.: Doubleday, 1964), p. 318—implies the characters' progression to infinity on parallel, untouching lines. More faithful to the spirit of Imlac and the book is Mary Lascelles' reminder that the whole—especially the account of the curing of the astronomer—enjoins readers, "do not withdraw yourself," "acknowledge your kinship with your fellow beings." "*Rasselas*: A Rejoinder," *Review of English Studies* (1970), 21:54.

23. *The Achievement of Samuel Johnson* (1955; rpt. New York: Oxford University Press, 1961), p. 63.

24. Wimsatt, p. 119.

25. *The Rambler*, No. 151, 5:40. There is also a parallel with Rasselas' dream of his own blissful later life in ch. 12.

26. E. L. McAdam, Jr., affirming the judgment of Hill (note 14, above), writes of this passage: "Once more Johnson uses a character to point up the relative maturity of the three young people, and the order is the same as before. . . ." *Johnson and Boswell: A Survey of Their Writings* (Boston: Houghton Mifflin, 1969), p. 59.

27. "Structural Patterns of Control in *Rasselas*," in John H. Middendorf, ed., *English Writers of the Eighteenth Century: Essays in Honor of James Lowry Clifford* (New York: Columbia University Press, 1971), p. 215. Regarding the issue of Rasselas' remaining concerned with temporal in addition to eternal life, see J. P. Hardy's judicious comments in *Samuel Johnson: A Critical Study* (London, Boston, and Henley: Routledge & Kegan Paul, 1979), pp. 144–48.

28. To John Taylor of Ashbourne, April 13, 1775, *The Letters of Samuel Johnson*, R. W. Chapman, ed. (Oxford: Clarendon, 1952), 2:24, quoted by Paul Fussell, *Samuel Johnson and the Life of Writing* (New York: Harcourt, 1971), p. 225. Fussell's perception that the various fantasies of the characters expressed in chapter 44 are alike in revealing the wish for domination (pp. 241–43) provides another example of Rasselas' competitiveness.

29. Wimsatt, pp. 115, 117.

10. Self-Assessment in *Les Liaisons dangereuses* and *Northanger Abbey*

1. This comparison is not unprecedented: see Frank W. Bradbrook, "Jane Austen and Choderlos de Laclos," *Notes and Queries* (1954), N.S. 1:75; *Jane Austen and Her Predecessors* (Cambridge: Cambridge University Press, 1966), pp. 122–23.

2. Austen admired Johnson's writing, and various commentators have probed the similarities between the two authors, especially in the areas of ethics and prose style: Frank W. Bradbrook, "Dr. Johnson and Jane Austen," *Notes and Queries* (1960), N.S. 7:108–12, and *Jane Austen and Her Predecessors*, pp. 10–19; Robert Scholes, "Dr. Johnson and Jane Austen," *Philological Quarterly* (1975), 54:380–90; Peter L. De Rose, *Jane Austen and Samuel Johnson* (Washington, D.C.: University Press of America, 1980)—this with some attention to the Lockean heritage as it affects *Northanger Abbey* (pp. 15–35). Among commentators alert to incidental parallels, Lloyd W. Brown compares Emma's imaginings with the delusions of the astronomer in *Rasselas—Bits of Ivory: Narrative Techniques in Jane Austen's Fiction* (Baton Rouge: Louisiana State University Press, 1973), p. 46. A. Walton Litz usefully describes the novels as a response to *Rambler* 4; "Obviously Johnson's arguments were still potent at the end of the century"—*Jane Austen: A Study of Her Artistic Development* (London: Chatto & Windus, 1965), pp. 56–57. The closest any commentator has come to considering the possibility of a large-scale formal resemblance between the novels and the philosophical tale is Darrel Mansell's remark, in *The Novels of Jane Austen: An Interpretation* (New York: Barnes & Noble, 1973), pp. 35–36, that when Catherine Morland has to choose between the values of the young Thorpes and the young Tilneys "There is something here not far from the aggressive intellectual purposefulness of *Rasselas*." Mansell's subject, "Jane Austen's use of her fictional material to further a rather brittle plan for the psychological reformation of her heroine" (p. xiii) is generally to my point, though seeing the novels in the perspective of the philosophical tale calls for diction less pejorative. My perspective gives me a different view of the issues, as I explain at the beginning of my concluding chapter. On *Northanger Abbey* see his pp. 22–45.

3. Choderlos de Laclos, *Les Liaisons dangereuses*, *Œuvres complètes*, Maurice Allem, ed., Pléiade Ed. (Paris: Gallimard, 1951), p. 200. Parenthetical references in my text are to this edition.

4. The best commentators on the dénouement include: Jean-Luc Seylaz, *Les Liaisons dangereuses et la création romanesque chez Laclos* (Genève: Droz; Paris: Minard, 1958), pp. 46–47, 130–31; Georges May, *Le Dilemme du roman au XVIIIᵉ siècle: Étude sur les rapports du roman et de la critique (1715–1761)* (New Haven: Yale University Press; Paris: Presses Universitaires de France, 1963), p. 255; Laurent Versini, *Laclos et la tradition: Essai sur les sources et la technique des* Liaisons dangereuses (Paris: Klincksieck, 1968), pp. 221–24; 628–31; Yvon Belaval, *Choderlos de Laclos* (Paris: Pierre Seghers, 1972), pp. 66–67; English Showalter, Jr., *The Evolution of the French Novel, 1641–1782* (Princeton: Princeton University Press, 1972), pp. 344–46; and, in a book very attentive to the problems of interpretation, Ronald C. Rosbottom, *Choderlos de Laclos* (Boston: Twayne, 1978), pp. 114–36.

5. See John Pappas, "Le Moralisme des *Liaisons dangereuses*," *Dix-huitième Siècle* (1970), 2:284–87.

6. B. C. Southam concludes that any changes in *Northanger Abbey* after 1803 were "probably slight." *Jane Austen's Literary Manuscripts: A Study of the Novelist's Development Through the Surviving Papers* (Oxford: Clarendon, 1964), p. 61. In a convenient chronology of the composition of Austen's works, A. Walton Litz agrees, placing *Northanger Abbey* after *Lady Susan*, which was written for the most part ca. 1794 (pp. 174–76). Dated 1818 on the title page, *Northanger Abbey* and *Persuasion* were actually published in December 1817 (p. 173). On the relation of *Northanger Abbey* to *Persuasion* and the rest of the canon, see Karl Kroeber's brief, thoughtful "Subverting a Hypocrite Lecteur," in Joel Weinsheimer, ed., *Jane Austen Today* (Athens: University of Georgia Press, 1975), pp. 33–45.

7. Susan Morgan gives interesting attention to such revelations: *In the Meantime: Character and Perception in Jane Austen's Fiction* (Chicago and London: University of Chicago Press, 1980), e.g., pp. 176–80. Scholars especially concerned with Austen's relation to the eighteenth century include Henrietta Ten Harmsel, *Jane Austen: A Study in Fictional Conventions* (The Hague: Mouton, 1964); Frank W. Bradbrook, *Jane Austen and Her Predecessors*; Kenneth L. Moler, *Jane Austen's Art of Allusion* (Lincoln: University of Nebraska Press, 1968); Stuart M. Tave, *Some Words of Jane Austen* (Chicago and London: University of Chicago Press, 1973); and Lloyd W. Brown. A more circumscribed but expert study is Jocelyn Harris' "'As if They Had Been Living Friends': *Sir Charles Grandison* into *Mansfield Park*," *Bulletin of Research in the Humanities* (1980), 83:360–405, which gains topicality from the recent publication of a short play based on Richardson's novel and attributed to Austen: *Jane Austen's "Sir Charles Grandison*," Brian Southam, ed. (Oxford: Clarendon, 1981).

8. Jane Austen, *Emma, Novels*, R. W. Chapman, ed., vol. 4, 3d ed. (1933; rpt. London: Oxford University Press, 1960), bk. 3, ch. 11, p. 408. Moler lays appropriate stress on the theme of self-knowledge in the novels, describing a particularly eighteenth-century notion of such knowledge (set against what he describes as a nineteenth-century notion, which Lionel Trilling applied to *Emma*). Moler explains, "Self-knowledge for Emma Woodhouse does not involve discovery or redefinition of the meaning of her existence; it does involve an awareness of failure in her given and accepted functions of life—and a discovery of the qualities in herself that have led to this failure" (p. 7). Drawing on Hannah More and other moralists, he emphasizes Emma's vices of vanity and arrogance, resulting from failure in "awareness of the tendencies of one's soul" (p. 10); the related but distinct questions, psychological rather than moral and social, of awareness of the way one's mind joins ideas, and why, are not separated out in Moler's account. Such psychological self-knowledge is the theme of the present chapter. To Angus Wilson's question, "For what has Miss Woodhouse learned?"—"The Neighbourhood of Tombuctoo," in B. C. Southam, ed., *Critical Essays on Jane Austen* (New York: Barnes & Noble, 1969), p. 198—I would reply: very little, in a psychological way, though like Tom Jones she has been conditioned, by failures, to be more prudent, and, though more intimately than Booth in *Amelia*, she has taken up allegorical residence with a personification of judgment, Mr. Knightley.

9. C. S. Lewis, "A Note on Jane Austen," in Ian Watt, ed., *Jane Austen: A Collection of Critical Essays* (Englewood Cliffs, N.J.: Prentice-Hall, 1963), p. 28. Cf. the list of words from *Mansfield Park* that David Lodge provides in *Language of Fiction: Essays in Criticism and Verbal Analysis of the English Novel* (London: Routledge and Kegan Paul; New York: Columbia University Press, 1966), pp. 100–4, a list centering on the word *judgment*, which itself mediates between social and moral codes. Lodge usefully argues that the concept of judgment presides over the novel, placing *all* the characters in a dramatic perspective. It may be added that, for Locke, judgment is the faculty whereby the mind distinguishes, "one from another, *Ideas*, wherein can be found the least difference, thereby to avoid being misled by Similitude, and by affinity to take one thing for another." Locke, *An Essay Concerning Human Understanding*, Peter H. Nidditch, ed. (Oxford: Clarendon, 1975), p. 156.

10. Paul Kent Alkon, *Samuel Johnson and Moral Discipline* (Evanston: Northwestern University Press, 1967), p. 26 and passim. D. D. Devlin, drawing on Locke, Butler, Johnson, and other moral philosophers, says Austen wanted to show "how the human spirit could sometimes break free from the strait-jacket of environment and early example." *Jane Austen and Education* (New York: Barnes & Noble, 1975), p. 28. His chapter 3 argues convincingly against Gilbert Ryle's opinion that Austen had intellectual debts to Shaftesbury and moral-

sense philosophy. But Devlin does not investigate the psychological dimension of the problem bearing on the association of ideas and self-love.

11. D. W. Harding situates Catherine "on the borderline between caricature and character," explaining the phenomenon by reference to *Northanger's* status as an early work of Austen's. "Character and Caricature in Jane Austen," *Critical Essays on Jane Austen*, p. 102. But in the perspective of the philosophical tale that borderline is precisely, formally, where Catherine belongs.

12. Jane Austen, *Northanger Abbey* and *Persuasion, Novels*, R. W. Chapman, ed., vol. 5, 3d ed. (1933; rpt. with revisions, London: Oxford University Press, 1965), vol. 1, ch. 1, p. 15. Parenthetical references in my text are to this edition, giving volume, chapter, and page numbers respectively (vol. 2 begins after chapter 15).

13. Locke, p. 399. On the same page Locke gives other examples illustrating associational aversion to certain books and rooms, and associational dependency: the dancer's need to have an "old Trunk" in view. I put this material in a note because I do not mean to argue that Austen was directly influenced by Locke; however, the mind evidenced especially by her *juvenilia* would certainly have delighted in these "cases." The well-known scene in *Northanger Abbey* which has Catherine say that there is something "shocking" coming out of London, a statement Eleanor Tilney takes to signify not a new Gothic novel but news of a political riot, her mistake calling forth Henry's "My dear Eleanor, the riot is only in your own brain" (1.14.113), is neatly explicable by reference to literalization of Locke's metaphor of mobbing association, mediated through Imlac's "riots" of the idle brain. Samuel Johnson, *Rasselas, Poems, and Selected Prose*, Bertrand H. Bronson, ed., 3d ed. (New York: Holt, Rinehart, and Winston, 1971), p. 694.

14. Charlotte Lennox, *The Female Quixote, or the Adventures of Arabella*, Margaret Dalziel, ed. (London: Oxford University Press, 1970), p. 329. Austen was repeatedly pleased by this novel, as she says in a letter to her sister, Cassandra, January 7, 1807; *Jane Austen's Letters* . . ., R. W. Chapman, ed., 2d ed. (London, New York, Toronto: Oxford University Press, 1952), p. 173.

15. Alkon, ch. 4.

16. Mary Lascelles, *Jane Austen and Her Art* (1939; rpt. London, Oxford, New York: Oxford University Press, 1968), pp. 145, 146, 145.

17. Lennox, p. 381. On Johnson's possible authorship of bk. 9, ch. 11, see Dalziel's note pp. 414–15 and the appendix by Duncan Isles (esp. p. 421).

18. Lascelles, p. 147.

19. *Ibid.*, pp. 61–62. Earlier, Lascelles says she does not think it "profitable" to search for evidence of Austen's "use of the *narrative material* which had served other novelists" (p. 42), but there is no consideration given to the heritage of the tale, nor—following the perception about Henry Tilney's function—to his significant fallibility as a mentor. A. Walton Litz partly supports his dating of this novel by alleging a lack of "narrative sophistication" (p. 59); he explains, ". . . Many of the characters are two-dimensional, and Jane Austen never seems quite sure of her relationship to Henry Tilney. She frequently allows him to usurp her authority, to voice her judgments and wield her irony, and the result is considerable ambiguity concerning her attitude toward the novel's 'hero'" (p. 58; cf. p. 69, and, regarding the more stable hero of *Emma*, p. 148). Mansell addresses the question of Henry's change and surveys other critics' remarks on it (pp. 36–38).

20. *The Spectator*, Donald F. Bond, ed. (Oxford: Clarendon, 1965), 3:495.

21. Alistair M. Duckworth ably brings in Smith's *Theory of Moral Sentiments* on sym-

pathy and imagination to explain the value as well as the error of Catherine's intuition about the General. *The Improvement of the Estate: A Study of Jane Austen's Novels* (Baltimore and London: Johns Hopkins University Press, 1971), pp. 98–100. Duckworth is also sensitive to Henry's fallibility and his peculiar relation to the narrator, issues resolved (p. 102) by reference to Robert C. Elliott's theme of the satirist satirized, in *The Power of Satire* (Princeton: Princeton University Press, 1960). I think, though, that this reasoning gives Austen's book too hard an edge; also, that Duckworth underestimates the "psychological development" of Catherine, which he compares unfavorably to Emma's (pp. 92, 100). Emma as a character illustrating psychology is richer than Catherine, but Catherine develops into a better psychologist of herself than Emma, and Catherine's development also illustrates psychology, not inconsiderably, while she is doing so.

22. Voltaire, *Candide*, René Pomeau, ed., *Complete Works*, vol. 48, William Barber et al., eds. (Oxford: Voltaire Foundation, 1980), p. 120.

23. *The Rambler*, W. J. Bate and Albrecht B. Strauss, eds., in John H. Middendorf, ed., *The Yale Edition of the Works of Samuel Johnson*, vols. 3–5 (New Haven and London: Yale University Press, 1969), 5:38. Parenthetical references in my text are to this edition.

24. Katrin Ristkok Burlin, "'The Pen of the Contriver': The Four Fictions of *Northanger Abbey*," *Jane Austen: Bicentenary Essays*, John Halperin, ed. (Cambridge: Cambridge University Press, 1975), pp. 90–91. There are also useful comments on Henry's fallibility (p. 101).

25. Ian Watt, *The Rise of the Novel: Studies in Defoe, Richardson and Fielding* (Berkeley and Los Angeles: University of California Press, 1959), pp. 296–97.

26. Ronald Paulson, *Satire and the Novel in Eighteenth Century England* (New Haven and London: Yale University Press, 1967), p. 298.

27. Ronald Paulson, *Popular and Polite Art in the Age of Hogarth and Fielding* (Notre Dame, Ind., and London: University of Notre Dame Press, 1979), pp. 157–71.

28. Avrom Fleishman, *Fiction and the Ways of Knowing* (Austin and London: University of Texas Press, 1978), pp. 35, 36.

29. Marvin Mudrick notes Henry's evasiveness here, assuming it is acceptable to Austen. *Jane Austen: Irony as Defense and Discovery* (Princeton: Princeton University Press, 1952), pp. 49–50.

30. This criticism of Henry differs from the objection, often expressed, that his common sense has its limitations. For a summary of opinions and a view of Henry different from mine, see Moler, p. 39. Henry's rigorism also shows in his reply to Catherine's remark that he is angry, after she has offended him: "I angry! I could have no right" (1.12.95).

31. Mansell, p. 45.

32. Johnson, *Rasselas, Poems, and Selected Prose*, p. 694.

33. *The Rambler*, 4:156. Richardson earlier in this paper alludes to the *Spectator's* rallying "forward young women" and says he himself used to call them "Seekers" (p. 154). Austen, of course, within two chapters, has some severe words for the *Spectator* (2.5.37–38).

34. James Edward Austen-Leigh, *Memoir of Jane Austen*, R. W. Chapman, ed. (1926; rpt. Oxford: Clarendon, 1951), pp. 157–58.

35. Graham Hough, "Narrative and Dialogue in Jane Austen," *Critical Quarterly* (1970), 12:209, 218.

36. Irène Simon, "Jane Austen and *The Art of the Novel*," *English Studies* (1962), 43:225–39—especially regarding what Simon sees as Austen's advice, "look for the implied meaning rather than take whatever [the narrator] says at face value" (p. 238); A. Walton Litz, p. 57 and passim. See also John Halperin, "Introduction," *Jane Austen: Bicentenary Essays*, pp. 35

and 42*n*, and, for a provocative intersection with Richardson, Harris, pp. 400–1, on Richardson's wish to make readers "all, if not Authors, Carvers."

37. Hough, p. 219.

11. "Delicious Consciousness" in *Persuasion*, via *Mansfield Park*

1. Susan Morgan's *In the Meantime: Character and Perception in Jane Austen's Fiction* (Chicago and London: University of Chicago Press, 1980) touches thoughtfully on this issue (e.g., pp. 176–80) as well as others I raise, including that of self-love (pp. 42, 70, 189–90), but takes an analytic standpoint explicitly dissociated from that furnished by "the inheritance of Locke" (p. 4). Morgan's main point, about Austen's sharing the Romantic appreciation of subjectivity and generosity as indispensable elements of true and satisfactory perception, is well taken, but associationism should be seen as variously linking the Romantics with Locke and eighteenth-century writers as well as variously distinguishing all of them from each other. Austen's revelations, as her terminology shows she realized, are an index to the associational processes of the heroines' minds which can make the revelations superfluous.

2. Darrel Mansell, *The Novels of Jane Austen: An Interpretation* (New York: Barnes & Noble, 1973), pp. 35–36, xiii, xi, 7.

3. Kenneth L. Moler compares the naivety of Fanny Price in *Mansfield Park* with that of Catherine in *Northanger Abbey* and cites other commentators on the matter. *Jane Austen's Art of Allusion* (Lincoln: University of Nebraska Press, 1968), p. 149.

4. Jane Austen, *Mansfield Park*, *Novels*, R. W. Chapman, ed., vol. 3, 3d ed. (London: Oxford University Press, 1934), vol. 3, ch. 17, p. 467. Parenthetical references in my text are to this edition, giving volume, chapter, and page numbers respectively (vol. 2 begins after chapter 18, and vol. 3 after vol. 2, chapter 13). The studies of *Mansfield Park* I have found most useful include: Joseph M. Duffy, Jr., "Moral Integrity and Moral Anarchy in *Mansfield Park*," *ELH* (1956), 23:71–91; Thomas R. Edwards, Jr., "The Difficult Beauty of *Mansfield Park*," *Nineteenth-Century Fiction* (1965), 20:51–67; and Avrom Fleishman, *A Reading of Mansfield Park: An Essay in Critical Synthesis* (Minneapolis: University of Minnesota Press, 1967).

5. Cf., from *Northanger Abbey*, "Fullerton had its faults, but Woodston probably had none." *Novels*, R. W. Chapman, ed., vol. 5, 3d ed. (1933; rpt. with revisions, London: Oxford University Press, 1965), vol. 2, ch. 11, p. 212.

6. Mansell, p. 125.

7. *Ibid.*, pp. 128, 136–37.

8. Norman Page, "Orders of Merit," in Joel Weinsheimer, ed., *Jane Austen Today* (Athens: University of Georgia Press, 1975), p. 100.

9. "Suggestion of a fairy-tale winding up of the various threads of the story," according to D. W. Harding, "Regulated Hatred: An Aspect of the Work of Jane Austen," in Ian Watt, ed., *Jane Austen: A Collection of Critical Essays* (Englewood Cliffs, N.J.: Prentice-Hall, 1963), p. 176.

10. John Bayley calls this strategy "mere abdication." "The Irresponsibility of Jane Austen," in B. C. Southam, ed., *Critical Essays on Jane Austen* (New York: Barnes & Noble, 1969), p. 18.

11. Cf., in the less somber *Sense and Sensibility*, the tone of the narrator at a comparable juncture that is less serious by far, after Edward Ferrars has been dismissed by a woman

he does not love, when he is working himself up to propose to the heroine Elinor: "How soon he had walked himself into the proper resolution, however, how soon an opportunity of exercising it occurred, in what manner he expressed himself, and how he was received, need not be particularly told." *Novels*, R. W. Chapman, ed., vol. 1, 3d ed. (London, New York, Toronto: Oxford University Press, 1933), p. 361.

12. Voltaire, Letter to Gabriel Cramer, July 1767, D14279, *Complete Works*, vol. 116, Theodore Besterman et al., eds. (Banbury: Voltaire Foundation, 1974), p. 207.

13. Jane Austen, *Northanger Abbey* and *Persuasion, Novels*, R. W. Chapman, ed., vol. 5, 3d ed. (1933; rpt. with revisions, London: Oxford University Press, 1965), vol. 3, ch. 11, p. 100. Parenthetical references in my text are to this edition, giving volume, chapter, and page numbers respectively. Note that volumes 1 and 2 of *Persuasion* are numbered 3 and 4. (The second volume of *Persuasion* begins after vol. 3, ch. 12.)

14. Beyond Blake's famous words in *The Marriage of Heaven and Hell* favoring a firm persuasion are John Locke's from the chapter on "Enthusiasm": "The Knowledge of any Proposition coming into my Mind, I know not how, is not a Perception that it is from GOD. Much less is a strong Perswasion, that it is true, a Perception that it is from GOD, or so much as true." *An Essay Concerning Human Understanding*, Peter H. Nidditch, ed. (Oxford: Clarendon, 1975), p. 701.

15. Samuel Johnson, *Rasselas, Poems, and Selected Prose*, Bertrand H. Bronson, ed., 3d ed. (New York: Holt, Rinehart and Winston, 1971), p. 677.

16. *The Rambler*, W. J. Bate and Albrecht B. Strauss, eds., in John H. Middendorf, ed., *The Yale Edition of the Works of Samuel Johnson*, vols. 3–5 (New Haven and London: Yale University Press, 1969), p. 25.

17. *Rasselas*, pp. 693–94. The application of this and other of Imlac's statements here to Austen has been made, in a different context, by Joseph A. Kestner III, *Jane Austen: Spatial Structure of Thematic Variations* (Salzburg: Institut für Englische Sprache und Literatur, 1974), pp. 68–69, 77.

18. For a quite (but not altogether) similar scene in which a character, Fielding's Sophia, lacks a perspective on her own thinking such as Anne displays, see *The History of Tom Jones a Foundling*, Fredson Bowers, ed., introd. Martin C. Battestin, *The Wesleyan Edition of the Works of Henry Fielding*, 2 vols. (Middletown, Conn.: Wesleyan University Press, 1975), 1:360–61 (bk. 7, ch. 9).

19. Howard S. Babb, *Jane Austen's Novels: The Fabric of Dialogue* (Columbus: Ohio State University Press, 1962), pp. 214–27. That intuition becomes still more intelligible, I think, when explained by reference to associationism, and Wentworth's speech can be seen as still more significant, in subtle ways. The importance of associationist thought and terminology in Austen's literary milieu (closer to her than is the "Preface" to *Lyrical Ballads*, which is suffused with such thought and terminology) appears by repeated references in a novel alluded to in *Northanger Abbey* (1.5.38), Maria Edgeworth's *Belinda* (1801), *Tales and Novels* (1893; rpt. New York: AMS Press, 1967), e.g., "'What a sudden transition!' said Lady Delacour. 'What association of ideas could just at that instant take you to [the topic of] Harrowgate?'" (3:112–13; see also pp. 151, 202–3). My attention was drawn to Edgeworth's novel by Marilyn Butler's *Jane Austen and the War of Ideas* (Oxford: Clarendon, 1975), where Edgeworth is credited with anticipating Austen's device of letting the heroine form judgments about the other characters by giving discriminating attention to their characteristic ways of speaking (pp. 141–45).

20. Jean H. Hagstrum, *Sex and Sensibility: Ideal and Erotic Love from Milton to Mozart* (Chicago and London: University of Chicago Press, 1980), p. 172. Cf. Chapman's note on

the word (*Sense and Sensibility*, p. 395) and also C. S. Lewis' comments in *Studies in Words*, 2d ed. (Cambridge: Cambridge University Press, 1967), p. 186, and K. C. Phillipps' remarks on "conscious" and "idea" in *Jane Austen's English* (London: Andre Deutsch, 1970), pp. 36–40, 71, 82.

21. Hagstrum, pp. 9–10 and passim.

22. Mansell, pp. 196, 202. Cf. Joseph Wiesenfarth, *The Errand of Form: An Assay of Jane Austen's Art* (New York: Fordham University Press, 1967), p. 139.

23. Morgan, pp. 194–95.

24. See Thomas Lockwood's very discriminating comments on this passage. "Divided Attention in *Persuasion*," *Nineteenth-Century Fiction* (1978), 33:312–13.

25. Henry Fielding, *Amelia*, Everyman's Library, 2 vols. in 1 (London: Dent; New York: Dutton, 1974), bk. 11, ch. 8; vol. 2, p. 260: "As in the delightful month of June . . . ."

26. David Hume, *A Treatise of Human Nature*, L. A. Selby-Bigge, ed., 2d ed., rev. P. H. Nidditch (Oxford: Clarendon, 1978), p. 283.

27. A. Walton Litz, drawing on W. J. Harvey, Martin Price, and other theorists of characterization, sees *Persuasion* as differing from Austen's other novels, illustrating a notion of the development of identity dependent on becoming rather than on being—a modern rather than an eighteenth-century view, he says, and a view allowing especially for "the disturbing possibility of alterations in the self." "'A Developement of Self': Character and Personality in Jane Austen's Fiction," Juliet McMaster, ed., *Jane Austen's Achievement* (New York: Barnes & Noble, 1976), p. 76. While that view is not characteristic of eighteenth-century novels, I hope I have shown that it is characteristic of eighteenth-century philosophy, and of the tales colored by that philosophy.

Index

Entries for authors of works in the tradition of the philosophical tale give topics first, then references to particular works. The titles of works in that tradition are abbreviated as follows:

C	Voltaire, *Candide*	NA	Austen, *Northanger Abbey*
GT	Swift, *Gulliver's Travels*	P	Austen, *Persuasion*
LP	Montesquieu, *Lettres persanes*	R	Johnson, *Rasselas*